MOON

D0981156

SAN DIEGO

IAN ANDERSON

Contents

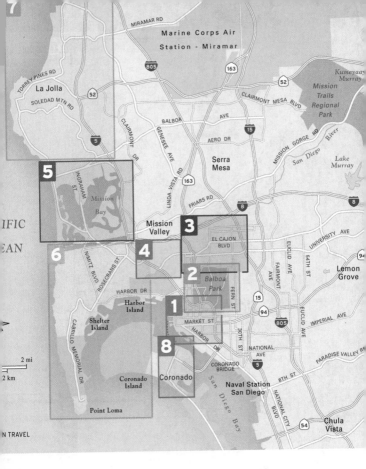

Maps

SEE MAP 4

SAN DIEGO
INTERNATIONAL
AIRPORT

W LAUREL ST

PACIFIC HWY

LITTLE ITALY

KALMIA ST

W JUNIPER ST

W IVY ST

W HAWTHORN ST

W GRAPE ST

W HAWTHORN ST

COLUMBIA ST

INDIA ST

KETTNER BLVD

W GRAPE ST

W FIR ST

LITTLE
ITALY

W ELM ST

5

W DATE ST

UNION ST

FRONT ST

Waterfront
Park

1

W CEDAR
ST

COUNTY
CENTER

INDIA ST

COLUMBIA ST

STATE ST

UNION ST

W BEECH ST

2

8

3

Maritime Museum
of San Diego

W ASH ST

W ASH ST

7

SEE MAP 6

W A ST

W A ST

1ST AVE

4

INDIA ST

COLUMBIA ST

W B ST

12

Santa Fe
Depot

9

CORONADO-BROADWAY PIER
FERRY

5

AMTRAK

AMERICA
PLAZA

10

11

CIVIC
CENTER

GASLAMP

USS Midway
Museum

6

BAYSHORE BIKEWAY

PACIFIC HWY

W BROADWAY

KETTNER BLVD

15

GAS

Tuna
Harbor Park

MARINA
DISTRICT

W F ST

W F ST

INDIA ST

W G ST

G ST

1ST AVE

16

SEAPORT
VILLAGE

W HARBOR DR

W MARKET ST

MAR

The New Children
Museum

22

GA

17

21

San Diego Bay

18

19

20

23

CONVENTION
CENTER

HARBOR DR

24

Embarcadero
Marina Park

SEE MAP 8

SIGHTS

3 Maritime Museum of San Diego
6 USS *Midway* Museum
22 The New Children's Museum
33 San Diego Central Library

RESTAURANTS

5 Carnitas' Snack Shack
8 Extraordinary Desserts
13 Donut Bar
17 Puesto
27 Cafe Chloe
28 Neighborhood
29 Cowboy Star
35 Lola 55
36 The Mission

NIGHTLIFE

7 Music Box
10 Karl Strauss Brewing Company
16 The Lion's Share
25 El Dorado Cocktail Lounge
32 Half Door Brewing Co.
37 Mission Brewery

ARTS AND CULTURE

9 Museum of Contemporary Art San Diego
12 San Diego Civic Theatre
14 Copley Symphony Hall
15 SDSU Downtown Gallery
20 Exclusive Collections Gallery

SPORTS AND ACTIVITIES

1 Waterfront Park
2 On the Water Adventures
4 Bayshore Bikeway
23 Seaforth Boat Rentals
24 Embarcadero Marina Park
30 East Village Tavern+Bowl
34 Petco Park

SHOPS

18 Tuna Harbor Dockside Market
19 Seaport Village

HOTELS

11 Hotel Republic
21 Manchester Grand Hyatt
26 Mudville Flats
31 Hotel Indigo San Diego

© AVALON TRAVEL

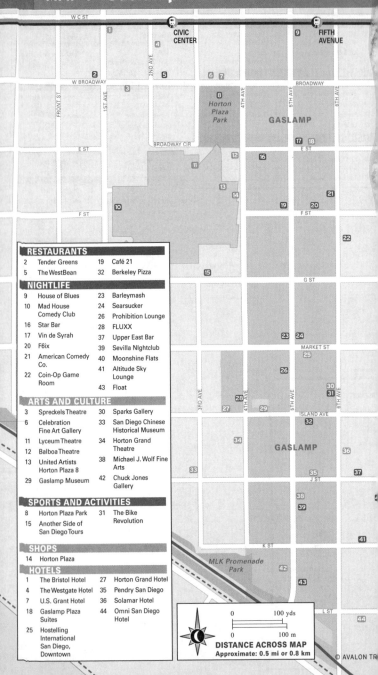

RESTAURANTS

2	Tender Greens	19	Café 21
5	The WestBean	32	Berkeley Pizza

NIGHTLIFE

9	House of Blues	23	Barleymash
10	Mad House Comedy Club	24	Searsucker
16	Star Bar	26	Prohibition Lounge
17	Vin de Syrah	28	FLUXX
20	F6ix	37	Upper East Bar
21	American Comedy Co.	39	Sevilla Nightclub
22	Coin-Op Game Room	40	Moonshine Flats
		41	Altitude Sky Lounge
		43	Float

ARTS AND CULTURE

3	Spreckels Theatre	30	Sparks Gallery
6	Celebration Fine Art Gallery	33	San Diego Chinese Historical Museum
11	Lyceum Theatre	34	Horton Grand Theatre
12	Balboa Theatre	38	Michael J. Wolf Fine Arts
13	United Artists Horton Plaza 8	42	Chuck Jones Gallery
29	Gaslamp Museum		

SPORTS AND ACTIVITIES

8	Horton Plaza Park	31	The Bike Revolution
15	Another Side of San Diego Tours		

SHOPS

14	Horton Plaza

HOTELS

1	The Bristol Hotel	27	Horton Grand Hotel
4	The Westgate Hotel	35	Pendry San Diego
7	U.S. Grant Hotel	36	Solamar Hotel
18	Gaslamp Plaza Suites	44	Omni San Diego Hotel
25	Hostelling International San Diego, Downtown		

0   100 yds

0   100 m

DISTANCE ACROSS MAP
Approximate: 0.5 mi or 0.8 km

© AVALON TR

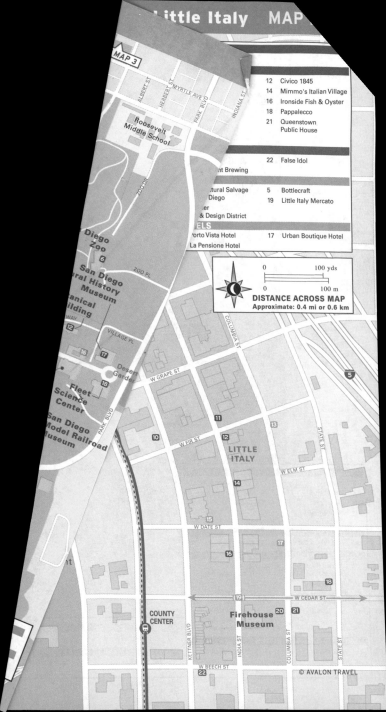

Little Italy **MAP**

MAP 3

12	Civico 1845
14	Mimmo's Italian Village
16	Ironside Fish & Oyster
18	Pappalecco
21	Queenstown Public House

| 22 | False Idol |

...nt Brewing

...tural Salvage ...Diego
...er & Design District

ELS

...orto Vista Hotel

...La Pensione Hotel

| 5 | Bottlecraft |
| 19 | Little Italy Mercato |

| 17 | Urban Boutique Hotel |

ALBERT ST
HERBERT ST
MYRTLE AVE
PARK BLVD
INDIANA ST

Roosevelt
Middle School

Diego
Zoo
6

San Diego
...ral History
Museum
...anical
...ilding
...WAY
12

VILLAGE PL
16 17
Desert
Garden
18

Fleet
Science
Center

San Diego
Model Railroad
...useum

PARK BLVD

ZOO PL

COLUMBIA ST

5

W GRAPE ST

11

12
LITTLE
ITALY

10
W FIR ST

STATE ST

W ELM ST

14

15
W DATE ST

17

16

18

19
W CEDAR ST

COUNTY
CENTER

KETTNER BLVD
INDIA ST
COLUMBIA ST
STATE ST

Firehouse
Museum

20 21

22
W BEECH ST

© AVALON TRAVEL

0   100 yds
0   100 m
DISTANCE ACROSS MAP
Approximate: 0.4 mi or 0.6 km

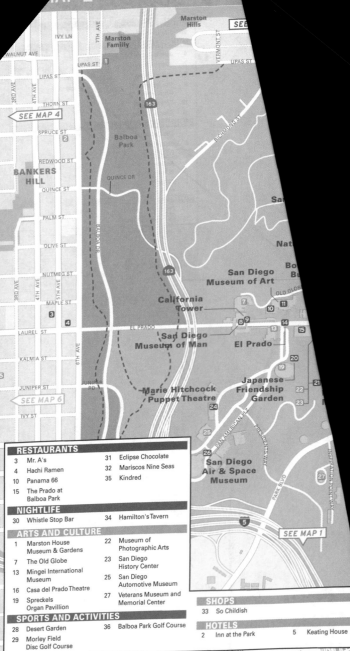

MAP 2

IVY LN

WALNUT AVE

UPAS ST

7TH AVE

Marston
Family

UPAS ST

Marston
Hills

VERMONT ST

SEE

UPAS ST

3RD AVE

4TH AVE

THORN ST

SEE MAP 4

SPRUCE ST

163

REDWOOD ST

BANKERS
HILL

QUINCE DR

Balboa
Park

QUINCE ST

PALM ST

OLIVE ST

NUTMEG ST

3RD AVE

4TH AVE

5TH AVE

MAPLE ST

RICHMOND ST

163

San Diego
Museum of Art

Bo
Bu

OLD GLOB

Sa

Nat

LAUREL ST

KALMIA ST

JUNIPER ST

SEE MAP 6

IVY ST

6TH AVE

EL PRADO

California
Tower

San Diego
Museum of Man

JUNIPER
RD

Marie Hitchcock
Puppet Theatre

El Prado

Japanese
Friendship
Garden

PARK AMERICAN PLZ

PRESIDENTS WAY

San Diego
Air & Space
Museum

PARK BLVD

INSPIRATION POINT WAY

SEE MAP 1

RESTAURANTS

3	Mr. A's	31	Eclipse Chocolate
4	Hachi Ramen	32	Mariscos Nine Seas
10	Panama 66	35	Kindred
15	The Prado at Balboa Park		

NIGHTLIFE

30	Whistle Stop Bar	34	Hamilton's Tavern

ARTS AND CULTURE

1	Marston House Museum & Gardens	22	Museum of Photographic Arts
7	The Old Globe	23	San Diego History Center
13	Mingei International Museum	25	San Diego Automotive Museum
16	Casa del Prado Theatre	27	Veterans Museum and Memorial Center
19	Spreckels Organ Pavillion		

SPORTS AND ACTIVITIES

28	Desert Garden	36	Balboa Park Golf Course
29	Morley Field Disc Golf Course		

SHOPS

33 So Childish

HOTELS

2	Inn at the Park	5	Keating House

CAPPS ST

North Park
Dryden

WILSHIRE TERR
FLORIDA ST
ALABAMA ST
MISSISSIPPI ST
LOUISIANA ST
TEXAS ST
ARIZONA ST
ARNOLD AVE
VILLA TERR
PERSHING AVE
30TH ST

UPAS ST

MORLEY FIELD DR

Bird
Park

BALBOA PARK

Tennis
Courts

Velodrome

Baseball
Fields

29

GRANADA AVE
28TH ST
29TH ST
DALE ST
GRIM AVE

QUINCE ST

PALM ST

GREATER
NORTH PARK

OLIVE ST

NUTMEG ST

Switzer
Canyon

MAPLE
ST

Burlingame

MAPLE
CT

LAUREL ST

SAN MARCOS AVE

28TH ST

KALMIA ST

30TH ST

FLORIDA DR

PERSHING DR

JUNIPER ST

30

IVY ST

31

HAWTHORN ST

US Naval
Hospital,
San Diego

GATE

Balboa Park

Golf Course

32

GRAPE ST

GRANADA AVE
DALE ST
28TH ST
30TH ST
FERN ST
GROVE ST

GRAPE ST

33

FIR ST

DATE ST

SOUTH
PARK

GOLF COURSE DR

26TH ST

8

36

34
35

28TH ST

RUSS BLVD

A ST

1ST ST

28TH ST

A ST

© AVALON TRAVEL

0   300 yds

0   300 m

DISTANCE ACROSS MAP
Approximate: 2.1 mi or 3.3 km

30TH ST. / UNIVERSITY

OHIO ST

ILLINOIS

LINCOLN AVE

30TH ST

30th St. / University

1

2

19

20

12 13 17

UNIVERSITY AVE

3

11

16

21

4

29TH ST

5
6

14

7

15

18

GRIM AVE

N PARK WY

8

9

RAY ST

10

0	100 yds
0	100 m

Old Trolley Barn Park

ADAMS AVE

Spalding Place

22

PARK BLVD

MISSION AVE

MEADE AVE

EL CAJON BLVD

HOWARD AVE

JOHNSON AVE

SEE MAP 4

163

LEWIS ST

LINCOLN AVE

WASHINGTON ST

NORMAL ST

32

POLK AVE

PARK BLVD

LINCOLN AVE

WASHINGTON ST

36 37 38

39

HILLCREST

CLEVELAND AVE

HARVEY MILK ST

NORMAL ST

CENTRE ST

UNIVERSITY AVE

UNIVERSITY AVE

33

34

41 40

7TH AVE

8TH AVE

VERMONT ST

35

HERBERT ST

CENTRE ST

CRESTWOOD PL

GEORGIA ST

ALABAMA ST

MISSISSIPPI ST

ROBINSON AVE

ESSEX ST

3RD AVE

4TH AVE

5TH AVE

42

6TH AVE

43

ROBINSON AVE

PENNSYLVANIA AVE

PENNSYLVANIA AVE

LANDIS S

44

CYPRESS AVE

RICHMOND ST

BROOKES AVE

BROOKES AVE

INDIANA ST

PARK BLVD

FLORIDA ST

Marston Hills

MYRTLE AVE

WALNUT AVE

Marston House

UPAS ST

MORLEY FIELD DR

0	300 yds
0	300 m

DISTANCE ACROSS MAP
Approximate: 2.8 mi or 4.5 km

BALBOA PARK

SEE MAP 2

© AVALON TRAVEL

RESTAURANTS

2	Caffé Calabria	27	Blind Lady Ale House
8	Waypoint Public House	30	Pomegranate
12	City Tacos	32	Great Maple
19	El Comal	37	Bread & Cie
20	Nomad Donuts	38	Snooze
21	URBN Pizza	44	Hash House a-go-go
24	Tajima Ramen		

NIGHTLIFE

1	Toronado	25	Lestat's West
3	West Coast Tavern	31	Lips
6	Bar Pink	33	Gossip Grill
13	North Park Beer Co.	34	Hillcrest Brewing Company
17	Seven Grand	35	Baja Betty's
18	Mike Hess Brewing	36	Urban MO's
23	Polite Provisions	42	The Rail

ARTS AND CULTURE

4	The Observatory North Park	22	Diversionary Theatre
14	Ray Street Arts District	39	Hillcrest Cinemas

SHOPS

5	George's Camera	16	Mimi & Red
7	Pigment	26	Bine & Vine Bottle Shop
9	Verbatim Books	28	Adams Avenue Bookstore
10	Visual	40	Vintage Shopping on 5th
11	Simply Local	41	Village Hat Shop
14	Ray Street Arts District		
15	Casa Artelexia		

HOTELS

29	Lafayette Hotel	43	ITH Zoo Hostel San Diego

SEE "30TH ST./UNIVERSITY" DETAIL

SEE "OLD TOWN" DETAIL

SEE MAP 6

SIGHTS

25	Heritage Park Victorian Village	36	Mason Street Schoolhouse
29	Robinson-Rose House	42	Old Town San Diego State Historic Park
31	San Diego Union Building	43	Whaley House Museum
33	Casa de Estudillo	45	El Campo Santo Cemetery
35	Wells Fargo Museum		

RESTAURANTS

4	El Agave	13	Gelato Verro Caffe
9	Lucha Libre	15	Starlite
10	Blue Water Seafood Market & Grill	17	Lefty's Chicago Pizzeria
11	El Indio	22	Casa Guadalajara

NIGHTLIFE

7	57 Degrees	14	Aero Club Bar
8	Blonde Bar	18	The Patio on Goldfinch
12	Shakespeare Pub & Grille		

ARTS AND CULTURE

1	Junípero Serra Museum	30	Seeley Stable
16	Cinema Under the Stars	32	Old Town Theatre

SPORTS AND ACTIVITIES

2	Presidio Park	23	Presidio Hills Golf Course
6	Electric Bike Central	41	Old Town Trolley Tours

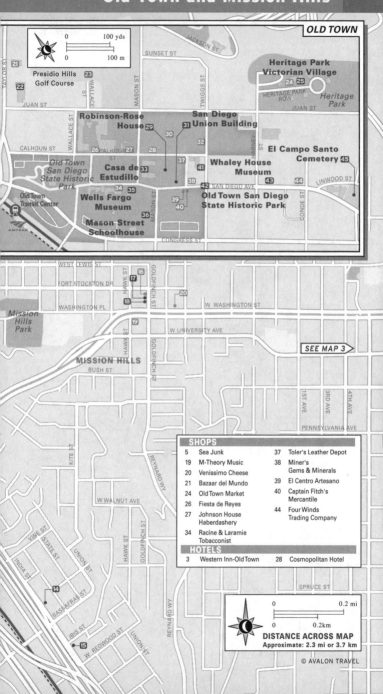

OLD TOWN

Presidio Hills Golf Course **23**
Robinson-Rose House **29**
San Diego Union Building
Casa de Estudillo **33**
Wells Fargo Museum
Mason Street Schoolhouse
Whaley House Museum
El Campo Santo Cemetery **45**
Heritage Park Victorian Village **24 25**
Old Town San Diego State Historic Park
Old Town Transit Center

SEE MAP 3

SHOPS
5	Sea Junk	37	Toler's Leather Depot
19	M-Theory Music	38	Miner's Gems & Minerals
20	Venissimo Cheese	39	El Centro Artesano
21	Bazaar del Mundo	40	Captain Fitch's Mercantile
24	Old Town Market		
26	Fiesta de Reyes	44	Four Winds Trading Company
27	Johnson House Haberdashery		
34	Racine & Laramie Tobacconist		

HOTELS
| 3 | Western Inn-Old Town | 28 | Cosmopolitan Hotel |

DISTANCE ACROSS MAP
Approximate: 2.3 mi or 3.7 km

© AVALON TRAVEL

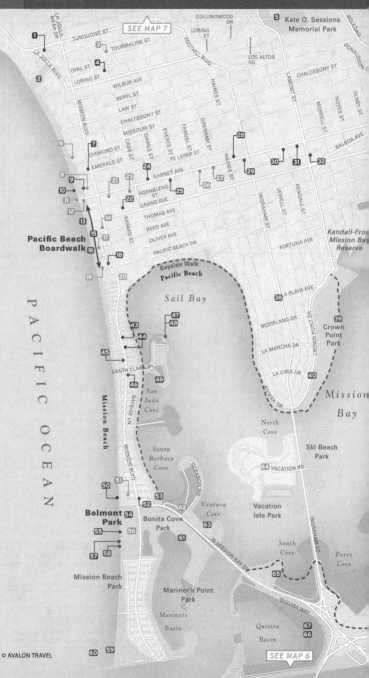

SEE MAP 7

SEE MAP 6

© AVALON TRAVEL

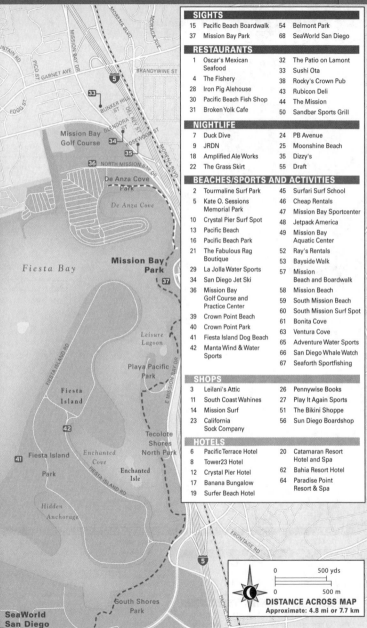

SIGHTS

15	Pacific Beach Boardwalk	54	Belmont Park
37	Mission Bay Park	68	SeaWorld San Diego

RESTAURANTS

1	Oscar's Mexican Seafood	32	The Patio on Lamont
4	The Fishery	33	Sushi Ota
28	Iron Pig Alehouse	38	Rocky's Crown Pub
30	Pacific Beach Fish Shop	43	Rubicon Deli
31	Broken Yolk Cafe	44	The Mission
		50	Sandbar Sports Grill

NIGHTLIFE

7	Duck Dive	24	PB Avenue
9	JRDN	25	Moonshine Beach
18	Amplified Ale Works	35	Dizzy's
22	The Grass Skirt	55	Draft

BEACHES/SPORTS AND ACTIVITIES

2	Tourmaline Surf Park	45	Surfari Surf School
5	Kate O. Sessions Memorial Park	46	Cheap Rentals
10	Crystal Pier Surf Spot	47	Mission Bay Sportcenter
13	Pacific Beach	48	Jetpack America
16	Pacific Beach Park	49	Mission Bay Aquatic Center
21	The Fabulous Rag Boutique	52	Ray's Rentals
29	La Jolla Water Sports	53	Bayside Walk
34	San Diego Jet Ski	57	Mission Beach and Boardwalk
36	Mission Bay Golf Course and Practice Center	58	Mission Beach
39	Crown Point Beach	59	South Mission Beach
40	Crown Point Park	60	South Mission Surf Spot
41	Fiesta Island Dog Beach	61	Bonita Cove
42	Manta Wind & Water Sports	63	Ventura Cove
		65	Adventure Water Sports
		66	San Diego Whale Watch
		67	Seaforth Sportfishing

SHOPS

3	Leilani's Attic	26	Pennywise Books
11	South Coast Wahines	27	Play It Again Sports
14	Mission Surf	51	The Bikini Shoppe
23	California Sock Company	56	Sun Diego Boardshop

HOTELS

6	Pacific Terrace Hotel	20	Catamaran Resort Hotel and Spa
8	Tower23 Hotel	62	Bahia Resort Hotel
12	Crystal Pier Hotel	64	Paradise Point Resort & Spa
17	Banana Bungalow		
19	Surfer Beach Hotel		

0   500 yds
0   500 m

DISTANCE ACROSS MAP
Approximate: 4.8 mi or 7.7 km

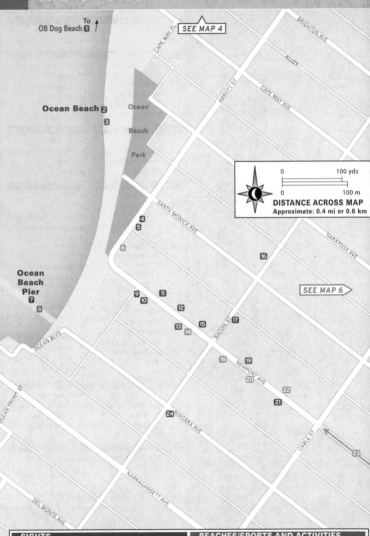

SIGHTS
2 Ocean Beach
7 Ocean Beach Pier

RESTAURANTS
4 OB Surf Lodge
9 South Beach Bar & Grille
10 Lighthouse Ice Cream & Yogurt
15 Hodad's
24 OB Noodle House

NIGHTLIFE
5 Wonderland Ocean Pub
11 The Holding Company
12 Sunshine Company Saloon
16 Pizza Port, Ocean Beach
17 Winstons Beach Club
21 Pacific Shores

BEACHES/SPORTS AND ACTIVITIES
1 OB Dog Beach
3 Ocean Beach
8 Ocean Beach Pier
13 South Coast Surf Shop
19 Ocean Experience Surf School

SHOPS
14 The Black
18 Galactic Comics
22 Miss Match
23 Ocean Beach Antique District

HOTELS
6 Ocean Beach Hotel
20 USA Hostels Ocean Beach

© AVALON TRA

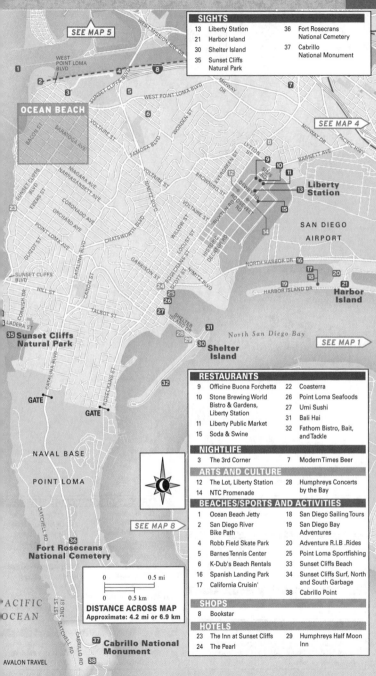

SEE MAP 5

WEST MISSION BAY DR

WEST POINT LOMA BLVD

OCEAN BEACH

MIDWAY DR

SEE MAP 4

SAN DIEGO AIRPORT

Liberty Station

North San Diego Bay

SEE MAP 1

Harbor Island

Shelter Island

Sunset Cliffs Natural Park

GATE

GATE

NAVAL BASE

POINT LOMA

SEE MAP 8

Fort Rosecrans National Cemetery

PACIFIC OCEAN

Cabrillo National Monument

AVALON TRAVEL

SIGHTS

13	Liberty Station	36	Fort Rosecrans National Cemetery
21	Harbor Island	37	Cabrillo National Monument
30	Shelter Island		
35	Sunset Cliffs Natural Park		

RESTAURANTS

9	Officine Buona Forchetta	22	Coasterra
10	Stone Brewing World Bistro & Gardens, Liberty Station	26	Point Loma Seafoods
11	Liberty Public Market	27	Umi Sushi
15	Soda & Swine	31	Bali Hai
		32	Fathom Bistro, Bait, and Tackle

NIGHTLIFE

| 3 | The 3rd Corner | 7 | Modern Times Beer |

ARTS AND CULTURE

| 12 | The Lot, Liberty Station | 28 | Humphreys Concerts by the Bay |
| 14 | NTC Promenade | | |

BEACHES/SPORTS AND ACTIVITIES

1	Ocean Beach Jetty	18	San Diego Sailing Tours
2	San Diego River Bike Path	19	San Diego Bay Adventures
4	Robb Field Skate Park	20	Adventure R.I.B .Rides
5	Barnes Tennis Center	25	Point Loma Sportfishing
6	K-Dub's Beach Rentals	33	Sunset Cliffs Beach
16	Spanish Landing Park	34	Sunset Cliffs Surf, North and South Garbage
17	California Cruisin'	38	Cabrillo Point

SHOPS

| 8 | Bookstar |

HOTELS

| 23 | The Inn at Sunset Cliffs | 29 | Humphreys Half Moon Inn |
| 24 | The Pearl | | |

| 0 | 0.5 mi |
| 0 | 0.5 km |

DISTANCE ACROSS MAP
Approximate: 4.2 mi or 6.9 km

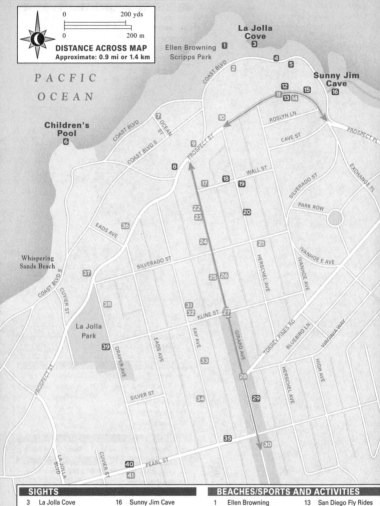

SIGHTS

3	La Jolla Cove
6	Children's Pool
16	Sunny Jim Cave

RESTAURANTS

5	Brockton Villa
8	Nine-Ten
12	George's at the Cove
18	Whisknladle
19	Burger Lounge
29	Harry's Coffee Shop
40	El Pescador Fish Market

NIGHTLIFE

18	Eddie V's
30	Herringbone
43	The Comedy Store

ARTS AND CULTURE

9	Madison Gallery
17	Athenaeum Music & Arts Library
33	THE LOT La Jolla
36	Tasende Gallery
37	Museum of Contemporary Art San Diego

BEACHES/SPORTS AND ACTIVITIES

1	Ellen Browning Scripps Park
4	Snorkel and Scuba
13	San Diego Fly Rides
39	La Jolla Tennis Club

SHOPS

11	Prospect Street
14	Jewels by the Sea
22	Bowers Jewelers
23	Geppetto's
24	Warwick's
25	Ascot Shop
26	Muttropolis
27	Girard Avenue
28	La Jolla Design District
30	D.G. Wills Books
31	Le Chauvinist
32	Echoes Too
34	Spoiled Rotten Boutique
41	Mitch's Surf Shop

HOTELS

2	La Jolla Cove Suites
7	Pantai Inn
10	La Valencia Hotel
21	La Jolla Village Lodge
38	The Bed & Breakfast Inn at La Jolla

© AVALON TRAVEL

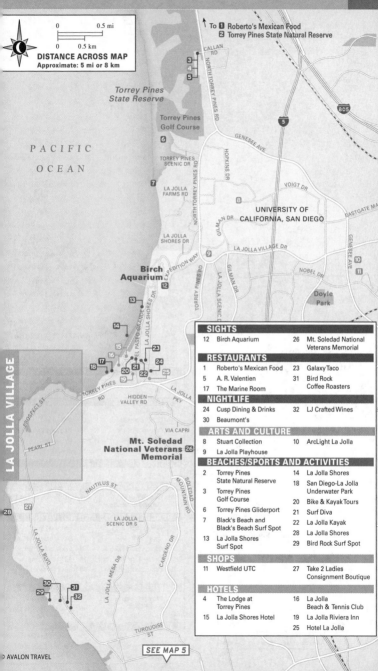

DISTANCE ACROSS MAP
Approximate: 5 mi or 8 km

0 .... 0.5 mi
0 .... 0.5 km

To ❶ Roberto's Mexican Food
❷ Torrey Pines State Natural Reserve

Torrey Pines State Reserve

PACIFIC OCEAN

Torrey Pines Golf Course

UNIVERSITY OF CALIFORNIA, SAN DIEGO

Birch Aquarium

Doyle Park

LA JOLLA VILLAGE

Mt. Soledad National Veterans Memorial

SEE MAP 5

© AVALON TRAVEL

SIGHTS		
12	Birch Aquarium	26 Mt. Soledad National Veterans Memorial

RESTAURANTS		
1	Roberto's Mexican Food	23 Galaxy Taco
5	A. R. Valentien	31 Bird Rock Coffee Roasters
17	The Marine Room	

NIGHTLIFE		
24	Cusp Dining & Drinks	32 LJ Crafted Wines
30	Beaumont's	

ARTS AND CULTURE		
8	Stuart Collection	10 ArcLight La Jolla
9	La Jolla Playhouse	

BEACHES/SPORTS AND ACTIVITIES		
2	Torrey Pines State Natural Reserve	14 La Jolla Shores
3	Torrey Pines Golf Course	18 San Diego-La Jolla Underwater Park
6	Torrey Pines Gliderport	20 Bike & Kayak Tours
7	Black's Beach and Black's Beach Surf Spot	21 Surf Diva
13	La Jolla Shores Surf Spot	22 La Jolla Kayak
		28 La Jolla Shores
		29 Bird Rock Surf Spot

SHOPS		
11	Westfield UTC	27 Take 2 Ladies Consignment Boutique

HOTELS		
4	The Lodge at Torrey Pines	16 La Jolla Beach & Tennis Club
15	La Jolla Shores Hotel	19 La Jolla Riviera Inn
		25 Hotel La Jolla

SEE MAP 1

GATE

NAVAL AIR STATION
NORTH ISLAND

GATE

GATE

SEE MAP 6

Ferry to Broadway Pier

Ferry to Convention Center

San Diego Bay

Centennial Park

1ST ST

2ND ST

3RD ST

4TH ST

5TH ST

6TH ST

7TH ST

8TH ST

9TH ST

10TH ST

ALAMEDA BLVD

PALM AVE

ORANGE AVE

POMONA AVE

GLORIETTA BLVD

Bayshore Bikeway

Tidelands Park

CORONADO BRIDGE

Coronado Golf Course

MARGARITA AVE

Coronado Bridge

Spreckels Park

J AVE
I AVE
H AVE
G AVE
F AVE
E AVE
D AVE
C AVE
B AVE
A AVE

OLIVE AVE

OCEAN BLVD

To Coronado Dog Beach

Coronado Museum of History and Art

DANA PL

ORANGE AVE

Coronado Beach

Glorietta Bay

SILVER STRAND BLVD

To
Glorietta Bay Park 28
AZ Kiteboarding 29
Silver Strand State Beach 30

PACIFIC

OCEAN

SIGHTS

6	Coronado Bridge	13	Coronado Museum of History and Art

RESTAURANTS

1	Coronado Coffee Company	11	Leroy's Kitchen and Lounge
3	Coronado Brewing Company	12	MooTime Creamery
		17	Lobster West
		24	Crown Room

NIGHTLIFE

21	Sunset Bar

ARTS AND CULTURE

8	Vintage Village Theatres Coronado	16	Lamb's Players Theatre

BEACHES/SPORTS AND ACTIVITIES

4	SUP Coronado	20	Coronado Beach
5	Bayshore Bikeway	27	Seaforth Boat Rentals
7	Coronado Golf Course	28	Glorietta Bay Park
10	Cruiser King	29	AZ Kiteboarding
19	Coronado Dog Beach	30	Silver Strand State Beach

SHOPS

2	Ferry Landing Marketplace	15	Orange Avenue
14	Bay Books	26	Shops at The Del

HOTELS

9	Cherokee Lodge	23	Glorietta Bay Inn
18	1906 Lodge	25	Hotel del Coronado
22	Villa Capri by the Sea		

0 400 yds

0 400 m

DISTANCE ACROSS MAP
Approximate: 1.5 mi or 2.4 km

© AVALON TRAVEL

SIGHTS

| 24 | Mission Basilica San Diego de Alcalá | 35 | Olympic Training Center |
| | | 36 | Aquatica San Diego |

RESTAURANTS

| 29 | Panchita's Bakery | 34 | ¡SALUD! |
| 31 | Las Cuatro Milpas | | |

NIGHTLIFE

| 10 | AleSmith Brewing Company | 14 | Societe Brewing Company |
| | | 28 | Brew Hop Brewery Tours |

ARTS AND CULTURE

11	Flying Leatherneck Aviation Museum	30	Bread & Salt
12	Quint Gallery	32	Chicano Park
26	Open Air Theatre	33	La Bodega Gallery
27	MCRD Museum	37	Mattress Firm Amphitheatre

BEACHES/SPORTS AND ACTIVITIES

1	Carlsbad State Beach	7	Fletcher Cove Beach Park
2	Oceanside City Beach	8	North Beach (Dog Beach)
3	North and South Ponto Beaches	9	Del Mar City Beach
4	Beacon's Beach	15	San Diego Sky Tours
5	Moonlight State Beach	16	Mission Trails Regional Park
6	Cardiff State Beach	23	SDCCU

To Rancho Bernardo and Escondido

1 Oceanside City Beach
2 Carlsbad State Beach
3 North and South Ponto State Beach
4 Moonlight Beach
5 Beacon's Beach

DISTANCE ACROSS MAP
Approximate: 5 mi or 8 km

0   0.5 mi
0   0.5 km

To Alpine and Anza-Borrego State Park →

To Campo

To Chula Vista Elite Athletic Training Center

To Mexico ↓

SHOPS

17	Siesel's Old Fashioned Meats	21	Fashion Valley
18	Bird's Surf Shed	22	Westfield Mission Valley
19	Catalina Offshore Products	25	Adventure 16

HOTELS

| 20 | Handlery Hotel | | |

© AVALON TRAVEL

A golden-hued playground beckoning thrill seekers, revelers, and soul searchers, San Diego boasts magnificent sunsets, sparkling waters, and a promise of the good life. A typical weather forecast is 72°F and sunny, and pretty much everybody wears sunglasses all the time.

On the beaches, locals sport board shorts, wetsuits, and bikinis, and the air carries the mingled scents of surf wax, sunscreen, and saltwater. On a clear day, sailboats traverse the bay, scuba divers explore underwater canyons, golfers tee up, and bicyclists cruise from beach to beach.

San Diego offers 80 miles of coastline, but with the resources of a major metropolitan city. For all its leisurely appearance, the city supports thriving industries—a vibrant performing arts scene, a taco-infused culinary identity, the finest craft brewing, and research institutions that attract some of the world's brightest scientific minds.

With a southern border and a western edge, San Diego collects people from every direction. Some come for the sunshine and the beaches, then stay to form a community of friendly, optimistic, and relaxed individuals who love and appreciate the natural resources of "America's Finest City." To make the most of your time in San Diego, all you need is a laid-back approach and a gentle push in the right direction.

Clockwise from top left: Seaport Village; a beach in La Jolla; a lifeguard stand on Ocean Beach; Botanical Building in Balboa Park.

Planning Your Trip

Where to Go

Downtown

San Diego's urban downtown was built around its huge, naturally protected harbor. Mere blocks from the city's skyscrapers are ships, bayside parks, and pleasant ocean breezes.

Within downtown are pocket neighborhoods with their own appeal and personalities. The **Marina District** is where the city meets the harbor; it's home to the tall antique ships of the **Maritime Museum of San Diego,** the **USS** *Midway* **Museum, San Diego Convention Center,** and plenty of visitor-friendly businesses. The **Gaslamp Quarter** is filled with **bars and clubs** that attract revelers to blow off steam. East of the Gaslamp, the **East Village** is a hip area home to **Petco Park** and the **San Diego Central Library.** On the northern border of downtown is **Little Italy.** While traditional Italian restaurants still populate this ethnic quarter, lately the **design-savvy neighborhood** has become a top destination for **California cuisine** as well as craft beer and artisanal coffee.

Balboa Park

Balboa Park's 1,200 acres are home to some of the city's best **museums** and **gardens,** as well as the famous **San Diego Zoo.** The heart of the park is **El Prado,** a Spanish colonial plaza that hosted an exposition celebrating the opening of the Panama Canal. The neighborhoods surrounding the park are among the oldest in the city, including upscale **Bankers Hill** and the quiet enclave **South Park** on its eastern border.

The city's nightlife buzzes around the Gaslamp Quarter.

a marina in San Diego

Uptown

Uptown actually comprises several neighborhoods, almost all of which abound with **great food** and craft beverages. **Hillcrest** has been an **LGBTQ hub** since the 1970s and stays lively with great bars and restaurants. In **North Park,** the city's tastemakers and creatives find a community among the area's century-old Craftsman homes.

Old Town and Mission Hills

Before Old Town was a town, it was a pueblo. The original Mexican village of San Diego has been faithfully restored within **Old Town San Diego State Historic Park,** preserving the city's adobe origins with plenty of gift and souvenir shops. Among the **historical museums,** you'll find homage to the city's **Mexican origins** and influence.

Mission Bay and Beaches

The **Mission Beach Boardwalk's** rides and attractions make family forays an adventure. The beach can be fantastic, while adjacent **Pacific Beach** provides a raucous playground for young adults both day and night. The real action takes place in **Mission Bay,** on fishing boats, Jet Skis, wakeboards, or other watercraft that don't need a good swell to be a blast.

Ocean Beach and Point Loma

Ocean Beach (better known as OB) offers a wild blend of hippies, surfers, bikers, and sailors that must be experienced to be believed. The character of the community extends to a sometimes hilarious **nightlife.** Or enjoy a quiet evening at **Sunset Cliffs Natural Park** watching the sun dip into the ocean each night.

The **Point Loma** peninsula sits across the bay from Coronado. On the

Sunset Cliffs near Ocean Beach

bay side of the peninsula, seafood lovers have access to the morning's fresh catch at **Shelter Island,** home to many of the area's yachts and fishing boats. At the tip of the peninsula, the **Cabrillo National Monument** commands the widest panoramic view of all of San Diego.

La Jolla

La Jolla is the city's most **upscale** neighborhood, with **fine dining,** high-end **shopping,** and multimillion-dollar homes. The views are just as rich below the ocean surface in protected **La Jolla Underwater Park. La Jolla Shores** is one of the county's best beaches for relaxing and splashing in the waves. Just to the north, the cliffs at **Torrey Pines State Natural Reserve** offer scenic hiking opportunities and undeveloped beaches, as well as a famous golf course.

Coronado

Just across the harbor from downtown, Coronado actually connects to a long sliver of peninsula, but the sleepy **upscale beach community** feels like an island. Coronado's claim to fame is the **Hotel del Coronado,** which made a starring appearance alongside Marilyn Monroe in the film *Some Like It Hot.*

Greater San Diego

Some sights are worth the drive, whether it be the **Mission Basilica San Diego de Alcalá** in Mission Valley, the Chicano heritage and local arts scene in colorful **Barrio Logan,** or a hop across the border and the rising food and beer scene in **Tijuana.**

When to Go

Spring

March and **April** see occasional spring showers with partly sunny days, small to medium crowds, and fluctuating surf. **May** and **June** are notoriously socked in with the marine layer (called "May Gray" and "June Gloom"). Days are warm but cloudy, with smaller crowds and surf.

Summer

July and **August** are **peak season**, with hot sunny days, very large crowds, and warm water with beginner-friendly surf. July consistently provides the year's best weather, but the crowds can be outrageous, especially during the long weekend around the immeasurably popular **Comic Con** (usually the second week of July). Hotel prices go through the roof that week, often triple the standard rate.

Fall

September and **October** are the "locals' summer," with warm, sunshiny days, medium crowds, and a mix of surf conditions.

Winter

In **November** and **December,** morning fog gives way to mild, partly cloudy afternoons. Crowds are small, with the exception of the last two weeks of December. Surfers can expect medium to very large waves.

Historically, **January** and **February** are the rainy months, though it's just as likely to have 90-degree days as it is three inches of rain. Considering most climes experience snow, 65°F with a chance of rain might seem pretty worthwhile. Crowds are small and surfers can expect large (sometimes very large) waves.

South Mission Beach volleyball courts

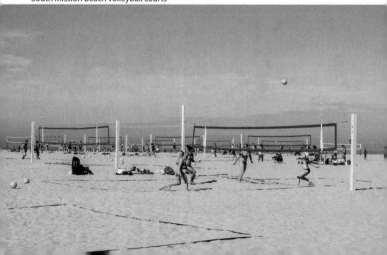

The Best of San Diego

Day 1

▶ Get an early start and head to the **San Diego Zoo**, where the animals are always livelier in the morning. Watch the pandas cuddle and the polar bears swim, then go next door to **Balboa Park** for lunch at **Panama 66**, a sculpture garden-restaurant with hot sandwiches and a terrific tap list.

▶ Your first stop for an afternoon of museum-hopping is to peruse the minor masterpieces at the **San Diego Museum of Art**. Study humankind at the **San Diego Museum of Man**, marvel at aeronautic engineering in the **San Diego Air & Space Museum**, then catch your breath in the **Botanical Building**.

▶ Head up to **North Park** for happy hour at **Polite Provisions**; its beautiful cocktail lounge may hook you up with some small plates if you're hungry. Save the appetite, though—North Park's Restaurant Row is nearby.

▶ Grab a couple of gourmet tacos at **City Tacos**, a great first stop before exploring the local beer scene. Start at **North Park Beer Co.**, then walk around the corner to visit **Toronado**.

Day 2

▶ Take the ferry to **Coronado** and wander the impressive **Hotel del Coronado**. Spend some time on **Coronado Beach**, then grab lunch at **Coronado Brewing Company** before heading back on the ferry.

A panda climbs a tree at the San Diego Zoo.   Balboa Park

Ocean Beach

Choosing the best beach for you depends upon whether you have children to entertain or are on your own looking for entertainment.

- **Coronado Beach** (page 75) is a long stretch of sand that starts at historic Hotel del Coronado and runs north to a dog-friendly beach. In between are families and couples quietly appreciating its beauty.

- **La Jolla Shores** (page 72) offers a wealth of water sports, a playground, more than a mile of gorgeous sand, and a large parking lot that fills quickly in summer.

- **Mission Beach** (page 66) has **Belmont Park,** a seaside amusement park with a roller coaster and an artificial wave where surfing performances are regularly staged throughout the day. Bikes and skateboards roll past on the boardwalk, giving even older children plenty to see and do.

- **Ocean Beach** (page 69) is a popular spot for young adults, who come here regularly to surf, swim, play volleyball, run their dogs, and gather around summer bonfires.

- **Pacific Beach** (page 66) offers fun surf and athletic beach games, but much of its character stems from the bars and cantinas fronting the boardwalk. The party vibe starts early and sometimes makes for a rowdy scene.

the Hotel del Coronado

- ▶ Stroll up the Embarcadero and visit the **Maritime Museum of San Diego** and the **USS _Midway_ Museum.** After gazing at ships both antique and modern, walk north to **Little Italy,** where you can sample more local beers at **Bottlecraft** before dining at one of the neighborhood's fantastic restaurants, such as **Herb & Wood.**

- ▶ After dinner, stroll through the charming neighborhood to reach decadent **Extraordinary Desserts.** The sugar rush should get you started for a night out in the **Gaslamp Quarter** club scene; if you prefer something chill, the swanky retro cocktail bar **Prohibition Lounge** is a great way to finish the night.

Day 3

- ▶ Start the day with donuts and coffee from **Nomad Donuts,** which will fuel you without leaving you too full for a day of action.

- ▶ Catch a morning surf lesson from **Surfari Surf School** at north **Mission Beach,** and enjoy some prime people-watching on the **Pacific Beach Boardwalk** while you catch your breath. You'll have worked up quite an appetite, so sate it the way a local surfer would—with fish tacos from **Oscar's Mexican Seafood.**

- ▶ Next up is **Mission Bay,** where you choose your speed: kayak, Jet Ski, wakeboard, or sail. (Hint: There's time to do two.) After playing all day, you'll need serious nourishment.

Best Craft Breweries

San Diego is crazy for beer and has dozens of small breweries. Beer drinkers come from all over to taste their wares.

Societe Brewing Company's Belgian-style blond ale

- **AleSmith Brewing Company** (page 172): In Miramar, next to the Marine Corps Air Station, AleSmith may have the greatest international reputation. The brewery shows off its stellar lineup of flagship beers and some rarely seen special issues.

- **Ballast Point Brewing** (page 150): The length of the tap list at the restaurant and tasting room in Little Italy makes its central location a benefit.

- **Modern Times Beer** (page 172): Everything on tap in this funky tasting room is worth trying; one or two may rank among the most sought-after beers in town. Check out the Michael Jackson Post-It mural.

- **Societe Brewing Company** (page 172): Societe is taking the region by storm with a deep roster of ales ranging from hoppy West Coasters to British and Belgian styles. Located in Kearny Mesa, it's not easy to find, but the beer is worth it.

- **Stone World Bistro & Gardens** (page 261): Located in Escondido, this gorgeous brewery sports indoor and outdoor bars, a restaurant, a desert garden, and an illuminating brewery tour. Many Stone beers are served here, as are some of the brewery's favorite craft beers.

- **Stone World Bistro & Gardens, Liberty Station** (page 167): This location may not have the cachet of its Escondido sibling, but it has plenty of space to serve up a huge variety of beers.

- **The Lost Abbey** (page 258): The Lost Abbey is a California outpost of brewing that's been handed down by Belgian monks for centuries. As far as West Coast beers go, this brewer's nailed it, with excellent craft beers in an unlikely location—a San Marcos business park.

Family-Friendly San Diego

Whatever your kids are into, there's probably a little something to keep *them* entertained. The question you need to ask yourself as a parent is: How much can you handle?

See the Animals

The San Diego Zoo is a no-brainer. However, its sister park, San Diego Zoo Safari Park, offers the opportunity to ride along in an off-road vehicle to see lions, tigers, and elephants in something closer to their natural habitats. SeaWorld San Diego delivers dolphin and killer whale shows where you're likely to get doused with water, while the smaller, drier Birch Aquarium exhibits fish that actually live in the region.

Ride the Rides

For action-packed theme-park experiences, check out the rides and games at Belmont Park, right by beautiful Mission Beach. Or make the drive north to Legoland, which smaller kids will especially love. In the summer, bigger kids will enjoy the water slides and wave pool at SeaWorld's Aquatica San Diego.

Water Sports Camps

If your kids are ready to go beyond the wave pool, sign them up for surf camp days with Surf Diva in La Jolla or Ocean Experience Surf School in Ocean Beach. To really get 'em going, sample the wakeboarding, kayaking, windsurfing, or sailing at camps offered by Mission Bay Sportcenter.

Planes, Boats, and Trucks

To see life-size versions of the toys kids love to play with, start at the San

roller coaster at Belmont Park

Diego Air & Space Museum and the USS *Midway* Museum. The ships of the Maritime Museum of San Diego skew older, though kids are just the right size to squeeze through a submarine. The Firehouse Museum offers fire trucks galore to explore.

Learn Something Fun

The Fleet Science Center teaches science lessons in the most fun way imaginable. Across the courtyard is the San Diego Natural History Museum, where the learning often involves dinosaurs. The New Children's Museum engages kids with interactive art installations that stimulate different parts of the brain.

sailing a catamaran on Mission Bay

▶ Roll up to **La Jolla** for seasonal ingredients with an ocean view at **George's at the Cove.** If you still have energy, nourish your mind with a destined-for-Broadway show at **La Jolla Playhouse.**

Day 4

▶ Spend a long morning in **Old Town San Diego State Historic Park,** exploring the adobe buildings and browsing the many gift shops. You'll be tempted to sit down for a Mexican lunch at one of the tourist restaurants, but save your appetite for a more genuine experience at **El Indio,** just up the street in **Mission Hills.**

▶ After lunch, ride over to **Ocean Beach** for a walk along the lengthy **Ocean Beach Pier,** a great vantage point for watching surfers. Grab your own spot of sand and enjoy the local color while you soak up some sun.

sunset over the Ocean Beach Pier

a cove in La Jolla

▶ Hit happy hour at **Wonderland Ocean Pub** when you get thirsty, then sit at the window to wait for an incredible sunset. Or, make your way up to **Sunset Cliffs Natural Park** to stroll the cliffs and experience the panoramic pink, purple, and bright-orange majesty as the sun goes down.

▶ Finish off the day over the hill at **Officine Buona Forchetta**, where some of the city's best Italian dishes include handmade pasta and authentic, wood-fired Neapolitan pizza.

Day 5

▶ Beat the crowds into La Jolla and grab a cup of local coffee at **Bird Rock Coffee Roasters**.

▶ Take advantage of the calm morning conditions to snorkel or scuba off **La Jolla Cove** and experience the vibrant below-sea-level nature reserve of **La Jolla Underwater Park**. This will prime your appetite for a fish taco plate at **El Pescador Fish Market**, in **La Jolla Village**.

▶ Walk it off along the famous shoreline, then spend the afternoon exploring neighborhood shops and art collections, including the **Madison Gallery** and the **Museum of Contemporary Art San Diego**.

▶ Prior to sunset, head up the hill to gape at the panoramic views from the **Mt. Soledad National Veterans Memorial**. Then roll south to the city's best sushi at **Sushi Ota** in Pacific Beach, followed by tiki cocktails and decor to match at **The Grass Skirt**.

Sights

Look for ★ to find
recommended sights

Highlights

★ **Oldest Fire Trucks:** The retired station hosting the **Firehouse Museum** has fire trucks, wagons, and hose carts dating from the mid-19th century (page 38).

★ **Most Historical Ships:** Check out both the **Maritime Museum of San Diego** and the **USS *Midway* Museum** to see amazing sea vessels, including an aircraft carrier, clipper ships, and two submarines (pages 38 and 39).

★ **Most Culturally Rich Landmark:** Balboa Park's **El Prado** is an ornate Spanish Revival promenade lined with many of the city's best museums, gardens, and theaters (page 41).

★ **Best Kid-Friendly Attraction:** There's no topping the **San Diego Zoo**— millions of parents have brought their children here to view lions, tigers, and… pandas—oh my (page 46)!

★ **Best Historic Birthplace:** Old Town San Diego State Historic Park preserves the surviving structures that made up the original Mexican pueblo of San Diego, down to the furniture and dining table place settings (page 47).

★ **Best Watery Playground: Mission Bay Park** has sailing, kayaking, and stand-up paddleboarding along a 4,200-acre waterway (page 50).

★ **Best Views:** On the Point Loma Peninsula, **Cabrillo National Monument** looks west across the ocean, south past Coronado into Mexico, and east facing the bay and city skyline (page 52).

★ **Best Place to Watch Surfers Strut Their Stuff:** Walk out a little ways on the **Ocean Beach Pier** and you'll find yourself looking down on the local lineup, who aren't above showing off a little if the waves are up (page 54).

★ **Best Place to Catch a Sunset:** The sandstone cliffs at **Sunset Cliffs Natural Park** face a western sky known to put on a show when the sun drops behind scattered clouds (page 55).

★ **Most Historic Building:** The original, all-wood **Hotel del Coronado** may not be considered the modern resort it was in 1888, but it's still gorgeous and one of a kind (page 59).

Cabrillo National Monument

What should people see in San Diego while they're here? It's not a question every visitor thinks to ask.

To be fair, there are plenty of people who've lived here for years who are far too distracted by the great weather and beaches to explore many of the city's interesting historical or culturally significant sights.

There are exceptions. Many of your fellow explorers in Balboa Park and Old Town are residents visiting or revisiting a favorite museum or historic home. Some locals maintain annual memberships to the San Diego Zoo so they can visit often. And hey—anything involving a beach? We're all over it.

San Diego's actually a fairly old city, at least as far as the West Coast is concerned—a frontier town first settled by boat rather than overland passage, a desert by the sea, with an undercurrent of both sailor and cowboy cultures, built on indigenous and Mexican foundations, with strong military ties and millions invested in tourism. There's a lot to see and do once you've had your fill of the beach.

Previous: the Coronado Bridge; a polar bear at the San Diego Zoo.

★ FIREHOUSE MUSEUM

Also known as the Pioneer Hook and Ladder Museum, this former home of San Diego Fire Station No. 6 offers a stunning visual history of firefighting, including antique gear, the fire badges of several nations, and a glimpse into the living quarters of on-call firefighters. While you can't slide down the fire pole, you will be impressed by the museum's collection of vintage fire trucks, wagons, and hose carts, some dating back to the mid-19th century. The museum is staffed by former and current firefighting volunteers and includes a 9/11 memorial. While it's fascinating to fire truck-loving kids, adults will also find plenty to marvel at.

Map 1: 1572 Columbia St., Little Italy, 619/232-3473, www.sandiegofirehousemuseum. com; Thurs.-Fri. 10am-2pm, Sat.-Sun. 10am-4pm; $3 adults, $2 children, $2 seniors

★ MARITIME MUSEUM OF SAN DIEGO

Cruising down Harbor Drive, it's tough to miss the *Star of India*, canvas unfurled from its 127-foot top mast. After all, how many 19th-century merchant sailing vessels do you see on a daily basis? The striking ship is the oldest active clipper of its type, and just one of many boats that make up the Maritime Museum. Beside it is the HMS *Surprise*, a replica 17th-century British frigate best known for its role in the film *Master and Commander*. Nearby is the *Berkeley*, a steamboat that once served as a ferry in early-20th-century San Francisco. Museum guests board each vessel to explore the deck and cabins, and stand where the captain once stood.

Perhaps none of these vessels is more intriguing than the pair of Cold War-era submarines. The USS *Dolphin* holds the distinction of having dived deeper than any other operational sub, and its compact decks and sailors' quarters aren't for the claustrophobic. More confining still is the B-39 Soviet sub, which cannot be traversed end-to-end walking upright. History is alive within these watercraft, providing one of San Diego's most memorable museum experiences.

Map 1: 1492 N. Harbor Dr., 619/234-9153, www.sdmaritime.org; daily 9am-8pm; $18 adults, $8 ages 3-12, $13 seniors, $13 ages 13-17, $13 military

THE NEW CHILDREN'S MUSEUM

Interactive artwork stokes the imagination of kids who engage with educational pieces by touching and climbing, or by playing with art supplies. Various permanent and revolving exhibits are based on a specific educational theme, which shifts every two years (previous themes have included *Animal Art, Child's Play,* and *Feast,* devoted to teaching kids about food and nutrition). Parents will enjoy watching their kids' brains light up and may even have occasion to marvel at the ingenuity behind some of the hands-on pieces in this stylish glass-and-steel space.

Map 1: 200 W. Island Ave., 619/233-8792, www.thinkplaycreate.org; Mon. 9:30am-4pm, Wed.-Sat. 9:30am-4pm, Sun. 11am-4pm; $13 adults, $13 children, $8.50 seniors, $6.50 military

SAN DIEGO CENTRAL LIBRARY

San Diego's main public library opened in late 2013 as one of the most ambitious new libraries in the nation, and it's certainly not your traditional stuffy institution. At half a million square feet, it boasts more than 1.25 million books and roughly 1,200 comfortable places to sit down and read, with panoramic windows and modern architectural flourishes such as a rooftop deck with a killer view of the Coronado Bridge and the South Bay. Information technology runs throughout, with adaptive computer devices for those with special needs, media editing suites, and a 3-D printing lab for those with more advanced know-how (most likely the students of the high-tech high school housed on the sixth and seventh floors of the nine-story building). Terrific (and separate) kid and teen sections make it a great family stop on a rainy day, or you may want to stop by just to redefine in your mind's eye what a library can be. Validation at an information desk nets you two hours free parking in the underground lot.

Map 1: 330 Park Blvd., 619/236-5800, www.sandiego.gov/public-library; Mon.-Thurs. 9:30pm-7pm, Fri.-Sat. 9:30am-6pm, Sun. noon-6pm; free

★ USS *MIDWAY* MUSEUM

The museum tag almost does a disservice to this 64-ton historical artifact—a true-to-life aircraft carrier. Commissioned at the end of World War II, the USS *Midway* was the world's largest ship when it was built, and it served as a temporary home to more than 200,000 sailors before retiring to its current location after nearly half a century in service. Each year, one million visitors explore the close confines experienced by those service members, inspecting their bunks, examining the bulwarks, and comparing them to the relative luxury of the captain's quarters.

Complimentary audio tours offer insights to the inner workings of the sonar and engine rooms. When it gets too claustrophobic, head up to the massive flight deck, where many of the museum's 29 vintage military aircraft have been restored to original condition. To gain an even more dynamic understanding of just how vital a role behemoths like this play in our nation's military defenses, check out one of the ship's flight simulators, where you can experience the vertigo of aerial combat and discover just how much skill it takes to land planes on an ocean vessel.

Map 1: 910 N. Harbor Dr., 619/544-9600, www.midway.org; daily 10am-5pm; $20 adults, $10 ages 6-12, $17 seniors, $15 students, $10 retired military

Top: the *Star of India* at the Maritime Museum of San Diego. Bottom: fighter jets and helicopters on the decks of the USS *Midway* Museum.

BOTANICAL BUILDING

The domed, rust-colored lath Botanical Building stands as a striking departure from the ornate Spanish architecture surrounding it on Balboa Park's El Prado. Fronted by a large reflecting pool populated by lily pads, the building hosts a tropical oasis of more than 2,000 flowers and fronds, including orchids, ferns, and palms. Take a brief stroll through the lush, shady rooms; these gorgeous plants are well tended, and for many, this stop turns out to be a highlight.

Map 2: 1549 El Prado, 619/239-0512, www.balboapark.org; Fri.-Wed. 10am-4pm; free

CALIFORNIA TOWER

For 80 years, the iconic tower gracing the main entrance to El Prado was closed to the public. Only recently has it been made accessible to the public through ticketed tours. Free lockers store your belongings during the 40-minute tour, which includes ascent of a narrow, 125-step staircase to the tower's viewing deck, which features a glorious 360-degree view of San Diego and its outskirts. The tower is accessed through the Museum of Man, and tour tickets include entrance to the museum. They may be purchased at the museum, but it's a safer bet to book ahead of time through the website, especially if you want to book a sunset viewing during summer months.

Map 2: 1350 El Prado, 619/239-2001, www.museumofman.org; daily tours every 40 minutes 10:20am-4:20pm, till 8pm Memorial Day-Labor Day; $22.50 adults, $20 over age 61, $18 students, $20 military, $16 ages 6-12, no entry under age 3

★ EL PRADO

Balboa Park houses a number of museums, theaters, and gardens, but the central promenade known as El Prado (translated as "the meadow") serves as a sight in itself. Locals regularly stroll the 0.5-mile-long Prado just for the pleasure of wandering its fountains, plazas, and ponds and appreciating the Spanish revival architecture throughout the park. Others hop on and off a circling tram that shuttles between parking lots and popular attractions. During the park's December Nights events (usually the first weekend in December), thousands arrive to enjoy the park's holiday decorative light show, while select attractions stay open late Fridays between Memorial Day and Labor Day for Balboa Park After Dark.

Map 2: El Prado between Cabrillo Bridge and Park Ave.

FLEET SCIENCE CENTER

Interactive exhibits at the Fleet Science Center offer kids hands-on instruction about electricity, space, optical illusions, and the human body, including a video program that predicts what you might look like at age 70. More relaxed entertainment includes planetarium shows, magic shows, and IMAX screenings of documentaries that virtually place you in the

One Day at Balboa Park

There's more to see and do at Balboa Park than can comfortably be accomplished in one day. If you're only going to make one pass through the treasured cultural center of San Diego, here's how to prioritize your visit with kids and without.

- **San Diego Museum of Art.** It doesn't have the most outstanding collection of paintings, but it's always reliable for enchanting visual moments, and the visiting exhibitions tend to be quite good.

- **California Tower and the San Diego Museum of Man.** It can be thought of as a museum of anthropology, topped by a tower with a panoramic view.

- **Mingei International Museum.** This museum doesn't get enough credit for bringing in unusual exhibits involving artisanal handiwork. Some objects are baffling in the sense that you can't believe it came out of someone's imagination; others baffle for different reasons altogether (see *Arts and Culture* chapter, page 180).

- **Botanical Building.** The flora inside is as lovely as the building, and while you may not remember their Latin names, some flowers may create a lasting image.

- **San Diego Air & Space Museum.** A stealth bomber is on display in front; inside there is much more.

Children will get pretty bored if you try to fill a whole day with museums. Bring them to these Balboa Park sights and they'll have fun despite themselves.

- **Fleet Science Center.** Blow everybody's mind with hundreds of

middle of a black hole, at the bottom of the ocean, or on the top of Mount Everest. Performances and screening schedules vary, and may include an additional entry fee.

Map 2: 1875 El Prado, 619/238-1233, www.rhfleet.org; Mon.-Thurs. 10am-5pm, Fri. 10am-8pm, Sat.-Sun. 10am-6pm; $20 adults, $18 seniors, $17 ages 3-12, $18 military

JAPANESE FRIENDSHIP GARDEN

The Japanese made gardening an art form, and the Japanese Friendship Garden, sequestered between El Prado and the Spreckels Organ Pavilion, demonstrates this art with elegance. A winding path leads past bonsai trees,

Botanical Building in Balboa Park

learning stations that trick you with optical illusions or turn common sense on its ear.

- **Marie Hitchcock Puppet Theatre.** If there's not a puppet theater in your town, expose your child to this sort of culture with the theater's puppet shows, sometimes involving very large puppets.

- **San Diego Natural History Museum.** Frankly, some parts of this museum on the natural history of San Diego are kind of ho hum, but there's a mastodon skeleton, a 3-D theater, and some pretty engaging temporary exhibits.

- **San Diego Model Railroad Museum.** Children love miniatures and trains, and this exhibit is huge and remarkably well detailed.

- **San Diego Air & Space Museum.** On this point, kids and parents may agree: Everybody's going to have fun here.

a koi pond, and a rock garden. A small exhibition house features culturally relevant artwork with picture windows overlooking the garden's manicured grounds and the canyon beyond.

Map 2: 2215 Pan American Plaza, 619/232-2721, www.niwa.org; daily 10am-7pm; $10 adults, $8 seniors, students, and military, free under age 7

MARIE HITCHCOCK PUPPET THEATRE

The oldest continuously active puppet theater in the country stages puppet shows of all types, with marionettes and hand puppets (both glow-in-the-dark and life-size). Kid-friendly plays and musicals are adapted from folklore or written specifically to take advantage of the production company's talent pool and venue.

Map 2: 2130 Pan American Plaza, 619/544-9203, www.balboaparkpuppets.com; shows Memorial Day-Labor Day Wed.-Sun. 11am, 1pm, and 2:30pm; Labor Day-Memorial Day Wed.-Fri. 10am, 11:30am, Sat.-Sun. 11am, 1pm, 2:30pm; $5 adults, $4 seniors, $4 military, $5 children, free under age 2

SAN DIEGO AIR & SPACE MUSEUM

You can't miss this museum devoted to flight—just look for the giant SR-71 stealth bomber out front. Inside are more thrills, with a close-up of the Apollo 9 space capsule, the World War II carrier-based Hellcat fighter, and a full-size replica of Charles Lindbergh's *Spirit of St. Louis.* Rotating exhibitions offer a taste of different technologies and wonders, but you can always count on the myriad aircraft built from years of humankind looking at the sky and thinking, "I can go there." Try out one of the flight simulators on hand to see if you've got the right stuff.

Map 2: 2001 Pan American Plaza, 619/234-8291, www.sandiegoairandspace.org; daily 10am-4:30pm; $19.75 adults, $16.75 seniors, students, and retired military, $10.75 ages 3-11, free active duty military, free under age 3

SAN DIEGO MODEL RAILROAD MUSEUM

This museum contains a small universe built around one of America's best-loved hobbies. Vast, incredibly detailed model towns and landscapes are on display, with working vintage trains chugging through them. Wonder at the craftsmanship behind these toys elevated to the status of collectibles, including some pristinely preserved vintage models.

Map 2: 1649 El Prado, 619/696-0199, www.sdmrm.org; Tues.-Fri. 10am-4pm, Sat.-Sun. 11am-5pm; $11 adults, $9 seniors, $6 students, $8 military, $5 ages 6-14, free under age 6

SAN DIEGO MUSEUM OF ART

San Diego doesn't boast one the greatest art collections in the world, but this Balboa Park favorite certainly houses its share of minor masterpieces. Paintings by such luminaries as Monet, Degas, Dalí, O'Keeffe, Modigliani, and Matisse are on permanent display, along with works by some of their lesser-known contemporaries. Ongoing museum highlights include East and South Asian pieces and an Art of the Americas exhibit that illustrates colonial through Civil War-era portraiture and frontier landscapes. Check out the ground-floor western gallery for visiting exhibitions, and pause to enjoy the building's entryway, with its ornately festooned Plateresque facade depicting famous statues, ships, and coats of arms.

Map 2: 1450 El Prado, 619/232-7931, www.sdmart.org; Mon.-Tues. 10am-5pm, Thurs.-Sat. 10am-5pm, Sun. noon-5pm; $15 adults, $10 seniors, $8 students, $10 military, free under age 18

Clockwise from top left: California Tower at the Museum of Man; a panda at the San Diego Zoo; Spanish colonial architecture along El Prado.

SAN DIEGO MUSEUM OF MAN

The study of humankind covers a lot of ground, so this anthropological museum continually finds captivating ways to keep people coming back. Recent exhibits have focused on the history of brewing beer and instruments of torture, while more permanent exhibits include castings of Mayan monoliths and displays of the ancient civilization's hieroglyphics, a comparable collection of ancient Egyptian artifacts, and the illuminating *Footsteps Through Time*, which traces four million years of evolution, from primates to humans and beyond (think cyborgs). Here you'll see such diverse items as fossil records, Neanderthal skulls, and a life-size C-3PO.

Map 2: 1350 El Prado, 619/239-2001, www.museumofman.org; daily 10am-5pm; $13 adults, $10 seniors, military, and students 6-17, free under age 6

SAN DIEGO NATURAL HISTORY MUSEUM

"The Nat," as it's sometimes known, focuses on the natural history of San Diego. Exhibits feature fossils and dinosaur bones of animals that once lived in and around Southern California and the Baja Peninsula, including mastodons, whales, and a giant shark, all of whom are depicted in 3-D films throughout the day. As you wander amid all this history, gaze at a large animated globe as it visualizes the continental shifts that have defined and redefined the Earth's landscape over the past 600 million years.

Map 2: 1788 El Prado, 877/946-7797, www.sdnhm.org; daily 10am-5pm; $19 adults, $17 seniors, military, and students, $12 ages 3-17, free under age 3

★ SAN DIEGO ZOO

With more than 600 species covering 100 acres smack in the middle of Balboa Park, the "world famous" San Diego Zoo covers a lot of ground, both literally and figuratively. Popular beasts include massive polar bears (occasionally known to wrestle in their aquarium-like tank), gorgeous tigers, charming elephants, majestic lions, and no shortage of monkeys, chimps, and gorillas. But the zoo's pride and joy is its family of pandas. Technically on loan from China, the pandas have been actively breeding, and park visitors line up for the chance to see panda cubs doing their thing (which is almost always cute).

Most of the zoo grounds are built into canyons, which means lots of walking—often up and down hills—which can be especially tiring on sunny days. Fortunately, the zoo operates an aerial tram that offers gondola rides from the lower zoo level to its top, as well as bus tours with a quick overview of the park. Mornings are the best time to visit by far, offering easier parking, cooler weather, and livelier animals, though late hours in summer offer a chance to see the zoo at night. During the winter holidays, special decorative lighting makes evening visits a real treat.

Map 2: 2920 Zoo Dr., 619/231-1515, www.sandiegozoo.org; July-Aug. daily 9am-9pm; Mar., May-June, and Sept.-Oct. daily 9am-6pm; Apr. daily 9am-7pm; Jan-Feb. and Nov.-early Dec. daily 9am-5pm; Dec. holidays daily 9am-8pm; $54 adults, $44 ages 3-11, free under age 3, free parking

EL CAMPO SANTO CEMETERY

Is it really haunted? Some say it is, but you won't find out unless you've got the nerve to visit at night. San Diego's original graveyard attracts its share of visitors during daylight hours. Wooden crosses and burial markers of the 447 San Diegans buried here between 1850 and 1880 include Yankee Jim Robinson, an accused boat thief hanged at nearby Whaley House while still proclaiming his innocence. The 2,000-square-foot "holy field" used to be much larger, but many graves were moved or paved over to create the shopping district now surrounding it. Now *that's* scary.

Map 4: 2410 San Diego Ave., 619/220-5422, www.hiddensandiego.net

CASA DE ESTUDILLO

Two centuries ago, this Spanish colonial home was considered among the grandest in northern Mexico. Times have changed, but the restored adobe hacienda remains both a state and a U.S. historic landmark. Beneath a pointed bell tower and lined with terra-cotta ceramic tile rooftops, the building's 13 rooms are decorated with period furniture that illustrates how the family of a presidio commandant may have lived—from table settings to sitting rooms, including household tools and accessories available at the turn of the 19th century.

Map 4: 4000 Mason St., 619/220-5422, www.parks.ca.gov; daily 10am-5pm; free

HERITAGE PARK VICTORIAN VILLAGE

Just southeast of Old Town's historical park are seven unique Victorian structures that were moved here from their original locations in order to preserve their historical architecture. The vibrant avocado-green Sherman-Gilbert House arrived first; the delicate stick structure of its mid-19th-century turret survived the truck ride from Bankers Hill. These gorgeous brightly colored buildings have been faithfully restored but sit quiet and closed up; they can only be admired from outside—with two exceptions. The modest Senlis Cottage reveals what San Diego's average working-class abode was like in the 19th century. San Diego's first synagogue, Temple Beth Israel, was built in 1889 and moved here in 1978 from its original location in the downtown neighborhood of Cortez Hill. Both buildings remain open during park hours and for occasional private events.

Map 4: 2454 Heritage Park Row, 858/565-3600, www.hiddensandiego.net; daily 9am-5pm; free

★ OLD TOWN SAN DIEGO STATE HISTORIC PARK

The name San Diego once referred to this tiny strip of land tucked under a hill next to where the I-5 and I-8 freeways now meet. Though most of its residents left more than a century ago, many of the original buildings remain. The city's oldest standing structures are now historic landmarks preserved within Old Town San Diego State Historic Park. A visit here gives

Top: one of the Victorian houses in Heritage Park. **Bottom:** El Campo Santo Cemetery in Old Town.

a sense of how the original settlement developed: a combination of Spanish
colony tinged with the American Old West.

Built between the 1820s and the 1850s, most buildings are old family residences, including the homes of Spanish soldiers who came here to fortify the presidio just up the hill. The restored adobe buildings are furnished to their period; each tells a story about daily life here in the early 19th century. Dining tables in the **Commercial Kitchen** are set with old-fashioned plates and utensils, as if dinner were about to be served.

Strolling around the park, you can bear witness to how the city matured. Later generations of wood and eventually brick buildings reflect the influx of American settlers from the East Coast. The **Mason Street Schoolhouse** depicts a reconstructed 19th-century classroom complete with desks and chalkboards. The **San Diego Union Building** features the typesetting tables and a printing press of the city's first newspaper. The Colorado House, site of the **Wells Fargo Museum**, invites guests inside an old bank vault.

Many of the old structures now house shops and restaurants, turning the park into a mall of sorts. The overall experience retains its historical character, though, with Mexican food and crafts commemorating the decades San Diego belonged to what was then a Spanish colony. A visit here is a must for anyone keen on gaining a sense of local history.

Map 4: 4002 Wallace St., 858/220-5422, www.parks.ca.gov; May-Sept. daily 10am-5pm, Oct.-Apr. Mon.-Thurs. 10am-4pm, Fri.-Sun. 10am-5pm; free

ROBINSON-ROSE HOUSE

Now the Old Town San Diego State Historic Park's **visitors center,** this replica of the original 1853 Robinson-Rose House primarily consists of one very functional room open to the public. But it's worth a visit if only for one reason: the large scale-model of Old Town as it looked in 1872. This mesmerizing reference point will flesh out your imagination as you explore the park. It's also the starting point for the free and educational walking tours that begin daily at 11am and 2pm.

Map 4: 4098 Mason St., 619/220-5422, www.parks.ca.gov; May-Sept. daily 10am-5pm, Oct.-Apr. Mon.-Thurs. 10am-4pm, Fri.-Sun. 10am-5pm; free

WHALEY HOUSE MUSEUM

In 1857, the Whaley House was the first of its kind in town, built with bricks and the addition of a second story. The former home of Thomas Whaley, it would go on to serve as a general store, a courthouse, and a theater after the Whaleys moved to a newer residence in New Town, better known today as downtown. Inside, the rooms are decorated with period furniture and include detailed histories of the house—ghost stories long associated with murders and untimely deaths that took place here, as well as public hangings staged on the front steps during its time as a courthouse. The Whaley

House's reputation as one of the most haunted houses in the country makes nighttime visits especially spooky and popular among ghost hunters.

Map 4: 2476 San Diego Ave., 619/297-7511, www.whaleyhouse.org; Memorial Day-Labor Day daily 10am-9:30pm, Labor Day-Memorial Day Sun.-Tues. 10am-5pm, Thurs.-Fri. 10am-4:30pm and 6pm-9:30pm, Sat. 10am-9:30pm; daytime admission $8 adults, $7 military, $6 ages 6-12 and over 64, free under age 6; evening admission $13 adults, $8 ages 6-12 and over 64, under age 6 not recommended

Mission Bay and Beaches   Map 5

BELMONT PARK

Since 1925, there has been an amusement park on Mission Beach. While the amusements may change, there are still plenty of bells and whistles attempting to lure visitors from the gorgeous beach right next door. One of the park's biggest attractions is the Wave House, an outdoor beachfront restaurant and lounge built around a pair of wave machines. The standing waves are always up at the push of a button; would-be surfers can try it on the beginner-friendly FlowRider. The bigger and faster FlowBarrel rides are reserved for the seasoned pros who stage acrobatic surfing shows on the hour. Belmont Park also features a small roller coaster, bumper cars, a laser maze, an arcade, and a carousel. Parking and admission are free; prices for rides and other amusements vary.

Map 5: 3146 Mission Blvd., 858/228-9283, www.belmontpark.com; Mon.-Thurs. and Sun. 11am-8pm, Fri.-Sat. 11am-10pm; free

★ MISSION BAY PARK

While surfing reigns up and down the coast, Mission Bay is the undeniable epicenter of all action water sports—from Jet Skis and wakeboard-toting powerboats to sailboats, kite-surfers, and kayaks. This artificial bay is really a network of parks and peninsulas, which split the 4,200-acre park into a couple of bays, six or seven small coves, and at least one "basin." For every small waterway filled with rowdy pontoons speeding along, there is a tranquil cove for stand-up paddleboarding or a romantic cruise in a paddleboat. If you prefer to stay on dry land, there are plenty of beaches, picnic areas, and playgrounds, along with a scenic bike path that circles the entire bay.

Map 5: 2688 E. Mission Bay Dr., 619/525-8213, www.sandiego.gov; daily 4am-midnight

PACIFIC BEACH BOARDWALK

Technically called Ocean Front Walk, this concrete bike, skate, and pedestrian path actually begins at the south end of Mission Beach and continues north between the sand and oceanfront homes to the Crystal Pier and Pacific Beach Park. All along are people riding beach cruisers, men

The SeaWorld Controversy

In 2013, a documentary titled *Blackfish* investigated the circumstances of the death of a SeaWorld trainer who was killed by a captive orca she was working with at SeaWorld Orlando. The film prompted a nationwide discussion about the practice of keeping killer whales and other large aquatic mammals in captivity, posing questions about its impact on the animals' psychological health and life spans. Amid the backlash stirred up by the film's publicity, a number of popular performing artists cancelled scheduled appearances at SeaWorld parks, which also became the sites of frequent demonstrations by animal welfare activists calling for a boycott.

SeaWorld San Diego was not immune to this. While the company initially insisted ticket sales were up in the wake of the movie's widespread release, it later admitted that attendance figures did decline as potential visitors were turned off by the prospect that the captive animals—and main attractions—at many of its parks were sensitive to the conditions of their confinement. (SeaWorld's Aquatica park in Chula Vista features only turtles and flamingos.)

Since the film came out, SeaWorld has announced plans to improve its captive habitats and to phase out killer whale shows once the current orcas have passed on.

flexing tattoos, and women parading in bikinis. The party starts somewhere around Pacific Beach Drive, as beachfront restaurants serve drinks on patios and decks overlooking the action on the beach. Pacific Beach's "PB" party reputation begins here, usually pretty early in the day, and it's a place where young adults tan and preen, drink and flirt, and generally live it up from ocean to bar. It may not always be family-friendly, but it rarely fails in the people-watching department.

Map 5: Ocean Front Walk, between Pacific Beach Dr. and Garnet Ave.

SEAWORLD SAN DIEGO

Combine the most popular parts of a zoo, aquarium, and circus and you'll get something a lot like SeaWorld. The aquatic mammal theme park features thousands of sea creatures in observable habitats as well as trained performances, none more famous than the killer whale Shamu. While several of the iconic black-and-white whales have donned the Shamu mantle over the years, the idea behind the shows remains the same: Spectators watch as four-ton orcas leap athletically out of the water, creating massive splash waves that soak large sections of the delighted audience. Plenty of other attractions may be found in the park, including dancing dolphins and a couple of hilarious vaudevillian sea lions.

Map 5: 500 Sea World Dr., 619/222-4732, www.seaworld.com/sandiego; daily 10am-5pm; peak summer and winter holidays daily 10am-9pm; $90 adults, $85 ages 3-9

Ocean Beach and Point Loma

Map 6

★ CABRILLO NATIONAL MONUMENT

Named for the first European explorer to sail into San Diego Bay, the monument to Juan Rodríguez Cabrillo is only a small part of what draws people to the "most southwesterly spot in the contiguous United States." Comprising 144 acres at the tip of the long, narrow Point Loma Peninsula, the monument centers on a statue of Cabrillo that commands a breathtaking panorama with views of the Pacific Ocean, San Diego, and, on a clear day, all the way to county's eastern mountain ranges.

At the peninsula's highest point stands the **Old Point Loma Lighthouse,** a preserved 19th-century structure that only ceased operation because low clouds and fog too often obscured its signal (it was retired in favor of a newer lighthouse down the hill).

Trails crisscross the monument, including the **Bayside Trail** (2.5 miles), a scenic trek overlooking the bay while traversing rare coastal sage scrub habitat on the peninsula's eastern side. It's just a short drive down the hill to the new lighthouse and the 0.5-mile **Coastal Tidepool Trail,** which winds past protected tidepools. These play home to entire ecosystems of starfish, anemones, and other exotic sea life that has evolved to survive within the shallow pools of seawater left behind at low tide. Time your visit by consulting a daily tide schedule.

Map 6: 1800 Cabrillo Memorial Dr., Point Loma, 619/557-5450, www.nps.gov/cabr; daily 9am-5pm; $15 per vehicle, $7 per walk-in

FORT ROSECRANS NATIONAL CEMETERY

A worthy view commends this 77.5-acre burial ground for fallen servicemen and -women, dating back to the Mexican-American War. It was first established in 1882, when remains of the American casualties of the 1846 Battle of San Pasqual were transferred here, and it continued to be a final resting place for fallen troops through World War II. With the bay, the ocean, and the city skyline, there's plenty of beautiful backdrop for grave markers and several memorials built to commemorate specific battles, including Guadalcanal and the Battle of Leyte Gulf. Notable service members interred here include Major Reuben H. Fleet (after whom the Balboa Park science museum is named) and Major General Joseph H. Pendleton, a career marine and eventual mayor of Coronado who advocated for a major marine base in the San Diego area.

Map 6: 1800 Cabrillo Memorial Dr., Point Loma, 858/658-7360, www.cem.va.gov; daily sunrise-sunset

HARBOR ISLAND

Harbor Island is an artificial peninsula designed to form long, protected yacht basins for the thousands of boats that moor here. It's home to a couple

Top: Belmont Park. Bottom: sandstone bluffs at Sunset Cliffs National Park.

of hotels and restaurants boasting excellent city views across the bay, as well as a few boating and sailing charters. The easiest way to enjoy Harbor Island is to walk or bike along the path through the park on its outer edge.
Map 6: south of N. Harbor Dr., across from San Diego International Airport

LIBERTY STATION

What used to be a naval training base has been reclaimed as a burgeoning commercial arts district. The once Spartan military buildings now host creative workshops and spacious restaurants, with new and interesting organizations moving in on a regular basis. On its eastern edge is grassy NTC Park, and along its western border is a shopping center with familiar food and drink franchises. The place gets most lively on the first Friday of the month, when a regular arts event brings people out to explore various studios, galleries, and special performances.
Map 6: bounded by Barnett Ave., N. Harbor Dr., Rosecrans St., and Chauncey Rd., www.libertystation.com

OCEAN BEACH

Ocean Beach may be called a lot of strange things (and most are true), but the name that sticks is "OB." Backpackers, teenagers, bikers, surfers, service members, yoga adepts—all types congregate on this stretch of coastal un-real estate, which began its days amid the carnival atmosphere of a beachfront amusement park built in the early 1900s. The park closed 100 years ago, but the vibe remains. Visitors will find ocean-themed souvenirs, bead shops, swimwear boutiques, and plenty of countercultural businesses kept alive by wave after wave of the wild diversity this little beach town with a quirky reputation tends to attract.
Map 6: 4800-5000 block of Newport Ave., between Abbott St. and Cliffs Blvd., Ocean Beach, www.oceanbeachsandiego.com

★ OCEAN BEACH PIER

It's said that the Ocean Beach Pier is the longest concrete pier on the West Coast. Whether or not that's true, its 1,971 feet make a perfect distance for a scenic stroll. Where the waves break, stop for an unbeatable view of surfers practicing their moves directly below. Along the way you'll pass promenading families, the occasional romantic couple on a sunset walk, and a lot of recreational anglers trying their hand at a different kind of catch (usually herring). A café bravely does business in the middle of the pier, which may take a bath in monster waves during heavy winter swells.
Map 6: west of the 5000 block of Niagara Ave., Ocean Beach

SHELTER ISLAND

When it comes time to berth their vessels, members of the active boating community have options up and down the coast, but the most desirable may be found on this inside leg of Point Loma. Though not far on a map from with pretty houses peppering the hillside above and gorgeous sailboats and pleasure craft in the Shelter Island Yacht Basin and America's Cup Harbor. However, restaurants top the list of reasons to visit, particularly when it comes to fresh-catch seafood that comes directly off fishing boats that call this area home.

Map 6: southeast of Rosecrans St. between Nimitz Blvd. and Talbot St.

★ SUNSET CLIFFS NATURAL PARK

Sunset Cliffs delivers gorgeous, unobstructed Pacific views from the top of eroding sandstone cliffs. On the east side of Sunset Cliffs Boulevard are rows of beautiful homes built to appreciate the scenery. The west side is reserved for the rest of us: a narrow strip of trails that wind along the waxing and waning cliffs' edge, overlooking the rocky outcroppings below. More than a mile of walking offers plenty of opportunities to stop and watch the surfers who consider this long stretch of waves their greatest local resource.

At the southern end of the road, the park opens up to a wider embankment of short hiking trails and desert foliage, as well as a large parking lot. The lot fills up in spring and fall evenings, when partly cloudy days culminate in vibrant orange and electric pink sunsets, and onlookers flock to the cliffs hoping to spot the elusive green flash, rumored to appear the moment the sun finally touches below the horizon.

A word of caution: These sandstone cliffs are in a perpetual state of decay, and while many ledges are fenced off for safety, that's not to say the unfenced areas are safe. Lives have been lost by people trying to capture the perfect photo only to find the ground giving way beneath them. Always stay a few feet back from a cliff's edge, and avoid navigating the tricky goat trails down to the beach without guidance from a seasoned local.

Map 6: 700-1300 block of Sunset Cliffs Blvd., between Adair St. and Ladera St. and extending south of Ladera St., www.sunsetcliffs.info; free

La Jolla

Map 7

BIRCH AQUARIUM

The Birch Aquarium is overseen by the Scripps Institution of Oceanography and includes plenty of interesting exhibits devoted to local aquatic life—reef ecosystems, kelp forests, lagoons, and underwater canyons. A great deck features touchable tide pools and boasts a fantastic view of La Jolla below. Jellyfish, anemones, and leopard sharks are always fascinating, but it's tough to imagine another creature as marvelous as the leafy sea dragon.

Map 7: 2300 Expedition Way, 858/534-3474, www.aquarium.ucsd.edu; daily 9am-5pm; $18.50 adults, $14 ages 3-17, $15.50 over age 59, $15 students, $15 military

It may sound like a place for children to swim, but it's not anymore. In 1931 Ellen Brown Scripps commissioned construction of a seawall to create a wave barrier along the beach so that small children could play safely at the water's edge. Over time, the local seal population decided to start bringing their pups here, to the point that bacteria levels in the water became too high for humans. Today, a rope barrier keeps people off the beach and the seawall serves as a perfect vantage point to stand and watch the seals belly along and roll around in the sand.

Map 7: 850 Coast Blvd.

LA JOLLA COVE

It's a wonder how so many folks flock onto this little stretch of sand just a few steps from La Jolla Village. The cove teems with underwater life, making it a popular spot for scuba divers and snorkelers, often seen floating just a few dozen yards offshore. Sea lions lounge on the large rocks sitting on either side of the beach, lolling on top of each other, barking, and catching some sun. Most of the year, waves are small or nonexistent, making for a fun swimming beach. But in the winter, uncommonly large swells may kick up a wave known as the Sleeping Giant, and local big-wave surfers head to the cove to give onlookers an exhilarating show.

Map 7: 1100 Coast Blvd.

MT. SOLEDAD NATIONAL VETERANS MEMORIAL

A 29-foot cross stands atop Mount Soledad, La Jolla's highest point, which boasts a panoramic view that surveys the entire county on a clear day. It's currently the centerpiece of a Korean War memorial enumerating the names of thousands of veterans who served their country during that conflict. However, ownership of the cross has changed hands several times over the years as legal battles were waged to have it removed from government land. Whether or not the cross remains, the view isn't going anywhere. Bring something to eat, picnic in the grass, and enjoy the beauty of greater San Diego.

Map 7: 6905 La Jolla Scenic Dr. S., 858/459-2314, www.soledadmemorial.com; daily 7am-10pm, free

SUNNY JIM CAVE

One of seven La Jolla smugglers' caves, Sunny Jim allegedly received its name from L. Frank Baum, author of *The Wizard of Oz*. Apparently the shape of the cave mouth reminded Baum of the original cartoon serial cereal box mascot, Sunny Jim, who first appeared on a box of Force Wheat Flakes in 1903.

There are two ways to see the cave: from the ocean or through the Cave Store (which rents snorkeling gear and sells souvenirs). A steep, slippery set of stairs leads into the cave from above and through a tunnel carved

Scenic Walks

a home in Mission Hills

These leisurely walks can be a great way to notice the understated sights of the city.

- The **Harbor Walking Path** (downtown) extends north from Marina Park (500 Kettner Blvd.) and leads along the waterfront past boats, parks, and monuments as well as San Diego Bay.

- The **Mission Bay Trail** (850 W. Mission Bay Dr.) offers a biking and walking path that circles almost the entire inside edge of Mission Bay, though you can always stick to a fraction of the 27-mile loop.

- **Sunset Cliffs Natural Park** (Point Loma) passes between big homes and sandstone cliffs rising above the ocean. It's an easy mile-long scenic walk along Sunset Cliffs Boulevard that can be extended into a 0.5-mile circuit of light trails once the road ends at Ladera Street.

- The **Coast Walk Trail** (La Jolla) picks up just left of the Sunny Jim Cave Store (1325 Coast Blvd.) and winds along the ocean toward La Jolla Shores, passing some ridiculous oceanfront properties in a mere 0.3 mile.

- For a pleasant stroll past beautiful homes, pay a visit to one of the city's oldest neighborhoods, **Mission Hills,** which has more than 300 historical homes ranging from Spanish revival homes to Craftsman bungalows to modern mansions. To see the highest concentration, start walking west on Fort Stockton Drive from West Lewis Street, turn left on Willoughby Street to Sunset Boulevard, then turn right to return to Fort Stockton Drive. Any side streets will take you past more beautiful estates.

Top: La Jolla Cove. Bottom: harbor seals at Children's Pool in La Jolla.

by immigrant laborers to smuggle more immigrant laborers and, during
Prohibition, booze. Daily kayak tours are also available.

Map 7: 1325 Coast Blvd., 858/459-0746, www.cavestore.com; daily 9am-6pm summer, Mon.-Thurs. 10am-5pm, Fri.-Sun. 9am-5pm winter; $5 adults, $3 under age 17

Coronado

Map 8

CORONADO BRIDGE

If there is a signature piece of San Diego architecture, the bridge connecting Coronado to downtown is it. The Coronado Bridge arches up to a 200-foot clearance (high enough for tall ships to pass under) before curving hard upon approaching Coronado, forming a swoop of blue steel and gray concrete that appears far less rigid than the sum of its parts. An artistic lighting project promising to make nighttime views just as inspiring is scheduled to be completed in 2019.

Map 8: 1825 Strand Way, www.coronado.ca.us

CORONADO MUSEUM OF HISTORY AND ART

How did Coronado come to be and why? This museum tells the story of the island that's really the tip of a peninsula. View pictures of early vacationers at Tent City, a canvas resort built beside the Hotel del Coronado as a friendly option for budget travelers. Examine vintage military costumes while learning how the U.S. Navy's presence has impacted the community. The small museum packs a lot of Coronado into its three exhibits—it's certainly not a full-day or even half-day activity, but it's great for establishing context on the area.

Map 8: 1100 Orange Ave., 619/435-7242, www.coronadohistory.org; Mon.-Fri. 9am-5pm, Sat.-Sun. 10am-5pm summer, daily 10am-4pm winter; free

★ HOTEL DEL CORONADO

It's rare that a hotel can be considered a sight in its own right, but then few carry the panache of Hotel Del. Built in 1888, the all-wood Victorian construction of the original building can take your breath away, particularly the grandly furnished lobby and the iconic dome over its historic **Crown Room,** which hosts a lavish Sunday brunch. Once the world's largest resort, the Del has been a popular destination among Hollywood VIPs for nearly a century; movie buffs will remember it as the location of Billy Wilder's comedy classic *Some Like It Hot.* Much of the luxury resort is open to the public: Sip a drink at the outdoor **Sunset Bar** or enjoy the outdoor ice-skating rink set up between Thanksgiving and New Year. Of course, the main attraction is what inspired the hotel's construction—just outside is one of the nation's finest beaches. Rent a cabana for the day and enjoy cocktail service on the sand as you watch sailboats, U.S. Navy ships, and the occasional breaching whale enhance the panoramic Pacific view.

Map 8: 1500 Orange Ave., 619/435-6611, www.hoteldel.com

Greater San Diego
Map 9

AQUATICA SAN DIEGO

This SeaWorld water park doesn't rely on splashing dolphins or whales to get you sopping wet. A series of individual and group water slides, a wave pool, an inner-tube float, and an interactive area with geysers and jets and a few other tricks offer excuses to dump water on the unsuspecting. Though not open year-round (or even weekdays most of the year), hot summer days see a lot of slippery sliding and splashing action in Chula Vista.

Map 9: 2052 Entertainment Cir., Chula Vista, 619/222-4732, www.aquaticabyseaworld. com; June-Aug. daily 10am-6pm, Apr.-May and Sept.-Oct. Sat.-Sun. 10am-6pm; $36 adults, $30 ages 3-9

MISSION BASILICA SAN DIEGO DE ALCALÁ

When the first California mission was established in 1769, it was originally to sit on the hill above Old Town. However, in 1774 this site was chosen in part to distance the mission from the garrison of Spanish soldiers, whose presence intimidated the indigenous people the mission meant to convert. In 1775, hundreds of indigenous people sacked and burned the mission; it has been rebuilt three times since. The current building has stood since 1931, and it still holds regular Roman Catholic Masses at 7am, 8am, and 9am on Sunday, as well as 5:30pm on Saturday and weekdays. The whitewashed adobe structure is instantly recognizable by its unique stacked bell tower, which features five bells. The large lower-right bell is original, dating to 1802 and notably topped by a crown representing the king of Spain.

Map 9: 10818 San Diego Mission Rd., Mission Valley, 619/283-7319, www.missionsandiego.com; Mon.-Fri. 8am-4:30pm; free

CHULA VISTA ELITE ATHLETIC TRAINING CENTER

No, you don't get to work out at this complex built to train world-class athletes for the Olympics, but you can walk an established mile-long path past those facilities for BMX, rugby, archery, and track-and-field hopefuls. For self-guided phone tours, you only need to show up, call 619/215-9070, and walk the Olympic Path, which passes by the mostly outdoor training fields. You may learn a lot about how the athletes work leading up to competition, and may feel a little closer to the team when the next summer Olympics takes place. For more in-depth information, come at 11am on Saturday for a free tour with a guide who can answer any questions.

Map 9: 2800 Olympic Pkwy., Chula Vista, 619/656-1500, www.easchulavista.com; Mon.-Fri. 9am-4:30pm; free

Beaches

Highlights

★ **Best Beach for Small Children:** **Bonita Cove,** located on the bay, offers a gentle waterfront and playgrounds (page 65).

★ **Beach Closest to the Party:** College students and singles liven up the nights around **Pacific Beach**—the parties often start early, on the beachfront (page 66).

★ **Best Dog Beach:** While it's sandy and spacious, with ocean and river coastline, what really makes **OB Dog Beach** great is how much locals and their dogs love to spend time there (page 69).

★ **Beach with the Most Character:** A unique mash of personalities and lifestyles coexist at **Ocean Beach,** which attracts a wild cross section of humanity (page 69).

★ **Best Secret Beach:** Down below **Sunset Cliffs,** this hard-to-get-to beach is becoming more and more popular (page 69).

★ **Best Family Beach:** A great beach for just about everybody, **La Jolla Shores** offers playful yet safe summer waves and loads of beach activities (page 72).

★ **Prettiest Beach:** Don't be fooled by the name; the turquoise waters of **Moonlight State Beach** are just as beautiful in sunlight (page 80).

surfers on Ocean Beach

They're the reason most people come to San Diego—and the biggest reason many people never leave.

With 80 miles of coastline, San Diego's got more than its fair share of beaches. It's hard to be humble: They're pretty fantastic. Most of them are just how people imagine them, with sparkling water and sand, golden light reflecting off sunglasses and smiles, and the scent of sunscreen and surf wax.

But there's a decent variety as well. San Diego's bays offer beaches that are similar to lakes, meaning the water is flat, with space enough for boats and water sports. They're also gentle enough for very young children to splash around without concern about strong currents.

Some of our best beaches are framed by wind-hewn cliff faces, creating gorgeous scenery when you're on the beach looking out at the water as well as when you're out in the water looking back at the beach. Everybody has a favorite beach in San Diego—even the dogs. Look through these pages to find yours.

Previous: cyclists on Mission Bay Beach; Windansea beach in La Jolla.

San Diego Beaches

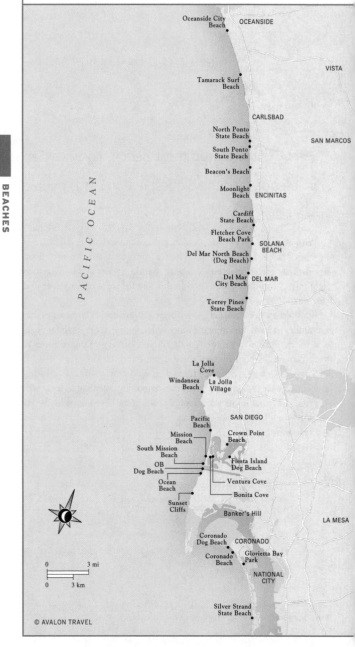

Oceanside City Beach OCEANSIDE

VISTA

Tamarack Surf Beach

CARLSBAD

North Ponto State Beach

SAN MARCOS

South Ponto State Beach

Beacon's Beach

Moonlight Beach ENCINITAS

PACIFIC OCEAN

Cardiff State Beach

Fletcher Cove Beach Park

SOLANA BEACH

Del Mar North Beach (Dog Beach)

Del Mar City Beach DEL MAR

Torrey Pines State Beach

La Jolla Cove

Windansea Beach La Jolla Village

Pacific Beach SAN DIEGO

Crown Point Beach

Mission Beach

South Mission Beach

Fiesta Island Dog Beach

OB Dog Beach

Ventura Cove

Ocean Beach

Bonita Cove

Sunset Cliffs

Banker's Hill

LA MESA

Coronado Dog Beach CORONADO

Coronado Beach Glorietta Bay Park

NATIONAL CITY

0   3 mi
0   3 km

Silver Strand State Beach

© AVALON TRAVEL

★ BONITA COVE

More than a mile of bayfront beach wraps around the inside edge of this cove located across Mission Boulevard from Mission and South Mission Beaches. The beach ends at grassy Mission Point Park at its southwestern shore, and after looping clockwise the other direction it winds up at the sandy peninsula Mariner's Point Park. Because the continuous stretch of sand almost completely encloses the cove, it's protected from surf and most watercraft, and it's a popular destination to bring young children; there's even a playground and tot lot at the grassy park area at the cove's northernmost curve, where three large parking lots may be accessed from either Mission Boulevard or West Mission Bay Drive. There are restrooms, picnic tables, barbecue grills, and fire rings near each parking lot and a shower on the east cove. Lifeguards are usually on duty.

Map 5: 1100 W. Mission Bay Dr., Mission Bay, 619/235-1169, www.sandiego.gov; daily 4am-10pm

CROWN POINT BEACH

A large inner-bayside beach with grassy areas and picnic tables, barbecue grills, and fire rings, Crown Point sees a lot of parties. It's loosely split into north, middle, and south parks, and permits may be acquired for large events up to 200, 400, and 350 people, respectively. The middle section features a boat ramp, making it a destination for light watercraft launches, including kayaks, motorboats, catamarans, and Jet Skis. The north and south parks feature small tot lots, while the middle has a public basketball court. Lifeguards monitor the north park daily during summer months.

Map 5: 1759-1799 Moorland Dr., Mission Bay, 619/525-8213, www.sandiego.gov; daily 4am-2am, parking lot closes at 10pm

FIESTA ISLAND DOG BEACH

Thanks to a narrow strip of land just wide enough for Fiesta Island Road to access it, Fiesta Island is technically Mission Bay's largest peninsula. Nevertheless, it's completely undeveloped save for the **San Diego Youth Aquatic Center** on its north end—which is reserved for organized activities sponsored by public and private children's organizations. The real reason most people visit year-round is that most of the island outside the aquatic center is a large off-leash dog park with nearly five miles of calm beach. Since people like to drive off-road vehicles on some parts of the island, the best bet for dogs is the southwest corner, where a dirt parking lot off the looping Fiesta Island Road delineates a dog-friendly section and provides plastic bags to clean up after your pet. Beyond that, there's endless sand and scrub, plus birds to chase.

Map 5: 1750 Fiesta Island Rd., Mission Bay, 619/525-8213; daily 6am-10pm

You can cruise about two miles along Mission Beach Boardwalk and still not run out of beach or boardwalk. Dubbed the "Golden Strand," it runs from South Mission all the way north to Pacific Beach. That long stretch in the middle? *That's* Mission Beach. It's most commonly identified with the beach in front of Belmont Park, where crowds congregate all summer. Runners, cyclists, and skaters of every stripe cruise past year-round. The large parking lot by the park is set up with restrooms, showers, picnic tables, volleyball nets, and fire rings, but the whole thing stretches more than a mile, so if you can find street parking along Mission Boulevard north of there, you'll find relatively uncrowded stretches of beach, which the lifeguards split intermittently into swim and surf zones. You may go where all the action is, or you may choose to settle on an empty spot on the sand and enjoy.

Map 5: Ocean Front Walk, between Pacific Beach Dr. and N. Jetty Rd., Mission Beach, www.sandiego.gov; daily 24 hours

★ PACIFIC BEACH

Pacific Beach offers a beach experience with a party atmosphere, with people (mostly young adults, including lots of singles) partying at the edge of the sand. They used to party *on* the sand until a city beach alcohol ban was put into effect, but the beachfront bars and restaurants ensure that the good times continue, especially south of Crystal Pier. North of the pier tends to be a little quieter, with swimming, surfing, and beach volleyball just a few of the popular activities. Fishing is allowed on the pier itself, and close by you'll find showers, restrooms, and lifeguards always on duty.

Map 5: Ocean Front Walk, between Pacific Beach Dr. and Law St., 619/221-8899, www.sandiego.gov; daily 24 hours

SOUTH MISSION BEACH

The Mission Beach most people see is directly around the large complex of parking, restaurants, shops, and amusements around Belmont Park. However, the beach continues south, and there you'll find locals sunning and sporting year-round, without regard for what tourists might be doing a half mile north. Lifeguards are regularly on duty, monitoring designated areas allowing swimming, surfing, and fishing. There are nets for beach volleyball and a basketball court, and amenities include picnic tables, fire rings, bathrooms, and showers. Access is via the parking lot at the southern terminus of Mission Boulevard.

Map 5: South end of Mission Blvd. at N. Jetty Rd., Mission Beach, www.sandiego.gov; daily 24 hours

VENTURA COVE

Another protected bay beach, most of Ventura Cove abuts the Bahia Resort Hotel, accessible via a parking lot across West Mission Bay Drive to the north from Bonita Cove. Lifeguards are on duty only in the summer,

Top: paddleboarding on Mission Bay. Bottom: a playground at Bonita Cove.

when picnic tables, fire rings, and a grassy park section make the splashy little beach a picnic and small-party destination. It also features a public restroom and beach shower.

Map 5: 3209 Gleason Rd., Mission Bay, 619/235-1169, www.sandiego.gov; daily 4am-2am

Nearby Activities

The biggest attraction near the beaches along the Golden Strand of Mission Beach is the amusement and entertainment venue **Belmont Park** (3146 Mission Blvd., 858/228-9283, www.belmontpark.com; Mon.-Thurs. 11am-8pm, Fri.-Sat. 11am-10pm, Sun. 11am-8pm; free), along with its **Wave House.** If you feel like scoping the bay scenery after some beach time, order up a bike (with kid trailer if needed) from **K-Dub's Beach Rentals** (619/630-9343, http://kdubsbeachrentals.com; $15 minimum) and enjoy a ride around the **Bayside Walk** bike and pedestrian path (Mission Bay, www.sandiego.org). To get more adventurous, rent a kayak, paddleboard, or catamaran at **Mission Bay Sportcenter** (1010 Santa Clara Pl., 858/488-1004, www.missionbaysportcenter.com; summer Mon.-Fri. 10am-7pm, Sat-Sun. 9am-7pm, winter daily 10am-5pm; sailboats from $30/hr, powerboats from $75/hr, kayaks from $18/hr, pedal boats from $20/hr, SUP from $18/hr) and hit the bay.

Nearby Restaurants

If you're hungry, eating in this part of town is all about fish. Post-beach lunches or snacks don't get any better than the fish tacos at **Oscar's Mexican Seafood** (703 Turquoise St., Pacific Beach, 858/488-6392, www.oscarsmexicanseafood.com; Sun.-Thurs. 8am-9pm, Fri.-Sat. 8am-10pm). For dinner, raise the stakes; either dig into beautifully cooked local seafood at the upscale fish market and restaurant **The Fishery** (5040 Cass St., Pacific Beach, 858/272-9985, www.thefishery.com; daily 10am-10pm), or book a seat at the city's best sushi restaurant, **Sushi Ota** (4529 Mission Bay Dr., Pacific Beach, 858/270-5670; Mon. 5:30pm-10:30pm, Tues.-Fri. 11:30am-2pm and 5:30pm-10:30pm, Sat.-Sun. 5pm-10:30pm). If in search of cocktails to finish the night in style, see about getting in at dazzling tiki bar **The Grass Skirt** (910 Grand Ave., Pacific Beach, 858/412-5237, www.thegrassskirt.com; daily 5pm-2am).

Nearby Hotels

When traveling with children, the best place to spend the night anywhere in the vicinity of Mission Bay will be the **Bahia Resort Hotel** (998 W. Mission Bay Dr., Mission Bay, 858/488-0551, www.bahiahotel.com), with its calm bayside beaches and playful Polynesian theme. If you're out to take advantage of the Pacific Beach nightlife, make a worthy crash pad of the affordable **Surfer Beach Hotel** (711 Pacific Beach Dr., Pacific Beach, 858/483-7070, www.surferbeachhotel.com), or do yourself one better with an upgraded ocean view at **Tower23 Hotel** (723 Felspar St., Pacific Beach, 858/270-2323, www.t23hotel.com).

Ocean Beach and Point Loma

★ OB DOG BEACH

Accessible via the parking lot at the end of Voltaire Street, the wide swath of beach between the lifeguard tower north of the lot and the shallow San Diego River is an off-leash dog park. Sun-worshippers and surfers still visit this beach daily, but they accept the notion dogs may run up to them, splash them with water, and possibly pee on their stuff. Dogs that don't like waves swim and play on the river shore, while bona fide beach dogs frolic with balls and Frisbees where the surf meets the sand.

Map 6: Voltaire St., west of W. Point Loma Blvd.; daily 24 hours

★ OCEAN BEACH

This half-mile stretch of sand runs from the OB Pier in the south to the shallow San Diego River bordering the beach's northern edge. Around the pier are surfers and some saltier souls who earn the place comparisons to Venice Beach. Move north to find a welcoming stretch of sand with beach volleyball courts and areas designated for swimming and bodyboarding. Beach bonfires (within designated fire rings) are popular on summer nights, and fishing off the pier takes place daily. Parking lots are at the ends of Voltaire Street and Santa Monica Avenue, with showers and restrooms beside each. Lifeguards monitor the beach daily.

Map 6: West of Abbott St., between Newport Ave. and Voltaire St., 619/221-8899, www.sandiego.gov; daily 24 hours

★ SUNSET CLIFFS BEACH

Most of Sunset Cliffs Natural Park overlooks rocky shoreline, with no discernible beachfront. However, there's a 400-foot section of sand wide enough to coax local sunbathers and surfers down from the clifftops. Accessible by a steep, tricky dirt path that descends from the west side of Sunset Cliffs Boulevard just north of its intersection at Hill Street, the small beach has neither lifeguards nor amenities. You'll need a reasonable level of fitness to get down the path and then traverse a pile of loose boulders at its base. Your reward is ocean water with a rocky, sometimes sharp sea bottom not conducive to swimming. Nevertheless, it can get crowded in the summer, and most days you'll find people down there, watching surfers or merely working on their tans, away from the OB beach life.

Map 6: Sunset Cliffs Blvd. north of Hill St.; daily 24 hours

Nearby Activities

K-Dub's Beach Rentals (619/630-9343, http://kdubsbeachrentals.com; $15 minimum) can meet you at the pier with a board to rent or, if you'd rather, a beach cruiser to go take a ride along the **San Diego River Bike Path** (end of Voltaire St., west of W. Point Loma Blvd., 619/645-3183,

BEACHES
OCEAN BEACH AND POINT LOMA

Dog-Friendly San Diego

Dogs have it pretty good here. Plenty of parks around town are designated off-leash (at least part of the time), and entire chunks of beach are given over to rollicking pooches eager to swim (some even learn to surf).

- **Fiesta Island Dog Beach** (1590 E. Mission Bay Dr., 619/235-1169, www.sandiego.gov; daily 6am-10pm): Shallow water and endless shoreline make this massive bayside beach the park of choice for dogs who feel the urge to cover some ground. It's mostly sand and scrub, but to a dog, the myriad smells and long runs are the hallmarks of a favorite destination.

- **OB Dog Beach** (western end of Voltaire St.): A wide and very deep patch of beach at the north end of OB has been given over to the dogs. Pups range in size from small to large, and most are deliriously happy to splash and fetch in the shallow waves and sandbars that form along the beach. Visits to the city's only 24-hour off-leash beach are usually during daylight hours. Animal temperament is the responsibility of the owners, so stay vigilant with regards to your pets, and clean up after them with the plastic bags provided.

- **OB Dog Wash** (4933 Voltaire St., 619/523-1700, www.dogwash.com; daily 10am-9pm): If you're doing it right, a visit to OB Dog Beach leaves you with a dirty pup. This shop offers raised tubs and gentle sprays ideal for getting the sand out, with options like hypoallergenic shampoo and blow-dryers available.

- **Coronado Dog Beach** (north end of Ocean Blvd., before the gated military base, 619/522-7342, www.coronado.ca.us; daily 5am-11pm): On the other end of Coronado Beach from the Hotel del Coronado, local dogs love to frolic off leash on this beach with a view of Point Loma.

www.sdrc.ca.gov), at the north end of Ocean Beach. Later in the afternoon, stick around the area to take a long walk along the cliffs at **Sunset Cliffs Natural Park** (Sunset Cliffs Blvd. between Adair St. and Ladera St. and extending south of Ladera St., www.sunsetcliffs.info; free)—and definitely stick around to watch for one of the area's legendary colorful sunsets, which are especially likely when it's partly cloudy. The OB nightlife can be worth sticking around for, if only to marvel at the mash-up of personalities out for a given evening. Check out the bands playing at **Winston's Beach Club** (1921 Bacon St., Ocean Beach, 619/222-6822, www.winstonsob.com; daily 1pm-2am; $0-15 cover), or wade deep into the blacklit fluorescence of underwater-themed dive bar **Pacific Shores.**

Nearby Restaurants

If you've got time for a long lunch, wait in line for San Diego's most famous burgers over at **Hodad's** (5010 Newport Ave., Ocean Beach, 619/224-4623, www.hodadies.com; daily 11am-10pm); if you've got to wait anyway, hold

Dogs enjoy the sand and waves at OB Dog Beach.

- **Grape Street Dog Park** (Grape St. and 28th St., www.balboapark.org; Mon.-Fri. 7:30am-9pm, Sat.-Sun. 9am-9pm): This sprawling, grassy, five-acre off-leash dog park is surrounded by eucalyptus and edges a canyon off the Balboa Park city golf course. The park is not fully fenced in, so it might not be suitable for runners. Most of the dogs are pampered and friendly, and they tend to run in packs. There are restrooms on-site and water fountains for the dogs.

- **South Bark Dog Wash** (2037 30th St., 619/232-7387, www.southbark. com; daily 10am-7pm): Just around the corner from Grape Street Dog Park, this little shop has a dedicated furry clientele, often in need of a wash in one of the raised basins or just a little post-run treat.

out for a seat at the window counter so you can people-watch while you eat. The best dining in Point Loma is just over the hill from OB, in Liberty Station. Check out **Officine Buona Forchetta** (2865 Sims Rd., Liberty Station, 619/548-5770, www.officinebuonaforchetta.com; Mon.-Thurs. noon-3pm and 5pm-9:30pm, Fri. noon-3pm and 5pm-10:30pm, Sat. noon-10:30pm, Sun. noon-9pm) for divinely authentic Italian wood-fired pizza and handmade pasta. A few minutes away you'll find San Diego's hottest brewery; **Modern Times Beer** (3725 Greenwood St., Point Loma, 619/546-9694, www.moderntimesbeer.com; Mon.-Fri. noon-10pm, Sat.-Sun. noon-midnight) shows impeccably good taste in craft beer and quirky interior design.

Nearby Hotels

Shelter Island may be in the most out-of-the-way part of Point Loma, but it offers the best places to stay. **The Pearl** (1410 Rosecrans St., Point Loma, 619/226-6100, www.thepearlsd.com) took a midcentury roadside hotel and made it into one of the coolest places to stay in San Diego. **Humphreys Half Moon Inn** (2303 Shelter Island Dr., Shelter Island, 619/224-3411, www.halfmooninn.com) isn't just a bayside hotel and resort—it's got the city's top live music venue, which brings in incredible talent for sunset performances all summer long.

La Jolla

Map 7

BLACK'S BEACH

The hardest beach in San Diego to get to is one of its best. Black's sits at the bottom of high cliffs forming south of Torrey Pines—cliffs that also block its access from La Jolla Shores. As a result, the secluded beach is tough to get to, and not usually monitored by lifeguards, which makes it an unsanctioned tanning destination for nudists. However, for the most part, the beach only gets crowded with surfers, and the bluffs in either direction emphasize the beach's unspoiled beauty. Black's Beach may be accessed from a path beginning at the Torrey Pines Gliderport (2800 Torrey Pines Scenic Dr.) or by walking down a gated vehicular access road that winds steeply from La Jolla Farms Road (9601 La Jolla Farms Rd.).

Map 5: Ocean Front Walk, between Pacific Beach Dr. and N. Jetty Rd., Mission Beach, www.sandiego.gov

LA JOLLA COVE

It's a wonder how so many folks flock onto this little stretch of sand just a few steps from La Jolla Village. The cove teems with underwater life, making it a popular spot for scuba divers and snorkelers, often seen floating just a few dozen yards offshore. Sea lions and seals lounge on the large rocks sitting on either side of the beach, lolling on top of each other, barking, and catching some sun. Most of the year, waves are small or nonexistent, making for a fun swimmers' beach. But in the winter, uncommonly large swells may kick up a wave known as the Sleeping Giant, and local big-wave surfers flock to the cove to give onlookers an exhilarating show. Showers and restrooms are found above the rock faces surrounding the cove, along with a lifeguard tower.

Map 7: 1100 Coast Blvd., 619/221-8899, www.sandiego.gov; daily 24 hours

★ LA JOLLA SHORES

One of the most popular beaches in town, La Jolla Shores offers more than a mile of sand where beach lovers can swim, surf, bodyboard, play volleyball, scuba dive, and launch small watercraft. A beachside park and playground round out the family-friendliness of the place, which also has restrooms, showers, picnic tables, and fire rings near a public parking lot. It's extremely crowded in summer, when small, easy waves and warm water are the norm.

Map 7: 8200 Camino Del Oro, 619/221-8899, www.sandiego.gov; daily 24 hours

Top: Windansea. Bottom: La Jolla Shores.

Sandstone cliffs add a little scenic oomph at this state beach that sits below Torrey Pines State Natural Reserve. You may access the beach via hiking trails from the reserve, but it's easier to park in the lot beside the beach. If the lot's full, loop around to park on Carmel Valley Road, where it's just a short walk to the sand via the McGonagle Road underpass. The long, wide stretch of sand here offers plenty for swimmers and bodyboarders, as well as surfers toward the north end. That's also where you'll find showers and restrooms, and lifeguards on duty year-round. In calm conditions people enjoy diving.

Map 7: 12600 N. Torrey Pines Rd., 858/755-2063, www.parks.ca.gov; daily 7:15am-sunset

WINDANSEA

A small beach by any standards, this picturesque neighborhood spot amounts to a small sandy cove surrounded by rocky outcroppings. It's not a great place to swim; however, some locals just enjoy the sand here, as it's away from the larger beach crowds farther up the coast. Skilled surfers grab speedy, sculpted waves at a popular reef offshore, but while lifeguards monitor the beach daily, it's best used as a beautiful place to catch some rays.

Map 7: 6800 Neptune Pl., 619/221-8899, www.sandiego.gov; daily 9am-sunset

Nearby Activities

La Jolla's got no end of interesting things to do around its beaches. For one, rather than simply swim or gather sun, you may wish to get active, hooking up with **La Jolla Kayak** (2199 Avenida de la Playa, 858/459-1114, www.lajollakayak.com; daily 8am-6pm; from $45 pp) for a guided tour exploring the La Jolla sea caves. If you'd like to stay dry, simply heading uphill to visit the **Mt. Soledad National Veterans Memorial** (6905 La Jolla Scenic Dr. S., 858/459-2314, www.soledadmemorial.com; daily 7am-10pm, free) will earn you a special view of the whole county on a clear day. Or, if you prefer a little cultural enrichment, dust off the sand and pay a visit to the **Madison Gallery** (1055 Wall St., Ste.100, 858/459-0836, www.madisongalleries.com; Mon.-Sat.10am-6pm, Sun. by appt.) for a glimpse of what's current in contemporary art.

Nearby Restaurants

There are enough incredible dining options to keep you in La Jolla for days; half of the county's top restaurants are in La Jolla Village. When in doubt, try the seasonally inspired, Caribbean-by-way-of-California cuisine of **Nine-Ten** (910 Prospect St., La Jolla Village, 858/964-5400, www.nine-ten.com; Mon.-Sat. 6:30am-11am and 11:30am-2:30pm, Sun. 10:30am-2pm, Sun.-Thurs. 6pm-9:30pm, Fri.-Sat. 6pm-10pm), or treat yourself to one of the best restaurants in San Diego, **George's at the Cove** (1250 Prospect St., La Jolla Village, 858/454-4244, www.georgesatthecove.com; Sun.-Thurs. 11am-10pm, Fri.-Sat. 11am-11pm), which also happens to boast one of

the best oceanview patios, overlooking La Jolla Cove. If you don't feel like
dressing up, consider the decades-old local favorite for fresh seafood served
as you like it: **El Pescador Fish Market** (634 Pearl St., La Jolla Village,
858/456-2526, www.elpescadorfishmarket.com; daily 11am-9pm).

Nearby Hotels

You don't need to be a golf fan to appreciate the classically upscale perks of
staying at **The Lodge at Torrey Pines** (11480 N. Torrey Pines Rd., Torrey
Pines, 858/453-4420, www.lodgetorreypines.com), but if you do want a tee
time at Southern California's most famous seaside golf course, it makes
the decision easy. For Mediterranean-style accommodations conveniently
located within La Jolla Village, book a stay at **La Valencia Hotel** (1132
Prospect St., La Jolla Village, 858/454-0771, www.lavalencia.com) and
simply walk everywhere. Or, for oceanfront charm at a more budget-
conscious mind-set, the view from most rooms at **La Jolla Cove Suites**
(1155 Coast Blvd., La Jolla Village, 858/459-2621, www.lajollacove.com)
shows you practically everything you came here to see.

Coronado

Map 8

CORONADO BEACH

Routinely listed among the best beaches in the United States, Coronado
Beach is what makes this place a dreamy summer destination. Even during
fall and winter months, the beach is protected from both large surf and
the atmosphere's marine layer by the whale-shaped point of Point Loma,
visible on the north horizon; so while beaches elsewhere may be overcast
and full of rip currents, Coronado should be just about right. Bear in mind
that when big waves do hit this beach, it ceases to be an ideal place for
less-experienced swimmers. There are several access points from Ocean
Boulevard along the mile-long beach. In front of the Hotel del, you may
rent cabanas and order drinks; you'll find fire rings at the north end, while
volleyball courts, bathrooms, and showers are near the main lifeguard
tower manning the central beach.

Map 8: Ocean Blvd. from Hotel del Coronado to Ocean Dr., 619/522-7346,
www.coronado.ca.us; daily 24 hours

CORONADO DOG BEACH

At the north end of Coronado Beach, just before the fence bordering the
North Island Naval Air Station, a small stretch of sand is designated off-
leash for dogs. Note there's a long, sandy alley you must walk from Ocean
Boulevard to get to this beach, and the white sand can heat up and burn feet
and paws while walking a couple hundred yards to the water.

Map 8: North end of Ocean Blvd., before the gated military base, 619/522-7342,
www.coronado.ca.us; daily 5am-11pm

Which Beach is for You?

San Diego's beaches have different personalities, so choosing the right beach begins with finding the personality that suits you.

- **Pacific Beach (PB):** Attracts lots of athletic **students** and **young adults** who like to **party** and who usually try to find ways to impress other singles with their fit bodies or acts of incomprehensible stupidity. Great beaches for **surfing** and quick access to Mission Bay.

- **Mission Beach:** Stretching two miles south and north, the north end bleeds into PB, while farther south the mood becomes decidedly less rowdy. The southern and northern stretches pass through **quiet residential areas** and comfortable **vacation rentals,** on either side of the tourist hub around Belmont Park, with its **rides, games,** and **souvenir shops.** Hotels around Mission Beach give you the option of visiting beaches on either side of its narrow peninsula: the oceanfront, with its waves and sunsets, or the bay side, with sandy coastline on calm waters that feel safer for **young children.**

- **Ocean Beach (OB):** OB whoops it up, though the atmosphere is decidedly more of a **laid-back party** than PB (at least during the day). There is also a more **eclectic crowd:** At night hippies, surfers, military folk, and misfits mingle at the bars, which skew a little wider in age range and have a slightly reduced meat-market feel. These are also great beaches for **surfing,** with easy access to Mission Bay and the burgeoning **restaurant scene** over the hill in Point Loma.

- **La Jolla:** La Jolla Shores is one of the better **family beaches** in town. While the long strip of sand is served by only a handful of hotels

GLORIETTA BAY PARK

A grassy, tree-lined park with a small, sandy bayside beach is a great spot for family days. There are picnic tables, restrooms, and a playground suitable for small children, who can play in the calm bay water. There's also a boat launch for more rousing bay activities.

Map 8: 1975 Strand Way, 619/437-8788, www.coronado.ca.us; daily 24 hours

SILVER STRAND STATE BEACH

Thanks to its somewhat remote location, this 2.5-mile-long state beach tends to be among the least trafficked in the county. It's the sort of unspoiled beach experience that can be hard to come by. Even the waves are relatively uncrowded (mostly because they're not that great), but that just means more practice for the novice and plenty of opportunity to bodyboard or bodysurf. Campfires and bonfires within designated fire rings help warm summer nights, with restrooms and picnic areas near

Cabanas are available on Coronado Beach beside the Hotel del Coronado.

and a tiny two-block commercial district, it's the stuff beach getaways are made of. It's also remarkably crowded in summer with youngsters splashing around in the waves. **La Jolla Village,** just up the road, is entirely different—an **upscale** pocket of **glamour** with a few tiny beach coves and parks running parallel to its **shops, galleries,** and **restaurants.** Plenty of fine hotels juggle urban and beach amenities.

· **Coronado:** Across the bay from downtown, Coronado offers the relaxed atmosphere of a **beach resort town. Seniors** and **families** will thrive here, as something about being across that bridge seems to temper the crowds just a bit. Orange Avenue, Coronado's main drag, is only a few blocks inland and offers **convenient restaurants** and **shopping.** The legendary **Hotel del Coronado** sits at the south end of the beach, always worth a visit if only for historical interest and a beachfront cocktail.

the parking lot at the center of the beach. Follow a highway underpass by the parking lot to access the Silver Strand's much smaller, and waveless, bayside beach.

Map 8: 5000 Hwy. 75, 619/435-5184, www.parks.ca.gov; daily 8am-7pm; $10 parking

Nearby Activities

If you're going to hit the beach in Coronado, you've probably already decided to visit the **Hotel del Coronado** (1500 Orange Ave., 619/435-6611, www.hoteldel.com)—and with good reason, because the historic resort has still got it. While in the area, take the time to head over to the Coronado Ferry Landing to enjoy the view—there's a great perspective of the San Diego skyline. If you've got energy to burn, rent a bike and tackle a section of the **Bayshore Bikeway** (1000 N. Harbor Dr., www.keepsandiegomoving. com), down **Silver Strand State Beach** (5000 Hwy. 75, 619/435-5184, www. parks.ca.gov; daily 8am-7pm; $10 parking).

You'll find **Coronado Brewing Company** (170 Orange Ave., Coronado Ferry Landing, 619/437-4452, www.coronadobrewingcompany.com; Sun.-Thurs. 10:30am-9pm, Fri.-Sat. 10:30am-10pm) near the ferry landing; the award-winning craft beer brewpub has set a tone for drinking beer with food around here for decades. For local produce served with craft cocktails, grab a table at **Leroy's Kitchen and Lounge** (1015 Orange Ave., Coronado, 619/437-6087, www.leroyskitchenandlounge.com; Mon.-Thurs. 11am-10pm, Fri. 11am-midnight, Sat. 10am-midnight, Sun. 10am-10pm). If you're around on a Sunday with money to burn and loose attire, don't miss the gloriously over-the-top brunch buffet in the **Crown Room** (1500 Orange Ave., 619/522-8490, www.hoteldel.com; Sun. 9:30am-1pm) at the Hotel del; dozens of individual food stations will serve you any kind of food you've ever considered brunch fare, and you will stuff yourself silly.

Nearby Hotels

It goes without saying the best stay on Coronado will be at the legendary **Hotel del Coronado,** but there are other fine options. Many of the rooms at **Glorietta Bay Inn** (1630 Glorietta Blvd., 800/283-9383, www.gloriettabayinn.com) reside within a repurposed mansion, shedding light on a little Coronado history. The **1906 Lodge** (1060 Adella Ave., 619/437-1900, www.1906lodge.com) shows off a little vintage of its own, with beautiful Arts and Crafts architecture contributed by San Diego's most influential architect, Irving Gill.

Greater San Diego   Map 9

BEACONS BEACH

Officially, this neighborhood beach is **Leucadia State Beach,** but everybody simply knows it as Beacons. A small public parking lot leads to a winding path down a shallow hillside to the beach, where cliffs and rocks form on either side to help the place feel just the right amount of removed from civilization. In addition to swimming and surfing, people come here for boating, fishing, and diving activities.

Map 9: 948 Neptune Ave., Leucadia, 760/633-2740, www.beaconsbeach.com; daily 24 hours

CARDIFF STATE BEACH

Longboard-friendly reefs off the shore attract surfers to this state beach, right beside the San Elijo beach campground. But it's just as good for lounging in the sand and swimming. People also fish and dive here when

Clockwise from top left: Moonlight State Beach; Oceanside City Beach; Del Mar City Beach.

conditions accommodate. Parking is available along the highway and in a day-use parking lot ($8), where you'll find restrooms and showers.

Map 9: 2500 S. Coast Hwy. 101, Cardiff-by-the-Sea, 760/753-5091, www.parks.ca.gov; daily dawn-sunset

CARLSBAD STATE BEACH

Accessible from Carlsbad Village, Carlsbad State Beach is fronted by resort hotels and street parking, lending to its resort town appeal. Popular activities include swimming, surfing, diving, and fishing. Restrooms and showers are available near Pine Street, and at the south end of Carlsbad beach, at the Tamarack surf beach, which also benefits from a free public parking lot.

Map 9: 7201 Carlsbad Blvd., Carlsbad Village, 760/438-3143, www.parks.ca.gov; daily dawn-sunset

DEL MAR CITY BEACH

Del Mar Beach runs the length of Del Mar, mostly found at the ends of residential streets and best accessed at the town center around 15th and 17th Streets. The mile-long stretch of beach is popular among local surfers and casual beachgoers, and many like to walk along the cliffs rising to the south when beaches appear during low tide. Restrooms and showers are available by the main lifeguard tower at 17th Street, with public parking across Coast Boulevard. Picnic tables and a tot lot are available at a pair of grassy parks on either side of railroad tracks above the beach: Powerhouse Park (1658 Coast Blvd.) and Seagrove Park (15th St. and Coast Blvd.).

Map 9: West of Coast Blvd. from 15th St. to 29th St., Del Mar, 858/755-1556, www.delmar.ca.us; daily 24 hours

FLETCHER COVE BEACH PARK

The central beach in Solana Beach sometimes gets called the "Pillbox" from the term for the type of defensive enclosed gun fort standing sentry here during World War II. Today, the small, pretty beach is used for surfing, surf-fishing, and swimming. It has free public parking, public showers, and restroom facilities as well as picnic tables, a playground, and a basketball court on the bluffs above. Lifeguards are on duty daily.

Map 9: 111 S. Sierra Ave., Solana Beach, 858/720-2400, www.ci.solana-beach.ca.us; daily 24 hours

★ MOONLIGHT STATE BEACH

Moonlight Beach is a sight to behold, with turquoise waters and light-sand beaches backed by sandstone cliffs—you won't really get Encinitas until you've seen its beach. Sun worshippers abound, and surfers usually show up when (typically mild) waves come through, though it's also good for diving and fishing. A parking lot features restrooms and showers, though it's just a couple blocks from town. Visit during the day, although it also happens to be pretty nice when the moon is out.

Map 9: 400 B St., Encinitas, 760/633-2740, www.parks.ca.gov; daily 5am-10pm

NORTH AND SOUTH PONTO BEACHES

Separated by the ocean outlet for the Batiquitos Lagoon, North and South Ponto Beaches are both on the southern end of South Carlsbad State Park, each offering swimming, surfing, and sunbathing. North Ponto is larger and arguably more scenic, but it also charges $8 in its day-use parking lot. Meanwhile, South Ponto boasts volleyball courts, free parking, and showers in addition to restrooms. Those things make the smaller beach more popular.

Map 9: 6325 Carlsbad Blvd., Carlsbad, 760/720-7001, www.parks.ca.gov; daily 6am-11pm

NORTH BEACH (DOG BEACH)

A small section north of Del Mar City Beach on the San Dieguito Lagoon, North Beach offers volleyball courts and leashed pets. But it gets the name Dog Beach between Labor Day and June 15, when canines are allowed off-leash to play in the sand and surf. The beach is not fenced in and is close to the highway, so only bring a dog that responds faithfully to voice commands.

Map 9: 3200 Camino Del Mar, 858/755-1556, www.delmar.ca.us; daily 24 hours

OCEANSIDE CITY BEACH—THE STRAND

Also known as The Strand, Oceanside City Beach runs straight for about four miles, from Carlsbad north to Oceanside Harbor. Most of the beach is free of heavy crowds, except in the peak of summer. Surfers tend to stick near the harbor and a quarter-mile pier jutting out from the center of town, but wide swaths of sand stretch the entire length, with shallow swimming areas good for kids and beginning surfers. Amenities include picnic tables, grills, fire rings, restrooms, and showers, while an amphitheater at the base of the pier hosts summer concerts.

Map 9: 301 The Strand N., Oceanside, 760/435-4018, www.ci.oceanside.ca.us; daily 24 hours

Nearby Activities

Oceanside's top tourist draw is considered the king of California's 21 missions, the **Mission San Luis Rey de Francia** (4050 Mission Ave., 760/757-3651, www.sanluisrey.org; Mon.-Thurs. 9:30am-5pm, Sat.-Sun. 10am-5pm; $5 adults, $4 seniors and ages 6-18, free military). But you can also spend a good couple of hours enriching your surf history at the **California Surf Museum** (312 Pier View Way, Oceanside, 760/721-6876, www.surfmuseum. org; Fri.-Wed. 10am-4pm, Thurs. 10am-8pm; $5 adults, $3 seniors, military, and students, free under age 12). Other than the beach, the biggest and best reason to visit Carlsbad has to be Legoland (1 Legoland Dr., 877/376-5346, www.legoland.com; daily from 10am, closing hours vary, $95-119 adults, $89-113 ages 3-12); the toy-brick-themed amusement park is supposedly best enjoyed by young children, but all ages seem to have a blast.

Nearby Restaurants

In Carlsbad, the relatively new Campfire (2725 State St., Carlsbad, 760/637-5121, www.thisiscampfire.com; Mon. 5pm-11pm, Tues.-Thurs. 11:30am-11pm, Fri. 11:30am-1am, Sat. 10am-1am, Sun. 10am-11pm) is already one of the most outstanding restaurants in all of North County. But if you want to delve into something experimental and truly memorable, make sure you make it to dinner at unorthodox sushi specialist Wrench & Rodent Seabasstropub (1815 S. Coast Hwy., Oceanside, 760/271-0531, www.seabasstropub.com; Mon. 4pm-9pm, Tues.-Sun. 4pm-10pm); its creative cuisine exists nowhere in the world but Oceanside. With that in mind, a humble pub dinner and beer at Bagby Beer Company (601 S. Coast Hwy., Oceanside, 760/512-3372, www.bagbybeer.com; Sun.-Thurs. 11am-10pm, Fri.-Sat. 11am-11pm) actually yields tasty food and world-class craft beer covering a refreshing range of traditional styles, as well as hoppy San Diego ales.

Nearby Hotels

To stay conveniently close to Legoland, Carlsbad by the Sea Hotel (850 Palomar Airport Rd., Carlsbad, 760/438-7880, www.carlsbadhotelbythesea.com) offers reasonable accommodations, despite not being next to the ocean. If you are looking for that oceanfront stay, head to charming Carlsbad Village and book a room at ideally located Tamarack Beach Resort (3200 Carlsbad Blvd., 800/334-2199, www.tamarackresort.com).

Sports and Activities

Highlights

★ **Sailing in San Diego Bay:** You may learn a thing or two about ropes and knots while out on a boat with **Seaforth Boat Rentals,** located downtown and in Coronado (pages 86 and 107).

★ **Cycling Around Mission Bay:** You'll get a good view of the water while riding along **Bayside Walk,** a path circumnavigating the entire bay (page 92).

★ **Best Spot for a Picnic:** Pick up some picnic items from Bread & Cie or Siesel's Old Fashioned Meats and head up to the grassy slopes of **Kate O. Sessions Memorial Park** for a panoramic view of the city and water (page 93).

★ **Best Surfing for a Novice:** It may not be the top choice for experienced surfers, but for the novice, a mild day at **Tourmaline Surf Park** will feed your stoke (page 95).

★ **Jet Skiing in Mission Bay:** The easiest way to learn how to Jet Ski around the bay is by checking out **Adventure Water Sports** (page 97).

★ **Best Golf Swing with a View:** Try your mettle at **Torrey Pines Golf Course,** the site of the 2021 U.S. Open and one of the most scenic courses in California (page 102).

★ **Paragliding at Torrey Pines:** At **Torrey Pines Gliderport** it's tough to call the better thrill—winds lifting you up to greater heights or the view of the cliffs and the coastline while it happens (page 103).

★ **Best Surfing for an Expert:** It takes a hike to get there, but the almond-shaped barrels of **Black's Beach** are well worth the effort (page 105).

★ **Best Underwater Encounters:** The protected marine habitats of the **La Jolla Underwater Park** offer a great scuba and snorkel environment (page 106).

sailboats in San Diego Bay

M any people come to San Diego to relax on the beach and let all of life's stresses melt away—and that's always a great reason to visit.

But when you get a look at just how many different kinds of thrills you can experience with two large bays and 80 miles of coastline at your disposal, you might want to get off your beach blanket and live a little. There are a lot of fun things to do in San Diego that you simply can't experience most other places, and sometimes that's motivation enough for seizing the day by flying, riding, skiing, or diving.

Some come here to surf, but it's not all about action sports. There are so many ways to engage; it's really more about setting your tempo and going with it. Kayak on Mission Bay, sip drinks on a sailboat, swing a club on the greens at Torrey Pines, hold tight to a tow-line while gliding across the water's surface, or practice yoga on a stand-up paddleboard. Some enterprising souls find a way to do it all, even squeezing in a little time to lounge on the sand between activities and following it up by drinking a couple of the region's celebrated craft beers before enjoying a most satisfying and well-earned night of sleep.

Previous: Torrey Pines Golf Course; a young surfer checking out the waves.

BOATING

ON THE WATER ADVENTURES

Most summer weekends, the Maritime Museum offers unique, four-hour tours of the harbor on replica sailing vessels from bygone centuries. There's the 1848 cutter the SS *Californian*, a tall ship that chased down gold rush era smugglers and tax evaders; and the San Salvador, a replica of the Spanish galleon that first brought explorer Juan Rodríguez Cabrillo into San Diego in 1542.

Map 1: 1492 N. Harbor Dr., Marina District, 619/234-9153, www.sdmaritime.org; summer only Sat.-Sun. 11:30am-4pm; $99 adults, $94 seniors, students, and military, $59 ages 3-12

★ SEAFORTH BOAT RENTALS

If you didn't bring your sailboat or yacht with you, this company has you covered, with charters and rentals available for each. Larger boats head out from downtown or other locations in Harbor Island (955 Harbor Island Dr., Ste. 130) and Coronado (1715 Strand Way). For smaller craft, look to Mission Bay (1641 Quivera Rd.).

Map 1: 333 W. Harbor Dr., Gate 1, Marina District, 888/834-2628, www.seaforthboatrental. com; Mon.-Fri. 10am-5:30pm, Sat.-Sun. 9am-5:30pm; watercraft rentals $40-1,500

BOWLING

EAST VILLAGE TAVERN+BOWL

With only six lanes, this place gives a little more real estate to the tavern than the bowl, but that shouldn't keep anyone from whiling away a rainy day shooting pool and knocking down pins while drinking better beer than most bowlers in the world.

Map 1: 930 Market St., 619/677-2695, www.tavernbowl.com; Sun.-Thurs. 11am-midnight, Fri.-Sat. 11am-2am; $20-46/hr

CYCLING

BAYSHORE BIKEWAY

The Bayshore Bikeway's 24-mile route begins or ends at the Broadway Pier, depending on how you look at it. Your best bet is to take the ferry to Coronado and ride south through Silver Strand State Beach and back. Or take a more leisurely course from Marina Park South (1 Marina Park Way) and pedal north along Harbor Drive.

Map 1: 1000 N. Harbor Dr., www.keepsandiegomoving.com

THE BIKE REVOLUTION

The Revolution is the sort of bike shop where the mechanics on staff can set up your rental bike and tune it to your needs. Whether you're looking to just roll over to Little Italy or tackle the Bayshore Bikeway, Revolution has mountain bikes, road bikes, and cruisers for rent and even offers delivery service.

Map 1: 522 6th Ave., Gaslamp, 619/564-4843, www.thebikerevolution.com; daily 9am-5pm; bike rentals $8-12/hr, $20-35/day

PARKS
EMBARCADERO MARINA PARK

Marina Parks North and South are two parks built around the Embarcadero marina that offer grassy fields, shoreline access, and terrific views of San Diego Harbor. Park South features basketball courts with a view of the Coronado Bridge, while Park North connects to Seaport Village shops and restaurants. They're not bad places to picnic or fly a kite. The Embarcadero is occasionally the site of music, food, and cultural festivals.

Map 1: 400 Kettner Blvd., Marina District, 619/686-6200, www.portofsandiego.org; daily 6am-10:30pm; free

HORTON PLAZA PARK

After being closed to the public for years, this recently reconstructed urban plaza fronting the Horton Plaza mall finally reopened in 2016. Inspired by amphitheater-style public parks in Portland and Seattle, it's the site of occasional public markets, performances, and other events, but most days it provides a place for local professionals to find a relaxing lunch spot. The park's main attraction is the 1908 Broadway Fountain, a domed fountain designed by legendary local architect Irving Gill.

Map 1: 900 4th Ave., 619/544-8180, www.hortonplazapark.com; daily 5am-midnight; free

WATERFRONT PARK

Just across Pacific Highway from the Maritime Museum, this county park includes a grassy field, playground equipment, and ankle-deep fountains with lots of water jets to keep you cool in summer—all within view of unfurled sails and the harbor beyond. It's occasionally the site of music and food festivals.

Map 1: 1600 Pacific Hwy., 619/232-7275, www.sdcounty.ca.gov/parks; daily 6am-10pm; free

SPECTATOR SPORTS
PETCO PARK

When the home of the **Padres** opened in 2004, local fans rejoiced. Though the Padres still didn't make the postseason, we do love the stadium, which easily boasts the best beer selection in the Major Leagues. An iconic brick Western Metal Works building backs up the left field fence, while an ingenious Park within the Park (open to the public during nongame times) sits behind the center field bullpen, a grassy slope with a partial view into the stadium and a large screen televising any game action hidden from view. Anyone with a ticket can check out this brilliant seventh-inning stretch

Clockwise from top left: the Old Town Trolley Tours bus; Waterfront Park; Petco Park

territory, which also happens to be served by favorite local vendors, including Stone Brewing, Green Flash, Hodad's, and Phil's BBQ.

Map 1: 100 Park Blvd., 619/795-5000, www.petcoparkevents.com; hours and admission vary

TOURS

ANOTHER SIDE OF SAN DIEGO TOURS

These Segway tours guide you throughout San Diego, with packages designed to tour downtown, Balboa Park, and the beach areas. You'll ride along with ease, silently mocking pedestrians using their own two feet, and probably being mocked back on occasion.

Map 1: 300 G St., 619/239-2111, www.anothersideofsandiegotours.com; daily 8am-6pm; Segway tours $75-200 pp

Balboa Park

Map 2

DISC GOLF

MORLEY FIELD DISC GOLF COURSE

Between the Frisbee and golf influences, this isn't exactly an action sport. But it's a great way to spend a few hours walking around Morley Field, tucked within the tree-lined northeast corner of Balboa Park, one of the city's greenest areas. It's a casual course for a casual game, and everybody seems to enjoy themselves. Discs are for sale or rent; if you want to do the course right, you'll need at least a couple of different sizes.

Map 2: 3090 Pershing Dr., 619/692-3607, www.morleyfield.com; daily sunrise-sunset; $3 weekdays, $4 weekends, rentals available

GOLF

BALBOA PARK GOLF COURSE

Certainly not the best-known city golf course, Balboa Park's 18 holes deserve better notice, if only for the view. One end of the course looks out at the bay and skyline, while another strolls past the beautiful Craftsman homes of the North Park and South Park neighborhoods. Warm up on one of the 14 station driving ranges, practice on the putting green, or beef up your technique with instruction from one of the PGA-certified golf pros on staff.

Map 2: 2600 Golf Course Dr., 619/235-1184, www.sandiego.gov; daily 7am-4pm; $14-32 resident, $18-40 nonresident

PARKS

DESERT GARDEN

At the eastern end of El Prado, cross the pedestrian bridge over Park Boulevard to find this richly diverse desert garden. Succulents and drought-resistant plants typical of the Mojave and Colorado Deserts are displayed across 2.5 acres. Time your visit in January-March for wildflower blooms.

Map 2: 2525 Park Blvd., 619/525-8213, www.balboapark.org; daily 24 hours; free

Old Town and Mission Hills Map 4

CYCLING

ELECTRIC BIKE CENTRAL

Helmets and locks are included with bike rentals from this shop, whether you plan to go with traditional pedal power or zip around more effortlessly on an electric bike.

Map 4: 1851 San Diego Ave., Ste. 100B, Old Town, 619/564-7028, http://electricbikecentral. com; Tues.-Sat. 10am-5pm, Sun. 10am-3pm; $30/2 hrs electric, $8/hr traditional bike

GOLF

PRESIDIO HILLS GOLF COURSE

Established in 1932, this small course is the oldest in town, featuring 18 par-3 holes for a cheap, short course central to the city. Pay special attention to the clubhouse, which predates the golf course by more than a century (built in 1820, it would be the oldest residential structure in San Diego were it not part of the golf course). Weekly clinics and by-appointment lessons are offered for adults and children.

Map 4: 4136 Wallace St., 619/295-9476; daily 8am-4pm; $12-18

PARKS

PRESIDIO PARK

The grassy slopes of this Old Town park catch a cool western breeze; on a clear day, you might see out to SeaWorld, Mission Bay, and the ocean. Find shade in the tree-covered arbor in the lower southern section of the park, or enjoy a view of Mission Valley from Inspiration Point in the northern part.

Map 4: 2811 Jackson St., 619/692-4918, www.sandiego.gov; daily 6am-10pm

TOURS

OLD TOWN TROLLEY TOURS

You'll see the orange and green Old Town Trolley buses all over town, providing hop-on, hop-off tours to visitors, originating from Old Town every 30 minutes. A tour can be a convenient way to see some of the top city sights, with 10 stops in key locations, including the Maritime Museum, Seaport Village, Horton Plaza, the Gaslamp, the Embarcadero Marina, Coronado, Balboa Park, and Little Italy. It takes two hours to complete a loop, with guides offering a running narrative along the way.

Map 4: 4010 Twiggs St., 619/298-8687, www.trolleytours.com/san-diego; daily 9am-5pm; $36 adults, $23 children 4-12

Top: cycling the Bayside Walk. Bottom: view from Kate O. Sessions Memorial Park.

BEACH RENTALS

CHEAP RENTALS

Rent surfboards, bikes, kayaks, paddleboards, wetsuits, snorkeling gear, beach umbrellas, and chairs from this, as they say, cheap spot. Other items for rent include a GoPro camera to attach to the front of your surfboard to capture the highs and lows of your wave session. The main shop sits on Mission Boulevard, a short walk from the beach or bay.

Map 5: 3689 Mission Blvd., Mission Beach, 858/488-9070, www.cheap-rentals.com; daily 10am-5pm; surf rentals $7-15/hr, $20-30/day; bike rentals $6-12/hr, $15-30/day; boat rentals $15/hr, $40-50/day

K-DUB'S BEACH RENTALS

You can pretty much rent gear for any beach activity from this delivery service, and employees will bring it wherever you are in Ocean Beach, Pacific Beach, Mission Beach, or Mission Bay. That includes surfboards, paddleboards, boogie boards, volleyball and net, beach chairs, beach umbrellas, corn hole sets, and coolers. You can even rent a bike in one location and have it picked up at another.

Map 5: Mission Bay and beaches, Ocean Beach, 619/630-9343, http://kdubsbeachrentals.com; $15 minimum

CYCLING

★ BAYSIDE WALK

A biking, walking, and jogging path hugs almost the entire inner circumference of Mission Bay, offering 27 miles to explore. You can pretty much pick your starting point: a block east of Mission Boulevard in Mission Beach, or a block south of Pacific Beach Drive at Fanuel Street Park. You can also pick up the trail as it cuts through Crown Point Park. Wherever you are in Mission Bay, look for the narrow paved path running alongside the water's edge.

Map 5: multiple access points around Mission Bay, www.sandiego.org

RAY'S RENTALS

All sorts of bikes, Rollerblades, and skateboards can be rented at this spot that clearly caters to the boardwalk cruising lifestyle. Choose from tandem bikes, beach cruisers, and BMX wheels, or rent a towable cruiser for those too young to ride. A second location is up the road in Pacific Beach (4655 Mission Blvd.).

Map 5: 3221 Mission Blvd., Mission Beach, 866/488-7297, www.rays-rentals.com; daily 9am-7pm; bike rentals $8/hr, $12/day; surfboards $10-15/hr, $20-30/day; kayaks $15/hr, $35/day

FISHING

SEAFORTH SPORTFISHING

Heading out into deep waters to troll for big fish is what this outfit is all about. You'll go as far as coastal Mexican waters on half-day or overnight trips in search of active spots. Choose from large boats with dozens of people or smaller private charters.

Map 5: 1717 Quivira Rd., Mission Bay, 619/224-3383, www.seaforthlanding.com; daily 5am-9:30pm, from $48, $38 children, seniors, and military

GOLF

MISSION BAY GOLF COURSE AND PRACTICE CENTER

This small and aging city course has a couple of things going for it: location and lights. Located at the northeast corner of Mission Bay, it's easy to get to whether you're staying in Mission Beach or Pacific Beach. The 18-hole, mostly par-3 course is the only lighted one in town, making it the best bet for a late round on a quick, inexpensive course.

Map 5: 2702 N. Mission Bay Dr., Mission Bay, 858/581-7880, www.sandiego.gov; daily 6:45am-9:30pm; $29 non-resident, $24 resident

KITEBOARDING

MANTA WIND & WATER SPORTS

A variety of kiteboarding packages aim to get you into the air and out on the sea, with pricing designed to benefit groups. Rental boards and harnesses are available for those traveling to the area with their own kite.

Map 5: 2203 Denver St., Mission Bay, 858/610-6000, www.mantawatersports.com; daily 9am-6pm, from $179

PARKS

CROWN POINT PARK

A large inner-bayside beach with grassy areas and picnic tables, Crown Point sees a lot of grilling and light watercraft activities. A popular place for birthday parties or just a friendly gathering for a game of horseshoes or Frisbee, the beach also has a boat ramp where you can launch kayaks, motorboats, catamarans, and Jet Skis. Parking is plentiful.

Map 5: 1759-1799 Moorland Dr., Mission Bay, 619/525-8213, www.sandiego.gov; daily 24 hours, lot closes at 10pm; free

★ KATE O. SESSIONS MEMORIAL PARK

One of the best parks in San Diego for a picnic, this grassy hillside space is named for the celebrated horticulturist and so-called "Mother of Balboa Park." While it may not have quite as many nonnative plants as Sessions would have liked, she would admire the view, which extends from the downtown skyline through Mission Bay north into Pacific Beach. It has a small playground, picnic tables, and restrooms, but mostly just green slopes and a smattering of relaxed people enjoying the gorgeous scenery.

Map 5: 5115 Soledad Rd., Pacific Beach, 619/525-8213, www.sandiego.gov; daily 24 hours

Clockwise from top left: kayakers on Mission Bay; a rental sailboat on Mission Bay; a surfer at Tourmaline Surf Park.

Surf Spots
CRYSTAL PIER SURF SPOT
Because the waves breaking next to Crystal Pier tend to be soft, fun rides right in the middle of central Pacific Beach, they become a popular testing ground for lots of beginners on rental boards during the summer. It's lighter on the crowds fall-winter, but as long as everybody keeps it friendly and safe, it can be a good time regardless. Best accessed down stairs at the end of Felspar Street, with mostly street parking in the area.

Map 5: Mission Blvd. at Felspar St., Pacific Beach

MISSION BEACH SURF SPOT
There's crowded, beginner-appropriate surf in front of the shops and restaurants around Belmont Park. But this beach stretches 1.5 miles north, and when you get away from the big parking lots and public amenities, the shifting beach breaks along this stretch draw fewer crowds, particularly during the week. In small conditions, it can provide an opportunity for beginners to practice on average waves without getting in an experienced surfer's way. Keep an eye out for designated surf and swim zones. Waves show up year-round but are often smaller in the summer.

Map 5: Mission Blvd. from Belmont Park to Santa Rita Pl., Mission Beach

SOUTH MISSION SURF SPOT
South of Belmont Park, a residential neighborhood fronts a long stretch of sand that continues until it hits the channel where Mission Bay boats access the Pacific, cordoned off from the beach by a long jetty. There are designated beach-break surf areas along this beach, where beginners may find accessible spots, but experienced surfers will find the best rides going left off the jetty. There's a parking lot to access the area at the south terminus of Mission Boulevard, along with showers and bathrooms.

Map 5: 3071 Mission Blvd. and N. Jetty Rd., Mission Beach

★ TOURMALINE SURF PARK
A dedicated surf park in every sense of the word, Tourmaline's charm begins in the parking lot, where crusty old surfers congregate over longboards and listen to classic rock anthems on the stereo of someone's VW bus. The waves breaking along the beach often favor longboards, but the way waves spread out across this length of coast makes it possible for different levels of surfers to coexist. South of the parking lot is an area for novice surfers to improve, though watch out for kelp beds floating in to the beach (the ropey seaweed can wrap around your arms, legs, and surfboard leash). North of the lot, farther out, expert surfers will find plenty to like in a large swell when PB Point starts to take off. However, when the surf forecast is 2-4 feet, the free parking, lifeguards, restrooms, showers, ease of access, and gentle surf make Tourmaline a great spot to be part of the surf community.

Map 5: Tourmaline St., west of La Jolla Blvd., Pacific Beach

Beginners' Surf Spots

There's a lot of beach in San Diego, but there are only a few surf spots appropriate for beginners—and even then, only on days when the waves don't go much higher than your kneecaps.

Stick to these breaks on calm, easy days and remember—there are probably other surfers trying to catch the same waves as you. (The person closest to the middle of the wave has the right of way, so look over your shoulder and make sure there isn't someone else riding in behind you.)

a stack of surfboards ready for the day's lesson

- **Tourmaline Surf Park** (Tourmaline St., west of La Jolla Blvd.): This wide beach offers a number of different areas; better surfers tend to stick to the north end. Beginners can't compete for waves against experienced riders, so stick to the smaller waves while you learn.

- **La Jolla Shores** (8200 Camino Del Oro): There are several designated surf zones along La Jolla Shores. As you move south, the breaks are safe bets for beginners. Just keep an eye out for swimmers who veer into the surf zone by mistake.

- **Coronado Beach** (Ocean Blvd. from Hotel del Coronado to North Island Naval Air Station): Coronado isn't known as a great surf destination, which makes it a good option for learners. Provided there are small breaking waves, the lack of experienced surfers will give beginners a chance to catch a few waves, which is really the only way to learn.

Surf Shops and Schools
SURFARI SURF SCHOOL

If you don't learn to surf during your first lesson, your second is free. Such is the guarantee from this North Mission Beach rental shop and surf school. Lessons head out at 9am, 11am, 1pm, and 3pm, each lasting 1.5 hours plus an extra hour with the board for practice. Class sizes run 3-5 people per instructor, with prices favoring groups signing up together. Stand-up paddleboarding classes and rentals are also available.

Map 5: 3740 Mission Blvd., Mission Beach, 858/337-3287, www.surfarisurfschool.com; daily 9am-5pm; $55-85 pp

WATER SPORTS

★ ADVENTURE WATER SPORTS

Mission Bay is a watery playground, and this place has all the toys and equipment you need to join in the fun. Rent a powerboat and cruise the bay, go wakeboarding or waterskiing, ride Jet Skis, or take it slow with pedal boats, aqua cycles, and stand-up paddleboards. All their gear offers direct access to the south portion of the bay; there's a second location on the north end at Campland on the Bay (2211 Pacific Beach Dr., 858/581-9300).

Map 5: 1710 W. Mission Bay Dr., Mission Bay, 619/226-8611, www.adventurewatersports. com; daily 8:30am-4pm; boat rentals from $130/hr, Jet Skis from $110/hr

JETPACK AMERICA

Jetpack America uses water jets to aerially propel (or "jetpack") you over water. While it may not be the fiery flight of science fiction, it can be a lot of exhilarating fun. Packages include classroom instruction, with options for a video of your efforts set to the music of your choice.

Map 5: 1010 Santa Clara Pl., Mission Beach, 888/553-6471, www.jetpackamerica.com; daily 10am-5pm; from $99

MISSION BAY AQUATIC CENTER

A lot of Mission Bay water sports take a little instruction the first time. This large instructional facility offers lessons to help you get your sea legs. Windsurfing, wakeboarding, stand-up paddleboarding, kayaking, sailing: Just listing all the classes this place offers is enough to wipe you out. It's certainly the kind of coursework that can make for a memorable vacation.

Map 5: 1001 Santa Clara Pl., Mission Beach, 858/488-1000, www.mbaquaticcenter. com; Tues.-Sun. 8am-5pm; classes from $49, kayak rentals from $21, sail rentals from $31, windsurf rentals from $31, SUP rentals from $26

MISSION BAY SPORTCENTER

Water sports rentals abound at this large Mission Bay facility, which covers tow sports, paddle sports, wave and wind sports—basically a little bit of everything you might want to do in San Diego. Rentals don't require any pre-instruction or certification, so you can enter your small catamaran on the bay right there and see how well your instincts handle turning a small sail into the wind. If you want to rent a powerboat and add a couple of wakeboards or Jet Skis, this is your spot.

Map 5: 1010 Santa Clara Pl., 858/488-1004, www.missionbaysportcenter.com; summer Mon.-Fri. 10am-7pm, Sat-Sun. 9am-7pm, winter daily 10am-5pm; sailboats from $30/hr, powerboats from $75/hr, kayaks from $18/hr, pedal boats from $20/hr, SUP from $18/hr

SAN DIEGO JET SKI

If you already know how to Jet Ski and would like to keep your rental for a while, visit this shop. It's not on Mission Bay, but it does offer tow equipment so that you can take the rental wherever you'd like to go. Your best bet is the Ski Beach launch located at Crown Point (1799 Moorland Dr.).

Map 5: 4275 Mission Bay Dr., Mission Bay, 858/272-6161, www.sdjetski.com; daily 9am-6pm, from $75

UNDERWATER SPORTS

LA JOLLA WATER SPORTS

These guys will take you to look at sharks or dive for lobster, or teach you how to spear fish. Or simply motor along the water's surface with a water scooter, goggles down, watching the underwater life unfold as you explore La Jolla Cove and caves.

Map 5: 2710 Garnet Ave. #110, Pacific Beach, 619/788-6416, www.lajollawatersports.com; daily 9am-5pm; from $40 pp

WHALE-WATCHING

SAN DIEGO WHALE WATCH

San Diego's ocean is teeming with life, and it's ironic that the largest creatures out there may be the toughest to spot. These three-hour whale-watching tours help seek them out, hopefully on days they're willing to breach. The boat departs from this bayside facility; snacks and drinks are available during the tour, and there are some activities for kids. Bring a jacket, as it's usually cooler out on the ocean than it is on land.

Map 5: 1717 Quivira Rd., Mission Bay, 619/839-0128, www.sdwhalewatch.com; daily 5am-10pm, from $48 adults, $44 seniors, military, children 2-17

Ocean Beach and Point Loma

Map 6

BOATING

CALIFORNIA CRUISIN'

Want to sleep on a yacht? You can—and that's only one of the choices offered by this charter boat service, which includes private dinner cruises, sailing charters, and houseboat rentals on San Diego Bay.

Map 6: 1450 Harbor Island Dr., Harbor Island, 619/296-8000, www.californiacruisin.com; daily 8:30am-5:30pm; call for pricing

SAN DIEGO BAY ADVENTURES

Mission Bay doesn't get to have all the fun. Jet Ski and stand-up paddleboard rentals and tours from this outfit put you out in the big bay, within view of skyscrapers, clipper ships, and active naval vessels.

Map 6: 1880 Harbor Island Dr., Harbor Island, 619/889-4294, www.sdbayadventures.com; daily 9am-6pm; Jet Skis $99/hr, kayaks $20/hr, stand-up paddleboards $20/hr

These guys offer shared sailing packages to individuals and small groups, taking up to six people at a time for 2-4-hour tours of San Diego Bay. You can help work the boat or sit back and enjoy complimentary drinks and snacks. Reasonable private packages are also available.

Map 6: 1450 Harbor Island Dr., Harbor Island, 619/786-0173, www.sandiegosailingtours. com; daily 9am-9pm; from $79 pp

CYCLING

SAN DIEGO RIVER BIKE PATH

This bike path will eventually extend from the ocean to the mountains. For now, it's a somewhat manageable five or six miles from OB Dog Beach, heading east through parts of Mission Valley and almost entirely removed from car traffic. This trail also connects to the Mission Bay Trail just north, for a longer day of beach riding.

Map 6: End of Voltaire St., west of W. Point Loma Blvd., 619/645-3183, www.sdrc.ca.gov

FISHING

OCEAN BEACH FISHING PIER

The simplest way to fish in San Diego is at the end of a pier, where you don't need a license or a boat. As you head toward the end of the pier, the bites get fewer but the fish get bigger—anything from mackerel and halibut to white sea bass and the rare yellowtail. Bait and tackle (and tacos) are available in a café set in the middle of the pier.

Map 6: 5091 Niagara Ave., Ocean Beach, 619/226-3474, www.sandiego.gov; daily 24 hours

POINT LOMA SPORTFISHING

With regularly scheduled half-day and one-day trips, long-range excursions, and charters, this sportfishing outfit offers a chance to hit the open sea and chase down some yellowtail. In addition to a small fleet of fishing boats, the shop sells equipment rentals and fishing licenses and secures permits for trips to the well-populated waters off Mexico. Earn your dinner by bringing home some fresh catch.

Map 6: 1403 Scott St., Point Loma, 619/223-1627, www.pointlomasportfishing.com; daily 5am-7pm; from $48

PARKS

CABRILLO NATIONAL MONUMENT

The southwesternmost point of the contiguous U.S. has a nice statue and great views, but it is best enjoyed for seaside hikes. Trails crisscross the monument grounds, including the 2.5-mile **Bayside Trail.** From the Old Point Loma Lighthouse, this scenic trek looks east across the bay while traversing rare coastal sage scrub habitat. On the west side of the monument, the 0.5-mile **Coastal Tidepool Trail** winds past a series of protected tide pools that reveal unique, self-contained ecosystems in low tide. The trail can be found off the parking lot beside the New Point Loma Lighthouse on Cabrillo Road; it continues north to connect to a second parking lot farther up Cabrillo Road.

Map 6: 1800 Cabrillo Memorial Dr., Point Loma, 619/557-5450, www.nps.gov; daily 9am-5pm; $10 per vehicle, $5 per walk-in

SPANISH LANDING PARK

Perhaps the greatest feature of this harborside park is its location just across the street from the airport. It's a pretty nice spot to kill time if you're waiting for a flight, are early to catch your flight, or simply want to relax or have a picnic before returning the rental car.

Map 6: 3900 N. Harbor Dr., Harbor Island, 619/686-6200, www.portofsandiego.org; daily 6am-10:30pm

SKATEBOARDING
ROBB FIELD SKATE PARK

Roll past the grassy fields of Robb Field and you'll come upon this specialized 40,000-square-foot concrete playground, designed street-style, with bowls, ledges, and rails for skateboarders to ply their techniques. Children under 12 should be accompanied by an adult.

Map 6: 2525 Bacon St., Ocean Beach, 619/236-5555, www.sandiego.gov; daily 10am-sunset

SURFING
Surf Spots
OCEAN BEACH JETTY

Accessible from the OB Dog Beach at the northernmost end of Ocean Beach, a long jetty juts out where the San Diego River meets the ocean, creating a unique subterranean terrain that can connect long, structured rides fun for long- and shortboarders of intermediate ability and above. The waves break right, similar to a point break, but when the angled second wave of a set bounces off the jetty, it gets a little extra juice on the bounce and hollows out a little more. Paddling out is easiest following the river close to the jetty. Waves break best in winter but turn up year-round. A large parking lot provides easy access.

Map 6: Voltaire St. and Abbott St., Ocean Beach

OCEAN BEACH PIER

The waters adjacent to the OB Pier are reserved for surfers at all times; anyone wishing to swim or bodyboard must move north of a yellow-checkered flag posted in front of the lifeguard tower. Surfers should respect this delineation, or the lifeguards will let you hear about it. During modest 2-4-foot conditions, this can be a decent beginner's beach—but try to sneak any waves away from well-established locals and they will also let you hear about it. Waves typically break left off the pier on any western swell;

newbies are better off trying some fun left and right beach breaks farther down the line. Whichever section you surf, paddling out is usually easier via the channel running close to the pier. Once these waves begin to surpass the six-foot range, leave it to the pros and watch from the pier for an amazing close-up look. Look for public parking lots in front of the pier and beside the main lifeguard tower, where showers and bathrooms are also available.

Map 6: Newport Ave. and Abbott St., Ocean Beach

SUNSET CLIFFS, NORTH AND SOUTH GARBAGE

Many waves break below Sunset Cliffs Boulevard; getting to most requires a risky descent down steep, narrow paths or even jumping from rock faces—best undertaken only with guidance from an experienced local. But if you take the road all the way till it ends, a long set of stairs brings you down to some low, flat rocks just above sea level. It's a matter of timing to plunge down into the water between waves, but the real tricky part is trying to navigate the jagged shallows when it's time to get out of the water, and it can be dangerous during active surf and high tides. Once in the water, it's a paddle of a couple hundred yards, usually made easier by a wide, calm channel running all the way out between two main breaks, called North Garbage and South Garbage. Waves out there can get up to 18 feet when huge storm swells hit in the winter, but an average day provides well-paced, long rides conducive to longboarding in an absolutely gorgeous environment. Good for intermediate and above, depending on size. Best at low tide, Garbage is mostly active in fall and winter, on northwest swells, usually rights and occasionally lefts, and flat in the summer. Street parking is available, and a dirt parking lot may be accessed from Ladera Street.

Map 6: Sunset Cliffs Blvd. and Ladera St., Sunset Cliffs

Surf Schools and Rentals
OCEAN EXPERIENCE SURF SCHOOL

Barneys, kooks, grommets, and beginners of all ages can sign up for group or private surf lessons, including stand-up paddleboard instruction and skateboard lessons. Equipment is provided and classes are taught by experienced local surfers, delivering a combination of detailed on-beach instruction and in-water guidance, with the hope of getting you up your first time out.

Map 6: 4940 Newport Ave., Ocean Beach, 858/225-2317, www.oceanexperience.net; Mon.-Sat. 9am-7pm, Sun. 9am-6pm; from $95 pp

SOUTH COAST SURF SHOP

Local board shapers and riders have made this shop an OB surfer hub for 40 years, buying wetsuits, board shorts, bikinis, and surf wax on the reg. Even if you're not a surfer, there's still plenty of gear to help you look the part, as well as surfboard rentals should conditions favor the pier a block away. Women can seek out a better-suited selection at **Wahines** (5037 Newport

Ave., 619/223-8808), the South Coast's sister shop a few doors down. Another shop is located in Pacific Beach (740 Felspar St. #A, 858/483-7660).

Map 6: 5023 Newport Ave., Ocean Beach, 619/223-7017, www.southcoast.com; Mon.-Sat. 10am-6pm, Sun. 10am-5:30pm; from $12/hr

TENNIS
BARNES TENNIS CENTER

Low rates and two dozen courts keep this family-friendly tennis center popular. Most options are hard courts, but you might find one of the four clay surfaces available. Turn on the lights to keep your match going.

Map 6: 4490 W. Point Loma Blvd., Point Loma, 619/221-9000, www.barnestenniscenter. com; Mon.-Thurs. 8am-9pm, Fri.-Sun. 8am-7pm; court fees $6-10 pp adults, $2 pp under age 18

WHALE-WATCHING
ADVENTURE R.I.B. RIDES

Once you hear what a R.I.B. is, you'll think this whale-watching trip is a lot cooler. Rigid inflatable boats (R.I.B.) were built for Navy Seal missions. Six- or 12- passenger boats head out in search of whales and dolphins, moving fast enough to find and follow. This badass outfit also conducts scuba charters and offers "Adventure Picnics."

Map 6: 1380 Harbor Island Dr., Harbor Island, 619/808-2822, www.adventureribrides. com; daily 8am-5pm; $85 adults, $70 age 5-12

La Jolla
Map 7

CYCLING
SAN DIEGO FLY RIDES

Specializing in electric bikes, this shop offers both rentals and tours, along with some pretty cool cruisers for purchase. The so-called electric assist can really be a boon to riders trying to navigate the canyons and mesas that define San Diego, but you'll still get your pedal on in the flats.

Map 7: 7444 Girard Ave., La Jolla Village, 619/888-3878, www.sandiegoflyrides.com; daily 10am-5pm; from $40/4 hrs

GOLF
★ TORREY PINES GOLF COURSE

Believe it or not, this home of the 2021 U.S. Open is a city golf course, which means that it's open to the public. It can be tough to get a tee time on the most famous course in town, particularly for nonresidents. Reservations (nonrefundable booking fees) are accepted up to 90 days out, with short-term allotments available via a lottery system. The reward is playing at one of two world-class William P. Bell-designed 18-hole courses atop bluffs overlooking the Pacific—either the north course or the challenging legendary south course.

Map 7: 11480 Torrey Pines Park Rd., 858/581-7171, www.sandiego.gov; daily 6am-6pm; from $93 resident, from $237 nonresident

KAYAKING

BIKE & KAYAK TOURS

Specializing in bicycle, kayak, and snorkel excursions—with an increasing emphasis on stand-up paddleboards—these guys help you make the most of La Jolla outdoors, providing guidance and gear to show you exactly what you came to see.

Map 7: 2158 Avenida de la Playa, La Jolla Shores, 858/454-1010, www.bikeandkayaktours.com; daily 8am-8pm; kayak tours $39 pp, snorkeling tours $39 pp, bike tours $49 pp

LA JOLLA KAYAK

This popular outfit offers kayak tours of La Jolla's seven sea caves—*and* a snorkeling tour as part of the kayak tour. It's a nice all-in-one way to explore local coastal life. If you want to get a land-based view from the seat of a bicycle, this shop offer tours for that, too.

Map 7: 2199 Avenida de la Playa, 858/459-1114, www.lajollakayak.com; daily 8am-6pm; from $45 pp

PARAGLIDING

★ TORREY PINES GLIDERPORT

The ocean cliffs of Torrey Pines provide the scenic backdrop for tourism of the high-flying variety. Hang gliding and paragliding excursions are available, and surprisingly little experience or ability is required. An experienced glider rides tandem with you, offering some sense of safety as you float high above the trees and the beach.

Map 7: 2800 Torrey Pines Scenic Dr., Torrey Pines, 858/452-9858, www.flytorrey.com; daily 9am-5:30pm; paragliding $175, hang gliding $225

PARKS

ELLEN BROWNING SCRIPPS PARK

From this grassy park next to La Jolla Cove, picnickers, sunbathers, and frolicking children are privy to a great view of the ocean and the cliffs of Torrey Pines. Though the shops, restaurants, and busy sidewalks of Prospect Street are merely a couple blocks away, this spot feels like it's in the middle of a summer vacation.

Map 7: 1133 Coast Blvd., 619/235-1169, www.sandiego.gov; daily 4am-8pm; free

TORREY PINES STATE NATURAL RESERVE

The Torrey pine is San Diego's only native five-needled pine, but that's not what really brings people here for hiking. That would be the ocean air, wind-sculpted landscapes, and scenic cliffs overlooking an unspoiled

Clockwise from top left: paragliding at Torrey Pines; a statue at Cabrillo National Monument; views while hiking at Torrey Pines State Natural Reserve.

either to the beach or looping back around through more vistas.

Map 7: 12600 N. Torrey Pines Rd., Torrey Pines, 858/755-2063, www.torreypine.org; daily 7:15am-sunset; free, parking $12

SURFING
Surf Spots
BIRD ROCK

A rare bit of reef surfing in San Diego, two spots break next to the namesake rock and should be reserved for more advanced surfers. When surf's up, the waves can get crowded with longtime locals, and outsiders can get shut out; patience and etiquette are required. The two breaks react differently to different tidal conditions, so one or the other usually shows up throughout the year. Street parking only.

Map 7: Bird Rock Ave. and Dolphin Pl., Bird Rock

★ BLACK'S BEACH

This underwater canyon off the coast lines up some of the best waves in town, and difficult access never prevents surfers from hitting this beach when the waves are breaking. Getting to the sand from the cliffs above requires a hike, whether down a path from the Torrey Pines Gliderport (2800 Torrey Pines Scenic Dr.) or down a gated, steep, and winding paved road off La Jolla Farms Road (9601 La Jolla Farms Rd.). Between the waves, crowds, and nudists (users consider the beach clothing-optional), it's definitely not for families or beginners. The break pulls fast waves with almond-shaped barrels when it's firing; it works year-round and usually gets the best shape on falling mid- to low tide.

Map 7: La Jolla Farms Rd. at Blackgold Rd.

LA JOLLA SHORES

Most days the smaller waves, shallow water, and lifeguards make this beach break hospitable enough for beginners, but when the swell picks up, the breaks at La Jolla Shores are quick and powerful. Whatever your level, obey the separate surf and swim zones, designated by checked flags placed throughout the long beach. Bodyboarders can play among swimmers, but surfers cannot, and vice versa. Stingrays often lurk along the ocean floor, so to avoid an encounter with one of their painful, barbed stingers, shuffle your feet to disrupt the sand ahead of you so they'll swim away. Look for waves year-round to break throughout the day, usually larger in winter. Showers and bathrooms are available by the parking lot.

Map 7: 8200 Camino del Oro, 619/221-8899, www.sandiego.gov; daily 24 hours

Surf Schools and Rentals
SURF DIVA

Every family member can benefit from the surf lessons, clinics, and camps offered by this female-friendly shop. Kids' camps in the summer get boys and girls out in the water and up on their boards. Multiday clinics offer women a chance to get into the swing of it, while men may opt for coed group or private lessons.

Map 7: 2160 Avenida de la Playa, La Jolla Shores, 858/454-8273, www.surfdiva.com; daily 8:30am-6:30pm; lessons from $75 pp

TENNIS
LA JOLLA TENNIS CLUB

This club has nine courts open to the public, so you stand a good chance of getting court time, though calling ahead to reserve is a good idea. The facility also hosts leagues and tournaments, and offers private lessons by its staff of tennis pros should you need help with your backhand.

Map 7: 7632 Draper Ave., 858/454-4434, www.ljtc.org; daily dawn-9pm; court fees $10/day

UNDERWATER SPORTS
★ SAN DIEGO-LA JOLLA UNDERWATER PARK

Two underwater canyons, a couple of reefs, and a kelp forest are some of the highlights of San Diego's deepest water park, which spans the equivalent of 6,000 acres off the coast between La Jolla Cove and La Jolla Shores. Plentiful marine life may be seen by those willing to snorkel or scuba—look for several nonthreatening species of shark, dolphins, sea lions, starfish, anemones, and hundreds of colorful fish and flora. Several shops offer kayak and snorkeling tours, or rent your own to access the south end of the shores.

Map 7: Launch from 2000 block of Avenida de la Playa, La Jolla Shores

Lessons and Rentals
SNORKEL AND SCUBA

Snorkel and Scuba offers regular dives for scuba-certified clients (including night dives), as well as guided tours below the surface of La Jolla. Newbies can sign up for the beginner's tour or select options from a snorkeling menu.

Map 7: 1188 Coast Blvd., La Jolla Shores, 858/539-0054, www.snorkelsandiegoscuba. com; tours daily 9am, noon, 3pm, 6pm, and sunset; from $195 pp

BOATING

★ SEAFORTH BOAT RENTALS

Learning to sail doesn't happen in an afternoon, but San Diego's protected bays offer a perfect environment to get started. Offering lessons here, as well as at other locations in Harbor Island (955 Harbor Island Dr., Ste. 130) and Mission Bay (1641 Quivira Rd.), Seaforth will teach you how to skipper a 22-foot sloop in moderate conditions. Return for more advanced classes later.

Map 8: 1715 Strand Way, 619/437-1514, www.seaforthboatrental.com; daily 9am until 30 minutes before sunset; from $249

CYCLING

BAYSHORE BIKEWAY

The Bayshore Bikeway's 24-mile route begins and ends at the Coronado Ferry Landing. You can ride the whole circuit (which requires taking the ferry and passing south through Chula Vista, then back up through Imperial Beach) or just stick to the Coronado peninsula, arguably the best part of the route.

Map 8: 1201 1st St., www.keepsandiegomoving.com

CRUISER KING

Coronado is pretty well fixed for bicycles even without this place, but having it nearby helps. It has some pretty good cruisers and hybrids for getting around the island or hopping the ferry downtown, plus electric bike rentals to make it easy.

Map 8: 957 Orange Ave., 619/522-6967, www.kruiserking.com; daily 10am-6pm; $7/hr, electric bike $40/4 hrs

GOLF

CORONADO GOLF COURSE

This 6,500-yard, par-72 course looks up at the Coronado Bridge and across the south bay. For more than 50 years, it has been considered among the top public courses in town (probably because it requires a collared shirt and prohibits flip-flops). Reserve tee times in advance.

Map 8: 2000 Visalia Row, 619/522-6590, www.golfcoronado.com; daily 5:30am-8pm; $53 resident, $55 nonresident

KITEBOARDING

AZ KITEBOARDING

Gaining skill at kiteboarding doesn't happen overnight, but take a few lessons from the experienced instructor at AZ and you might get the hang of it after a few days. At a reasonable $150 per two-hour lesson, it's worth booking to find out if you've got the mettle. Set an appointment and meet your instructor at Silver Strand State Beach for your lesson.

Map 8: 5000 Hwy. 75, 918/740-2894, www.kiteboardcoronado.com; by appointment only; $150 pp

STAND-UP PADDLEBOARDING
SUP CORONADO

Coronado is a great place for learning stand-up paddleboarding. Between the Pacific Ocean and San Diego Bay, the island offers ideal water conditions and scenery; most of the time it's going to be mellow. SUP Coronado offers lessons, tours, and even some SUP yoga sessions.

Map 8: 2000 Mullinex Dr., 619/888-7686, www.supcoronado.com; by appointment only; lessons from $50 pp

Greater San Diego   Map 9

PARKS
MISSION TRAILS REGIONAL PARK

These 5,800 acres of open-space preserve will give you a little idea of what San Diego's natural landscape is truly like. Popular hikes include trails up to the 1,500-foot Cowles Mountain and the 6.5-mile hike around scenic Lake Murray.

Map 9: 1 Father Junipero Serra Trail, Santee, 619/668-3281, www.mtrp.org; daily 9am-5pm; free

SPECTATOR SPORTS
SDCCU STADIUM

Formerly known as Qualcomm Stadium, and before that Jack Murphy Stadium, this Mission Valley sports venue plays home field to the Aztecs of San Diego State University. It also comes alive every so often hosting international club soccer matches.

Map 9: 9449 Friars Rd., Mission Valley, 619/641-3100, www.sandiego.gov/qualcomm

TOURS
SAN DIEGO SKY TOURS

I'm assuming every city offers aerial tours from the open cockpit of a biplane? It's an adventurous way to see the city, and only slightly less so to book a small party in a small, enclosed plane instead.

Map 9: 3717 John J Montgomery Dr., 619/757-6419, www.sandiegoskytours.com; from $175

Restaurants

Look for ★ to find
recommended restaurants

Highlights

★ **Best Burger:** You might be surprised that pork specialist **Carnitas' Snack Shack** turns out the area's best burger—but honestly, the casual outdoor eatery on the waterfront does everything well (page 113).

★ **Best Celebrity Chef Restaurant:** *Top Chef* alum Brian Malarkey sets the bar high with **Herb & Wood,** where incredible ingredients are cooked to perfection in a wood-fired kitchen (page 113).

★ **Best Dessert:** Want to justify dessert? Go to **Extraordinary Desserts** for cakes, pastries, and more made with artistic integrity and decadently great taste (page 113).

★ **Best Seafood:** With tasty food and stylish decor, **Ironside Fish & Oyster** creates a memorable meal, beginning with oysters (page 118).

★ **Best Steak House:** A classic American steak house updated for the 21st century, **Born & Raised** takes excessive to another realm (page 118).

★ **Best Pizza:** San Diego loves its pizza, especially the authentic Neapolitan pies coming out of the brick oven at **Officine Buona Forchetta** (page 135).

★ **Best California Cuisine:** Enjoy a view of famous La Jolla Cove while feasting on the chef's tasting menu at **George's at the Cove** (page 139).

★ **Finest Dining:** You'll enjoy French-inspired seafood while the ocean laps against the windows at **The Marine Room.** It's an elite dining experience (page 140).

★ **Best Brunch:** Come hungry to the extravagant Sunday brunch buffet in the **Crown Room** at Hotel del Coronado (page 141).

★ **Best Mexican Food:** Locals stand in line every day for the nation's best flour tortillas at **Las Cuatro Milpas** (page 144).

oysters at Ironside Fish & Oyster

PRICE KEY

💲 Entrées less than $10

💲💲 Entrées $10–20

💲💲💲 Entrées more than $20

San Diego may not be the most diverse metropolis around, but you can typically find quality samplings of any notable cuisine. For the best dining experience, stick to what we do best: seafood or Mexican.

The city's Mexican restaurants range from delicious little taco trucks to restaurants where someone makes fresh guacamole at your table. Avoid the tourist traps along San Diego Avenue in Old Town and you'll be hard-pressed to find one that doesn't at least taste good.

The local fishing industry provides all manner of fresh catch, and our taste for it means we get some pretty great fish flown in from out of town as well. Most local sushi restaurants have been declared "best in town" by enthusiastic customers, but more unique to the region are the fresh-catch fish counters. Customers line up at a well-stocked glass counter to choose whichever cut of fish looks best that day. These popular, casual spots have popped up all over town—if you love grilled fish, make visiting one a priority.

California's farm-to-table movement has also caught on locally. Thanks to the state's year-round growing season, locally sourced meat and produce are a rich prospect, and more and more talented chefs have embraced locavore principles. The result: You can support those principles yourself while enjoying some of the best restaurants in town.

Of course, there are classic staples. Burger lovers debate a number of places that do them well, Sunday brunch spots have some of the longest wait times in town, and starting a dessert bar has become a legitimate

---

Previous: Officine Buona Forchetta; roasted branzino at Herb & Wood.

business opportunity. Eating well in San Diego proves remarkably easy if you stick to the basics.

Downtown
Map 1

BREAKFAST
DONUT BAR $

The real beauty of the Donut Bar folks is their willingness to push the boundaries of donut-dom. There's the standard maple bacon bar, and they'll take a stab at the cronut hybrids, but they also incorporate flavors by creating fruity sandwiches or turning the concept of a PB&J into a donut. Go early, because they always sell out; or visit Friday or Saturday evening for fresh donuts and craft beer.

Map 1: 631 B St., Gaslamp, 619/255-6360, www.donutbarsandiego.com; Mon.-Fri. 7am until sold out, Sat.-Sun. 8am until sold out, Fri.-Sat. 5pm-10pm

THE MISSION $

The Mission's menu draws heavily from Mexican and American traditions, and the café has become a favorite among locals for its pancakes and egg dishes as well as breakfast burritos and *chilaquiles* (sort of like breakfast nachos). The Mission bakes its own bread, and does so rather well, so expect outstanding sandwiches and the best cinnamon-bread French toast in town. You'll find the same menu at its other locations in North Park (2801 University Ave.) and Mission Beach (3795 Mission Blvd.), with paintings by local artists on the walls and Southwestern decorative motifs throughout.

Map 1: 1250 J St., East Village, 619/232-7662, www.themissionsd.com; daily 7am-3pm

CAFÉS
JAMES COFFEE CO. $

With a rock-and-roll approach to specialty coffee, this local artisanal roaster in Little Italy occupies a large garage space, where a co-op of pop-up shops might include a shaving parlor or an eyewear shop. Popular among musicians, graphic designers, software developers, and tattooed creative types, the shop manages to feel like a workspace without losing street cred in the process.

Map 1: 2355 India St., Little Italy, 619/756-7770, www.jamescoffeeco.com; daily 7am-9pm

THE WESTBEAN $

Choose between a fruity bean or a chocolaty roast, and enjoy some of the most balanced local coffee within the bar's slick modern-rustic interior. If tea's your thing, try the shop's offering by Mad Monk, a local tea purveyor that keeps it simple and sensuous.

Map 1: 240 Broadway, Gaslamp, 619/542-9124, www.thewestbean.com; Mon.-Fri. 6am-6pm, Sat.-Sun. 8am-3pm

JUNIPER & IVY ⑤⑤⑤

Top Chef All-Stars winner Richard Blais found a receptive audience when he opened this "Refined American Food with Left Coast Edge" eatery in Little Italy, and San Diego foodies have enthusiastically embraced his creative approach. Blais's liquid nitrogen tricks come into play while crafting the horseradish "pearls" that top oysters with a melon mignonette. Blais and his team constantly redraft the imaginative menu with dozens of intriguing dishes. When making reservations, request one of the few circle booths for the best seats in the house. The lively and comfortable industrial dining room is a place to be seen, so dress casually cool and enjoy excitedly discussing your meal.

Map 1: 2228 Kettner Blvd., Little Italy, 619/269-9036, www.juniperandivy.com; Sun.-Thurs. 5pm-10pm, Fri.-Sat. 5pm-11pm

CONTEMPORARY

★ CARNITAS' SNACK SHACK ⑤

You don't need to dig swine to enjoy Carnitas', but you'll sure love this harborside casual outdoor eatery if you do. Between the braised pork belly appetizer, pulled pork tacos, and fries served with bacon ketchup, hog heaven becomes a delectable possibility. Other regular menu items include a cheese bread and sliced rib-eye steak sandwich; one of the city's best burgers; and a terrine made from beets, spinach, and goat cheese (in case there's a vegetarian in your group). Local carnivores line up all day for this, even when the über-decadent poutine isn't on the menu.

Map 1: 1004 N. Harbor Dr., Marina District, 619/696-7675, www.carnitassnackshack.com; Mon.-Thurs. 11am-9pm, Fri. 11am-10pm, Sat. 9am-10pm, Sun. 9am-9pm

★ HERB & WOOD ⑤⑤⑤

Celebrity chef Brian Malarkey sources the world's finest ingredients for the wood-fired kitchen visible from the dining room of this large yet comfortable restaurant. Highlights include roasted branzino, grilled Iberian pork, smoked trout, house pâtés, and a host of creative vegetable dishes, but in reality everything from apps to desserts is delicious, and best when shared.

Map 1: 2210 Kettner Blvd., Little Italy, 619/955-8495, www.herbandwood.com; Sun.-Thurs. 4:30pm-10pm, Fri.-Sat. 4:30pm-11pm

DESSERT

★ EXTRAORDINARY DESSERTS ⑤

This sweets specialist offers the best desserts in town. You'll have trouble choosing, but you'll definitely be singing its praises if you order a slice of cake with some of the handcrafted small-batch ice cream. Lines always seem to be out the door, but you'll want to stand in this one to get a good look at each of the daily offerings, whether you're grabbing dessert to go or eating in the spacious modern dining room. If all that's too daunting, you may try the stellar bakery's smaller location in nearby Bankers Hill (2929 5th Ave.).

Map 1: 1430 Union St., Little Italy, 619/294-7001, www.extraordinarydesserts.com; Sun.-Thurs. 10am-11pm, Fri.-Sat. 10am-midnight

PAPPALECCO $

Pappalecco's gelato is made on the premises daily, and there are usually dozens of creamy and delicious flavors. Choose a regular hazelnut or Nutella, which adds a ribbon of the popular hazelnut spread to the melt-in-your-mouth frozen treat, or marvel over the refreshing fruitier options. There's not much seating, so on crowded evenings it may be best to grab a cup or cone to go for a walk around Little Italy. Or try the larger second location in Hillcrest (3650 5th Ave.).

Map 1: 1602 State St., Little Italy, 619/238-4590, www.pappalecco.com; Mon.-Thurs. 7am-10:15pm, Fri. 7am-11pm, Sat. 7:30am-11pm, Sun. 7:30am-10:15pm

FARM-TO-TABLE
CAFÉ 21 $$$

Avocado fries, duck wings, and lamb ribs paired with a tasting flight of six different sangrias make this a great happy-hour spot. For dinner, the kitchen turns out great dishes featuring a rotating selection of local and sustainable ingredients. Live music sometimes accompanies the grass-fed steak or fresh catch of the day in this stylish restaurant, which boasts a warm brick bar, a colorful dining room, and a bank of large windows looking out onto the lively Gaslamp sidewalk.

Map 1: 802 5th Ave., Gaslamp, 619/795-0721, www.cafe-21.com; Sun.-Thurs. 8am-10pm, Fri.-Sat. 8am-11pm

TENDER GREENS $$

Technically a fast food chain, this California franchise breaks the mold by practicing farm-to-table principles. Each restaurant is overseen by a pedigreed executive chef who works to make the most out of seasonal ingredients and natural meats, including cured-in-house salami, marinated steak, and buttermilk fried chicken. You won't get fries with that; instead, enjoy assorted grilled vegetables and some of the best salads available downtown.

Map 1: 110 W. Broadway, Gaslamp, 619/795-2353, www.tendergreens.com; daily 11am-9pm

FRENCH
CAFÉ CHLOE $$$

Nestled pleasantly in the sweet spot between casual and fine dining, this local favorite serves up Parisian embellishments and quality French cuisine. Start the day with a *croque madame* (hot ham-and-cheese sandwich topped with a fried egg) or bistro salad on the dog-friendly patio, or swing by late for a romantic meal in the quaint dining room. Enjoy traditional dishes

Top: Ironside Fish & Oyster. Bottom: Herb & Wood.

like *steak frites* (steak and fries) or pan-roasted duck breast, expertly paired with a *vin rouge* (red wine), of course.

Map 1: 721 9th Ave., East Village, 619/232-3242, www.cafechloe.com; Tues.-Thurs. 11am-10pm, Fri.-Sat. 8:30am-10:30pm, Sun. 8:30am-9:30pm

ITALIAN
BERKELEY PIZZA 💲

Stuffed, deep-dish Chicago pies have a home in San Diego thanks to Berkeley Pizza. The pizza is the real deal, thick with toppings and a delicious chunky marinara—a single slice will fill most. Berkeley started as a farmers market booth, then opened a storefront to keep up with the high demand caused by excellent word of mouth. Its small barebones storefront reflects its demand as a delivery spot. Same with its North Park location (3934 30th St.).

Map 1: 539 Island Ave., Gaslamp, 619/937-0808, www.berkeleypizza.net, Sun.-Wed. 11am-11pm, Thurs.-Sat. 11am-3am

MIMMO'S ITALIAN VILLAGE 💲💲

Mimmo's dining room literally resembles a small Italian village, with a traditional Italian menu and dining experience. Feast on pasta, olives, and caprese, then choose from cannoli, tiramisu, or mascarpone for dessert. A sidewalk dining patio proves a popular spot to eat and people-watch.

Map 1: 1743 India St., Little Italy, 619/239-3710, www.mimmos.biz; Mon.-Thurs. 11am-9pm, Fri. 11am-11pm, Sat. noon-11pm, Sun. noon-9pm

MEXICAN
LOLA 55 💲

This new fast-casual taco concept places great importance on both the use of quality ingredients and where they come from. The tortillas are made from non-GMO corn, for example. The wide range of tacos on the menu might source local fish and produce or sustainably raised meats. However, the ultimate goal here is producing the terrific flavors and warmth of the Mexican culinary tradition.

Map 1: 1290 F St., East Village, 619/727-9282, www.lola55catering.com; Mon.-Fri. 11am-10pm, Sat.-Sun. 7am-10pm

PUESTO 💲💲

When you're craving tacos near the Marina, this is the spot to visit. Mix-and-match tacos include lobster, nopal cactus, or filet mignon served in a house-made corn tortilla with crispy melted cheese, avocado, and pistachio jalapeño salsa. The large restaurant also offers traditional fish dishes such as ceviche and several variations on guacamole. Sample some of the great tequila-based cocktails to wash it down, and if you truly enjoy living, order the flan.

Map 1: 789 W. Harbor Dr., Marina District, 619/233-8880, www.eatpuesto.com; daily 11am-10pm

Gastropubs

A happy consequence of the city's romance with all things beer, San Diego's dining scene has witnessed an increase in gastropubs: restaurants built around the idea that drinking and eating well should go hand in hand.

You may find traditional pub fare like fish-and-chips, sausages, and burgers at **Queenstown Public House** (1557 Columbia St., Little Italy, 619/546-0444, www.queenstownpublichouse.com; Mon.-Tues. 11am-10pm, Wed.-Thurs. 11am-11pm, Fri. 11am-midnight, Sat. 9am-midnight, Sun. 9am-10pm), **Waypoint Public House** (3794 30th St., North Park, 619/255-8778, www.waypointpublic.com; Mon.-Tues. 4pm-9pm, Wed.-Thurs. 4pm-10pm, Fri. 4pm-midnight, Sat. 9am-midnight, Sun. 9am-9pm), and **Neighborhood** (777 G St., East Village, 619/446-0002, www.neighborhoodsd.com; Sat.-Wed. 11:30am-midnight, Thurs.-Fri. 11:30am-1:30am), but these restaurants go the extra mile to ensure their menus appeal to foodies and even—dare I say it—health-conscious beer drinkers. In Pacific Beach, the **Iron Pig Alehouse** (1520 Garnet Ave., Pacific Beach, 858/412-4299, www.ironpigalehouse.com; Mon.-Sat. 11:30am-close, Sun. 11am-close) gives beer drinkers an excellent reason to gorge on Texas-style barbecue, smoked slow and low on hickory and oak.

Spots like **OB Noodle House** (4993 Niagara Ave., Ocean Beach, 619/255-9858, www.obnoodlehouse.com; Mon.-Thurs. noon-11pm, Fri.-Sat. 11:30am-11pm, Sun. 11am-11pm) bucks the pub tradition, offering Asian favorites to pair with its terrific tap lists. The way San Diegans have responded suggests that noodles and IPA are meant to go together. Meanwhile, **Blind Lady Ale House** (3416 Adams Ave., Normal Heights, 619/255-2491, www.blindladyalehouse.com; Mon.-Thurs. 5pm-midnight, Fri.-Sun. 11:30am-midnight) and **Urbn Pizza** (3085 University Ave., North Park, 619/255-7300, www.urbnnorthpark.com; Sun.-Mon. noon-10pm, Tues.-Thurs. noon-midnight, Fri.-Sat. noon-2am) back a more common beer pairing: pizza.

Stone World Bistro & Gardens, Liberty Station (2816 Historic Decatur Rd., Ste. 116, Liberty Station, 619/269-2100, www.stonelibertystation.com; Sun.-Thurs. 11:30am-9pm, Fri.-Sat. 11:30am-10pm) takes it all the way, pairing sustainable, made-from-scratch, farm-to-table world cuisine with local and far-flung world-class beers. Beer snobs can now maintain high drinking standards without missing out on a good meal.

RESTAURANTS
DOWNTOWN

PUBS
NEIGHBORHOOD $

Burgers are the specialty of this minimalist gastropub near the ballpark, with a number of well-crafted sauces to top them, including cranberry habanero aioli and cumin mayo. The only caveat worth mentioning is that you won't find ketchup, so if that's an all-American deal-breaker, stick to the beer-braised short ribs, meatball pita, or steak tacos. Local drafts are featured, although the rotating selection always has a few out-of-town gems as well.

Map 1: 777 G St., East Village, 619/446-0002, www.neighborhoodsd.com; Sat.-Wed. 11:30am-midnight, Thurs.-Fri. 11:30am-1:30am

QUEENSTOWN PUBLIC HOUSE $$

Featuring a mostly local tap list and British comfort food by way of New Zealand, this converted Craftsman home offers unique decor, a dog-friendly patio, and an overall enjoyable dining experience. You can't go wrong with perennial favorites like fish-and-chips or the pot pie, which has a roasted Cornish game hen in the middle of the crust. The staff is always willing to recommend standouts from the current spate of beers.

Map 1: 1557 Columbia St., Little Italy, 619/546-0444, www.queenstownpublichouse.com; Mon.-Tues. 11am-10pm, Wed.-Thurs. 11am-11pm, Fri. 11am-midnight, Sat. 9am-midnight, Sun. 9am-10pm

THE WATERFRONT BAR AND GRILL $

The Waterfront opened back in 1933, just as Prohibition ended, making it San Diego's oldest continually operating bar. Known for its burgers, the menu also includes a Mexican brunch with classic salsa and egg dishes such as *chilaquiles* (served over tortilla chips) and huevos rancheros (served with fresh tortillas). The bar opens to a dining patio and serves enough beer to keep it lively and easy to spot from the sidewalk, all day long.

Map 1: 2044 Kettner Blvd., Little Italy, 619/232-9656, www.waterfrontbarandgrill.com; daily 6am-2am

SEAFOOD

★ IRONSIDE FISH & OYSTER $$

Mermaids, fish skulls, and brass tables set the tone in this design-savvy raw bar and seafood restaurant. Start with oysters, mussels, clams, or ceviche, then move on to San Diego's best lobster roll or a whole roasted fish. This place knows seafood—cold or cooked—so you could even try the "fries with eyes" while marveling at mermaid statues and a wall made from barracuda skulls.

Map 1: 1654 India St., Little Italy, 619/269-3033, www.ironsidefishandoyster.com; Sun.-Thurs. 11:30am-midnight, Fri.-Sat. 11:30am-2am

STEAK HOUSE

★ BORN & RAISED $$$

Based on a traditional U.S.-style chophouse, this snazzy $7 million restaurant takes the steak house concept to greater heights than any midcentury American steak house dared ever dream. Portraits of late hip-hop stars adorn the walls, and leather booths surround marble tabletops, where customers receive top-shelf service, including rolling table carts where side dishes are prepared on the spot. Of course, top billing goes to the steaks, ranging from archaic dishes like steak Diane, a massive porterhouse for two, and tournedos Rossini topped by seared foie gras.

Map 1: 1909 India St., Little Italy, 619/202-4577, www.bornandraisedsteak.com; daily 4pm-midnight

COWBOY STAR 💲💲💲

Combine a Western steak house with sustainable principles and European fine-dining standards and you'll have a fair approximation of Cowboy Star. Enjoy prime-grade rib eye or "intensely marbled" Wagyu beef while comfortably seated in a leather booth beneath a painting of John Wayne. Impeccable service comes from a supremely knowledgeable waitstaff prepared to suggest a wine pairing for the exquisite filet mignon steak tartare (complete with a quail egg). Everything—from the cocktails to the wine list to the long list of hormone- and antibiotic-free meats—is top-shelf, with several selections cured or dry-aged in the restaurant's own butcher shop.

Map 1: 640 10th Ave., East Village, 619/450-5880, www.cowboystarcs.com; Mon. 5pm-10pm, Tues.-Thurs. 11:30am-2:30pm and 5pm-10pm, Fri. 11:30am-2:30pm and 5pm-10:30pm, Sat. 4pm-10:30pm, Sun. 5pm-9pm

VEGAN

CAFE GRATITUDE 💲💲

One of the city's best restaurants is also among its healthiest. The plant-based dishes served all day prove nourishing and fulfilling, but most important they taste terrific. Standouts include a macrobiotic grain bowl with mashed yams, adzuki beans, and sea vegetables; a kelp noodle pesto; cold pressed juices; and a $6 community rice bowl (great if you're short on cash) with kale, black beans, and tahini. When you're tired from traveling, rejuvenate yourself here.

Map 1: 1980 Kettner Blvd., Little Italy, 619/736-5077, www.cafegratitude.com; daily 8am-10pm

CIVICO 1845 💲💲

An Italian restaurant first, this authentic eatery just happens to furnish a full plant-based menu in addition to its more traditional one. You're in luck whichever way you decide to go; the food's just as well received by devout vegans as it is omnivores, from the meatless Bolognese to the dairy-free tiramisu.

Map 1: 1845 India St., 619/431-5990, www.civico1845.com; Sun.-Thurs. 11am-10pm, Fri.-Sat. 11am-11pm

RESTAURANTS
DOWNTOWN

Top: Born & Raised. Bottom: Mariscos Nine Seas.

ASIAN
HACHI RAMEN $

These days, you can't go to any restaurant district without being a stone's throw from a ramen bar. This ramen bar happens to be within a stone's throw of Balboa Park and to offer a balanced menu of healthy *poke* (seasoned or marinated raw fish) salads and sushi rolls to complement its terrific noodle creations. During the summer, cold ramens include the option to add sashimi, creating unique, affordable, nutritionally balanced meals that taste great and refreshing on the hottest of days.

Map 2: 2505 5th Ave., Bankers Hill, 619/231-0700, www.hachiramen.com; Mon.-Thurs. 11:30am-9pm, Fri.-Sat. 11:30am-10pm

MR. A'S $$$

Atop a 12-story high-rise off Balboa Park, the west-facing dining room and patio of this French-inflected restaurant overlooks San Diego Bay, with views of downtown, the Coronado Bridge, Mission Bay, and the Pacific Ocean. Mr. A's serves modern American cuisine with a focus on fresh, locally-sourced ingredients. Take care to heed the dress code—while this upscale spot accepts business casual during the day, it won't even seat a man for dinner if he's wearing shorts.

Map 2: 2550 5th Ave., Bankers Hill, 619/239-1377, www.asrestaurant.com; Mon.-Fri. 11:30am-9pm, Sat. 5pm-9:30pm, Sun. 10am-9pm

BREAKFAST
ECLIPSE CHOCOLATE BAR & BISTRO $$

A terrific artisanal chocolatier, Eclipse turns concepts like burned-chili caramel into tantalizing reality. Stop in for a box of chocolates, then stick around to devour one of the sweet and savory meals (especially brunch). Incorporating chocolate into just about every dish is accomplished with complexity and grace: maple-bacon blueberry pancakes with toasted white chocolate shavings will start your day brilliantly. Especially great on cool date nights, the clean, midcentury-style bistro sports a menu of rich drinking chocolates that can be enjoyed with a shot of espresso.

Map 2: 2145 Fern St., South Park, 619/578-2984, www.eclipsechocolate.com; Mon.-Thurs. 9am-10pm, Fri.-Sat. 9am-11pm, Sun. 9am-4pm

CALIFORNIA
THE PRADO AT BALBOA PARK $$

When exploring El Prado, many visitors stop here for lunch, happy hour, or dinner for one good reason: The dining patio overlooks a particularly verdant section of the park. The layout makes it tough on waitstaff, who probably log more miles per shift than any park visitor, so don't expect to rush through the menu's California comfort food items. Instead, order a drink at the bar and leisurely choose from a menu of tacos, sandwiches, and large salads.

Map 2: 1549 El Prado, Balboa Park, 619/557-9441, www.cohnrestaurants.com/theprado; Mon. 11:30am-3pm, Tues.-Thurs. 11:30am-10pm, Fri. 11:30am-9:30pm, Sat. 11am-9:30pm, Sun. 11am-10pm

FARM-TO-TABLE
PANAMA 66 $$

Tucked in a courtyard beside the San Diego Museum of Art's sculpture garden, this locally sourced gastropub features midcentury-style cocktails and a rotating selection of San Diego's best beers to help wash down tasty sandwiches, salads, and charcuterie plates. Live jazz is featured Wednesday nights, while local rock, folk, and soul musicians often perform on weekends.

Map 2: 1450 El Prado, Balboa Park, 619/696-1966, www.panama66.blogspot.com; Mon. 11:30am-3pm, Tues.-Thurs. 11:30am-10pm, Fri. 11:30am-11pm, Sat. 11am-11pm, Sun. 11am-10pm

MEXICAN
MARISCOS NINE SEAS $

A truth peculiar to fish tacos is that some of the tastiest in town come off the back of a truck. The best of those trucks parks in the Target parking lot in South Park, serving ridiculously delicious fried and grilled fish tacos as well as soups, ceviche, and other seafood delights.

Map 2: 3030 Grape St., South Park, 619/279-0010, www.mariscosnineseasseafood.com; daily 9:30am-7:30pm

VEGAN
KINDRED $$

Whatever stereotype you might apply to a vegan restaurant, this exceptionally stylish bar and eatery will turn it upside down. It specializes in decadent plates of food, matching rich sauces and comfort dishes without losing sight of its plant-based approach. It doubles as a cocktail lounge, serving a lengthy list of spirits and cocktails to a crowd of stylishly dressed young people who socialize breezily despite the restaurant's subtle death metal soundtrack.

Map 2: 1503 30th St., South Park, 619/546-9653, www.barkindred.com; Mon.-Thurs. 4pm-midnight, Fri. 4pm-1am, Sat. 10am-1am, Sun. 10am-midnight

ASIAN
TAJIMA RAMEN $

This local favorite also features stylish ramen bars in Hillcrest (3739 6th Ave.) and East Village (901 E St.) as well as two larger restaurants in Kearny Mesa. Whichever you visit, expect killer *tonkotsu* (breaded and fried pork cutlet) served with pork belly over skinny, fat, or spinach noodles; killer vegan ramen with asparagus and fried tofu; and refreshing *poke* (raw fish salad) bowls. It's a great late-night option, especially on weekends.

Map 3: 3015 Adams Ave. #102b, North Park, 619/756-7517, www.tajimasandiego.com; Sun.-Thurs. 11:30am-10:30pm, Fri.-Sat. 11:30am-3am

BREAKFAST
HASH HOUSE A GO GO $$

Heaping portions of farm-style breakfasts keep this eatery busy during breakfast and brunch, especially on weekends, when locals line up for pancakes, waffles, Benedicts, and meaty hashes. The simple farmhouse interior will do, but for the best experience, hold out for patio seating. Consider splitting a meal, or be prepared to walk away with a full belly as well as leftovers.

Map 3: 3628 5th Ave., Hillcrest, 619/298-4646, www.hashhouseagogo.com; Mon. 7:30am-2pm, Tues.-Thurs. 7:30am-2pm and 5:30pm-9pm, Fri. 7:30am-2pm and 5:30pm-9:30pm, Sat. 7:30am-2:30pm and 5:30pm-9:30pm, Sun. 7:30am-2:30pm and 5:30pm-9pm

NOMAD DONUTS $

Michelin-starred pastry chef Kristianna Zabala could likely work anywhere in town, but she's found a welcome niche creating artisan donuts and wood-fired Montreal-style bagels. The bagels run pretty true to form, with a traditional variety of schmears and sandwiches. However, the donuts are like no other, incorporating unique flavors such as ube taro coconut, blueberry ginger, and pomegranate rose. Many vegan options are available for both donuts and bagels, and there is full coffee service.

Map 3: 2911 3102 University Ave., North Park, 619/431-5000, http://nomaddonuts.com; Mon.-Thurs. 6am-2pm, Fri. 6am-2pm and 5pm-10pm, Sat. 7am-3pm and 5pm-10pm, Sun. 7am-3pm

SNOOZE $

Pancake lovers will find the wait at Snooze worth it. The variety of specialty flavors includes sweet potato, strawberry malted, and pineapple upside-down cakes, with a rotating selection of daily specials. Savory eaters will find solace in traditional and experimental egg dishes, including Benedicts

with lox, prosciutto, or pulled pork. Be ready to share, because you will want to try everything. Despite a large dining room, wait times can be long.
Map 3: 3940 5th Ave., Hillcrest, 619/500-3344, www.snoozeeatery.com; daily 6:30am-2:30pm

CAFÉS

CAFFÉ CALABRIA $

Freshly roasted beans make superior coffee, and if you already know this you'll want to check out this Italian-style roaster. A variety of dark roasted, single-origin beans and blends can be purchased in bulk or brewed into your preferred coffee drink, and they'll taste great, because they were recently roasted on the premises. Inside, TV screens show Italian league soccer or cycling races, or opt for parklet seating outside.
Map 3: 3933 30th St., North Park, 619/683-7787, www.caffecalabria.com; Mon.-Tues. 6am-3pm, Wed.-Fri. 6am-11pm, Sat.-Sun. 7am-11pm

CONTEMPORARY

BREAD & CIE $

It's no accident you'll come across Bread & Cie baked goods in restaurants and markets all over town; the French-style bakery bakes some of the best bread in San Diego. Stop in for sandwiches, either to dine in or take out for a picnic, and grab some desserts while you're here—you'll have to have one once you see them. The macarons in particular deliver a decadently sweet dose of Parisian nostalgia, perfect for nibbling on the restaurant's bistro-style dining patio.
Map 3: 350 University Ave., Hillcrest, 619/683-9322, www.breadandcie.com; Mon.-Fri. 7am-7pm, Sat. 7am-6pm, Sun. 7:30am-6pm

GREAT MAPLE $$

With a cobbled stone exterior and polished interior, this slick and welcoming restaurant feels like the contemporary version of a mountain town diner. Hardwood floors, green vinyl booths, and white marble countertops give it a clean look that matches its impeccable menu, which strikes an unusually good balance between meat and vegetable dishes. You may choose between steak tartare and beet tartare, and for every succulent grass-fed burger there's a creatively assembled salad. Nevertheless, keep reading; the list goes on and includes occasional surprises like Maine lobster poutine. Also, save room for dessert—the place is known for its pies as well as a decadent take on the maple-bacon donut.
Map 3: 1451 Washington St., Hillcrest, 619/255-2282, www.thegreatmaple.com; Mon.-Thurs. 8am-2pm and 5pm-9pm, Fri. 8am-2pm and 5pm-9:30pm, Sat. 8am-2:30pm and 5pm-9:30pm, Sun. 8am-2:30pm and 5pm-9pm

WAYPOINT PUBLIC HOUSE $$

With 30 rotating taps, including two nitro beers, you won't have trouble finding fantastic beer at Waypoint, but if you need pointers, the menu always recommends a couple of worthy beer pairings for each dish. The corner restaurant's a lot brighter and airier than the name might suggest, with huge rows of windows open on warm days, which are, of course, most of them. The breezy contemporary decor matches the playful menu, which bounces creatively between comfort food and light California cuisine.

Map 3: 3794 30th St., North Park, 619/255-8778, www.waypointpublic.com; Mon.-Tues. 4pm-9pm, Wed.-Thurs. 4pm-10pm, Fri. 4pm-midnight, Sat. 9am-midnight, Sun. 9am-9pm

EUROPEAN
POMEGRANATE $$

The Georgian cuisine served here has nothing to do with the American South; instead, this Georgia refers to the former Soviet state, now an independent republic bordering the Black Sea. Pickled vegetables and barbecued meats satisfy a loyal customer base, while the stewed lamb and roasted chicken dishes prove most tender. Handwritten positive reviews line the white walls; bring a felt-tip pen and add your own. Cash only.

Map 3: 2312 El Cajon Blvd., North Park, 619/298-4007, www.pomegranatesd.com; Sun.-Thurs. 5pm-10pm, Fri.-Sat. 5pm-11pm

MEXICAN
CITY TACOS $

Eating tacos must be done in San Diego, and a number of places serve them, whether authentic Baja street tacos or some traditional local take on fried fish. Then there's City Tacos, which turns tradition on its head for foodies looking to enjoy traditional flavor profiles in creative new ways. The chile relleno taco invokes the classic dish with mild spice and a gloriously melted cheese blend. The mahi-mahi adobo sears a lovely piece of fish and pairs it with mango salsa. Then there's the Borrego taco—lamb, mushroom, and fried leeks. You won't find the likes of it elsewhere, much to the detriment of elsewhere.

Map 3: 3028 University Ave., North Park, 619/296-2303, www.citytacossd.com; Mon.-Thurs. 11am-11pm, Fri.-Sat. 11am-2am, Sun. noon-11pm

EL COMAL $$

If you're ready to experience homemade Mexican food, this family-owned restaurant offers a delicious and down-to-earth experience. *Comal* translates to "griddle," a reference to the restaurant's *antojitos*, traditional small dishes built around the ground hominy dough masa, used to make tamales and some of the best corn tortillas you'll ever taste. Consequently, any taco on the menu is a go, especially the goat *barbecoa* (barbecue). To see what else masa can do, try the *mulitas* (like a corn tortilla grilled cheese), *gorditas* (like a pita sandwich), *huaraches* (like a corn tortilla pizza), or the green mole enchiladas, if they're available. And if you see a soup you like, just order it—they're all fantastic.

Map 3: 3946 Illinois St., North Park, 619/294-8292, www.elcomalsd.com; Mon.-Wed. 10am-3pm and 5pm-9pm, Thurs.-Fri. 8am-10pm, Sat. 8am-10pm, Sun. 8am-9pm

PIZZA

BLIND LADY ALE HOUSE 💲💲

Tasty Napolitano pizza and 26 craft beers on tap would probably be enough to keep this place popular. But a comfortable wood dining room filled with community tables elevates this to a joy-filled space where families and friends bond over great ales. Whether you order a pie with house-made chorizo and sausage toppings, *moules frites* (mussels and fries), or a charcuterie board, it's tough to go wrong, especially if you try one of the beers brewed in-house by Automatic Brewing Co.

Map 3: 3416 Adams Ave., Normal Heights, 619/255-2491, www.blindladyalehouse.com; Mon.-Thurs. 5pm-midnight, Fri.-Sun.11:30am-midnight

URBN PIZZA 💲💲

The best crust in town hails from the coal-fired ovens of this chic pizza spot—and yes, pizza spots can be chic. A full bar turns out tasty cocktails as well as local craft beer, so the place often fills up with thirsty pretty things, hipsters, and cocktail connoisseurs. But excellent pizza is the root of Urbn's success, with toppings like sausage-stuffed peppers, fresh clams, and mashed potatoes. Great happy hour specials make a visit worth your while.

Map 3: 3085 University Ave., North Park, 619/255-7300, www.urbnnorthpark.com; Sun.-Mon. noon-10pm, Tues.-Thurs. noon-midnight, Fri.-Sat. noon-2am

Old Town and Mission Hills Map 4

CONTEMPORARY

STARLITE 💲💲

The fact its kitchen is open late would make this stylish, cocktail savvy restaurant a favorite post-bar dinner stop for San Diego's creative set. That it happens to serve some of the best dishes in town is just a bonus that keeps the place a perennial favorite. Whatever the hour you drop by, start with the kale Caesar salad and mac and cheese before moving on to the *jidori* chicken or grilled octopus.

Map 4: 3175 India St., Mission Hills, 619/358-9766, www.starlitesandiego.com; Sat.-Thurs. 5pm-1am, Fri. 4pm-1am

DESSERT

GELATO VERO CAFFE 💲

Holding down its little corner for more than 30 years, this gelato shop is a great place to go for dessert after indulging in one of the block's many good restaurants. Classic Italian flavors include *gianduia* (chocolate hazelnut) and spumoni (cherry chocolate amaretto) as well as fruit-flavored *sorbettos*.

Map 4: 3753 India St., Mission Hills, 619/295-9269, www.gelatoverocaffe.com; Mon.-Thurs. 6am-midnight, Fri. 6am-1am, Sat. 7am-1am, Sun. 7am-midnight

CASA GUADALAJARA $$

Old Town's historic park has no shortage of "authentic" Mexican restaurants vying for tourist attention. If you're intent on finding the classic Mexican margarita and Latin-music dining-patio experience, do as the locals do and head to Casa Guadalajara, the best of the bunch. Dishes like *chile colorado* (tender beef with a spicy red sauce) and carne asada *tampiqueña* (chili-rubbed) offer all the flavors you seek, though tacos, enchiladas, and fajitas always prove popular. Sit on the patio, order some chips and guacamole, and savor the experience.

Map 4: 4105 Taylor St., Old Town, 619/295-5111, www.casaguadalajara.com; Mon.-Thurs. 11am-9pm, Fri. 11am-10pm, Sat. 10am-10pm, Sun. 10am-9pm

EL AGAVE $$$

El Agave creates a "Mexican gastronomy," crafting a menu of authentic dishes that range from the usual to the exotic, including an appetizer called *tlacoyos cuitlacoche* (a rarely found delicacy of blue masa and corn fungus). For the less adventurous, the menu's safest bets include any of its 10 moles, each a worthy excuse to dine here. The restaurant doubles as a tequila museum, and its walls are lined with more than 2,000 bottles, which add a beautiful brightness to the rustic decor.

Map 4: 2304 San Diego Ave., Old Town, 619/220-0692, www.elagave.com; daily 11am-10pm

EL INDIO $

For 75 years, this *tortilleria* has been churning out homemade tortillas and tortilla chips. During most of that time, it has also been serving up beloved and authentic Mexican food to a loyal following of locals and visitors. The founder of the family-owned mainstay is said to have invented the term *taquito,* so the rolled tacos are worth a try. Sit down in the busy casual dining room or on the patio, or order to go.

Map 4: 3695 India St., Mission Hills, 619/299-0385, www.elindiosandiego.net; daily 8am-9pm

LUCHA LIBRE $

If you like your Mexican food with a side of extreme kitsch, dive into this campy masked wrestling-themed taco and burrito shop. Wrestler murals and a mask gallery liven up the bright pink walls, while luchadores wrestle on TV screens, playing up the wild vibe. You'll find prototypical San Diego-style Mexican food here, as well as a few modern takes along the lines of a lettuce-wrapped taco and a great salsa bar. It's a kooky way to eat like a local while still living like a traveler. With 24 hours' notice, you can even reserve the Champion's Booth, which must be seen to be believed.

Map 4: 1810 W. Washington St., Mission Hills, 619/296-8226, www.tacosmackdown.com; Sun.-Thurs. 10am-11pm, Fri.-Sat. 10am-2:30am

Must-Try Mexican Food

To make the most of San Diego's local specialties, look for these menu items at their recommended restaurants, along with other mainstays like enchiladas, chiles rellenos, shredded pork carnitas, and the rotisserie lamb-inspired pork *al pastor*. Don't forget to hit the salsa bar and use it generously.

- **Baja-style fish tacos** consist of beer-battered fish fillets deep-fried and served on corn tortillas with cabbage and a white *crema* (cream) sauce. Add-ons like *pico de gallo* (fresh salsa), onions, and guacamole are great, but eat them with just a little Cholula or Valentina hot sauce instead. Try them at **Oscar's Mexican Seafood** (703 Turquoise St., Pacific Beach, 858/488-6392, www.oscarsmexicanseafood.com; Sun.-Thurs. 8am-9pm, Fri.-Sat. 8am-10pm) or **Mariscos Nine Seas** (3030 Grape St., South Park, 619/279-0010, www.mariscosnineseasseafood.com; daily 9:30am-7:30pm).

- *Antojitos* are like Mexican tapas: small plates, usually dishes made with masa, a corn dough commonly associated with tamales and corn tortillas. The handmade tortillas at **El Comal** (3946 Illinois St., North Park, 619/294-8292, www.elcomalsd.com; Mon.-Wed. 10am-3pm and 5pm-9pm, Thurs.-Fri. 8am-10pm, Sat. 8am-10pm, Sun. 8am-9pm) are phenomenal, and their *sopes, mulitas,* and *gorditas* incorporate beans, cheese, and other ingredients, resembling tiny pizzas, grilled sandwiches, and empanadas, respectively.

- **California burritos** or **carne asada fries:** California's great contribution to Mexican food? French fries. The Cali burrito adds fries to a beefy carne asada burrito, with melting cheddar cheese, and maybe a little sour cream or guacamole. Carne asada fries pile all the same ingredients on a plate, resulting in a nachos-like dish with fries instead of chips. Try them at **Roberto's Mexican Food** (2206 Carmel Valley Rd., Torrey Pines, 858/436-7189, www.robertos.us; Sun.-Thurs. 9am-9pm, Fri.-Sat. 9am-10pm).

PIZZA

LEFTY'S CHICAGO PIZZERIA $

Chicago may be a far cry from our sun-drenched beach lifestyle, but who doesn't love deep-dish pizza, Polish sausage, and Italian beef sandwiches? The family behind Lefty's came straight from the Windy City with authenticity on their minds. Both this Mission Hills outpost and the original North Park location (3448 30th St.) have become standbys for Chicago expatriates and longtime locals, who keep coming back for the eatery's thin- or thick-crust pizzas and excellent char-grilled burgers.

Map 4: 4030 Goldfinch St., Mission Hills, 619/299-4030, www.leftyspizza.com; Sun.-Thurs. 11pm-9pm, Fri.-Sat. 11am-10pm

a classic Baja fish taco from Oscar's Mexican Seafood

- **Mole** is a smooth sauce made from chilies and other ingredients, including almonds, ground pumpkin seeds, and chocolate. Moles are usually ordered by color—brown, green, white, or red (a.k.a. *colorado*). With 10 moles to choose from, ordering one from **El Agave** (2304 San Diego Ave., 619/220-0692, www.elagave.com; daily 11am-10pm) may be a little more complicated, but it's entirely worth it.

- *Taquitos* (rolled tacos) are rumored to have been invented at **El Indio** (3695 India St., 619/299-0333, www.el-indio.com; daily 8am-9pm). The rolled tacos are available with shredded beef, chicken, or potato and garnished with cheese and guacamole for the proper effect. The *flautas* are prepared the same way as a *taquito,* but with flour tortillas instead of corn.

SEAFOOD
BLUE WATER SEAFOOD MARKET & GRILL $$

The secret got out about Blue Water when the beloved fresh-catch seafood spot was covered on TV's *Diners, Drive-Ins and Dives,* but the line out the door always existed near lunchtime. That line moves quickly, though, guiding you past the market counter, where you can linger over the different cuts of fish available. Decide which looks best and then order it as a sandwich, a salad, a taco, or on a plate with your choice of seasoning. The place always looks packed, but tables open up frequently; grab one on the patio if you can.

Map 4: 3667 India St., Mission Hills, 619/497-0914, www.bluewaterseafoodsandiego.com; Mon.-Thurs. 11am-9pm, Fri. 11am-10pm, Sat. 11:30am-10pm, Sun. 11:30am-9pm

AMERICAN
IRON PIG ALEHOUSE $$

The best barbecue by the beach is served by this Texas-style, oak and hickory smokehouse. Its gastropub environment gets a boost from a top-notch craft beer menu, but there's little doubt people come here for the brisket, pulled pork, and chicken. There's even a smoked gouda and cheddar grilled cheese for vegetarians to join in on the hickory-infused fun.

Map 5: 1520 Garnet Ave., Pacific Beach, 858/412-4299, www.ironpigalehouse.com; Mon.-Thurs. 11:30am-10pm, Fri.-Sat. 11:30am-11pm, Sun. 10am-10pm

ROCKY'S CROWN PUB $

Pacific Beach's legendary local burger bar doesn't need special toppings or gimmicky burgers in its recipe for success, just tried and true burger fixings that have earned it decades of devoted clientele, *Food Network* accolades, and a spot on many San Diegans' best burger lists.

Map 5: 3786 Ingraham St., Pacific Beach, 858/273-9140, www.rockyburgers.com; daily 11am-midnight

ASIAN
SUSHI OTA $$$

Make reservations, because the esteemed chef Ota is the city's most storied sushi chef, and his place has long been considered the best in town. Legend has it, he happened upon San Diego while traveling and fell in love with the taste of local sea urchin *(uni)*. Although you'll probably want to order his *uni,* you will always be best off going chef's choice, or *omakase*—another legend has it that each morning Ota gets first pick of the best local catch.

Map 5: 4529 Mission Bay Dr., Pacific Beach, 858/270-5670; Mon. 5:30pm-10:30pm, Tues.-Fri. 11:30am-2pm and 5:30pm-10:30pm, Sat.-Sun. 5pm-10:30pm

BREAKFAST
BROKEN YOLK CAFÉ $$

If you can stand the wait, hold out for rooftop seating at this PB brunch institution. The massive menu includes classic Mexican egg dishes like *chilaquiles* and *huevos con chorizo;* a griddle menu of pancakes and waffles; and a litany of Benedicts and massive omelets. Gather your friends, order a couple rounds of mimosas, and feast. Other locations include Gaslamp (355 6th Ave.) and Point Loma (3577 Midway Dr.).

Map 5: 1851 Garnet Ave., Pacific Beach, 619/270-9655, www.thebrokenyolkcafe.com; daily 6am-3pm

CONTEMPORARY

THE PATIO ON LAMONT ⑤⑤⑤

What's better at the Patio: the food or the decor? It's a tough call. The menu features braised short ribs, braised octopus, seafood risotto, and a 21-day-aged bone-in rib eye. Seating options include a romantically lit interior dining room and a bright spot beneath the living wall of plants that adorn the eatery's namesake covered patio. If you think these decisions are tough, wait until you see the cocktail list! Of course, first you've got to decide between this and a possibly more gorgeous Mission Hills location (4020 Goldfinch St.).

Map 5: 4445 Lamont St., Pacific Beach, 858/412-4648, www.thepatioonlamont.com; Sun.-Thurs. 9am-11pm, Fri.-Sat. 9am-midnight

SANDBAR SPORTS GRILL ⑤⑤

Sandbar is not just a nice piece of real estate on Mission Beach—though it is that. Set on the boardwalk just north of Belmont Park, its windows capture the beach vibe, the ocean breeze, and plenty of people-watching. Order a drink while you wait for tasty tacos or burgers.

Map 5: 718 Ventura Pl., Mission Beach, 858/488-1274, www.sandbarsportsgrill.com; Sun.-Wed. 9am-midnight, Thurs.-Sat. 9am-2am

DELI

RUBICON DELI ⑤

This local sandwich chain lays a solid foundation for its subs with a variety of house-baked breads, including pesto, jalapeño jack, and Dutch crunch. All the favorite lunch meats are available, or opt for one of the more intriguing house specials, such as the Whale's Veg—spinach, kale, cabbage, carrot, bell pepper, avocado, tomato, onion, cucumber, hummus, tarragon Dijon mustard, balsamic vinaigrette, and jack cheese. You'll find a second location in Mission Hills (3715 India St.).

Map 5: 3819 Mission Blvd., Mission Beach, 858/488-3354, www.therubicondeli.com; daily 10:30am-7pm

MEXICAN

OSCAR'S MEXICAN SEAFOOD ⑤

Why do lines of people keep forming beside the taco truck mural of that hole-in-the-wall in north PB? Because the fish tacos demand it. Oscar's excels at the classic Baja-style battered fish, available for a buck on weekday afternoons. Smoked fish, shrimp, and steak tacos also go great with the house ceviche or fish stew. There's a less charming central Pacific Beach location (746 Emerald St.) and another in East Village (927 J St.).

Map 5: 703 Turquoise St., Pacific Beach, 858/488-6392, www.oscarsmexicanseafood.com; Sun.-Thurs. 8am-9pm, Fri.-Sat. 8am-10pm

SEAFOOD

THE FISHERY $$$

No finer restaurant in town shows a greater dedication to local seafood than The Fishery. Chef Paul Arias works on the principle that food tastes best when it's perfectly in season, so the availability of local seafood and produce factors heavily into a menu that is comprehensive, yet totally fish-centric. Don't expect a beef or chicken dish, but delight in the variety of shellfish, sushi, and chowders, plus freshly caught specimens either grilled, roasted, braised, or pan-roasted.

Map 5: 5040 Cass St., Pacific Beach, 858/272-9985, www.thefishery.com; daily 10am-10pm

PACIFIC BEACH FISH SHOP $$

Line up for grilled fish, sandwiches, or tacos at the counter of this locals' favorite. It's easy to spot thanks to a marlin trophy out front. Order your choice of fish based on what looks good that day, accompanied by marinades such as blackened lemon-butter or chipotle. Or keep it crudo with ceviche, oysters, a shrimp cocktail, or sashimi of the day. Take it to the patio with a draft beer and relish where you are.

Map 5: 1775 Garnet Ave., Pacific Beach, 858/483-4746, www.thefishshoppb.com; daily 11am-10pm

Ocean Beach and Point Loma

Map 6

AMERICAN

FATHOM BISTRO, BAIT, AND TACKLE $

Located in the middle of a bayside fishing pier, this bait and tackle shop makes and serves hot dogs, sausage sandwiches, and burgers meant to be washed back with one of many local beers on draft. Grab a seat on the pier and check out the view of downtown and Coronado. Fries are not an option, but you might like the *lumpia* (Filipino spring rolls).

Map 6: 1776 Shelter Island Dr., Shelter Island, 619/222-5835, www.fathombistro.com; Tues.-Thurs. 3pm-9pm, Fri. 3pm-10pm, Sat. 10am-10pm, Sun. 10am-8pm

HODAD'S $

The *Food Network* inexorably changed the face of Ocean Beach a few years back when it named Hodad's among the nation's best burgers. Now lines run half a block long on sunny days. Whether the basic burger selection here is worth the hype or just another greasy beneficiary of TV fame, you're in for a wait. Hold out for the prime people-watching real estate at the counter overlooking the sidewalk. Otherwise, prepare to spend your meal

Map 6: 5010 Newport Ave., Ocean Beach, 619/224-4623, www.hodadies.com;
daily 11am-10pm

ASIAN

OB NOODLE HOUSE $$

The popularity of the original **OB Noodle House** (2218 Cable St.), down
the road, led to its recent expansion into this larger location a block from
the OB Pier. Locals love the place and seek out their favorite dishes among
udon, pho, lo mein, and other pan-Asian pastas, as well as a fine rotation
of local craft brews and cocktails to drink with them. It's never a bad
place to be on a warm evening; enjoy a beer on the outdoor patio as the
neighborhood's nightlife starts to pick up.

Map 6: 4993 Niagara Ave., Ocean Beach, 619/255-9858, www.obnoodlehouse.com;
Mon.-Thurs. noon-11pm, Fri.-Sat. 11:30am-11pm, Sun. 11am-11pm

UMI SUSHI $$

For gorgeous sushi boats and shoji decor, give this Shelter Island sushi joint
the nod. You can eat your fill of clean, beautifully cut fish, or order from
the impressive list of rolls. Try the Mountain Roll, spicy tuna topped with
baked salmon, or opt for more standard fare with the Crazy Boy, a tempura-
fried California roll. Umi offers a traditional feel yet welcomes novice sushi
eaters looking to try delicious raw seafood.

Map 6: 2806 Shelter Island Dr., Shelter Island, 619/226-1135, www.umisushisandiego.
com; Mon.-Sat. 11:30am-2pm and 5pm-9pm, Sun. 5pm-9pm

BREAKFAST

OB SURF LODGE $$

Across the street from the beach, this new restaurant goes for a midcentury
beach vibe, though its outward-facing view makes it the best place for an
OB breakfast. From-scratch biscuits make for fully satisfying breakfast
sandwiches, though Benedicts, pancakes, *chilaquiles,* French toast, and
American classics round out any taste.

Map 6: 5083 Santa Monica Ave., Ste. 1F, Ocean Beach, 619/955-5475, www.obsurflodge.
com; Mon.-Thurs. 9am-9pm, Fri. 9am-10pm, Sat. 8am-10pm, Sun. 8am-9pm

CONTEMPORARY

BALI HAI $$$

This bay-view restaurant opened during the 1950s Polynesian craze,
so you'll still spot some tiki decor and catch live Hawaiian tunes some
evenings. The menu covers Pacific Rim dishes, including seafood, meat,
vegetarian, and gluten-free options. There's something for everyone,
especially if everyone enjoys potent cocktails. Share a scorpion bowl or
add another to the tally of 2.3 million mai tais served in this warm and

Dining with a View

A view of the skyline is reason enough to dine at Coasterra.

Whether you're looking for a romantic dinner with a sunset view or just want to gaze out the window, a number of fine establishments offer excellent views, especially if you call ahead to reserve a good table.

For the most up-close interaction with the Pacific Ocean, try **The Marine Room** (2000 Spindrift Dr., 858/459-7222, www.marineroom.com; Sun.-Thurs. 5:30pm-9:30pm, Fri.-Sat. 5:30pm-10pm), which boasts reinforced windows that keep the water out during high tide. Waves crashing against a dining room window isn't likely something you'll experience elsewhere.

George's at the Cove (1250 Prospect St., La Jolla Village, 858/454-4244, www.georgesatthecove.com; Sun.-Thurs. 11am-10pm, Fri.-Sat. 11am-11pm) overlooks the jewel of La Jolla, its cove. Fine seasonal cuisine from its terrace proves a can't-miss experience.

To check out the city skyline, book a table at **Coasterra** (880 Harbor Island Dr., Harbor Island, 619/814-1300, www.cohnrestaurants.com/coasterra; Sun.-Thurs. 11:30am-9pm, Fri.-Sat. 11:30am-10pm) on Harbor Island. The Mexican restaurant sits on the water, boasting San Diego's most stunning downtown view.

Bali Hai (2230 Shelter Island Dr., 619/222-1181, www.balihairestaurant.com; Mon.-Thurs. 11:30am-10pm, Fri.-Sat. 11:30am-11pm, Sun. 9:30am-10pm) has a broader perspective of the bay, including a glimpse at some of the naval vessels coming out of Coronado, which aren't always pretty but can be fascinating.

Dress well to enjoy the view from **Mr. A's** (2550 5th Ave., Bankers Hill, 619/239-1377, www.asrestaurant.com; Mon.-Fri. 11:30am-9pm, Sat. 5pm-9:30pm, Sun. 10am-9pm). The 12th-story restaurant has a dress code. It's worth heeding to enjoy the French-inspired cuisine and stunning city-meets-coast panorama.

The greenest views come courtesy of the golf course at Torrey Pines. Check it out from the deck of the terrific **A.R. Valentien** (11480 N. Torrey Pines Rd., Torrey Pines, 858/777-6635, www.arvalentien.com; Mon.-Fri. 7am-11am, 11:30am-2:30pm and 5:30pm-10pm, Sat. -Sun. 7am-11:30am, noon-2:30pm, and 5:30pm-10pm), one of the most pleasant lunch spots in town. It also happens to face west, delivering golf course greenery, an ocean sunset, and incredible food: the trifecta.

welcoming space. Reserve in advance for a window seat, so you can catch an up-close glimpse of U.S. Navy vessels traversing the harbor.

Map 6: 2230 Shelter Island Dr., 619/222-1181, www.balihairestaurant.com; Mon.-Thurs. 11:30am-10pm, Fri.-Sat. 11:30am-11pm, Sun. 9:30am-10pm

SODA & SWINE $

A 20-foot foosball table makes a conversational centerpiece of this stylishly wacky indoor/outdoor fast-casual joint. Craft beer and cocktails support a menu featuring no fewer than six kinds of meatball (or veggie ball) sandwiches, served on slider buns, on a hoagie roll, or over pasta. Mix up different cheeses and sauces as you see fit, and share an amazing menu of side dishes, including Brussels sprouts, crispy polenta, and a decadent mac and cheese.

Map 6: 2750 Dewey Rd. #104., Liberty Station, 619/501-9989, www.sodaandswin.com; Sun.-Thurs. 11am-10pm, Fri.-Sat. 11am-midnight

DESSERT
LIGHTHOUSE ICE CREAM & YOGURT $

You'll smell this ice cream and frozen yogurt shop before you see it, specifically the made-on-site waffle-ice cream sandwiches. If you come within sniffing distance, you will wind up standing in line trying to decide between an apple-cinnamon waffle sandwich filled with sea salt-caramel ice cream or a cone of huckleberry topped with bacon. Or keep it simple with a blueberry-cheesecake ice cream banana split.

Map 6: 5059 Newport Ave., Ocean Beach, 619/222-8600; daily 11am-10pm

FARM-TO-TABLE
STONE WORLD BISTRO & GARDENS, LIBERTY STATION $$

Stone reigns as one of the biggest and most successful craft brewers in town. It's also a 40,000-square-foot organic farm-to-table restaurant with 40 taps of Stone special releases, collaborations, and dozens of handpicked guest beers. The huge outdoor patio is the place to be on warm days; half the taps are out here, along with bocce ball courts and outdoor movie screenings. Amid such amenities, it's easy to forget about the food, which is made from scratch, often with produce grown at Stone's very own farm. Asian-inspired dishes include *yakisoba* (noodle stir-fry) and Korean barbecued ribs, plus intriguing takes on duck tacos, a corned lamb Reuben, and a *jidori* chicken schnitzel.

Map 6: 2816 Historic Decatur Rd., Ste. 116, Liberty Station, 619/269-2100, www.stonelibertystation.com; Sun.-Thurs. 11:30am-9pm, Fri.-Sat. 11:30am-10pm

ITALIAN
★ OFFICINE BUONA FORCHETTA $$

The original location of this molto autentico Italian restaurant got so popular it would take two hours to get a table, so it opened this much larger space featuring copious indoor and outdoor seating, including a modified vintage Fiat convertible that serves as a romantic two-person booth. While it's far shorter a wait, Buona Forchetta's signature hand-made pastas and wood-fired Neapolitan pizzas are just as outrageously great here.

Map 6: 2865 Sims Rd., Liberty Station, 619/548-5770, www.officinebuonaforchetta.com; Mon.-Thurs. noon-3pm and 5pm-9:30pm, Fri. noon-3pm and 5pm-10:30pm, Sat. noon-10:30pm, Sun. noon-9pm

MARKETS
LIBERTY PUBLIC MARKET ⑤

Modeled after public markets such as Seattle's famous Pike Place, this food-centric market features dozens of artisan vendors operating independent booths. Food options include empanadas, ramen, Mediterranean food, hot sandwiches, and Maine lobster rolls, in addition to locally roasted coffee and locally brewed craft beer (which you may drink while you browse). A communal dining room and large patio provide places for everybody to eat together once they've ordered their pick of food.

Map 6: 2820 Historic Decatur Rd., Liberty Station, 619/487-9346, www.libertypublicmarket.com; daily 11am-8pm

MEXICAN
COASTERRA ⑤⑤

Offering an unparalleled view of the San Diego city skyline, this harborside restaurant brings you about as close to the water as you can get without getting wet. A little milder than most local Mexican restaurants, and a little more upscale, the tastefully curated dishes are bolstered by stretchy Oaxacan cheese, chipotle salsas, and roasted poblano peppers.

Map 6: 880 Harbor Island Dr., Harbor Island, 619/814-1300, www.cohnrestaurants.com/coasterra; Sun.-Thurs. 11:30am-9pm, Fri.-Sat. 11:30am-10pm

SOUTH BEACH BAR & GRILLE ⑤

With an upstairs deck overlooking the pier, OB's always-bustling South Beach Bar & Grille is a longtime favorite fish taco destination for locals and out-of-town guests. Choices range from traditional Baja battered-and-fried tacos to grilled options, including wahoo, mahi-mahi, lobster, and shark; wash these down with one of the local beers on tap. You're on your own finding an open table amid the constant rush, but once you've claimed your spot, you've earned the right to enjoy it awhile.

Map 6: 5059 Newport Ave., Ocean Beach, 619/226-4577, www.southbeachob.com; daily 11am-2am

SEAFOOD
POINT LOMA SEAFOODS ⑤

When do you know the seafood's truly fresh? When you pass a fleet of fishing boats outside the restaurant. Point Loma Seafoods has achieved cultlike status over the years, with a glass deli counter displaying your

Clockwise from top left: A vintage Fiat convertible doubles as a two-person booth at Officine Buona Forchetta; Liberty Public Market has become central to a rising Liberty Station culinary scene; Sea urchin is a local seafood delicacy.

choice of the latest catch. Line up at the counter and choose your fresh catch for fish tacos, seafood salad, sushi, or plates with fries and slaw. The best-known option may be the simplest: a piece of fish on freshly baked sourdough with tartar sauce—that's it. The freshness of the fish is all the frills this sandwich needs.

Map 6: 2805 Emerson St., Shelter Island, 619/223-1109, www.pointlomaseafoods.com; Mon.-Sat. 9am-7pm, Sun. 10am-8pm

La Jolla
Map 7

AMERICAN
BURGER LOUNGE ⑤

This cleanly designed local chain offers grass-fed hamburgers, free-range turkey burgers, organic quinoa veggie burgers, big salads, and gluten-free buns with fries and onion rings cooked in "100 percent refined peanut oil." Thing is, all of this stuff tastes great, granting an affordable meal that's relatively good for you. Other locations include Hillcrest (406 University Ave.) and the Gaslamp (528 5th Ave.).

Map 7: 1101 Wall St., La Jolla Village, 858/456-0196, www.burgerlounge.com; Sun.-Thurs. 10:30am-9pm, Fri.-Sat. 10:30am-10pm

BREAKFAST
BROCKTON VILLA ⑤⑤

Three things make Brockton Villa a favorite in La Jolla: a patio with views overlooking La Jolla Cove, the quaint 1894 beach bungalow setting, and the French toast. The soufflé-style toast is a fluffy, moist-in-the-middle treat that draws rave reviews decade after decade. A friendly warning: When the wind is blowing in from the cove, the scent of local animal life can take a few minutes to ignore.

Map 7: 1235 Coast Blvd., La Jolla Village, 858/454-7393, www.brocktonvilla.com; daily 8am-9pm

HARRY'S COFFEE SHOP ⑤

Hidden among the high-end boutiques and trendy restaurants is this anachronistic coffee shop embodying the classic American diner, complete with vinyl booths and a breakfast counter. The menu offers eggs dishes galore, from a list of omelets to eggs with bacon, sausage, chicken-fried steak, or corned beef hash. Order refills on that mug of joe, which is made from a special blend of beans roasted by local coffee mainstay Café Moto.

Map 7: 7545 Girard Ave., La Jolla Village, 858/454-7381, www.harryscoffeeshop.com; daily 6am-3pm

BIRD ROCK COFFEE ROASTERS $

This celebrated local roaster favors light-roasting its single-origin beans, which are usually the product of direct agreements between Bird Rock and a network of farmers around the globe. Bird Rock puts a lot of thought and craft into its coffee, and the staff welcomes questions about brewing techniques, especially about the daily selection of fresh beans. A newer location is in Little Italy (2295 Kettner Blvd.).

Map 7: 5627 La Jolla Blvd., Bird Rock, 858/551-1707, www.birdrockcoffee.com; Mon.-Fri. 6am-6pm, Sat.-Sun. 6:30am-6pm

CALIFORNIA

★ GEORGE'S AT THE COVE $$$

Routinely named San Diego's top restaurant, George's doesn't just offer a seasonally inspired "California modern" menu that evolves almost daily, it boasts prime real estate overlooking La Jolla Cove. Its ocean terrace offers one of the overall best dining experiences in Southern California, with pristine and occasionally surprising dishes that range from fish tacos to dry-aged rib eye to stellar vegan fare. You may order à la carte, but it's tough to go wrong with a tasting menu, especially if you just let the chef decide how to feed the table. All pairs well with the ocean and—if you time it right—the sunset.

Map 7: 1250 Prospect St., La Jolla Village, 858/454-4244, www.georgesatthecove.com; Sun.-Thurs. 11am-10pm, Fri.-Sat. 11am-11pm

NINE-TEN $$$

Chef Jason Knibb has earned accolades over the years for the "evolving California cuisine" served at the Grand Colonial Hotel's restaurant. Appetizers may include squid-ink spaghettini with bay scallops in an *uni* (sea urchin) emulsion, while entrée options range from a creatively dressed prime steak dish to succulent seafood prepared sous vide. Local produce dictates the weekly flavor profiles, and the excellently prepared staff can recommend perfect wine pairings all the way through dessert. Reserve a spot on the sidewalk patio for people-watching along Prospect Street, or request terrace dining for a partial sunset view of the Pacific.

Map 7: 910 Prospect St., La Jolla Village, 858/964-5400, www.nine-ten.com; Mon.-Sat. 6:30am-11am and 11:30am-2:30pm, Sun. 10:30am-2pm, Sun.-Thurs. 6pm-9:30pm, Fri.-Sat. 6pm-10pm

FARM-TO-TABLE

A.R. VALENTIEN $$$

Spearheading the farm-to-table movement in San Diego, the restaurant at The Lodge at Torrey Pines crafts delicious charcuterie and simple yet effective dishes, adhering to the principle that quality ingredients result in quality meals. Even something as simple as baked chicken under a brick tastes better when it's done right. The dining room is nice, but it's tough to beat lunch on the gorgeous deck overlooking the 18th hole of the famous Torrey Pines Golf Course.

Map 7: 11480 N. Torrey Pines Rd., Torrey Pines, 858/777-6635, www.arvalentien.com; Mon.-Fri. 7am-11am, 11:30am-2:30pm, and 5:30pm-10pm, Sat.-Sun. 7am-11:30am, noon-2:30pm, and 5:30pm-10pm

WHISKNLADLE $$$

The covered patio is where you'll find one of the best dining (and people-watching) experiences in San Diego. Executive chef Chris Powell crafts seasonal dishes prepared from scratch, usually dependent on which organic produce and sustainably sourced meats and seafood are available fresh. The result is out-of-this-world quality; even a routine charcuterie plate stands out, with exceptional house-cured meats, brined-in-house olives, and house-baked breads. You can't go wrong with any pasta entrée, especially a pork sausage *ragù* sauce over tagliatelle that will make you question every Italian restaurant you've ever visited.

Map 7: 1044 Wall St., La Jolla Village, 858/551-7575, www.whisknladle.com; daily brunch 9:30am-3pm, daily happy hour 3pm-6pm, dinner Sun.-Thurs. 5pm-9pm, Fri.-Sat. 5pm-9:30pm

FRENCH
★ THE MARINE ROOM $$$

This high-end restaurant has been a legendary draw since the 1940s, famous for being so close to the ocean that waves splash against the windows during high tide. Diners enjoy a little thrill each time the water splashes only inches away, but ultimately the food lives up to its reputation as well. Globally sourced seafood is supplemented by French gastronomy that includes everything from Maine lobster tail to lamb osso buco.

Map 7: 2000 Spindrift Dr., La Jolla Shores, 858/459-7222, www.marineroom.com; Sun.-Thurs. 5:30pm-9:30pm, Fri.-Sat. 5:30pm-10pm

MEXICAN
GALAXY TACO $$

This colorful, mostly outdoor restaurant brings a little attitude to La Jolla, offering a spread of traditional and gourmet tacos that prove perfect before, after, or in the middle of a beach day. Tortillas and tamales are made from scratch using heirloom corn, and while the regular fish, meat, and vegetarian tacos always satisfy, watch out for Tuesday night events, where highly regarded guest chefs (usually from non-Mexican restaurants) come by to offer their own creative takes on what a taco can taste like.

Map 7: 2259 Avenida de la Playa, La Jolla Shores, 858/228-5655, www.galaxytaco.com; Mon.-Sat. 11am-10pm, Sun. 10am-10pm

ROBERTO'S MEXICAN FOOD $

Overlooking Los Penasquitos Lagoon, which feeds into Torrey Pines State Beach, this casual local Mexican chain exemplifies the classic San

Diego-style burrito shop. Go for one of two regional specialties: California burritos or carne asada fries. Both feature marinated beef, French fries, cheese, guacamole, and salsa; they're wrapped in a tortilla for the former, served on a plate for the latter.

Map 7: 2206 Carmel Valley Rd., Torrey Pines, 858/436-7189, www.robertos.us; Sun.-Thurs. 9am-9pm, Fri.-Sat. 9am-10pm

SEAFOOD
EL PESCADOR FISH MARKET $

Fresh seafood in La Jolla has a long history. This newly expanded local staple dates back to the 1970s and offers a bounty of fresh-catch seafood, served in sandwiches, burritos, or tacos—all very satisfying. High ceilings and picture windows light up a long glass counter filled with local fish, including yellowtail, sea bass, and Mexican white shrimp. To truly embrace the beauty of this spot, grab the sashimi platter of the day.

Map 7: 634 Pearl St., La Jolla Village, 858/456-2526, www.elpescadorfishmarket.com; daily 11am-9pm

Coronado   Map 8

AMERICAN
CORONADO BREWING COMPANY $$

A local institution, CBC has been serving up pub grub for decades, which goes great with its award-winning beers. Order a tasting flight with appetizers, then settle on a pint to go with your burger, pizza, or taco plate. Aim for lunch or an early dinner to enjoy the shaded dining patio on a sunny day. With the city skyline within view, you can check a few items off your San Diego to-do list all in one place.

Map 8: 170 Orange Ave., Coronado Ferry Landing, 619/437-4452, www. coronadobrewingcompany.com; Sun.-Thurs. 10:30am-9pm, Fri.-Sat. 10:30am-10pm

BREAKFAST
★ CROWN ROOM $$$

The Hotel del Coronado's lavish all-you-can-eat brunch includes a truly dizzying number of buffet stations, all served in the Crown Room, one of the city's best architectural examples of jointed wood construction. Eggs are made to order, prime rib roasts are carved, pancakes flipped, and sushi rolled. Even if you go back for thirds, you won't get to it all. You may never even know what you missed by the time you've made it through your second dessert. Reservations are recommended, as the high cost of entry doesn't seem to keep the crowds away.

Map 8: 1500 Orange Ave., 619/522-8490, www.hoteldel.com; Sun. 9:30am-1pm

Top: the Hotel del Coronado's Crown Room. Bottom: Las Cuatro Milpas.

CAFÉS

CORONADO COFFEE COMPANY ⑤

A scenic location in Coronado's Ferry Landing Marketplace makes this large kiosk a good spot to grab a cup of coffee on the way to or returning from downtown, especially when beans from a local roaster are being served. If you're not taking the ferry, enjoy your cup of joe at the small park just to the left up the coastline.

Map 8: 1201 1st St., Ferry Landing Marketplace, 619/522-0217,
www.bluebridgehospitality.com; Mon.-Fri. 7am-8pm, Sat.-Sun. 7am-9pm

DESSERTS

MOOTIME CREAMERY ⑤

A rotating selection of handcrafted ice cream, sorbet, frozen yogurt, and sherbet includes unique flavors along the lines of *horchata,* cheesecake, coconut, Girl Scout mint, Irish cream, and Mexican chocolate. Top that with candy bars, marshmallows, gummies, nuts, fruit, or fudge. Then chop, smash, and mix it all together into a waffle cone or bowl, or a waffle cup, or a chocolate-dipped waffle cone. Enjoy.

Map 8: 1025 Orange Ave., Coronado, 619/435-2422, www.mootime.com;
Sun.-Thurs. 11am-9pm, Fri.-Sat. 11am-10pm

FARM-TO-TABLE

LEROY'S KITCHEN AND LOUNGE ⑤⑤⑤

A nearby organic farm supplies this welcoming Coronado eatery with the bulk of its produce, and the chefs respond by crafting the best of whatever's fresh. The menu changes seasonally, but you'll always find deliberately conceived salads, seafood, and meat dishes. Despite their local-source ethos, the restaurant reflects the world-wandering ways of its namesake into its repertoire; eastern and island influences usually pair well with seasonal cocktails, wine, or a stellar assortment of local craft beer.

Map 8: 1015 Orange Ave., Coronado, 619/437-6087, www.leroyskitchenandlounge.com;
Mon.-Thurs. 11am-10pm, Fri. 11am-midnight, Sat. 10am-midnight, Sun. 10am-10pm

SEAFOOD

LOBSTER WEST ⑤

Lobster rolls are a favorite meal in New England seaside resort towns; there's no reason they can't be in a San Diego seaside resort town too. This casual shop brings in Maine lobster to serve the traditional-style rolls, with a vertical cut down the center of the bun. Crab, shrimp, and scallops are also heavily featured.

Map 8: 1033 B Ave., Ste.102., Coronado, 619/675-0002, www.lobsterwest.com;
Sun.-Thurs. 11am-8pm, Fri.-Sat. 11am-9pm

Fresh-Catch Market Restaurants

Fish counters have sprung up all around San Diego—wherever you are, you're only a few minutes away from your fill of yellowtail, halibut, sea bass, salmon, or any number of available fillets. Seafood counters are built around the concept that the best way to order fish is to point at it and describe how you'd like it prepared. Meals are typically a grilled fish with a marinade on a plate, or built into a sandwich or a couple of tacos.

- **Blue Water Seafood Market & Grill** (3667 India St., Mission Hills, 619/497-0914, www.bluewaterseafoodsandiego.com; Mon.-Thurs. 11am-9pm, Fri. 11am-10pm, Sat. 11:30am-10pm, Sun. 11:30am-9pm) in Mission Hills has always attracted a big lunch crowd, mostly repeat visitors who can't get enough of the daily selections cooked with lemon-garlic butter, chipotle, or blackened seasonings.

- **El Pescador Fish Market** (634 Pearl St., La Jolla Village, 858/456-2526, www.elpescadorfishmarket.com; daily 11am-9pm) is a personal favorite, and one of the best lunch values in La Jolla, hands down.

- **Point Loma Seafoods** (2805 Emerson St., Shelter Island, 619/223-1109, www.pointlomaseafoods.com; Mon.-Sat. 9am-7pm, Sun. 10am-8pm) is a regional classic on Shelter Island as well as a good excuse to visit and see all the fishing boats moored in the marina next door.

- If you're in the vicinity of Mission Bay, cap off a fun-filled day by stopping in to **Pacific Beach Fish Shop** (1775 Garnet Ave., Pacific Beach, 858/483-4746, www.thefishshoppb.com; daily 11am-10pm), which offers great beers in addition to fish.

- Not all the fish market shops are casual eateries. **The Fishery** (5040 Cass St., Pacific Beach, 858/272-9985, www.thefishery.com; daily 10am-10pm) offers a full-service restaurant around its fish market, and the seafood's treated especially well.

Greater San Diego

Map 9

MEXICAN

★ LAS CUATRO MILPAS $

Don't be deterred by the ever-present line out the door. For one, it moves fast. But no line in San Diego offers so great a payoff for so little cost. Make a hearty Mexican breakfast of eggs and chorizo with beans and rice, or a lunch of tacos and impossibly succulent tamales, or eat any of it and all of it at any time of day. Whatever you get, make sure it includes plenty of warm flour tortillas to soak up the meal—they are the best in the United States, and possibly the only tortillas you'll remember for the rest of your life.

Map 9: 1857 Logan Ave., Barrio Logan, 619/234-4460; Mon.-Fri. 8:30am-3pm, Sat. 6:30am-3pm

Mexican pastries, or *pan dulce*, are a departure from those found in most bakeries. Depending on the source, many vary in quality and simply aren't worth trying. If you happen by Panchita's, make the effort. Grab a pair of tongs and a self-serve tray and browse shelves filled with the city's best, which often range from cookies to shortbreads. Look for sugar-crusted *conchas*, glazed *campechanas*, and pineapple-stuffed empanadas, which are especially worth remembering.

Map 9: 1879 Logan Ave., Ste. K, Barrio Logan, 619/338-9331, www.panchitasbakery.com; daily 5:30am-9pm

¡SALUD! $

Chicano street culture influences the decor of this gourmet taco shop, giving the place a piquant vibe to match its neighborhood. The tacos match as well, beginning with the signature Barrio taco, made with beans, beef, and nopal cactus. Creative tacos include a fried egg and bacon breakfast taco served in the morning, a steak and fries taco, beer-battered fish, and "soyrizo" veggie. Join the line for the popular Taco Tuesday, when tacos are three for $2.

Map 9: 2196 Logan Ave., Barrio Logan, 619/255-3856, www.saludsd.com; Mon.-Thurs. 10am-9pm, Fri.-Sat. 10am-11pm, Sun. 9am-5pm

Nightlife

S an Diego's Gaslamp Quarter is the epicenter for rowdy nightlife downtown. Most nights—especially weekends—the bars, clubs, and restaurants bring out large crowds from all over the city.

Businesses cater to this flood of revelers. Most are set up to handle high volume, posting beautiful hostesses and fast-talking pitchmen on the sidewalks to lure customers. It's a competitive market, and places open and close all the time, so when you stroll the area at night you may see some new flash-in-the-pan bar or club attracting a lot of attention.

Avoiding downtown may be the impetus for the growth of North Park's nightlife. The Uptown neighborhood has flourished as a destination for creative and design-savvy types, as well as service industry vets. It's also a major hub for craft beer aficionados, with a slew of tap houses and new brewery tasting rooms opening seasonally. The 30th Street Restaurant Row entices many to stick around and imbibe craft cocktails as the night wears on.

Nearby Hillcrest caters to the LGBTQ community, with gleeful dance clubs and pickup scenes. The community is proud, and proudly open to everyone, so many nightspots cater to different niche interests on rotating nights of the week.

When the sun goes down, there's nothing like the beach communities. In Ocean Beach (OB), Newport Avenue brings in a wild mixture of surfers, bohemians, military members, bikers, and locals attracted to the laid-back atmosphere and cheap drinks. Nights in OB prove anything but predictable, and you may be surprised at the friends you make. Pacific Beach may be a little easier to peg; those cruising the beach and Garnet Avenue are usually out to drink and meet members of the opposite sex. It's a casual party

Previous: the Gaslamp Quarter; a pint of San Diego craft beer.

Look for ★ to find
recommended nightlife

Highlights

★ **Best Dance Club:** A little bit of Vegas showed up in San Diego when **FLUXX** opened its doors. The splashy club features interesting live shows as well as the occasional superstar DJ. It's not for the shy or the budget conscious (page 151).

★ **Best Rock Club: The Casbah** has been the go-to destination for in-the-know fans to catch under-the-radar bands, sometimes only a year or two removed from playing giant festivals and arenas (page 154).

★ **Best Tap House: Hamilton's Tavern** isn't huge, and everybody knows how great its tap list can be, so there's usually a crowd—sometimes even during the dog-friendly happy hour (page 158).

★ **Best Craft Cocktails: Polite Provisions** bartenders know exactly what they're doing. The lengthy cocktail list will entice whether you like sweet and fruity or prefer quality spirits to shine (page 158).

★ **Best Whiskey Bar:** An extensive menu of bourbons, scotches, and ryes gives **Seven Grand** its allure. A tasty take on an old-fashioned doesn't hurt; neither does the backroom stage with entertaining jazz acts most nights (page 159).

★ **Best Tiki Bar:** Dress lively; **The Grass Skirt** embodies the tiki trend and so should you. Make a reservation for a smooth entrance to order tropical fruity tiki mug cocktails (page 163).

★ **Best Craft Breweries: Stone World Bistro & Gardens, Liberty Station** clearly has the widest brand recognition; **AleSmith Brewing Company,** with a newly expanded brewery and tasting room, probably has the most awards; and relative newcomer **Societe Brewing Company** just has delicious IPAs across the board (pages 167, 172).

★ **Best Wine Bar:** Ocean Beach doesn't seem the most likely community for wine aficionados, but **The 3rd Corner** brings great selections to town (page 167).

The Grass Skirt

the scene, and then settle in with your choice for the night. The best part
about partying near the beach is heading over to catch the moon's reflection
over the ocean after last call . . . and deciding where to pick up a late-night
burrito while you sober up.

Downtown

Map 1

BARS
BARLEYMASH
This bar is open throughout the day to serve food and drink with a party
vibe, but when the Gaslamp nightlife kicks up, Barleymash kicks up with
it, making room for popular music and the heavy flirting that epitomizes
San Diego on a Saturday night. Dress to impress at this open-street club,
which clears out the dining room at night so people can dance.

Map 1: 600 5th Ave., Gaslamp, 619/255-7373, www.barleymash.com; Mon.-Fri.
11:30am-2am, Sat. 10am-2am, Sun. 9am-2am

COIN-OP GAME ROOM
The 1980s live on in this beautiful arcade bar featuring dozens of nostalgic
stand-up video game cabinets, Skeeball lanes, and pinball machines. Beside
all the games you'll find a place to set your drink, courtesy of a legitimate
bar serving craft cocktails and beer, and a restaurant serving elevated pub
food. If you can grab one of the large multiplayer tabletop game booths to
the left of the entrance, you can even continue to play video game classics
in between bites.

Map 1: 789 6th Ave., Gaslamp, 619/546-6441, www.coinopsd.com; Mon.-Fri. 4pm-2am,
Sat.-Sun. noon-2am

SEARSUCKER
Searsucker sets the table for a swanky cocktail hour. A tasty cocktail menu
and killer small plates bring in well-dressed young professionals looking to
meet and unwind while chill dance music plays. The large bar holds a good
number of people; scattered low sofas separate the dining room a few feet
away. It doesn't get wild, but it often feels like it could.

Map 1: 611 5th Ave., Gaslamp, 619/233-7327, www.searsucker.com; Mon.-Thurs.
11:30am-3:30pm and 4:30pm-10pm, Fri. 11:30am-3:30pm and 4:30pm-2am, Sat.
10am-2pm and 5:30pm-2am, Sun. 10am-3pm and 5:30pm-10pm

STAR BAR
In case the 6am opening time didn't clue you in, this is a dive—and it
doesn't have much more going for it than that. If you start to feel detached

Legacy of the Stingaree

Between 1860 and 1880, San Diego gained a wharf and a rail connection to the rest of the United States, resulting in exponential population growth by land and sea. The newly formed downtown expanded rapidly, and the area spreading out from the wharf up to Market Street (between 1st Ave. and 5th Ave.) began to take on a life of its own. Nicknamed the Stingaree, for the stingray-like "sting" a night out in the district provided, the area developed into a bawdy district rife with opium, gambling dens, more than 100 bars, and an estimated 120 brothels. The Stingaree drew comparisons to San Francisco's Barbary Coast and New York's Bowery. When the 20th century began, it was a hotbed of debauchery, mischief, and crime.

With the completion of the Panama Canal in 1914, San Diego was set to become the first western port for an onslaught of ships that would bring an even greater number of visitors west; some would attend the Panama-California Exposition at what eventually became Balboa Park. Its location near the wharf meant the Stingaree was the first thing visitors would see when entering San Diego Bay.

In 1912, city officials decided to crack down, raiding gambling houses and opium dens, and giving prostitutes one-way tickets out of town. They also drafted more stringent health and safety codes, which led to the condemnation and demolition of more than 100 buildings that couldn't meet the new standards. The Stingaree was flattened in an attempt to rid the nascent harbor town of its bad influences.

Unfortunately for San Diego's **Chinatown**, its borders overlapped with large sections of the Stingaree. Home to many immigrant laborers who came to build the railroads or work on developments in Coronado, the eight-square-block community got caught up in both the Stingaree's nighttime activities and its downfall. Buildings in Chinatown were hit especially hard by the new health codes. The impoverished inhabitants could not afford to rebuild, effectively dismantling the quarter to such a degree that many San Diegans today don't even know a Chinatown ever existed here.

While the Stingaree was gone, its vices were not. In the aftermath of the 1912 raids, drinking and prostitution actually increased, and spread to other parts of the city. The **Gaslamp Quarter** remained an unsavory place for decades; businesses were loath to build here because potential customers refused to cross south of Broadway. When the seminal Macy's department store came to San Diego in 1957, it passed up downtown in favor of on a site in Mission Valley, cementing an urban flight that continued into the mid-1980s, when the revitalization of San Diego's downtown was finally able to overcome the lasting legacy of its Stingaree.

from the Gaslamp scene, the stiff-drink, no-pretense baseness of Star Bar will snap you out of it. Cash only.

Map 1: 423 E St., Gaslamp, 619/234-5575; daily 6am-2am

BREWERIES
BALLAST POINT BREWING

Ballast Point Brewing is a large production with many locations in San Diego and elsewhere. The tasting room and restaurant in Little Italy has plenty of seating, including an outdoor patio, which accompanies favorites like Sculpin IPA, Sculpin with habanero, and frequent experimental releases.

Map 1: 2215 India St., Little Italy, 619/255-7213, www.ballastpoint.com; Mon.-Sat. 11am-11pm, Sun. 11am-9pm

CLUBS

★ FLUXX

High-concept decor, incredible-sounding bands and DJs, bottle service, and go-go dancers are what you can look forward to after standing in line to get into FLUXX. It's almost like Vegas came to San Diego.

Map 1: 500 4th Ave., Gaslamp, 619/232-8100, www.fluxxsd.com; Thurs.-Sat. 9pm-2am; $15 cover

F6IX

A big sound system gives this basement club some bass, with hip-hop on the decks to keep those bodies moving. A wraparound bar fronts the dance floor, but bottle service is the way to go if you're out to impress *before* showing off your moves.

Map 1: 526 F St., Gaslamp, 619/238-0138, www.f6ixsd.com; Thurs.-Sun. 9pm-2am; $10-25 cover

MOONSHINE FLATS

Cheap beer, Jack Daniels, and line dancing: If that's what you look for in a night out, here you are. Jeans are acceptable but are much better paired with a cowboy hat and a pair of boots. Music takes on a country tone; sometimes the place feels like a large barn with a disco ball.

Map 1: 344 7th Ave., East Village, 619/255-7625, www.moonshineflats.com; Thurs. 8pm-1:30am, Fri.-Sat. 8pm-2am; $10 cover after 9pm

SEVILLA NIGHTCLUB

This close to the border, you'd better believe there's a top-flight Latin music club, and *caliente* (hot) doesn't begin to describe it. By the time the late-night line has formed out front, you'll wish you had reserved a spot on the guest list.

Map 1: 353 5th Ave., Gaslamp, 619/233-5979, www.sevillanightclub.com; Mon.-Thurs. 8pm-2am, Fri.-Sat. 10pm-2am, Sun. 5pm-2am; $10-20 cover

VIN DE SYRAH

A *Through the Looking Glass* theme makes this basement nightclub a little more fun than the typical wine parlor its name suggests, beginning with a front door that's tricky to find. Be careful while you search for the handle—your image is being beamed via closed circuit to a TV screen inside, much to the amusement of those at the bar. Other head-trips await, along with late-night DJ sessions and plenty of wine, beer, and cocktails.

Map 1: 901 5th Ave., 619/234-4166, www.syrahwineparlor.com; Tues.-Wed. and Sun. 5pm-midnight, Thurs.-Sat. 5pm-2am; no cover

COCKTAIL LOUNGES

EL DORADO COCKTAIL LOUNGE

The wild nights of the Gaslamp don't appeal to everyone. For those looking to inch away from the downtown crowds, this cowboy-style bar farther afield in East Village does the trick. Nightly DJs play different grooves—from soul to EDM and hip-hop. It's one of the later last calls in town, making it a worthy last stop any night.

Map 1: 1030 Broadway, East Village, 619/237-0550, www.eldoradobar.com; Fri.-Sat. 5pm-2am, Sun.-Thurs. 7pm-2am

FALSE IDOL

Accessed via a "secret" entrance inside notable comfort food restaurant **Craft & Commerce** (www.craft-commerce.com), this tiki bar seems to exist in another time and place, designed with cave walls and a ceiling filled with colored lamps made from glass fishing floats. Fruity drinks served in tiki mugs abound, and reservations are suggested.

Map 1: 675 W. Beech St., Little Italy, 619/269-2202, www.falseidoltiki.com; daily 6pm-2am

THE LION'S SHARE

Game is on the menu of this restaurant and bar, including antelope, quail, and rabbit. However, regardless of your taste for exotic meats, the craft cocktails rank among the best in town, with a deep and constantly moving drinks menu that finds interesting turns on cocktail classics, at times with locally produced spirits.

Map 1: 629 Kettner Blvd., Marina District, 619/564-6924, www.lionssharesd.com; daily 4pm-2am

PROHIBITION LOUNGE

Speakeasy style keeps this small below-ground bar fashionable, with expertly made drinks you might have found back in the day (order dealer's choice and pay attention to how it's done). Dress appropriately (think dress pants and cocktail dresses; jeans and T-shirts won't fly here) and you should get past the doorman to enjoy the retro vibe and nightly jazz or blues performances.

Map 1: 548 5th Ave., 619/501-1919, www.prohibitionsd.com; Tues.-Sun. 8pm-1:30am

COMEDY CLUBS

AMERICAN COMEDY CO.

Featuring open mic nights and hosting touring comics, this Gaslamp comedy club brings plenty of laughs downtown, with the help of a full bar. Well-known comedians to grace its stage in recent years include Norm MacDonald, Hannibal Buress, Tig Notaro, and Whitney Cummings.

Map 1: 818 6th Ave., Gaslamp, 619/795-3858, www.americancomedyco.com; Tues. 6pm-10pm, Wed.-Thurs. 5pm-10pm, Fri.-Sat. 5pm-11:30pm, Sun. 6pm-10pm; tickets $10-30, 2 drink min.

Clockwise from top left: the Gaslamp Quarter; The Casbah; Coin-Op Game Room.

Tucked into an off-the-street location on the top floor of the Horton Plaza shopping mall, this Gaslamp comedy club offers a loose environment, great for local comics and up-and-comers alike, whether scheduled events or regular open mics.

Map 1: 502 Horton Plaza, Gaslamp, 619/702-6666, www.madhousecomedyclub.com; Mon.-Wed. 6pm-11:30pm, Thurs.-Sun. 6pm-1:30am; $0-25 tickets/cover, 2 drink min.

CRAFT BEER
HALF DOOR BREWING CO.

Built in a century-old house, this family-run brewpub takes after an Irish pub inside, but much of the seating is found on large balconies facing the street outside Petco Park. It can be a great place to visit around baseball games and during the off-season.

Map 1: 903 Island Ave., East Village, 619/232-9845, www.halfdoorbrewing.com; Mon.-Fri. 11am-2am, Sat.-Sun. 9am-2am

KARL STRAUSS BREWING COMPANY

Back in 1989, Karl Strauss kicked off what is now a nearly billion-dollar craft beer industry in San Diego. The county's oldest brewpub has since expanded to a dozen other locations, including La Jolla (1044 Wall St.) and Carlsbad (5801 Armada Dr.), but the original location pours its award-winning beer with food all day, a short walk from the marina.

Map 1: 1157 Columbia St., Gaslamp, 619/234-2739, www.karlstrauss.com; Mon.-Thurs. 11am-10pm, Fri. 11am-11pm, Sat. 11:30am-11pm, Sun. 11:30am-10pm

MISSION BREWERY

Located across the parking lot from Petco Park, this former Wonder Bread factory dates to 1894 and provides a redbrick atmosphere for enjoying a sampling of Mission's brewed-on-site award-winning *hefeweizen* and ales before, after, or during games.

Map 1: 1441 L St., East Village, 858/544-0555, www.missionbrewery.com; Sun.-Thurs. noon-10pm, Fri.-Sat. noon-midnight, opens 2 hours before Padres home games

LIVE MUSIC
★ THE CASBAH

San Diego's indie rock scene has a clear epicenter, and it's The Casbah, which has brought the nation's best burgeoning talent to its intimate club stage since 1989. Some of the grayer rockers sipping drinks in the courtyard between sets might reminisce about before-they-were-big shows by Nirvana, No Doubt, or Arcade Fire. Meanwhile, young local and touring bands still know the Little Italy venue to be a vital stop along the way to making it.

Map 1: 2501 Kettner Blvd., Little Italy, 619/232-4355, http://casbahmusic.com; daily 8:30pm-2am; tickets $6-40

Top: Polite Provisions. Bottom: Moonshine Flats.

HOUSE OF BLUES

The national club chain has a San Diego location in the Gaslamp, equipped with a second basement venue hosting smaller scope performances. But the potent volume of its main stage books known touring bands for all genres of popular music, including rock, electronic, hip-hop, dance, country, jazz, Latin, and of course blues. Every Sunday it hosts a gospel brunch.

Map 1: 1055 5th Ave., Gaslamp, 619/299-2583, www.houseofblues.com/sandiego; Tues.-Sun. 4pm-11pm, happy hour 4pm-6pm; tickets $12-60

MUSIC BOX

This multiple-story music venue draws interesting acts ranging from bluegrass to burlesque, though mostly books rock, jazz, and blues. The well-designed sound system and acoustics can handle bigger shows, but it's great to catch the venue during more intimate events. Either way, drinks at the upscale club run steep.

Map 1: 1337 India St., Little Italy, 619/795-1337, http://musicboxsd.com; daily 7:30pm-2am; tickets $18-80

ROOFTOP LOUNGES

ALTITUDE SKY LOUNGE

On the 22nd floor of the Marriot Gaslamp, the panoramic views of the city and harbor may almost distract you from the well-dressed clientele of this upscale bar. Not thoroughly impressed? Take your drink to the rooftop and take in one of the highest vantage points in the city.

Map 1: 660 K St., Gaslamp, 619/696-0234, www.sandiegogaslamphotel.com; daily 5pm-1:30am; no cover

FLOAT

The rooftop lounge at the Hard Rock Hotel finds any excuse to become a sexy open-air nightclub. During the day, lounge seating and poolside drinks set against the San Diego skyline couldn't feel cooler. Weekend nights and Sunday afternoons in the summer, world-famous DJs turn the club inside out, with beautiful young people dancing four stories above the hustling Gaslamp scene. Look your best to get in; some days it can be difficult.

Map 1: 207 5th Ave., Gaslamp, 619/764-6924, www.hardrockhotelsd.com; daily 11am-2am; no cover, ticketed events $10-25

UPPER EAST BAR

The rooftop lounge at the Salomar Hotel entices with an outdoor bar, poolside cocktails, cabanas, and plenty of lounge chairs from which to lord over East Village from above. Umbrellas shade the daylight, while heat lamps warm up the night, providing everything you need to stay comfortably warm while looking cool.

Map 1: 616 J St., East Village, 619/531-8744, www.hotelsolamar.com; Sun.-Thurs. noon-9pm, Fri.-Sat. noon-11pm; no cover

Best Happy Hours

Enjoy happy hour oysters and cocktails at Herringbone.

You could wait until dark to enjoy a drink at some of San Diego's best bars and restaurants, but why miss out? You'll find great drink and snack specials to go with amazing views and supremely cool atmospheres.

Located within a sculpture garden at Balboa Park, **Panama 66** (1450 El Prado, Balboa Park, 619/696-1966, www.panama66.blogspot.com; Mon. 11:30am-3pm, Tues.-Thurs. 11:30am-10pm, Fri. 11:30am-11pm, Sat. 11am-11pm, Sun. 11am-10pm) offers the ideal way to wind down from a day of culture seeking.

OB's **Wonderland Ocean Pub** (5083 Santa Monica Ave., Ocean Beach, 619/255-3358, www.wonderlandob.com; Mon.-Fri. 11am-close, Sat.-Sun. 9am-close) overlooks the beach, serving food and drinks in front of what usually turns out to be a gorgeous sunset.

Sunsets at the swank **Cusp Dining & Drinks** (7955 La Jolla Shores Dr., 858/551-3620, www.cusprestaurant.com; daily 7am-10pm, bar open 11am-10pm, happy hour 4pm-6pm) in La Jolla come with complimentary champagne and an 11th-floor picture window to enjoy them by. Closer to town, take the elevator ride to **Mr. A's** (2550 5th Ave., Bankers Hill, 619/239-1377, www.asrestaurant.com; Mon.-Fri. 11:30am-9pm, Sat. 5pm-9:30pm, Sun. 10am-9pm) for happy hour specials and a look at the sun descending over Point Loma and San Diego Bay.

If you've seen enough of the ocean, La Jolla's **Herringbone** (7837 Herschel Ave., 858/459-0221, www.herringboneeats.com; Mon.-Wed. 11:30am-9pm, Thurs.-Fri. 11:30am-10pm, Sat. 10am-10pm, Sun. 10am-9pm) serves up top-notch cocktails and a variety of one-dollar happy-hour oysters within their dreamy dining room, which is decorated with olive trees.

And if you're really hungry, you can never go wrong with one of the city's best pies at **Urbn Pizza** (3085 University Ave., 619/255-7300, www.urbn-northpark.com; Sun.-Mon. noon-10pm, Tues.-Thurs. noon-midnight, Fri.-Sat. noon-2am), where happy hour specials include a free large pizza with a pitcher of craft beer.

BARS
★ HAMILTON'S TAVERN

Arguably the best tap house in a town filled with great tap houses, Hamilton's 28 handles and a pair of cask engines bring in pretty much every local craft beer worth drinking, and they rotate in top finds from out of town as well. Monthly events feature specific favorites of Hamilton's owner, who operates a couple of other bars and craft breweries nearby.

Map 2: 1521 30th St., South Park, 619/238-5460, www.hamiltonstavern.com; Mon.-Fri. 3pm-2am, Sat. 1pm-2am, Sun. 10am-2pm

WHISTLE STOP BAR

A longtime fixture in the local music and arts scene, Whistle Stop has a couple of weekly throwback DJ nights, hosts monthly storytelling and comedy events, brings in happy hour entertainment on weekends, and has a few quieter nights simply being a favorite neighborhood bar.

Map 2: 2236 Fern St., South Park, 619/284-6784, www.whistlestopbar.com; Mon.-Fri. 3pm-2am, Sat. 1pm-2am, Sun. 10am-2am; scheduled events $5 cover

Uptown   Map 3

BARS
BAR PINK

In 2007, this pink elephant-themed bar helped salvage a flagging North Park nightlife scene. Since that scene started thriving, Bar Pink simply shuffles along serving strong drinks in a dark lounge outfitted with pink pool tables and a stage for bands and DJs to occasionally rock the place out.

Map 3: 3829 30th St., North Park, 619/564-7194, www.barpink.com; daily noon-2am

WEST COAST TAVERN

This bar sits in what would have been the lobby of the historic theater that is now the Observatory music venue. It usually operates independently from whatever concert is playing. While pre- and post-show crowds may pack the place up, it often holds its own in between as a fun, boozy stop in a buzzing neighborhood.

Map 3: 2895 University Ave., North Park, 619/295-1688, www.westcoasttavern.com; Mon.-Fri. 4pm-2am, Sat. 10am-2am, Sun. 9am-2am

COCKTAIL LOUNGES
★ POLITE PROVISIONS

Between the skylights and the open windows, this may be the brightest daytime cocktail lounge you'll encounter short of being outdoors, which is another option. The marble and polished brass interior gleams—as does the unique floor layered with shiny nickels. Whatever time of day you visit, the beautiful bar space serves up an extensive list of delicious cocktails to some of the most style-savvy locals.

Map 3: 4696 30th St., North Park, 619/269-4701, www.politeprovisions.com; Mon.-Thurs. 3pm-2am, Fri.-Sun. 11:30am-2am

★ SEVEN GRAND

Somewhere between hunting lodge and jazz club, the main attraction at Seven Grand is whiskey—bourbon, scotch, rye, and Irish. The hunting trophies on walls of plaid wallpaper make the idea that there's a jazz stage in the back seem incongruous, but crowds keep coming back for both the music and the booze. A deep menu features single malts and single casks along with blends, oak-barrel-aged options, and reserves. Order a favorite right away, because you're going to be reading that menu for a while before deciding on your second.

Map 3: 3054 University Ave., North Park, 619/269-8820, www.213hospitality.com/sevengrandsd; Mon.-Sat. 4pm-2am, Sun. 8pm-2am

CRAFT BEER

MIKE HESS BREWING

When in North Park, drop by this large family- and dog-friendly space. There's usually a food truck parked in the loading dock, along with a mind-blowing selection of barely remembered vintage board games to play over crisp, tasty beers. They're brewed in the large shiny tanks visible downstairs from the bridge you cross as you enter.

Map 3: 3812 Grim Ave., North Park, 619/255-7136, www.mikehessbrewing.com; Sun.-Thurs. noon-10pm, Fri.-Sat. noon-midnight

NORTH PARK BEER CO.

The words "Ales & Lagers, Friends & Neighbors" greet you at the entrance to this urban brewery, and it's a pretty accurate description for how the neighborhood craft beer hub gets used. The bar is decorated to resemble a British pub, while the vast seating area lit by vintage-looking streetlamps adds a romantic night vibe. The house and guest beers are all excellent, and a kitchen in the back serves sausages when friends and neighbors get hungry.

Map 3: 3038 University Ave., 619/255-2946, www.northparkbeerco.com; Mon.-Thurs. 3pm-10pm, Fri. noon-midnight, Sat. 10am-midnight, Sun. 10am-10pm

TORONADO

Toronado is the rare San Diego bar that claims a focus on Belgian ales, but in truth its tap list is just as loaded with San Diego's best. Communal tables and patio seating give patrons the chance to compare and contrast, resulting in one heck of a social place to drink and obsess over everybody's favorite brew.

Map 3: 4026 30th St., North Park, 619/282-0456, www.toronadosd.com; Sun.-Wed. 11:30am-midnight, Thurs.-Sat. 11:30am-2am

GAY AND LESBIAN

BAJA BETTY'S

From mimosas to margaritas to shots, Betty's has the drinks to match every time of day. This popular gathering spot's impeccable Mexican decor and tequila cocktails make for raucous brunches and happy hours, with build-your-own nacho platters available until the kitchen closes at 11pm, just in case you drank through dinner.

Map 3: 1421 University Ave., Hillcrest, 619/269-8510, www.bajabettyssd.com; Mon.-Fri. 11am-1am, Sat.-Sun. 10am-1am

GOSSIP GRILL

The irreverent "home of the two-finger pour," this Hillcrest women's bar boasts cocktail names among the most poetically bawdy in all of Southern California. It's a lounge and patio space where simply ordering a round of drinks sets the tone.

Map 3: 1220 University Ave., Hillcrest, 619/260-8023, www.thegossipgrill.com; Mon.-Fri. noon-2am, Sat.-Sun. 10am-2am

HILLCREST BREWING COMPANY

Billing itself as "The first gay brewery in the world," this cheeky local brewer serves up suds with names like Banana Hammock scotch ale and an award-winning red ale called Crotch Rocket. Up to 15 guest beers from around San Diego round out the tap list.

Map 3: 1458 University Ave., Hillcrest, 619/269-4323, www.hillcrestbrewingcompany. com; Mon.-Fri. 4pm-11pm, Sat. noon-11pm, Sun. 9am-11pm

LIPS

Where in San Diego can you find a gender-bending Cher impersonator lip-syncing in an outlandish outfit? At Lips, the raunchy and playful drag shows cover any number of celebrity divas, and performers are far from shy about including audience members in their songs. It's a popular spot for bachelorette and birthday parties, with dinner shows most nights as well as a Sunday brunch.

Map 3: 3036 El Cajon Blvd., North Park, 619/295-7900, www.lipssd.com; Tues.-Thurs. 7pm-11pm, Fri. 6:30pm-midnight, Sat. 5:30pm-2am, Sun. 11am-3pm and 7pm-10pm

THE RAIL

If drinking and dancing makes a good formula for a gay bar, consider The Rail a rousing success. Theme nights set the mood, with an '80s night on

Monday and Latin vibes on Saturday, plus nights featuring go-go dancers, drag shows, and "boylesque."

Map 3: 3796 5th Ave., Hillcrest, 619/298-2233, www.thebrassrailsd.com; Mon. 11am-2am, Thurs.-Fri. 11am-8pm, Sat. 10am-2am, Sun. 10am-8pm

URBAN MO'S

MO's claims to be the "Best Gay Bar in San Diego," if not the world. The only way to find out for sure is to drop in on its burger-loving patio and find out. Chances are you're going to meet people in the process, drink another couple of rounds, and find yourself declaring something the best of somewhere before the night ends.

Map 3: 308 University Ave., Hillcrest, 619/491-0400, www.urbanmos.com; daily 9am-1:30am

LIVE MUSIC
LESTAT'S WEST

A local stop on the touring singer-songwriter circuit, this intimate venue, affiliated with the 24-hour Lestat's coffeehouse next door, stages mostly acoustic, lyric-driven music, including modest stars of the genre. A long-running open-mic night on Monday gives local troubadours a chance to practice their craft.

Map 3: 3341 Adams Ave., Normal Heights, 619/818-8013, www.lestats.com; show times vary

Old Town and Mission Hills Map 4

BARS
THE PATIO ON GOLDFINCH

The beautifully verdant "living wall" decor of this Mission Hills restaurant attracts diners all day long, but anyone who skips the tequila selection is missing out. Alternate between sips of tequila and the fruity, spicy, house *sangrita* and you'll never want to drink it any other way. The open patio restaurant also offers a lengthy list of barrel-aged cocktails worth delving into.

Map 4: 4020 Goldfinch St., Mission Hills, 619/501-5090, www.thepatioongoldfinch.com; Sun.-Thurs. 11am-11pm, Fri. 11am-midnight, Sat. 9am-midnight

SHAKESPEARE PUB & GRILLE

British pubs are really a global phenomenon. A San Diego favorite is this lower Mission Hills establishment, which serves traditional pub food, classic British ales, and footy on the telly, of course.

Map 4: 3701 India St., Mission Hills, 619/299-0230, www.shakespearepub.com; Mon.-Thurs. 10:30am-midnight, Fri. 10:30am-1am, Sat. 8am-1am, Sun. 8am-11pm

COCKTAIL LOUNGES

AERO CLUB BAR

For what is possibly the best whiskey selection in San Diego, look to this dive bar just off the freeway. Its detailed book runs through bourbon, scotch, rye, Irish, American whiskey, and moonshine; if for some reason that's not enough for you, the bartenders can throw together a nice few cocktails as well. Be sure to check the juke box lineup—also one of the city's best.

Map 4: 3365 India St., Mission Hills, 619/297-7211, www.aeroclubbar.com; daily 2pm-2am

STARLITE

This late-night kitchen also happens to be one of the city's craft cocktail leaders. The stylish interior (loosely sticking to the starlight theme) matches a rotating list of drinks that always includes one or two of its famous mules to be served in copper mugs.

Map 4: 3175 India St., Mission Hills, 619/358-9766, www.starlitesandiego.com; Sat.-Thurs. 5pm-1am, Fri. 4pm-1am

LIVE MUSIC

BLONDE BAR

Though a newcomer to the live music and club scene, Blonde is run by industry vets who know what it takes to get a night going. Regular dance events, retro music nights, and live bands keep the fairly small club happening.

Map 4: 1808 W. Washington St., Mission Hills, www.blondebarsd.com; daily 5pm-2am; $0-20 cover

WINE BARS

57 DEGREES

This is one of the larger wine bars in town, with high ceilings, an art gallery, a full-service bar, and a view of the skyline . . . and the back side of the airport. Okay, the view's not stellar, but the well-lit airiness of the place makes it a nice spot for drinks after a day at Old Town. And when the downtown lights up at night, the views improve.

Map 4: 1735 Hancock St., Mission Hills, 619/234-5757, www.fiftysevendegrees.com; Tues.-Wed. 4pm-10pm, Thurs. 4pm-11pm, Fri. 4pm-midnight, Sat. 11am-midnight

BARS
DUCK DIVE

Duck Dive often plays the part of a sports bar, but it also factors in the character of a beach community—hosting acoustic music performances, making cocktails with local farmers market fruit, and keeping the surf vibe alive. There's usually something worth digging here most of the day.

Map 5: 4650 Mission Blvd., Pacific Beach, 858/273-3825, www.theduckdive.com; Sun.-Fri. 10am-2am, Sat.-Sun. 9am-2am

CLUBS
MOONSHINE BEACH

With the motto "Sun down, party up," this country music and line dancing venue adds to PB nightlife with live music and DJs. The large venue a few blocks from the beach can fit a large audience or open the floor to a lot of revelers mixing it up into late night.

Map 5: 1165 Garnet Ave., Pacific Beach, 858/999-0158, www.moonshinebeachsd.com; Tues. 7pm-2am, Thurs.-Sat. 8pm-2am; $10 cover

PB AVENUE

PB Avenue offers a range of themed weeknights to attract young men and women who like to party. Karaoke Mondays, University Night Tuesdays, and Trivia Wednesdays end the same way, with DJs spinning popular music to encourage a little bumping and grinding on the dance floor. Lodge decor means wood panels and mounted buffalo heads, but when the flashing lights turn on, the only thing you'll look at is each other.

Map 5: 1060 Garnet Ave., Pacific Beach, 858/263-4514, www.thewoodgroupsd.com; daily 5pm-2am; no cover

COCKTAIL LOUNGES
★ THE GRASS SKIRT

About as tiki as it gets, this immersive bar pairs richly colored decor with richly flavored drinks, along with plenty of thatched fringe. The sterling lineup of cocktails draws from a 150-bottle collection of rums and an abundance of tropical fruit. It's wise to make reservations for this popular destination and to dress like a 1950s hipster.

Map 5: 910 Grand Ave., Pacific Beach, 858/412-5237, www.thegrassskirt.com; daily 5pm-2am

JRDN

With all the rowdy beachfront drinking that takes place on the boardwalk, JRDN (pronounced Jordan) proves the clear choice for those seeking a classier Pacific Beach experience. It's the bar at the swanky boutique hotel Tower23 (you might be inclined to think the place is some sort of Michael Jordan devotional, but the basketball player's name connected to his jersey number is just a coincidence). Marvel at the view and sip something delicious—you'll look great doing so.

Map 5: 723 Felspar St., Pacific Beach, 858/270-2323, www.t23hotel.com/jrdn; Sun.-Thurs. 9am-9:30pm, Fri.-Sat. 9am-10pm

CRAFT BEER
AMPLIFIED ALE WORKS

This brewery, tap house, and kebab restaurant doesn't stand out from the street or the beach, but when you find it on the second floor of its PB strip mall, you'll be grateful you did. Drink the tasty house beer, eat some *döner* (Turkish kebabs), or simply grab some sun with an ocean view on the killer west-facing deck, which alone is reason enough to visit.

Map 5: 4150 Mission Blvd. #208, Pacific Beach, 858/270-5222, www.amplifiedales.com; Mon.-Wed. 11am-11pm, Thurs.-Sat. 11am-midnight, Sun. 11am-11pm

DRAFT

Since a ban on drinking at city beaches went into effect a few years back, this Mission Beach spot might be the best place to imbibe a craft beer while enjoying the sun, surf, and sand. Located right on the boardwalk, the outdoor seating promotes people-watching while sipping a local brew. When done, simply reapply your sunscreen and head to the beach, only a few steps away.

Map 5: 3105 Ocean Front Walk, Mission Beach, 858/228-9305, www.draftsandiego.com; Mon.-Fri. 11:30am-9pm, Sat.-Sun. 9am-9pm, Fri.-Sat. bar open until 10pm

LIVE MUSIC
DIZZY'S

Dizzy's is more a concept than a jazz venue. It's had a number of locations over the years, but wherever it lands, it's always about the performances, usually by internationally respected talent covering a wide range of jazz and folk styles. Tickets are not available in advance; check the website calendar and choose a show that piques your interest.

Map 5: 1717 Morena Blvd., Mission Bay, 858/270-7467, www.dizzysjazz.com; $15-25 cover

Top: Modern Times. Bottom: Starlite.

Ocean Beach and Point Loma

Map 6

BARS
SUNSHINE COMPANY SALOON

The rooftop deck of the 'Shine hosts the most energetic happy hour in OB, and the vast space downstairs does a good job of keeping up with the crowds. On weekend nights, the place fills with locals of every stripe—surfers, military folk, college kids, and anyone with a deep tan to show off.

Map 6: 5028 Newport Ave., Ocean Beach, 619/222-0722, www. sunshinecompanyoceanbeach.com; Mon.-Fri. 11am-2am, Sat.-Sun. 10am-2am

WONDERLAND OCEAN PUB

Offering the best view in OB, Wonderland sits on the second floor facing the beach and pier, often getting an early start on the colorful OB nightlife. When the surf is up, you can watch local wave riders from the bay windows. Time it right and enjoy a few more beers while watching the reliably thrilling sunsets.

Map 6: 5083 Santa Monica Ave., Ocean Beach, 619/255-3358, www.wonderlandob.com; Mon.-Wed. 11am-midnight, Thurs.-Fri. 11am-2am, Sun. 9am-midnight

COCKTAIL LOUNGES
PACIFIC SHORES

No one seems to remember the last time they went to Pac Shores, but everybody kind of remembers the first. Strong, cheap cocktails are served in a decades-old "underwater" setting of black-lit mermaid and sea creature art. It's vintage OB.

Map 6: 4927 Newport Ave., Ocean Beach, 619/223-7549, www.pacshoresob.com; daily noon-2am

CRAFT BEER
MODERN TIMES BEER

With consistently fantastic beers and a commitment to design that's rare in the craft beer world, Modern Times creates visually rich places to enjoy its beer (and coffee), both here at its brewery and at its taproom in North Park (3000 Upas St.). From the bar made from vintage books to a Michael Jackson mural made from Post-It notes, you'll have plenty to look at while drinking highly sought IPAs, barrel-aged stouts, and sours. It fills up fast.

Map 3: 3725 Greenwood St., Point Loma, 619/546-9694, www.moderntimesbeer.com; Mon.-Fri. noon-10pm, Sat.-Sun. noon-midnight

PIZZA PORT, OCEAN BEACH

Part brewing company, tap house, and pizza spot, this local brewpub's proximity to the beach makes it ideal for post-sunset suds. House beers run the gamut from interesting to fantastic, and there are always a number of handles devoted to terrific craft-brewing friends and collaborators.

Map 6: 1956 Bacon St., Ocean Beach, 619/224-4700, www.pizzaport.com; Sun.-Thurs. 11am-10pm, Fri.-Sat. 11am-midnight

★ STONE WORLD BISTRO & GARDENS, LIBERTY STATION

Stone reigns as the biggest and most successful craft brewer in town. This 23,000-square-foot organic, farm-to-table restaurant offers 40 taps of Stone special releases, collaborations, and dozens of handpicked guest beers. Relax on the massive outdoor patio and enjoy a bocce ball game with your pint.

Map 6: 2816 Historic Decatur Rd., Suite 116, Liberty Station, 619/269-2100, www.stonelibertystation.com; Sun.-Thurs. 11:30am-9pm, Fri.-Sat. 11:30am-10pm

LIVE MUSIC

THE HOLDING COMPANY

THC spends much of its day as a typically OB-style bar, pouring drinks for the sunburnt and the surfed out. In the evening it usually pulls a lineup of local musicians, plus occasionally the sort of touring act with cachet in a hippie-leaning beach town.

Map 6: 5046 Newport Ave., Ocean Beach, 619/341-5898, www.thcob.com; Mon.-Fri. 3pm-2am, Sat.-Sun 11am-2am; $0-15 cover

WINSTONS BEACH CLUB

OB's live music mainstay, Winstons caters to the tastes of the neighborhood's laid-back inhabitants, usually offering lineups of reggae, funk, a little bit of crusty rock, and a Grateful Dead cover band Monday nights. Happy hour entertainment often includes comedy, karaoke, and a glimpse of local color bellying up to the bar.

Map 6: 1921 Bacon St., Ocean Beach, 619/222-6822, www.winstonsob.com; daily 1pm-2am; $0-15 cover

WINE BARS

★ THE 3RD CORNER

An island of elevated tastes in OB's oasis of grungy charm, this is the sort of wine bar where board shorts go well with a chardonnay. Increasingly higher rents in the neighborhood have gentrified it somewhat, but this place has captured the increased demand for quality drinks with a lovely bottle selection.

Map 6: 2265 Bacon St., Ocean Beach, 619/223-2700, www.the3rdcorner.com; Tues.-Fri. 11:30am-midnight, Sat. 10am-1am, Sun. 10am-11pm

Kid-Friendly Places for Beer Lovers

Drink pints by the Mission Beach Boardwalk at Draft.

Children don't care that San Diego is a beer mecca, but their parents might. Take heart; there are some places the kids can enjoy while Mom or Dad sneaks in a pint.

- **Blind Lady Ale House** (3416 Adams Ave., 619/255-2491, www. blindladyalehouse.com; daily 11:30am-midnight): If the kids love pizza, order a simple pie and enjoy the friendly atmosphere and 26 beers on tap.

- **Draft** (3105 Ocean Front Walk, Mission Beach, 858/228-9305, www. draftsandiego.com; Mon.-Fri. 11:30am-9pm, Sat.-Sun. 9am-9pm, Fri.-Sat. bar open until 10pm): If you're visiting Belmont Park at Mission Beach, grab a seat on or near the patio and order something from the menu while you explore the nearly 70 beers on tap.

- **Mike Hess Brewing** (3812 Grim Ave., North Park, 619/255-7136, www. mikehessbrewing.com; Sun.-Thurs. noon-10pm, Fri.-Sat. noon-midnight): North Park locals dig this pet- and child-friendly place, which supplies board games and some refreshing made-on-site suds.

- **Stone World Bistro & Gardens, Liberty Station** (2816 Historic Decatur Rd., Ste. 116, Liberty Station, 619/269-2100, www.stonelibert-ystation.com; Sun.-Thurs. 11:30am-9pm, Fri.-Sat. 11:30am-10pm): You'll find kid-friendly menus and plenty of outdoor space to enjoy here and at the Escondido location (1999 Citracado Pkwy., 760/294-7899, www. stonebrewing.com; Sun.-Thurs. 11am-10pm, Fri.-Sat. 11am-11pm).

BARS
BEAUMONT'S
Roughly between the raging nightlife of Pacific Beach and the rather staid evenings of La Jolla Village, this Bird Rock place offers a bar scene that's active and engaged without being overbearing; it's good for a nightcap and a little live music on weekends.

Map 7: 5662 La Jolla Blvd., Bird Rock, 858/454-2323, www.beaumontseatery.com; Mon.-Wed. 11:30am-midnight, Thurs.-Fri. 11:30am-2am, Sat. 9am-midnight, Sun. 8am-midnight

EDDIE V'S
The upstairs bar of this seafood restaurant offers one of the most scenic drinking venues in town. While nightly jazz performances play, sip drinks overlooking the La Jolla Caves with a view of the shores beyond.

Map 7: 1270 Prospect St., La Jolla Village, 858/459-5500, www.eddiev.com; Mon.-Thurs. 4pm-11pm, Fri.-Sat. 11am-midnight, Sun. 11am-10pm

COCKTAIL LOUNGES
CUSP DINING & DRINKS
It's all about the sunsets at this 11th-floor hotel bar and restaurant. A stellar cocktail list accompanies the view in the slick dining room; the bartender breaks out the champagne to celebrate when pinks, purples, and neon oranges fill the western sky. Enjoy a few drinks at the swank contemporary bar, and seriously consider sticking around for dinner.

Map 7: 7955 La Jolla Shores Dr., 858/551-3620, www.cusprestaurant.com; daily 7am-10pm, bar open 11am-10pm, happy hour 4pm-6pm

HERRINGBONE
Herringbone is a seafood spot offering a great cocktail environment. The best reason to drink here is the beautiful interior design: Olive trees are planted throughout the high-ceilinged, hangar-like space, softly lit by Edison bulbs. The $1 oyster happy hour doesn't hurt either.

Map 7: 7837 Herschel Ave., 858/459-0221, www.herringboneeats.com; Mon.-Wed. 11:30am-9pm, Thurs.-Fri. 11:30am-10pm, Sat. 10am-10pm, Sun. 10am-9pm

COMEDY CLUBS
THE COMEDY STORE
Friday and Saturday nights offer an opportunity to see some of the top touring comics pass through La Jolla, with the occasional legend popping up. The rest of the week, watch some of the best local comedians fine-tune their craft on the big stage.

Map 7: 916 Pearl St., 858/454-9176, www.lajolla.thecomedystore.com; Mon.-Thurs. noon-11pm, Fri.-Sat. noon-1am; $0-25 tickets/cover, 2 drink min.

Beeramar

The industrial neighborhood north of Marine Corps Air Station Miramar has become one of the most dense craft beer neighborhoods in the nation. With more than 20 breweries and tap rooms to explore, locals have taken to calling it Beeramar. The cornerstone of the area is the rather large and well-known **AleSmith Brewing Company** (9990 AleSmith Ct., Miramar, 858/549-9888, www.alesmith.com; Mon.-Thurs. 11am-10pm, Fri.-Sat. 11am-11pm, Sun. 11am-9pm), but there are plenty of high-quality breweries operating on a much smaller scale to explore, and even a few craft beverage producers branching out from beer to other potable drinks. These are just a few starting points for exploration.

Started by Denmark's famous gypsy brewer Mikkel Borg Bjergsø, **Mikkeller Brewing San Diego** (9366 Cabot Dr., 858/381-3500, www.mikkellersd.com; Sun.-Wed. noon-9pm, Thurs.-Sat. noon-10pm) brings his boundary-pushing creativity to San Diego's craft scene.

Pure Project (9030 Kenamar Dr. #308, 858/252-6143, www.purebrewing.org; Mon. 3pm-9pm, Tues.-Thurs. noon-9pm, Fri.-Sat. noon-10pm, Sun. noon-8pm) puts its focus on sustainable practices while adding flavors to its refreshing brews, including tropical fruits and Central American coffee. Right next door, you'll find a brewery of Pacific Beach brewpub **Amplified Ale Works** (9030 Kenamar Dr. #309, 858/800-2534, Mon.-Wed. 11am-11pm, Thurs.-Sat. 11am-midnight, Sun. 11am-11pm), which brings a rocker attitude to its craft.

On one Miramar block, more than a half dozen craft beverage companies occupy two adjacent buildings on Miralani Drive, which has come to be known as the **Miralani Makers District.** On one side of the street, three breweries are joined by a couple of urban wineries and a sake brewer, **Setting Sun Sake** (8680 Miralani Dr. #120, 951/757-1393, www.settingsunsake.com; Mon.-Thurs. 3pm-9pm, Fri.-Sat. noon-10pm, Sun. noon-9pm). On the other, craft mead and cider producers operate next door to the nanobrewery **Thunderhawk Alements** (8675 Miralani Dr. #100, 619/952-4832, www.thunderhawkbeer.com; Wed.-Thurs. 3pm-9pm, Fri.-Sat. noon-10pm, Sun. noon-6pm).

WINE BARS
LJ CRAFTED WINES

Bringing a taste of wine country to La Jolla, this urban winery sources grapes from Napa and Sonoma, where its award-winning winemaker creates breathtaking vintages meant to be drunk, not cellared. Rather than package in bottles, this sweet little wine bar pours straight from the barrel; if you want to take some home, you may fill a reusable growler.

Map 7: 5621 La Jolla Blvd., 858/551-8890, www.ljcraftedwines.com; Mon.-Thurs. 4pm-10pm, Fri.-Sat. 1pm-11pm, Sun. 2pm-8pm

beer sampler at Ballast Point Brewing

The largest brewery in the area is **Ballast Point Brewing** (9045 Carroll Way, 858/790-6900, www.ballastpoint.com; Mon.-Thurs. 11am-11pm, Fri.-Sat. 11am-midnight, Sun. 10am-10pm), with more locations around San Diego (see Little Italy listing) and elsewhere. This spot in Miramar operates a huge restaurant in its brewery. Meanwhile, its founders sold the company to a macro beer producer a few years ago and used some of the money to launch another business nearby—a craft distillery with a huge restaurant. **Cutwater Spirits** (9750 Distribution Ave., 858/672-3848, www.cutwater-spirits.com; Sun.-Thurs. 11am-10pm, Fri.-Sat. 11am-11pm) makes craft spirits on a 40-foot-tall still and offers distillery tours throughout the day.

Coronado

Map 8

COCKTAIL LOUNGES
SUNSET BAR

San Diego's most famous hotel might be thrilling enough to warrant perusing the cocktail list at the Sunset Bar, but its beachfront locale should not be dismissed. Bottom line: You get to drink at the beach. Cocktail service is provided to those who rent lounge chairs. In winter, an ice-skating rink dominates the view.

Map 8: 1500 Orange Ave., 619/435-6611, www.hoteldel.com; Tues.-Thurs. 4:30pm-10pm, Sat.-Sun. 4:30pm-11pm

CRAFT BEER

★ ALESMITH BREWING COMPANY

To many, AleSmith isn't just the best brewery in San Diego—it ranks among the best on the planet. After nearly two decades, the small but heralded company expanded its operations into this massive new building boasting the county's largest brewery taproom. It features a "secret" side bar where you can blend your own barrel-aged beers, as well as a free museum dedicated to Mr. Padre, Major League Baseball legend Tony Gwynn, who worked with AleSmith to make the recipe for San Diego Pale Ale .394 (named for his best season batting average).

Map 9: 9990 AleSmith Ct., Miramar, 858/549-9888, www.alesmith.com; Mon.-Thurs. 11am-10pm, Fri.-Sat. 11am-11pm, Sun. 11am-9pm

BREW HOP BREWERY TOURS

A wise solution to the problem of getting from brewery to brewery without a designated driver, these customized beer tours tote you to several of your preferred destinations. In addition to picking you up and dropping you off, drivers will be happy to offer guidance to ensure you hit the right places at the right times.

Map 9: 2330 1st Ave., Ste. 411, 858/361-8457, www.brewhop.com; from $75 pp

★ SOCIETE BREWING COMPANY

A couple of California's best up-and-coming craft brewers teamed up and moved to San Diego to join our flourishing beer scene—and just like that our beer scene got even better. Societe's roster of American- and European-style ales runs deep and delicious. This is a must-stop for beer lovers with a long afternoon and an unquenchable thirst who enjoy drinking in the shadow of brewing tanks.

Map 9: 8262 Clairemont Mesa Blvd., Clairemont Mesa, 858/598-5409, www.societebrewing.com; Mon.-Wed. noon-9pm, Thurs.-Sat. noon-10pm, Sun. noon-8pm

Arts and Culture

Look for ★ to find
recommended arts and culture

Highlights

★ **Most Underrated Museum:** Most locals admit they've never been to the **Mingei International Museum,** despite its central Balboa Park location. Its focus on the handmade is captivating (page 180).

★ **Best Place to See a Play:** Pretty much the best place to do anything here is outside, and the outdoor venue at **The Old Globe** stages terrific productions of Shakespeare each summer (page 181).

★ **Best Concert Venue:** You get to see the sunset over a yacht-filled marina followed by a stellar show at **Humphreys Concerts by the Bay.** It's tough to do better (page 187).

★ **If You Only Go to One Art Gallery:** La Jolla's contemporary art museum remains under renovation, but the spacious **Madison Gallery** keeps the village relevant (page 188).

★ **Best Sculpture Collection:** More than just an excuse to explore the UCSD campus, many of the sculptures in the **Stuart Collection** up the ante on experiential art (page 189).

★ **Most Likely to Spawn a Broadway Run:** A number of successful shows have premiered at **La Jolla Playhouse** before heading to New York—and there will be more (page 189).

★ **Must-See Murals:** A valuable bit of history unfolds with the murals at **Chicano Park,** a rich tapestry of socially relevant artwork presented in a context no museum could match (page 190).

Mingei International Museum in Balboa Park

San Diego's well-known image as a sun-drenched surfer's paradise may not merit comparison to major cultural offerings in other cities, but it can surprise you.

The theater scene is not only one of high quality, but it is also one of the most productive in the country, routinely assembling world-class productions and inspiring the curiosity and respect of out-of-towners and local alike.

While endeavors in other artistic areas might not have the same prestige, San Diego is a surprisingly intellectual town once the craft beer bottles and surfboards are put away. There are always interesting things brewing under the surface—outdoor cinemas under the stars, the historical and cultural museums of Balboa Park, and the vibrant art scene in Barrio Logan. It's tough to balance sunshine, coastline, beer, and culture, yet somehow San Diego manages.

CINEMA

UNITED ARTISTS HORTON PLAZA 8

Found inside the Horton Plaza mall, this eight-screen multiplex shows popular first-run films, including a screen equipped to handle digital 3-D movies. Three hours free parking is available in the mall parking garage with validation.

Map 1: 475 Horton Plaza, Gaslamp, 844/462-7342, www.regmovies.com

GALLERIES

CELEBRATION FINE ART GALLERY

Living artists are the focus of this densely packed gallery space just off the lobby of the U. S. Grant Hotel. At any given time, several distinct styles may be found—from traditionalist to contemporary. Though rarely edgy, these globally sourced paintings prefer a different mode of expression: mastery of technique over flashy subject matter.

Map 1: 326 Broadway, Gaslamp, 619/238-9111, www.celebrationfineart.com;
Mon.-Thurs. noon-7pm, Fri.-Sat. 11am-3pm and 6pm-9pm

CHUCK JONES GALLERY

A Wile E. Coyote statue greets you at the entrance to this gallery, which celebrates *Looney Tunes* creator Chuck Jones as both an artist and an inspiration. A Pepé Le Pew charcoal sketch may not be everyone's idea of fine art, but a number of interesting pieces exhibit Jones's fanciful vision, making for the rare art gallery an entire family may enjoy.

Map 1: 232 5th Ave., Gaslamp, 619/294-9880, www.chuckjones.com;
Mon.-Sat. 10am-9pm, Sun. noon-8pm

EXCLUSIVE COLLECTIONS GALLERY

This Seaport Village gallery features a small but talented group of active West Coast artists. The gallery focuses on a strong use of color in pieces alluding to past masters or channeling unique and fantastic visions. A slow walk through the small space is encouraged.

Map 1: 835 W. Harbor Dr., Ste. AB, Marina District, 619/232-1930, www.ecgallery.com;
daily 10am-9pm

MICHAEL J. WOLF FINE ARTS

Embracing both contemporary and pop-art movements, many of the pieces in this Gaslamp gallery may border on kitsch. But the range of art on offer doesn't overly rely on conceptual oddities and includes some legitimately stunning pieces by artists with the technical virtuosity to back up their forays into commercial appeal.

Map 1: 363 5th Ave., Ste. 102, Gaslamp, 619/702-5388, www.mjwfinearts.com;
Tues.-Sat. 11am-7pm, Sun. 10am-6pm

The location of this gallery representing San Diego State University's School of Art + Design is meant to help its students remain engaged with the active arts community in the city center. It brings culturally relevant exhibitions featuring both domestic and international artists.

Map 1: 725 W. Broadway, 619/501-6370, http://art.sdsu.edu; Thurs.-Mon. 11am-4pm

SPARKS GALLERY

More than 130 years old, the brick Sterling Hardware Building provides a beautiful historical space to feature contemporary artists hailing from San Diego and throughout Southern California. Sparks hosts opening receptions scheduled throughout the year to launch both solo and group shows.

Map 1: 530 6th Ave., Gaslamp, 619/696-1416, www.sparksgallery.com; Wed.-Fri. noon-7pm, Sat. 11am-7pm, Sun. 11am-5pm

MUSEUMS

GASLAMP MUSEUM AT THE DAVIS-HORTON HOUSE

The oldest wooden building downtown now serves as monument to the efforts of William Heath Davis, who first had the idea to settle San Diego around the bay. While his efforts failed, the idea obviously panned out. Davis's former home was originally shipped from Maine to San Diego in 1850. Walking tours originate from the house to explore the many historical buildings that subsequently sprang up in the Gaslamp—the real perk of a visit here. The **audio tour** ($10) starts at 11am on Saturday and lasts two hours.

Map 1: 410 Island Ave., Gaslamp, 619/233-4692, www.gaslampfoundation.org; Tues.-Sat. 10am-4:30pm, Sun. noon-3:30pm; self-guided tour $5, free under 8, audio tour $10 adults, $8 seniors and military, $5 students, free under 8

MUSEUM OF CONTEMPORARY ART SAN DIEGO

This downtown branch of the Museum of Contemporary Art San Diego (MCASD) features rotating exhibitions highlighting engaging artists, groups, and collections. Everything from street art to large installations fills the high ceilings of its two adjoining spaces. Admission is free the third Thursday every month for extended hours 5pm-8pm.

Map 1: 1100 and 1001 Kettner Blvd., 858/454-3541, www.mcasd.org; Thurs.-Tues. 11am-5pm; $10 adults, $5 seniors and students over age 26, free for students under age 26 and military

SAN DIEGO CHINESE HISTORICAL MUSEUM

Housed in a historic 1927 building, this museum preserves and documents Chinese culture and history, particularly local history. The old Chinese Mission building itself is symbolic, as it was saved from demolition in order to establish this museum, then moved several blocks to its current location. Inside are imported Chinese artifacts, like a 19th-century bridal

ARTS AND CULTURE
DOWNTOWN

carriage, plus photos and relics documenting the short-lived existence of San Diego's Chinatown. The museum hosts temporary exhibitions of Chinese and Chinese American art at its annex buildings, the **Dr. Sun Yat-Sen Memorial Extension** (328 J St.) and the **Chuang Archive and Learning Center** (541B 2nd Ave.).

Map 1: 404 3rd Ave., 619/338-9888, www.sdchm.org; Tues.-Sat. 10:30am-4pm, Sun. noon-4pm; $5 adults, under 12 free

PERFORMING ARTS
BALBOA THEATRE

This historic 1924 vaudeville and movie palace sat empty for decades before being faithfully restored and reborn as a state-of-the-art music and comedy venue. Its Southwestern appeal and Gaslamp location provide a great setting for some good shows.

Map 1: 868 4th Ave., Gaslamp, 619/570-1100, www.sandiegotheatres.org

COPLEY SYMPHONY HALL

Also known as the Jacobs Music Center, this home of the **San Diego Symphony** also brings in touring philharmonics and ballet companies. The 1929 building's exterior may not impress, but walk through the doors and the architectural splendor inside will take your breath away.

Map 1: 750 B St., 619/235-0800, www.sandiegosymphony.org

HORTON GRAND THEATRE

This intimate 250-seat Gaslamp venue stages entertaining shows with a modest price tag. These days, the red-velvet draped stage hosts productions by **Intrepid Theatre Company.** They say there's not a bad seat in the house.

Map 1: 444 4th Ave., Gaslamp, 760/295-7541, www.intrepidtheatre.org

LYCEUM THEATRE

Built as part of Horton Plaza shopping center in the mid-1980s, the Lyceum hosts the **San Diego Repertory Theatre,** whose shows often include social, political, countercultural, and other diverse materials. The two intimate stages include local premieres of edgy sensations and classic plays reimagined in different contexts. Recent shows have included *The Who's Tommy* and the musical *Evita*.

Map 1: 79 Horton Plaza, Gaslamp, 619/544-1000, www.lyceumevents.org

SAN DIEGO CIVIC THEATRE

The largest theater in town, in terms of both capacity and scope, the 3,000-seat Civic Theatre might bring a Broadway touring company or stage a large production of the San Diego Ballet. If it's playing here, it's worth seeing.

Map 1: 1100 3rd Ave., 619/570-1100, www.sandiegotheatres.org

Clockwise from top left: the historic Marston House; Spreckels Theatre; Spreckels Organ Pavilion.

SPRECKELS THEATRE

For more than 100 years this one-time vaudeville venue has seen every manner of cultural performance, ranging from dance companies and rock bands to the Chinese Circus. The beautifully kept space offers terrific lines of sight and acoustics, with plenty of Gaslamp restaurants and bars nearby to make a night of it.

Map 1: 121 Broadway, Ste. 600, Gaslamp, 619/235-9500, www.spreckels.net

Balboa Park   Map 2

MUSEUMS

MARSTON HOUSE MUSEUM & GARDENS

An excellent example of the arts and crafts movement, the Marston House was built in 1905 and belonged to San Diego's "First Citizen," George Marston. The retailer and philanthropist was integral to the inception of Balboa Park, and his magnificent home overlooks its northwest corner. A tour reveals myriad ingenious details added by architects William Hebbard and Irving Gill, including specialized built-in cabinetry and a turn-of-the-20th-century precursor to an intercom system. Tours of the garden are also available.

Map 2: 3525 7th Ave., 619/297-9327, www.sohosandiego.org; tours every half hour Fri.-Sun. 10am-5pm; $15 adults, $14 military, $12 seniors and students, $7 ages 6-12

★ MINGEI INTERNATIONAL MUSEUM

Mingei is a Japanese term (rough translation: "art of all people") used to distinguish traditionally handmade crafts from mass-produced industrial objects. The museum brings together handmade works from around the world, celebrating such diverse artifacts as surfboards and quilts, while its collection of theatrical masks represents cultures spanning the globe. Definitely check out Wednesday's Palace, a unique dollhouse constructed of found objects that include feathers, dried leaves, and seashells.

Map 2: 1439 El Prado, 619/239-0003, www.mingei.org; Tues.-Sun. 10am-5pm; $10 adults, $7 seniors, students, military, and ages 6-17, free under age 6, free third Tues. of month

MUSEUM OF PHOTOGRAPHIC ARTS

This small museum screens the occasional art film or documentary and offers rotating exhibits, balanced between students and local artists. Most often, exhibits feature internationally known photographic artists with an interesting point of view. A great example of work you can expect to find here is a recent retrospective of Brazilian photojournalist Sebastião Salgado.

Map 2: 1649 El Prado, 619/238-7559, www.mopa.org; Tues.-Sun. 10am-5pm; $5 suggested donation

SAN DIEGO AUTOMOTIVE MUSEUM

Classic car buffs won't want to skip this gearhead Shangri-La. Dozens of fully restored cars line this giant hall, beautifully illustrating changes in design and technology over the years. Highlights include a 1914 Model T, a 1931 Cadillac Roadster, a 1953 Jaguar XK120, and even a DeLorean. Motorcycle enthusiasts will find a 1913 Indian Big Twin with sidecar and a road-worn 1914 Harley Davidson.

Map 2: 2080 Pan American Plaza, 619/231-2886, www.sdautomuseum.org; daily 10am-5pm; $9 adults, $6 seniors, military, and students, $4 ages 6-15, free under age 6

SAN DIEGO HISTORY CENTER

Permanent exhibits offer an informative timeline of San Diego, beginning with the indigenous Kumeyaay people and continuing on through Spanish colonization, the Mexican revolution, and annexation to the state of California. Seasonal exhibits highlight specific regions, historical figures, or ties to industry that shaped the city for better or worse.

Map 2: 1649 El Prado, Ste. 3, 619/232-6203, www.sandiegohistory.org; daily 10am-5pm; $10 suggested donation

VETERANS MUSEUM AND MEMORIAL CENTER

Commemorating the American service members who lost their lives for their nation, this small museum in a former naval hospital chapel honors them the way these sacrificing individuals might have preferred, without too much pomp or frill. The stories of pivotal battles are told, along with a reminder of the costs of victory.

Map 2: 2115 Park Blvd., 619/239-2300, www.veteranmuseum.org; Tues.-Sun. 10am-4pm; $5 adults, $4 veterans and seniors, $2 students, free under 12

PERFORMING ARTS

CASA DEL PRADO THEATRE

The Casa Del Prado stages kid-friendly theatrical, musical, and dance performances Friday evenings and weekend afternoons. Shows star children working in classes and camps put on by the San Diego Junior Theatre, San Diego Civic Youth Ballet, and Civic Dance Arts Program. It's a nice place for kids to take the spotlight, and some of them have gone on to professional success.

Map 2: 1600 Village Pl., 619/239-8355, www.juniortheatre.com

★ THE OLD GLOBE

Gathered at the northwest end of El Prado, The Old Globe actually comprises three different theater spaces at the **Conrad Prebys Theatre Center.** The Old Globe is based on Shakespeare's Old Globe in London and features world-class theatrical talent. The 580-seat venue stages classics as well as new productions year-round.

The 600-seat, open-air **Lowell Davies Festival Theatre** stages some of Shakespeare's finest work during the annual **Summer Shakespeare**

Military History

San Diego culture is closely intertwined with the ongoing presence of the U.S. military. Naval bases pepper the bay and coastline, and the U.S. Marine Corps (USMC) Recruit Depot in the center of town turns young volunteers into USMC privates—in other words, they are sent to boot camp. Fittingly, a number of sights around town reflect the military's presence.

The **USS *Midway* Museum** (910 N. Harbor Dr., 619/544-9600, www.midway.org; daily 10am-5pm; $20 adults, $10 ages 6-12, $17 seniors, $15 students, $10 retired military) isn't so much a museum as a retired aircraft carrier loaded with vintage aircraft. It's an invaluable insight into how life on a ship might be (i.e., not entirely pleasant, as you might guess). It's even more cramped at the **Maritime Museum of San Diego** (1492 N. Harbor Dr., 619/234-9153, www.sdmaritime.org; daily 9am-8pm; $18 adults, $8 ages 3-12, $13 seniors, $13 ages 13-17, $13 military), which features many vessels, including the USS *Dolphin* submarine, which is not as claustrophobic as the Soviet-era sub on-site.

For a closer look at more aircraft, head to Balboa Park's captivating **San Diego Air & Space Museum** (2001 Pan American Plaza, 619/234-8291, www.sandiegoairandspace.org; daily 10am-4:30pm; $19.75 adults, $16.75 seniors, students, and retired military, $10.75 ages 3-11, free active duty military, free under age 3), which is always a crowd-pleaser. It's a short drive north on I-15 to Miramar and the Marine Corps's **Flying Leatherneck Aviation Museum** (4203 Anderson Ave., Miramar, 858/693-1723, www.flyingleathernecks.org; Tues.-Sun. 9am-3:30pm; free), a yard filled with recent and retired aircraft, many of which saw some serious action. The retired aviators who volunteer at the museum offer the best insights.

The Marines celebrate their land and sea history at the **Marine Corps**

Festival (June-Sept.). The outdoor venue is backed by Balboa Park, an excellent option on warm summer evenings (but bring a sweater or light jacket).

The smallest of the three, the **Sheryl and Harvey White Theatre** has a theater-in-the-round design—the audience literally surrounds the stage. None of the 250 seats in this intimate venue are more than five rows back, making it an ideal setting for small runs of usually artier fare.

Map 2: 1363 Old Globe Way, 619/234-5623, www.theoldglobe.org; ticket prices vary

SPRECKELS ORGAN PAVILION

Built in 1914 as a donation to the Panama-California Exposition, this 4,518-pipe beauty is the largest outdoor organ in the western hemisphere. Interesting events pop up seasonally (silent movie screenings accompanied by the pipe organ), and free concerts are offered Sunday at 2pm, rain or shine. In summer, Monday evening concerts (7:30pm-9:30pm) fill the 2,500-seat pavilion.

Map 2: 2125 Pan American Rd. E., Ste. 10, 619/702-8138, www.spreckelsorgan.org; free

a stealth bomber replica in front of the Air & Space museum

Command Museum (Marine Corps Recruit Depot, 1600 Hochmuth Ave., 619/524-6719, www.corpshistory.org; Mon. 8am-3pm, Tues.-Sat. 8am-4pm; free), located on the recruit depot—you might see young men and women in training.

And if you needed any more proof of the lengths these marines, sailors, and soldiers will go to in their service, honor the fallen with visits to the **Veterans Museum and Memorial Center** (2115 Park Blvd., 619/239-2300, www.veteranmuseum.org; Tues.-Sun. 10am-4pm; $5 adults, $4 veterans and seniors, $2 students, free under 12) in Balboa Park and the **Fort Rosecrans National Cemetery** (1800 Cabrillo Memorial Dr., Point Loma, 858/658-7360, www.cem.va.gov; daily sunrise-sunset) in Point Loma.

Uptown

Map 3

CINEMA
HILLCREST CINEMAS

This Uptown art-house theater hosts some of the year's best movies—just not major blockbusters. Indie comedies and intimate dramas are what fill this art deco-inspired Landmark theater, and great conversations can be overheard on the way out. Parking in this neighborhood is tough; validate your ticket for accessible parking in the basement of the building.
Map 3: 3965 5th Ave., Hillcrest, 619/298-2904, www.landmarktheatres.com

GALLERIES
RAY STREET ARTS DISTRICT

North Park's arts community peppers the neighborhood with ad hoc galleries within hair salons, coffee shops, wine bars, and restaurants. But the epicenter of the local visual arts scene is this little block of Ray Street, just off the happening corner of 30th Street and University Avenue. While the studios and galleries vary, classes, workshops, and exhibitions are kept alive by the **San Diego Art Department** (3830 Ray St.). Every second Saturday, during the **Ray at Night** art walk, artists display their creations, often accompanied by live music, food, and wine.

Map 3: Ray St. between University Ave. and North Park Way, North Park

PERFORMING ARTS
DIVERSIONARY THEATRE

With a mission to provide theatrical performance space for LGBTQ voices, the shows here range from serious, introspective, and soul-baring fare to the hilariously absurd, including the occasional *Big Gay Improv Show*, a fund-raising effort.

Map 3: 4545 Park Blvd., Ste. 101, 619/220-0097, www.diversionary.org

THE OBSERVATORY NORTH PARK

Once a venue for theatrical productions, this revamped 1929 theater now hosts concerts by well-known rock and pop music artists. Shows are usually all-ages but may be age restricted depending on the nature of the show (such as the recent *An Evening with John Waters*).

Map 3: 2891 University Ave., North Park, 619/239-8836, www.observatorysd.com

Old Town and Mission Hills Map 4

CINEMA
CINEMA UNDER THE STARS

Classic movies and cult films are screened in this comfortable outdoor venue, which has a retractable roof in case those stars come with a chance of showers. Reserve your zero-gravity recliner or cabana seating online or at the box office after 6pm on show night.

Map 4: 4040 Goldfinch St., Mission Hills, 619/295-4221, www.topspresents.com; Thurs.-Sun. 8pm

MUSEUMS
JUNÍPERO SERRA MUSEUM

Spain established its first permanent presence in San Diego on Presidio Hill in 1769. This small museum perched on its crest tells the stories of the settlers who came here, as well as the indigenous Kumeyaay people who lived in communities scattered throughout the region. Named for the Catholic priest who founded the original mission, the Spanish Revival building was not part of the original settlement, which fell into ruin more than a century ago. However, it does house relics of the mission, including an 18th-century

Movies in the Outdoors

Not every movie is best experienced in a multiplex. These outdoor venues take advantage of San Diego's great weather.

- **Cinema Under the Stars** (4040 Goldfinch St., Mission Hills, 619/295-4221, www.topspresents.com; Thurs.-Sun. 8pm) in Mission Hills provides a comfortable, open-air venue to experience classic films and cult favorites, with plenty of great restaurants nearby.

- During the summer, the **Spreckels Organ Pavilion** (2125 Pan American Rd. E., Ste. 10, 619/702-8138, www.spreckelsorgan.org; free) at Balboa Park presents silent film screenings, accompanied by live music performed on the venue's enormous pipe organ.

- Shelter Island boutique hotel **The Pearl** (1410 Rosecrans St., Point Loma, 619/226-6100, www.thepearlsd.com) projects classics and pop-culture favorites on a wall over its swimming pool, often attracting crowds and the occasional dangling of feet in the water.

- **Stone World Bistro & Gardens, Liberty Station** (2816 Historic Decatur Rd., Ste. 116, 619/269-2100, www.stonelibertystation.com; Sun.-Thurs. 11:30am-9pm, Fri.-Sat. 11:30am-10pm) serves some of the city's best beer and terrific food. It also projects cult and comedy classics onto one of its courtyard walls during the summer.

- The gorgeous **Hotel del Coronado** (1500 Orange Ave., Coronado, 619/522-8001, www.hoteldel.com; Sun. 8pm; free) hosts Sunday night screenings of family-friendly classics on its beach throughout the summer.

olive press and one of the cannons that guarded the walls of the fortified presidio built to protect it.

Map 4: 2727 Presidio Dr., 619/232-6203, www.sandiegohistory.org; Sat.-Sun. 10am-4pm; free

SEELEY STABLE

Stables were still a necessity when Old Town was founded, and this 1851 stagecoach station gives interesting insight into the way things were. The large barnlike space is filled with carriages, period saddles, and other tack from a time when paying a visit to La Jolla (currently a 20-minute drive) could take up to four hours.

Map 4: 2648 Calhoun St., 619/220-5427, www.parks.ca.gov; daily 10am-5pm; free

PERFORMING ARTS
OLD TOWN THEATRE

Home of the **Cygnet Theatre Company,** the Old Town Theatre has staged well-known shows by prominent playwrights, many of which had never

Clockwise from top left: The Junípero Serra Museum celebrates San Diego's early and indigenous history; Chicano Park boasts a large collection of murals; Old Town Theatre is home of the Cygnet Theatre Company.

been produced on a professional level in San Diego before. The company is responsible for producing high-caliber work, and their musicals and plays tend to be great successes.

Map 4: 4040 Twiggs St., 619/337-1525, www.cygnettheatre.com

Ocean Beach and Point Loma

Map 6

CINEMA
THE LOT, LIBERTY STATION

Leather recliners, cocktails, and dinner service contribute to this luxury theater being one of the most comfortable in the county. With first-run films and fan favorites making limited engagements, advance ticket purchase is recommended.

Map 6: 2620 Truxtun Rd., 619/566-0069, http://thelotent.com

GALLERIES
NTC PROMENADE

When the Naval Training Center (NTC) opened up its former barracks buildings to the Liberty Station District, creative and performing arts organizations moved in, resulting in a loose-knit community featuring galleries, performances, and workshops. Galleries are open during the **Friday Night Liberty Art Walks** (first Friday of the month), and you'll often find correlating events, such as capoeira performances or the riotous storytelling evening *So Say We All.* On a regular basis, different organizations within the NTC network offer workshops teaching topics in music, dance, jewelry-making, improv, visual arts, and creative writing. Notable groups include the Theatre Arts School of San Diego; San Diego Watercolor Society; San Diego Writers, Ink; and the San Diego Ballet Company.

Map 6: 2640 Historic Decatur Rd., Point Loma, 619/573-9300, www.ntclibertystation. com; hours vary

PERFORMING ARTS
★ HUMPHREYS CONCERTS BY THE BAY

People watch summer shows at this outdoor venue from their boats—kayaks, paddleboats, or one of the yachts moored next door to this Shelter Island venue. It's one of the best places in town to catch a music or comedy show. Most simply buy a ticket for a folding seat inside the outdoor amphitheater or reserve one of the hotel rooms connected to the balcony overlooking the stage; these high-end accommodations offer some of the best seats in the house.

Map 6: 2241 Shelter Island Dr., Shelter Island, 619/224-3577, www.humphreysconcerts. com; May-Oct.

CINEMA
ARCLIGHT LA JOLLA
State-of-the-art features of this next-generation mall multiplex include 3-D auditoriums and one outfitted with a sophisticated, 32-channel Atmos surround-sound system. A café serves food and drinks in the lobby, where guests may relax until just before show time (thanks to assigned seating). Select screenings for adults 21 and over permit bringing beer or wine into the theater.

Map 7: 4425 La Jolla Village Dr., 858/768-7770, www.arclightcinemas.com

THE LOT LA JOLLA
Located within ritzy La Jolla Village, this luxury theater was built to match. Reserved seats should be purchased ahead of time, though you may decide whether you'd like to order meals and drinks once you've arrived.

Map 7: 7611 Fay Ave., 858/77-0069, http://thelotent.com

GALLERIES
★ MADISON GALLERY
The largest of La Jolla's galleries, this 10,000-square-foot space is a relatively new location for one of the top galleries in the nation, but moving away from its longtime beachfront home hasn't impacted the quality of its curation. It hosts the work of up to 15 artists at a time, usually active and well-established names, with a few notable rising talents producing contemporary work across a variety of media.

Map 7: 1055 Wall St., Ste.100, 858/459-0836, www.madisongalleries.com; Mon.-Sat. 10am-6pm, Sun. by appt.

TASENDE GALLERY
Originally based in Acapulco, Jose Tasende's gallery has been showing modern artists in this La Jolla space for more than 38 years, though recent redesigns see the space growing, with plans to add a second story with an oceanfront view. The focus on established mid- to late-career artists means you're likely to encounter some familiar names, both inside and among the array of sculptures in front of the building.

Map 7: 820 Prospect St., 858/454-3691, www.tasendegallery.com; Tues.-Fri. 10am-5pm, Sat. 11am-5pm

MUSEUMS
MUSEUM OF CONTEMPORARY ART SAN DIEGO
This historic oceanfront museum began a $56 million expansion in 2017 and is due to reopen in mid-2020, presumably better than ever. While this

location is offline, the museum continues to draw relevant contemporary exhibitions to its sister location downtown (1100 and 1001 Kettner Blvd.).

Map 7: 700 Prospect St., 858/454-3541, www.mcasd.org

MURALS OF LA JOLLA

Since 2010, this project of the Athenaeum Music & Arts Library has been bringing a renowned cadre of artists to contribute public art pieces throughout La Jolla Village. Check the project website to find a map of over a dozen murals from the likes of John Baldessari, Heather Gwen Martin, and William Wegman.

Map 7: La Jolla Village, 858/334-9053, www.muralsoflajolla.com

★ STUART COLLECTION

The vast sculpture garden at UC San Diego boasts 18 striking, beautiful, and thought-provoking pieces—boulders in the shape of a giant teddy bear, a snake path, and a singing tree. However, the collection's most-discussed work sits on a seventh-floor rooftop, accessible only a few hours a week. Do Ho Suh's *Fallen Star* consists of a tiny blue cottage hanging off a ledge atop Jacobs Hall. While it can be viewed from beneath, it's only upon entering the meticulously constructed little home that you understand its purpose. Be warned; the sense of displacement may stay with you afterward.

Map 7: 9500 Gilman Dr., 858/534-2117, www.stuartcollection.ucsd.edu; daily 6am-midnight, *Fallen Star* installation Tues. and Thurs. 11am-2pm; free

PERFORMING ARTS
ATHENAEUM MUSIC & ARTS LIBRARY

An unusual and cherished institution, this lovely venue houses a library of books devoted to art and music that contains a small gallery of rotating work. An intimate music space also hosts a culturally rich lineup of mostly jazz or chamber music performances, with the occasional experimental artist. Lectures, art shows, film screenings, children's storytelling hours, and the occasional reception round out the many engagements of this cultural hub.

Map 7: 1008 Wall St., 619/454-5872, www.ljathenaeum.org

★ LA JOLLA PLAYHOUSE

With a reputation as incubator for Broadway productions, this nonprofit theater group located on the UCSD campus stages original productions with a remarkable success rate. Recent years have seen the world premieres of *Jersey Boys* and *The Who's Tommy*. The group was cofounded by Gregory Peck and manages to stay vital whether producing unknown shows of emerging talents or bringing the very best to local audiences.

Its four spaces include the original **Mandell Weiss Theater**, the lavish **Mandell Weiss Forum**, and the smaller **Shank and Potiker** black-box theater. Performances are held year-round, from experimental pieces to those destined for greatness.

Map 7: 2910 La Jolla Village Dr., 858/550-1010, www.lajollaplayhouse.org

Coronado

Map 8

CINEMA
VINTAGE VILLAGE THEATRES CORONADO

Don't be fooled into thinking this simple three-screen theater in the center of Coronado isn't state-of-the-art. A recent remodel brought the 65-year-old venue up to spec, with 4K digital projection technology as well as 3-D and surround sound. Come for first-run blockbusters as well as the occasional indie flick.

Map 8: 820 Orange Ave., 619/437-6161, www.vintagecinemas.com

PERFORMING ARTS
LAMB'S PLAYERS THEATRE

An "intimate" 350-seat venue used by a popular local production company, this auditorium was originally built in 1917 by notable Coronado resident John Spreckels. Lamb's has been in residence for more than 20 years, producing four or five shows annually, often crowd-pleasers.

Map 8: 1142 Orange Ave., 619/437-6000, www.lambsplayers.org

Greater San Diego

Map 9

ART
★ CHICANO PARK

Tucked under the base of the Coronado Bridge, this small park paints a picture of the suffering and resilience of Mexican-American San Diego. Barrio Logan has been predominantly Latino since refugees fleeing the Mexican revolution settled here at the end of the 19th century. Back then, the neighborhood extended to the waterfront, but naval installations built during World War II closed that off. When freeway construction cut the neighborhood in half, the bridge itself closed off part of the sky. In 1970, the city tried to pave this little bit of designated park space to put in a highway patrol parking lot. The Latino residents protested, occupying the park for nearly two weeks and forcing the city to invest in the park's preservation. Artists came to beautify the concrete pillars and walls with murals and sculptures, resulting in one of the city's most singular art collections and landscapes.

Map 9: 1949 Logan Ave., Barrio Logan, 619/232-1930, www.chicanoparksandiego.com; open 24 hours daily

GALLERIES

BREAD & SALT

Part gallery, art studio hub, and events space, this Barrio Logan arts hub brings interesting cultural happenings on a regular basis—there's even a craft brewery on-site. It often highlights a rotation of artists-in-residence to create compelling installations.

Map 9: 1955 Julian Ave., Barrio Logan, 619/851-4083, www.breadandsaltsandiego.com; Tues.- Sat. 11am-4pm; free

LA BODEGA GALLERY

Down the street from Chicano Park, this thriving young gallery organizes themed group shows that create a dialog among local artists and draw curious crowds—particularly during Barrio Art Walk events, the second Saturday night of each month. Recent shows have included skateboard deck art, Día de Los Muertos skull art, and Frieda Kahlo-inspired works.

Map 9: 2196 Logan Ave., Barrio Logan, 619/255-7036, www.labodegagallery.com; Tues.-Thurs. noon-6pm, Fri. noon-11pm, Sat. 6pm-10pm; free

QUINT GALLERY

For more than three decades, emerging and established artists from all over the world exhibited a wide range of contemporary works at Quint's La Jolla gallery. Despite moving to an industrial neighborhood east of the freeway, Quint still brings intriguing exhibitions highlighting the work of active artists.

Map 9: 5171 Santa Fe St., Ste. H., 858/454-3409, http://quintgallery.com; Thurs.-Sat. 10am-4pm; free

MUSEUMS

FLYING LEATHERNECK AVIATION MUSEUM

Marine Corps Air Station (MCAS) Miramar is home to some of the world's best jet pilots. Wander through the yard of this museum to watch the jets fly up close, then peruse the retired military planes, helicopters, and ground support vehicles often famous for their service, such as the *Sea Knight* chopper, whose heroic crew proved courageous and indispensable during the evacuation of Saigon. Inside you can get a close look at flight suits and read detailed stories about the heroics of military pilots, including Alfred A. Cunningham, the father of U.S. Marine Corps aviation.

Map 9: 4203 Anderson Ave., Miramar, 858/693-1723, www.flyingleathernecks.org; Tues.-Sun. 9am-3:30pm; free

The Marine Corps Recruit Depot (MCRD) Museum tells the history of the Marine Corps and its presence in San Diego with detailed information about the often unsung roles of these devil dogs who shaped modern history. Valid identification is required to gain entry to this military base in the Midway district, best accessed via the sentry gate on Barnett Avenue at Henderson Avenue.

Map 9: Marine Corps Recruit Depot, 1600 Hochmuth Ave., 619/524-4426, www.corpshistory.org; Mon.-Sat. 8:30am-4pm

PERFORMING ARTS

MATTRESS FIRM AMPHITHEATRE

The name has changed over the years (many, many times), but no matter who the corporate sponsor is, the suburban setting of this large outdoor stage results in great sound for some of the biggest rock, country, rap, and pop acts on tour.

Map 9: 2050 Entertainment Circle, Chula Vista, 619/494-5600, www.amphitheatrechulavista.com

OPEN AIR THEATRE

A beautiful outdoor venue on the San Diego State University campus, the outdoor Open Air Theater brings top-level talent on a regular basis, hosting some of the most popular bands in rock and pop music.

Map 9: 5500 Campanile Dr., 619/594-0234, www.as.sdsu.edu

Shops

Look for ★ to find
recommended Shops

Highlights

★ **Best Home and Design:** Little Italy has grown into one of the hippest neighborhoods in town, mostly due to the high levels of taste found in the **Kettner Art & Design District.** Ingenious designers and impeccably curated shops will make you want to hang around here too (page 196).

★ **Best Bottle Shop:** Spend a few days in San Diego and you'll want to fill your suitcase with beer. When the time comes, hit **Bottlecraft** to load up on the best of local craft, by the bottle or the can, mixed and matched as you see fit (page 196).

★ **Best Farmers Market:** The **Little Italy Mercato** is so popular and well run that farmers, artisans, and purveyors clamor to sell here. You'll find delicious organic produce to sample, fresh fish to taste, and more flavors than your appetite can handle (page 196).

★ **Best Children's Shop:** For young children's toys and gifts, look no further than **So Childish.** Many of the baby and toddler clothes, plushies, toys, musical instruments, and books manage to steer clear of commercial influence (page 200).

★ **Best Mexican Gift Shop for Design Fans: Casa Artelexia** turns out some stellar folk art. Come here for unique crafts, jewelry, and decorative wares (page 202).

★ **Best Gift Shop:** Finding something for anyone is a tall order, even in the best gift shops. But **Pigment** has something for drinkers, gardeners, pop culture buffs, design hounds, sentimentalists, children, and health nuts (page 202).

★ **Best Mexican Gift Shop for Tourists:** To take something home that feels like San Diego, head to the **Bazaar del Mundo** in Old Town, which has Spanish and Mexican influences (page 206).

★ **Best Fashions:** Whether you seek high-end designer fashions or the latest looks from nationally known labels, the boutiques on **Girard Avenue** in La Jolla have your shopping day pegged (page 212).

★ **Best Window Shopping:** Window-shopping on **Orange Avenue** in Coronado ranges from beachy to kitschy. It starts around 8th Street and continues all the way to the Hotel Del (page 215).

★ **Best Surf Shop:** There's only one **Bird's Surf Shed**—it's part museum, part epic surf story waiting to happen. Nose around for a glorious new or vintage board, or just hang out and let the locals sing tales of their SoCal adventures (page 217).

San Diego may be many things, but a world-class shopping destination is not one of them. While it may boast better-than-average surf shops and more swimsuits than most cities, rare is the person who plans a trip just to push the limit of his or her credit card.

Aside from surf and beachwear, San Diego's proximity to the Mexican border means access to a great deal of Mexican crafts, folk art, and decor, including pottery, textiles, and (sometimes kitschy) religious artifacts.

Like-minded shops tend to cluster together on a single street or district, providing window-shopping opportunities, and this is true of clothing boutiques around La Jolla, Pacific Beach, and North Park, as well as antiques (Ocean Beach) and home design shops (La Jolla and Little Italy).

When it comes to food and beverages, shopping gets hot, whether you're into fresh-catch local seafood or locally produced craft beverages. Retail shops in San Diego have a high turnover rate, but we're always looking to grill fish and drink beer.

Previous: Old Town Market; ceramic goods for sale at El Centro Artesano.

ANTIQUES AND VINTAGE
ARCHITECTURAL SALVAGE OF SAN DIEGO

When old and antiquated buildings are torn down or refurbished, the original construction materials have to go somewhere. The good stuff goes here. Stained-glass windows, vintage drawers and cabinet hardware, wooden doors, and iron gates are merely some of the fascinating items you'll uncover. Much of it can't even be categorized, and it's rarely things you'd expect. Homeowners will be thrilled, while dreamers and design enthusiasts will be inspired.

Map 1: 2401 Kettner Blvd., Little Italy, 619/696-1313, www.architecturalsalvagesd.com; Sun. 11am-5pm, Tues.-Sat. 10am-5:30pm

★ KETTNER ART & DESIGN DISTRICT

This loose cluster of furniture shops, art galleries, and design boutiques operates out of the north end of Little Italy. Some shops are temporary, some are well known, and some are obscure, but all hold potential. Interior and landscape design buffs should loop through the neighborhood, stopping at **AT-HOM Store & Design** (2310 Kettner Blvd. Ste. B, 619/744-9974, www. at-hom.com) and **The Atomic Bazaar** (2400 Kettner Blvd., 619/534-8397, www.theatomicbazaar.com) with occasional forays up side streets to check out places like **Love & Aesthetics** (621 W. Fir St., 619/546-6143, http:// loveandaesthetics.com). Keep your eyes open—any little door could lead to something amazing.

Map 1: Kettner Blvd. and India St. between Laurel St. and Hawthorn St., Little Italy

GOURMET TREATS
★ BOTTLECRAFT

San Diego's favorite beverage receives special treatment in this boutique bottle shop featuring the best of local brands plus rotating selections from the world's top craft brewers. Bottle shelves are arranged by geographic origin, while coolers split cold bottles and cans by style. Any bottle or can may be purchased individually, and a fantastic tap list allows you to drink while you shop or sit on the patio, enjoying the day. You'll find a lesser space but larger selection and a cheese counter at the North Park location (3007 University Ave.).

Map 1: 2161 India St., Little Italy, 619/487-9493, www.bottlecraftbeer.com; Mon.-Thurs. noon-10pm, Fri.-Sat. noon-midnight, Sun. 11am-10pm

★ LITTLE ITALY MERCATO

The city's best farmers market convenes every Saturday to sell produce, local seafood, and a few craft goods to happy throngs of locals who make a date of it week in and week out. Copious California sunshine helps regional farmers grow year-round, so there's always something in season,

Clockwise from top left: Architectural Salvage; Horton Plaza; Seaport Village.

and usually more than enough for a great meal. Walk away with some fresh avocados, or order breakfast or lunch to go at any number of booths. Upon completion of the Piazza della Famiglia, expected sometime in 2018, the Mercato will move to its location at India and Date Streets.

Map 1: Cedar St. from Kettner Blvd. to Front St., Little Italy; Sat. 8am-2pm

TUNA HARBOR DOCKSIDE MARKET

One day a week, local fishers sell fresh-catch seafood from an open-air market on the dock next to Seaport Village. Year-round fish include black cod, California halibut, mahi-mahi, octopus, crab, and sea urchin. Seasonal species rotating through include opah, swordfish, spiny lobster, and bluefin tuna.

Map 1: 598 Harbor Ln., Marina District, www.thdocksidemarket.com; Sat. 8am-1pm

SHOPPING MALLS
HORTON PLAZA

Horton Plaza opened in 1985 in an effort to revitalize downtown after rough times through the 1970s. Anchored by Macy's and Jimbo's (a natural grocery store), the colorful open-air mall fills about six square blocks with typical mall stores. There's an eight-screen movie theater, a playhouse and music venue, and an outdoor ice rink that opens in the winter. There is a vast parking garage, and most businesses validate up to one hour of parking there (Jimbo's and 24 Hour Fitness validate for two hours, and movie theaters validate for three). After that, it's $2 for every 15 minutes.

Map 1: 324 Horton Plaza, Gaslamp, 619/239-8180, www.westfield.com/hortonplaza;
Mon.-Sat. 10am-8pm, Sun. 11am-6pm

SEAPORT VILLAGE

Perched on the waterfront just off Marina Park, Seaport Village feels more like a collection of shops next to a beach park (along with a few uninspired restaurants). Scenery aside, most shops are focused on San Diego-themed souvenirs, sunglasses, and beach styles. The exceptions are Upstart Crow (619/232-4855, daily 9am-9pm), a bookstore and gift shop, and the always fun, occasionally functional Village Hat Shop (619/233-7236, daily 10am-9pm). It's worth a visit for the walk along the waterfront and for the hand-carved carousel that's been in operation since 1895.

Neighboring the village, The Headquarters (789 W. Harbor Dr., www.theheadquarters.com) extension opened in 2013 to create more retail space and to provide a venue for some decent restaurants, including Puesto (619/233-8880, daily 11am-10pm) and Gelato Paradiso (619/238-0307, Sun.-Thurs. 11am-9pm, Fri.-Sat. 11am-10pm). The extension was formerly the old police headquarters, and you can also check out the old jail cell. Shops include Geppetto's Toys (619/615-0005, Mon.-Sat. 10am-9pm, Sun.

Top: tomatoes at the Little Italy Mercato. **Bottom:** imported and local craft beer sold at Bottlecraft.

10am-8pm) and **Coco Rose** (760/213-7080, Mon.-Sat. 10am-7pm, Sun. 10am-6pm), which offers Balinese-inspired women's fashions.

Map 1: 849 W. Harbor Dr. and 789 W. Harbor Dr., 619/235-4014, www.seaportvillage.com; Mon.-Sat. 10am-9pm, Sun. 10am-9pm

Balboa Park

Map 2

KIDS AND PETS
★ SO CHILDISH

This children's boutique can only be characterized as "delightful," providing South Park locals with the perfect place to pick up a baby shower or kid's birthday gift. Ranging from adorable necessity to cherished keepsake, the curated selection makes big-box kid shops seem plastic and hollow.

Map 2: 1947 30th St., 619/238-0800, www.sochildish.com; Tues.-Sat. 10am-5pm, Sun. 10am-4pm

Uptown

Map 3

ART AND DESIGN
GEORGE'S CAMERA

Many San Diego photographers have benefitted from the knowledgeable staff of this longtime camera shop, which carries top digital brands, and also plenty of film cameras and accessories, including dark room supplies. High end cameras and gear are offered for rent, whether you like to try before you buy, or just want to give yourself a couple days to perfectly catch the colors of an ocean sunset. Keep an eye out for the shop's occasional photo classes and workshops.

Map 3: 3837 30th St, North Park, 619/297-3544, www.georgescamera.com; Mon.-Sat. 9am-6pm

VISUAL

Other than the occasional sketchbook, what you'll find at this North Park art store is paints, pens, and pencils—but they're great quality paints, pens, and pencils. Local visual artists may be here browsing color palettes or checking out the artwork displayed on its walls.

Map 3: 3776 30th St., North Park, 619/501-5585, www.visualshopsd.com; Mon.-Fri. noon-7pm, Sat.-Sun. noon-5pm

BOOKS

ADAMS AVENUE BOOKSTORE

Dating back to 1965, this independently run bookstore features a deep collection of used and rare books, plus a couple of cats who consider the stacks their turf. The two-story shop gets so packed to the gills with hardcovers and paperbacks that the stairwell is lined with bookshelves. Upstairs, cookbooks appropriately stock what used to be somebody's kitchen, and downstairs in back, a kids' play area occupies a room full of children's titles.

Map 3: 3502 Adams Ave., 619/281-3330, www.adamsavebooks.com; Mon.-Tues. and Thurs.-Sat. 10am-6pm, Wed. noon-8pm, Sun. noon-5pm

VERBATIM BOOKS

This little used and rare bookshop has brought a bit of literacy back to North Park. In addition to popular and hard-to-get selections from popular fiction and literature, the shop features a solid range of nonfiction, as well as titles from over 100 local authors and a zine corner devoted to small budget chapbooks and the like.

Map 3: 3793 30th St., North Park, 619/501-7466, www.verbatim-books.com; daily 10am-7pm

CLOTHING AND ACCESSORIES

MIMI & RED

If San Diego women have a unifying style, it's probably based around this hippie-chic boutique with a finger on the pulse of Southern California fashions. Expect plenty of summery and natural looks.

Map 3: 3041 University Ave., North Park, 619/298-7933, www.mimiandred.com; Sun.-Mon. 11am-6pm, Tues.-Sat. 11am-7pm

VILLAGE HAT SHOP

Let's be honest: There are few more entertaining things to shop for than hats. At this local hat shop, you'll try on Stetsons and Kangols, fedoras, pageboys and top hats, women's hats with floral or feather adornments, cowboy hats, and Panama hats. '80s music is often playing so that you can do your own montage. Ultimately you'll walk away with the perfectly styled hat for your head. Look for the smaller sister shop at Seaport Village (853 W. Harbor Dr.).

Map 3: 3821 4th Ave., Hillcrest, 619/683-5533, www.villagehatshop.com; Mon.-Thurs. 10am-6pm, Fri.-Sat. 10am-8pm, Sun. 11am-6pm

VINTAGE SHOPPING ON 5TH

A lot of fashionable folks live in the Hillcrest neighborhood, so it's not surprising to find this little pocket of vintage shops on 5th Avenue. Top among them is the funky foraging of **Flashbacks Recycled Fashion** (3849 5th Ave., 619/291-4200; Mon.-Sat. 10am-7pm, Sun. 11am-6pm). While you're sifting through the vintage racks on this short block, check out **Lost and Found** (3840 5th Ave., 619/955-8915; daily 10am-7pm), **Luigi Vera** (3823 5th Ave., 619/683-2199, www.luigivera.com; Mon.-Sat. 11am-7pm, Sun. 11am-6pm), and **Buffalo Exchange** (3862 5th Ave., 619/298-4411, www.buffaloexchange.com; Mon.-Sat. 10am-8pm, Sun. 11am-7pm).

Map 3: 5th Ave. between Robinson Ave. and University Ave., Hillcrest

GIFT AND HOME
★ CASA ARTELEXIA

Mexican folk art inspires many of the crafts, jewelry, and decorative wares at this shop, whether it's Roman Catholic mysticism, *papel picado*, or the skull-heavy styling of Día de los Muertos (Day of the Dead). It's unique, often kitschy, and usually enriching—you won't find the likes of it elsewhere.

Map 3: 3811 Ray St., North Park, 619/501-6381, www.artelexia.com; Mon.-Sat. 11am-6pm, Sun. 11am-4pm

★ PIGMENT

San Diego's best home and gift shop, Pigment became popular for its selection of air plants, plus a gorgeous variety of wall and ceiling planters, but there are dozens of great gifts and conversation starters here, from a make-your-own gin kit to electronics accessories made with polished wood. This North Park mainstay recently expanded into a larger space to offer more cleverly conceived decorative items. It's the kind of place where browsing is its own reward.

Map 3: 3801 30th St., North Park, 619/501-6318, www.shoppigment.com; Mon.-Thurs. 10am-7pm, Fri.-Sat. 10am-8pm, Sun. 10am-5pm

SIMPLY LOCAL

Made in San Diego is the ethos behind this locavore boutique. It's not the sort of shop filled with San Diego T-shirts. These goods are actually knit, stitched, carved, printed, cut, or otherwise produced within the community. Homegrown items range from stationery and gifts to fashions to freshly roasted coffee.

Map 3: 3013 University Ave., North Park, 619/756-7958, http://simplylocalsandiego.com; Sun.-Thurs. 10:30am-8pm, Fri.-Sat. 10:30am-9pm

GOURMET TREATS
BINE & VINE BOTTLE SHOP

Great taste guides this friendly craft beer and wine bottle shop. The curated selection balances the best of local products with desirable selections from elsewhere, and knowledgeable staff knows just where to find what you're looking for.

Map 3: 3334 Adams Ave., Normal Heights, 619/795-2463, http://bineandvine.com; daily 11am-10pm

ANTIQUES AND VINTAGE
SEA JUNK
You can't find nautical antiques just anywhere. This Maidhof Brothers shop, near the border of Mission Hills and Old Town, sells gorgeous wood stateroom furniture and oil lanterns, plus ridiculously cool items like spyglasses, sextants, portholes, ship's telegraphs, and inclinometers.
Map 4: 1891 San Diego Ave., 619/574-1891, www.seajunk.com; Mon.-Fri. 10am-5pm, Sat. 11am-5pm

CLOTHING AND ACCESSORIES
JOHNSON HOUSE HABERDASHERY
Where else are you going to go to find proper saloon garb? This small entertaining shop features vintage clothing, custom hats, and unique accessories, whether you're into steampunk or just enjoy the fineries of ye olde times.
Map 4: 2706 Calhoun St., 619/291-5170; daily 10am-6pm

MINER'S GEMS & MINERALS
While greater San Diego did experience a small and short-lived gold rush, this gem, rock, and fossil retailer does not technically match the historical accuracy of Old Town. Nevertheless, it offers a unique and interesting assortment of geodes, old bones, and precious stone jewelry.
Map 4: 2616 San Diego Ave., 619/688-1178, www.minersgemsandminerals.com; daily 10am-6pm

TOLER'S LEATHER DEPOT
Presumably, the residents of 19th-century Old Town wore a lot of leather—at least that's the conceit of this leather specialist. Plenty of belts, buckles, bolo ties, cowboy hats, and moccasins are on hand to help complete your Western outfit.
Map 4: 2625 Calhoun St., 619/295-7511; daily 10am-6pm

GIFT AND HOME
CAPTAIN FITCH'S MERCANTILE
Old Town teems with souvenir and gift shops; those searching for better offerings might appreciate this shop, which embraces both the cowboy and sailor sides of the city's history. Vintage compasses, marshal's stars, and model ships, in addition to quite a few children's books and assorted San Diego-themed trinkets, offer a more interesting variety to choose from.
Map 4: 2627 San Diego Ave., 619/298-3944; Mon.-Fri. 10am-6pm, Sat.-Sun. 10am-8pm

Mexican Folk Arts and Crafts

Mexico isn't just geographically close to San Diego—it's been less than 200 years since San Diego *was* Mexico. The city is steeped in Mexican culture, including food, architecture, and local crafts. Some of the best Made in San Diego products have Mexican origins and make for great shopping opportunities and souvenirs.

· **Papel Picado.** A precise and detailed paper-cutting craft (it translates to "perforated paper"), *papel picado* most often depicts floral patterns or sun and skull imagery. The brightly colored paper is often strung like Tibetan prayer flags. You'll find great examples in the booths of **Old Town Market** (4010 Twiggs St., 619/278-0955, www.oldtownmarketsandiego. com; daily 9am-8pm).

· **Pottery.** Head over to **El Centro Artesano** (2637 San Diego Ave., 619/297-2931; Mon.-Thurs. 9:30am-6pm, Fri.-Sun. 9:30am-9pm) to peruse the red terra-cotta and hand-painted clay work, ranging from simple and decorative planters to wind chimes and *chiminea* (small wood-burning fireplaces).

· **Religious Artifacts.** Mexican culture is predominantly Roman Catholic, but some of its indigenous folklore remains, infused into a Roman Catholic mysticism that manifests in a fascination with death. Hence you'll find skull iconography depicting Santa Muerte (Our Lady of the Holy Death) and the celebration of Día de los Muertos (Day of the Dead). Skulls adorn jewelry, bride and groom figurines, and colorful shrines. **Casa Artelexia** (3803 Ray St., North Park, 619/501-6381, www.artelexia.com; Mon.-Sat. 11am-6pm, Sun. 11am-4pm), in North Park, offers a trove of inspired products celebrating the tradition.

· **Talavera Tile.** These ornate, hand-painted tiles look great on their own,

EL CENTRO ARTESANO

Made-in-Mexico planters and wind chimes are the reasons to visit this pottery lot, which is both colorful and well stocked. It's also a great spot to get acquainted with the *chiminea;* many a local backyard uses this outdoor fireplace to keep warm on cool nights.

Map 4: 2637 San Diego Ave., 619/297-2931; Mon.-Thurs. 9:30am-6pm, Fri.-Sun. 9:30am-9pm

FOUR WINDS TRADING COMPANY

Featuring Native American and Mexican folk arts, crafts, and jewelry, this small shop doesn't focus strictly on artifacts from the region, but it does pride itself on the authenticity of its wares. It's a fine place to browse for the serious or casual collector.

Map 4: 2448 San Diego Ave., 619/692-0466; daily 10am-5pm

painted skulls celebrating Día de los Muertos

but together they become beautiful walls, floors, decorative trim, or garden decor. A whole shop is dedicated to them within **Fiesta de Reyes** (2754 Calhoun St., 619/297-3100, www.fiestadereyes.com; Mon.-Thurs 10am-9pm, Fri.-Sat. 10am-10pm, Sun. 9am-9pm).

· **Textiles.** You'll find plenty of Mexican-influenced clothes, blankets, rugs, and table settings at **Bazaar del Mundo** (4133 Taylor St., 619/296-3161, www.bazaardelmundo.com; Tues.-Sat. 10am-9pm, Sun.-Mon. 10am-5:30pm), just at the edge of Old Town. Based either on the brightly colored stripe and diamond patterns of the serape shawl (or poncho), or the airy, white, embroidered tunic called a *huipil,* these designs have evolved through colonial sewing and weaving methods from their indigenous inceptions.

RACINE & LARAMIE TOBACCONIST
San Diego's first cigar store dates back to 1868 and still sells stogies as well as pipes and other tobacco products. It also doubles as a museum of sorts, with a few vintage pipes, lighters, and matchbooks on display, making it the rare smoke shop of some interest to nonsmokers.

Map 4: 2737 San Diego Ave., 619/291-7833, www.racineandlaramie.com; Mon.-Sat. 10am-6pm, Sun. 10:30am-5pm

GOURMET TREATS
VENISSIMO CHEESE
If "All the best cheese from all over the world" sounds like something you want to experience, stop by San Diego's top dedicated cheese shop. Sample anything you see within the small shop's glass cases; you only have to ask the friendly and helpful staff. Color-coded labels identify whether the cheese was made from cow's milk, goat, sheep, or buffalo. If you get

hungry while nibbling away, order a cheese board or freshly made salami or *soppressata* sandwich. Other locations include **The Headquarters** (789 W. Harbor Dr.), in the Marina District, and **Bottlecraft** (3007 University Ave.) in North Park.

Map 4: 754 W. Washington St., Mission Hills, 619/491-0708, www.venissimo.com; Mon.-Sat. 10am-6pm, Sun. 11am-4pm

MARKETS

★ BAZAAR DEL MUNDO

Just around the corner from Old Town State Historic Park, this little complex of shops steps up the Mexican cultural experience by offering a better brand of wares in a less hectic environment. While there's still plenty of kitschy fun, there's also some seriously tasteful and colorful merchandise—from hand-painted textiles and clothing to Native American jewelry and Mata Ortiz pottery. You can accomplish some serious shopping here.

Map 4: 4133 Taylor St., 619/296-3161, www.bazaardelmundo.com; Tues.-Sat 10am-9pm, Sun.-Mon. 10am-5:30pm

FIESTA DE REYES

Tucked into the northern corner of Old Town San Diego State Historic Park, this courtyard complex holds three Mexican restaurants and has a small stage for traditional music and dance performances. You'll also find specialty shops devoted to Mexican Talavera tiles, olive oil, silver jewelry, beef jerky, and souvenirs galore. It's clearly designed to please visitors and much of the time succeeds.

Map 4: 2754 Calhoun St., 619/297-3100, www.fiestadereyes.com; Mon.-Thurs 10am-9pm, Fri.-Sat. 10am-10pm, Sun. 9am-9pm

OLD TOWN MARKET

A bazaar of more than 40 small shops, this enclosed open-air shopping center on the southern edge of Old Town San Diego State Historic Park offers a colorful collection of rustic and Mexican clothing, accessories, and decorative items, including Talavera tiles, *papel picado*, woven blankets, ornaments, and folk art.

Map 4: 4010 Twiggs St., 619/278-0955, www.oldtownmarketsandiego.com; daily 9am-8pm

MUSIC

M-THEORY MUSIC

Not a lot of independent music stores operate in San Diego anymore, but this favorite is still at it, serving up vinyl and CDs instead of downloads. It also stocks a fair number of local recordings, and the clerks will gladly turn you on to some of the best homegrown music.

Map 4: 827 W. Washington St., 619/220-0485, www.mtheorymusic.com; Mon.-Sat. 10am-8pm, Sun. 11am-7pm

BOOKS
PENNYWISE BOOKS
Pacific Beach may seem an unlikely place for a great used bookstore, but what better time to grab an old paperback than on your way to relax on the sand? If it gets a little wet, no big deal; it only cost a few bucks. This used and trade books shop stocks sci-fi, fantasy, romance, suspense, Westerns, and all manner of nonfiction, most of it small enough for a big pocket. Just don't get so wrapped up in the plot that you forget to reapply sunscreen.

Map 5: 1331 Garnet Ave., Pacific Beach, 858/270-1640, www.pennywisebooks.info; Tues.-Sat. 10am-5pm

CLOTHING AND ACCESSORIES
THE BIKINI SHOPPE
This shop's not 100 percent stocked with bikinis, but you get the idea. Women in need of new beachwear can look here, whether one-piece, two-piece, cover-up, beach sandals, or hats.

Map 5: 728-A Ventura Pl., Mission Beach, 858/488-8967, www.sandiegobikinishoppe.com; daily 9am-9pm

CALIFORNIA SOCK COMPANY
You might never fully grasp how many different ways something so simple as a sock can manifest without a visit to this specialty shop. This unlikely beach neighborhood shop nevertheless remains very SoCal about socks, delving into novelty patterns you'd never expect, such as cereal box graphics, pop culture phenomenon, and avocados.

Map 5: 959 Garnet Ave., Pacific Beach, 858/876-2578, http://californiasockcompany.com; Mon.-Sat. 10am-9pm, Sun. 10am-8pm

THE FABULOUS RAG BOUTIQUE
What does style look like to the women of Pacific Beach? This popular boutique has plenty of it to show you. From cute and flirty dress-down looks like short shorts and off-the-shoulder tops to evening attire such as cocktail dresses and jumpsuits, the shop outfits local gals all day long.

Map 5: 829 Garnet Ave., Pacific Beach, 858/270-1993, www.thefabulousrag.com; Mon.-Sat. 10:30am-6:30pm, Sun. 11am-6:30pm

LEILANI'S ATTIC
San Diego isn't Hawaii, but the closer you get to the ocean, the more Hawaiian style seems suitable, and the more need there is for a shop like this. Leilani's furnishes all the floral print shirts and dresses you could want, plus beachwear, leis, and maybe a ukulele or two.

Map 5: 5105 Cass St., Pacific Beach, 619/246-1494, www.leilanisattic.com; Mon.-Sat. 9am-6pm, Sun. 9am-5pm

SOUTH COAST WAHINES

A shop "for girls who surf or just want to look like they do," this local beach outpost dedicated to *wahines* (Hawaiian for "a young female surfer") sells both functional and fashionable surf clothing, including beach gear with a feminine touch.

Map 5: 4500 Ocean Blvd., Pacific Beach, 858/273-7600, www.southcoast.com; Mon.-Fri. 10am-6pm, Sat. 9:30am-6pm, Sun. 10am-5:30pm

SUN DIEGO BOARDSHOP

Surfer style takes front and center at this spot, which also sells some surf and skate gear with plenty of stuff for women. But it's dudes who'll benefit the most from the jeans, T-shirts, flannels, shorts, and hoodies that make up the pre- and post-surf uniforms favored by local wave riders.

Map 5: 3126 Mission Blvd., 858/866-0108, www.sundiego.com; Sun.-Thurs. 10am-8pm, Fri.-Sat. 10am-9pm

OUTDOOR GEAR
PLAY IT AGAIN SPORTS

If you're looking for some fun and games to play with at the beach, drop by this shop selling new and used gear, including bikes, bodyboards, and other kid-size stuff as well as some possible bargains.

Map 5: 1401 Garnet Ave., Pacific Beach, 858/490-0222, www.playitagainsportssd.com; Mon.-Fri. 10am-8pm, Sat. 9am-7pm, Sun. 10:30am-6pm

SURF SHOPS
MISSION SURF

For more than 20 years, surfers have been trying out boards from this full-service surf shop, conveniently located near the pier at Pacific Beach. Pick up fresh wax and a surf report in the morning and maybe some new threads in the afternoon after returning one of many rental options.

Map 5: 4320 Mission Blvd., Pacific Beach, 858/483-8837, www.missionsurf.com; Sun.-Thurs. 10am-6pm, Fri.-Sat. 10am-7pm

Ocean Beach and Point Loma

Map 6

ANTIQUES AND VINTAGE
OCEAN BEACH ANTIQUE DISTRICT

Just a couple of blocks from the beach, Ocean Beach's main drag suddenly becomes an antique-lover's dream. A half dozen well-stocked shops offer unique assortments of vintage furniture and decorative treasures. Some are connected to local history and culture, accumulated over 100 years of San Diego's importance as a shipping gateway to points international. Check out **Vignettes** (4828 Newport Ave., 619/222-9244, www.vignettesantiques.com; Mon.-Sat. 10:30am-5pm, Sun. 11am-5pm) or **Ocean Beach Antique Mall** (4926 Newport Ave., 619/223-6170; Thurs.-Tues. 11am-5:30pm) for starters.

Map 6: Newport Ave. between Cable St. and Sunset Cliffs Blvd., Ocean Beach

BOOKS
BOOKSTAR

While Bookstar is technically a Barnes & Noble, you won't know it from the sign out front, which is built into the neon-emblazoned marquee of the Loma Theater. The single-screen art deco theater was built in 1944 and became a bookstore about in the late 1990s. The large, full-service store still feels like a vintage theater, with paisley rugs, swirls and patterns painted on the ceiling, some original art deco fixtures, and even the old movie screen. It makes browsing books feel adventurous.

Map 6: 3150 Rosecrans Pl., 619/225-0465, www.barnesandnoble.com; Mon.-Sat. 10am-8pm, Sun. 10am-7pm

GALACTIC COMICS

Every funky beachside community needs a comic book store. Galactic jibes pretty well with OB's out-there mentality; it's just a couple of laid-back guys into graphic arts and storytelling, offering comics, video games, and rental DVDs to a dedicated clientele.

Map 6: 4981 Newport Ave., Ocean Beach, 619/226-6543, www.galacticcomics.com; Tues.-Sun. 11am-8pm, Mon. 1pm-8pm

CLOTHING AND ACCESSORIES
MISS MATCH

Ocean Beach fashion brings together beachy styles and hippie chic, and so does this Newport Avenue boutique that offers contemporary looks that are smart and comfortable, offering plenty of appeal without being flashy.

Map 6: 4932 Newport Ave., Ocean Beach, 619/223-5500, www.missmatchsd.com; daily 10am-7pm

GIFT AND HOME
THE BLACK

A whiff of incense hits you the moment you walk through the doors of this OB mainstay, which has been selling countercultural goods more than four decades. Locals come here for everything from replacement guitar strings and harmonicas to beaded jewelry and smoking implements.

Map 6: 5017 Newport Ave., Ocean Beach, 619/222-5498, www.theblackoceanbeach. com; Mon.-Sat. 10am-8pm, Sun. 10am-7pm

ART AND DESIGN
LA JOLLA DESIGN DISTRICT
Close to the ocean, fashionable Girard Avenue caters to apparel, but past Kline Street it turns into a top-notch home and design district, with antiques, designer interiors, high-end furniture, and architectural boutiques. Visit **Design Studio West** (7422 Girard Ave., 858/454-9133, http://designstudiowest.com; Mon.-Fri. 9am-5pm, Sat. 10am-4pm) for big ideas or **Everett Stunz** (7547 Girard Ave., 858/459-3305, www.everettstunz.com; Mon.-Sat. 10am-6pm) for designer beds. These shops thrive here for a reason—each ranges from interesting to outstanding, offering an amazing resource for decorators and dreamers.

Map 7: Girard Ave. between Kline St. and Genter St.

PROSPECT STREET
Decorative art shoppers will find plenty to browse with a short stroll on the north end of Prospect Street, which might be entirely devoted to artisanal goods were it not for the occasional restaurant. Specialty shops like **Africa and Beyond** (1250 Prospect St., 858/454-9983, www.africaandbeyond.com; daily 10:30am-6pm) offer cultural craft objects; **National Geographic Fine Art Gallery** (1205 Prospect St., 619/568-6790, www.natgeofineart.com; Mon.-Wed. 10am-9pm, Thurs.-Sat. 10am-10pm, Sun. noon-8pm) focuses on nature photography; and **Legends Fine Art Gallery** (1205 Prospect St., 858/456-9900, www.legendsgallerylajolla.com; Mon.-Wed. 10am-8pm, Thurs. 10am-9pm, Fri.-Sat. 10am-10pm, Sun. 11am-7pm) features prints by Dr. Seuss, among others. Browse the area for a range of fine-art prints, photography, sculptures, and digital creations.

Map 7: Prospect St. between Herschel Ave. and Cave St.

BOOKS
D.G. WILLS BOOKS
Exactly the sort of dusty old bookshop that bibliophiles fear will become extinct, D.G. Wills is stacked to the ceiling with a mixture of old, new, and collectible volumes crammed together on wooden shelves. The store hosts readings with venerable authors and is home to the La Jolla Cultural Society.

Map 7: 7461 Girard Ave., 858/456-1800, www.dgwillsbooks.com; Mon.-Sat. 10am-7pm, Sun. 11am-5pm

WARWICK'S
The Warwick family has been selling books, stationery, and gifts since 1896. Four generations have run this place, which moved to its La Jolla location

Clockwise from top left: Pigment; Prospect Street; Bird's Surf Shed.

more than 75 years ago. It's a book-tour stop for many best-selling authors and a great place to supplement your vacation reading list.

Map 7: 7812 Girard Ave., 858/454-0347, www.warwicks.com; Mon.-Sat. 9am-6pm, Sun. 10am-5:30pm

CLOTHING AND ACCESSORIES

ASCOT SHOP

Any man who wants his wardrobe to be absolutely on point should step inside this independently owned shop that has provided top fashions from this location since 1950. Aside from a turn-of-the-21st-century redesign by the architect of the Coronado Bay Bridge, this upscale destination operates as it has for decades, outfitting men with the finest selection of dress and casual threads in town.

Map 7: 7750 Girard Ave., 858/454-4222, www.ascotshop.com; Mon.-Sat. 10am-6pm

BOWERS JEWELERS

A beautifully presented shop by anyone's standards, this family-owned jewelry and gift boutique has served La Jolla for nearly 70 years. Polished wood cases display both affordable and lavish settings, with gorgeous jewels that make for fine romantic gestures. Decorative *objets d'art* throughout the store qualify as great and unique gift ideas.

Map 7: 7860 Girard Ave., 858/459-3678, www.bowersjewelersoflajolla.com; Mon.-Sat. 9:30am-5:30pm, Sun. 11am-4pm

ECHOES TOO

After perusing the designer apparel lining the sidewalks of Girard Avenue, step a couple of blocks over to check out the discounted wares of this small consignment boutique. Any designer jeans in your size are bound to be a score, and there'll surely be enough dresses, blouses, and accessories to stoke the imagination.

Map 7: 7705 Fay Ave., 858/459-6588; Mon.-Fri. 11am-5pm, Sat. 10am-4pm

★ GIRARD AVENUE

Fashion boutiques come and go, and vary by season or taste. What remains constant is that Girard Avenue (east from Prospect Street) plays home to a wealth of trendy and designer women's clothing and accessories boutiques. This is a window shopper's dream, with internationally known retailers along the lines of **Ralph Lauren** (7830 Girard Ave., 858/459-0554; Mon.-Sat. 10am-6pm, Sun. noon-5pm) and **Kate Spade** (7931 Girard Ave., 858/454-2548; Mon.-Thurs. 10am-6pm, Fri.-Sat. 10am-7pm, Sun. 11am-5pm), exquisitely curated local boutiques like **Francesca's** (7886 Girard Ave., 858/729-0350; Mon.-Sat. 10am-8pm, Sun. 11am-7pm) and **La Donna** (937 Silverado St., 585/459-3410; Mon.-Sat. 10am-7pm, Sun. 11am-6pm), and national retailers like **Chico's** (7855 Girard Ave., 858/456-6273;

(7925 Girard Ave., 858/459-2565; Mon.-Thurs. 10am-7pm, Fri.-Sat. 10am-8pm, Sun. 11am-6pm).

Map 7: Girard Ave. between Prospect St. and Kline St.

JEWELS BY THE SEA

With estate, vintage, and fashion jewelry—including those of several local designers—the selection at this independently owned shop differs from most jewelry retailers, which is part of the charm. Pieces range greatly in price; walk away with a fashionably affordable scarf or an exotic gemstone gift.

Map 7: 1237 Prospect St., 858/459-5166, www.jewelsbythesea.biz; Mon. and Wed.-Sat. noon-6pm, Sun. 1pm-6pm

LE CHAUVINIST

"There exists a substantial difference between being in style and having style," states the owner of this men's clothing and accessories shop, which offers a mix of new and consignment fashions. Prepared to outfit a guy for a business meeting, a rock concert, or opening day at the Del Mar racetrack, the shop's selection ranges from socks and cufflinks to seersucker suits and Panama hats.

Map 7: 7709 Fay Ave., 858/456-0117, www.lechauvinist.com; Tues.-Fri. 11am-5pm, Sat. 10am-4pm, Sun. 9am-2pm

TAKE 2 LADIES CONSIGNMENT BOUTIQUE

South of La Jolla Village, near Windansea Beach and away from the heavy foot traffic of Girard Avenue and Prospect Street, this designer boutique carries the rarely worn attire of local fashionistas who need to make room for next season's looks. It's an excellent place to find attire bearing the instantly recognizable names of the world's best-known designers, without the world's biggest price tags. Clothes this fine rarely go out of fashion; they merely stop being new.

Map 7: 6786 La Jolla Blvd., 858/459-0095, www.take2ladiesconsignor.com; Mon.-Fri. 11am-6:30pm, Sat. 11am-5pm

KIDS AND PETS
GEPPETTO'S

Consider this as much a warning to young parents as a recommendation: This fabulous local shop looks amazing and will lure your children from the sidewalk. You'll follow, too, because its unique toy selection is tough to beat. The prices aren't, however, so be prepared to dash your child's dreams or break out your wallet.

Map 7: 7850 Girard Ave., 858/456-4441, www.geppettotoys.com; Mon.-Sat. 9am-7pm, Sun. 10am-6pm

SHOPS
LA JOLLA

MUTTROPOLIS

This small Southern California chain has a full-service online shop, so you can get a pretty good idea what type of pampering pet products it offers for dogs and cats. But shopping is always more fun in person. This colorful, organized space presents tasteful leashes and collars, designer pet carriers, and food dishes representative of the La Jolla lifestyle.

Map 7: 7755 Girard Ave., 858/459-9663, www.muttropolis.com; Mon.-Fri. 10am-7pm, Sat. 10am-6pm, Sun. 10am-5pm

SPOILED ROTTEN BOUTIQUE

How do the upscale tots dress in a ritzy place like La Jolla? Find the answer in this children's boutique, which sells dapper duds and designer items of impossible cuteness. Show up at a baby shower with something from this shop and you win.

Map 7: 7556 Fay Ave., Ste. C, 858/459-1904, www.spoiledrottensd.com; Mon.-Sat. 10am-4:30pm

SHOPPING MALLS
WESTFIELD UTC

Possibly the best mall in town, UTC (a.k.a. University Towne Centre) includes upscale cineplex ArcLight, the best local food chain (Tender Greens), and all the relevant department stores (Macy's, Nordstrom) and mall franchises you'd expect, plus a number of stores you might have thought too highbrow to be seen within reach of a food court.

Map 7: 4545 La Jolla Village Dr., 858/546-8858, www.westfield.com/utc; Mon.-Sat. 10am-9pm, Sun. 11am-7pm

SURF SHOPS
MITCH'S SURF SHOP

La Jolla's go-to surf shop since the late 1960s, Mitch's sells great longboards, shortboards, paddleboards, wetsuits, and other beach gear for those inspired by the azure waters off the coast. Think of it as an important first stop in the pursuit of an endless summer.

Map 7: 631 Pearl St., 858/459-5933, www.mitchssurfshop.com; daily 10am-6:45pm

BOOKS
BAY BOOKS

Independently owned on Orange Avenue since 1991, this well-stocked local favorite carries current titles and magazines, as well as a deep inventory of must-read books. Various staff and regular customers have placed handwritten recommendations around the shop, calling attention to titles they've discovered and enjoyed through the years.

Map 8: 1029 Orange Ave., 619/435-0070, www.baybookscoronado.com; Mon.-Sat. 9am-7pm, Sun. 9am-6pm

SHOPPING MALLS
FERRY LANDING MARKETPLACE

Where the ferry lands in Coronado, a small circle of shops and restaurants has developed, including gift shops like the Paris-inspired **French Room** (619/437-4325), a branch of OB women's boutique **Miss Match** (619/435-5550, www.missmatchsd.com), and its men's fashions sister shop **Men's Mojo** (619/435-5552, www.mensmojosd.com).

Map 8: 1201 1st St., 619/435-8895, www.coronadoferrylandingshops.com; daily 10am-9pm

★ ORANGE AVENUE

Orange Avenue serves as Coronado's main drag. In the southwest corner of the island, near the Hotel del Coronado, it's home to a bevy of restaurants, gift shops, and boutiques. Most shops sell swimwear, housewares, funny T-shirts, or kitschy beach-themed souvenirs. There are few you'd go out of your way to visit, but Orange Avenue is a nice stroll.

Map 8: Orange Ave. between 8th St. and Dana Pl.

SHOPS AT THE DEL

A left turn from the lobby leads down to a small mall of shops within the Hotel del Coronado. Offerings include resort boutiques, travel goods, bath and body items, photography services, and designer sunglasses.

Map 8: 1500 Orange Ave., 619/435-6611, www.hoteldel.com; daily 8am-9pm, individual shop hours vary

SHOPS
CORONADO

GOURMET TREATS
CATALINA OFFSHORE PRODUCTS

San Diego has enough fresh seafood restaurants in town that going out of the way to pick up your own fish hardly seems worthwhile. And yet people do—this fish market is that good. Shop for local oysters, fillets of the best fish in season, and wild-caught Mexican shrimp, or crack open a sea urchin for some fresh *uni* and taste the ocean.

Map 9: 5202 Lovelock St., Morena, 619/297-9797, www.catalinaop.com; Wed.-Sun. 8am-5pm, Mon.-Tues. 8am-3pm

SIESEL'S OLD FASHIONED MEATS

To pick up a fine cut of meat, make this gourmet market your only stop. Prime and choice cuts are available at the butcher's counter (take a number), along with some of the best sausages in town. They always have a few surprises in stock, whether the exquisitely marbled Wagyu beef or pheasant. A freezer near the back wall contains an unheard-of variety of game meats, and the deli counter is nearly as good.

Map 9: 4131 Ashton St., Morena, 619/275-1234, www.bestmeatssandiego.com; Mon.-Sat. 9am-7pm, Sun. 10am-6pm

OUTDOOR GEAR
ADVENTURE 16

Hiking, camping, rock climbing—when San Diegans need outdoor gear, they stop by this local retail alternative to REI. It's staffed by outdoors enthusiasts who will be able to guide you to some great trails and secret spots if you ask.

Map 9: 4620 Alvarado Canyon Rd., Alvarado Canyon, 619/283-2374, www.adventure16.com; Mon.-Fri. 10am-8pm, Sat. 10am-6pm, Sun. 11am-5pm

SHOPPING MALLS
FASHION VALLEY

Not terribly far from Westfield Mission Valley (see below) is this similar though slightly higher-end mall with a movie theater complex, food court, shops, and the Nordstrom, Neiman Marcus, and Bloomingdale's department stores. Fashion Valley tends to be a little more high-concept and trending, and therefore more likely to be crowded. It's also accessible on the trolley line.

Map 9: 7007 Friars Rd., Fashion Valley, 619/688-9113, www.shopfashionvalley.com; Mon.-Sat. 10am-9pm, Sun. 11am-7pm

WESTFIELD MISSION VALLEY

Westfield Mission Valley is conveniently located, with loads of parking, a movie theater complex, and department stores such as Target as well as a number of places for cheap eats.

Map 9: 1640 Camino Del Rio N., Mission Valley, 619/296-6375, www.westfield.com/missionvalley; Mon.-Sat. 10am-9pm, Sun. 11am-6pm

SURF SHOPS

★ BIRD'S SURF SHED

The only true must-visit surf shop in town isn't found in a beach neighborhood. The Shed (really a Quonset hut) is a bit of a local legend, and often the site of celebrity surfer clinics, movie premieres, and the epic recounting of burly sessions after big swells hit. The huge selection of boards includes vintage models and custom rarities, and a devout wave rider can get lost for hours just soaking it all in.

Map 9: 1091 W. Morena Blvd., Morena, 619/276-2473, www.birdssurfshed.com; Mon.-Sat. 10am-6:30pm, Sun. 11am-5pm

Hotels

PRICE KEY

$ Less than $100 per night

$$ $100–200 per night

$$$ More than $200 per night

*S*an Diego is a sprawling city, with a mix of neighborhoods and attractions. Hotels spring up mostly around the areas where people visit most—downtown and the beach neighborhoods—with the exception of Balboa Park and Old Town, which would have to sacrifice charm for lodging.

Most hotels are pretty standard, with virtually every national chain represented, along with motels and budget inns. There are a few resorts around the beach areas, plus some hip boutique hotels and backpacker hostels. Mission Valley is home to most of the larger chain hotels, with rates more affordable than those downtown, but you'll need a car to see anything other than the I-8 freeway.

Picking a hotel for its location always makes sense, but in truth this is the kind of city where you may have breakfast in one neighborhood, lie on the beach in another, visit a museum across town, and then get dinner in the opposite direction before returning to your home base for drinks. In other words, where you stay may have more to do with where you want to be when you call it a night or what you want the first thing you see to be when you wake up in the morning.

CHOOSING A HOTEL

There is no shortage of hotel rooms in San Diego—unless the unbelievably popular Comic Con is taking place, in which case rooms fill up well in advance and rates triple. But aside from that one long weekend in July, you should have your pick of locations to lay your head at night. Deciding where is all about where you want to go and how you want to get around.

Previous: the famous Hotel del Coronado; cabanas at the Bahia Resort Hotel in Mission Bay.

Look for ★ to find
recommended hotels

Highlights

★ **Best Value:** Little Italy's **La Pensione Hotel** offers good, clean rooms on the cheap, some with harbor views. The neighborhood is within walking distance of the Gaslamp, great restaurants, the bay, and the trolley (page 224).

★ **Best Apartment-Style Hotel:** Beautiful Craftsman-style rooms with private kitchens and updated amenities make **Mudville Flats** in the East Village a satisfying place to return to at night (page 224).

★ **Best Hotel in a Non-Touristy Area:** A stay at North Park's well-appointed **Lafayette Hotel** allows a little respite from the heavily trafficked tourist areas that can wear you down during the day, but it's still close to some great evening entertainment (page 228).

★ **Best Beach Hotel for Adults:** A boutique hotel on the beach in a lively area, Pacific Beach's **Tower23 Hotel** is convenient to Mission Bay, Mission Beach, and the seemingly endless nightlife of Garnet Avenue. It even has its own hip restaurant and bar (page 230).

★ **Best Golf Resort: The Lodge at Torrey Pines** is hallowed ground—overlooking the ocean and close to the sights and shopping of La Jolla. Plus your stay earns you preferred tee times (page 235).

★ **Best Hotel You Never Need to Leave:** If you're just looking to unpack your bags and enjoy going nowhere for a few days, head to the legendary **Hotel del Coronado,** where you can eat, drink, shop, play by the pool, and enjoy a perfect beach in an idyllic setting. It's like vacationing in another era (page 236).

If you've got a car, quick freeway access will be easy but parking will not. Hotels in the downtown area typically charge $15-35 per night for parking on top of their room rates, and you won't be able to get around that by finding street parking unless you get really lucky, repeatedly. That said, if you plan to spend a lot of time around downtown—going to a ballgame in East Village, nightclubs in the Gaslamp, and harbor-front museums in the Marina District—having hotel parking can be a real plus, as you can explore other areas where spaces are easier to come by yet always have a spot waiting for you back at your place. Little Italy may be a few steps removed from these neighborhoods, but it's easy to get in and out, and rates are still low considering how hip the neighborhood has become and how great the restaurants are.

Decent walking neighborhoods like North Park, Hillcrest, and Mission Hills offer little choice of accommodations. In Mission Valley, a short freeway drive from these areas, there's a street called Hotel Circle, which features more than a dozen hotels alongside the east-west I-8. The easy freeway access of these establishments is undisputable, but other than a few sprawling malls, there's little to see and do within walking distance, and with few exceptions, these rooms are the kind you leave early in the morning and return to only to sleep at night.

Of course, everybody at some point wants to stay by the beach, and most of the beach communities can accommodate, in many cases right on the sand—although you'll find better values going even a block or two inland. If you score a Mission Bay-front hotel, you may even benefit from water-sports lessons and rentals right outside your door. While it's easy to spend entire sunny days on foot in the right beach area and never once regret it, none of them are really that easy to get to without a vehicle.

Downtown Map 1

THE BRISTOL HOTEL $$

A 2017 $7 million renovation updated this long-struggling hotel with modern in-room amenities and midcentury decor worthy of its terrific location. Walking distance from the Gaslamp Quarter, Marina District, and Little Italy, The Bristol may not offer the best accommodations in the immediate vicinity, but the now-1960s-themed hotel offers a more affordable stay than neighboring properties, with a touch of style; a few rooms are outfitted with record players and '60s pop vinyl.

Map 1: 1055 1st Ave., 619/232-6141, www.thebristolsandiego.com

GASLAMP PLAZA SUITES $$

Occupying San Diego's first skyscraper, this tidy, friendly hotel and time-share offers 64 rooms, each named for a famous author. While a stay in the Dr. Seuss room might sound special, the decor is fairly standard through-out. The building's 1913 charm shines through at every turn, whether in

Where to Stay for...

San Diego's beaches have different personalities, so choosing a beach hotel begins with finding the personality that suits you.

· **...That SoCal Beach Life:** A little secret about San Diego beach residents is that most of them rarely leave their neighborhoods unless they have to. Spend time in one of the city's self-contained beach communities and you'll see why. Aim for **Pacific Beach** if you're interested in sunny beach days, athletic pursuits, and finishing the night with drinks. Look a little farther south to **Mission Beach** if you're traveling with children and wish to enjoy its long boardwalk and bay beaches. If you enjoy a little funky counterculture with your beach activities, there's only one place to be: among the crusty soul-searchers of **Ocean Beach**.

· **...An Urban Experience:** San Diego's downtown area plays home to its most lively nightlife, some of its most active theaters, and its hottest dining scene. A number of hotels between the **Gaslamp Quarter** and **Marina District** offer quick access to the areas' respective tourist destinations and nightlife, while **Little Italy** is a perfect choice if you're interested in walking to the city's best restaurants.

· **...An Elegant Stay:** Although one of the most upscale communities on the West Coast, **La Jolla** is surprisingly accessible to vacationers and even includes a few hotels to accommodate modest budgets. Pretty beaches, the Torrey Pines nature reserve, and the central La Jolla Cove keep nature close at hand; however, the main draws are upscale dining, luxurious hotel stays, spa treatments, and high-end shopping. To vacation like a one-percenter, stay in La Jolla.

· **...History and Culture:** While Old Town represents the historic birthplace of San Diego, Balboa Park is its unquestioned cultural heart. To

marble, brass, mosaic, or carved wood. A comfortable 11th-floor roof deck offers a view of San Diego only a high-rise could provide.
Map 1: 520 E St., Gaslamp, 619/232-9500, www.gaslampplaza.com

HORTON GRAND HOTEL $$$

Originally built as two separate hotels during the 1880s, the architecture of this beautifully appointed boutique hotel leaves a fine impression. The two buildings connect to form a graceful, shady courtyard. No two rooms are alike, though a number do offer a lovely courtyard balcony.
Map 1: 311 Island Ave., Gaslamp, 619/544-1886, www.hortongrand.com

HOSTELLING INTERNATIONAL SAN DIEGO, DOWNTOWN $

This central Gaslamp hostel offers 60 dorm beds, 38 private rooms, and a fully equipped shared kitchen, providing clean accommodations at bargain prices. A no-alcohol policy keeps the place quiet, and reading and TV

North Park's hip Lafayette Hotel

spend time accessing its museums, performances, architecture, gardens, and zoo, stay in one of the uptown communities surrounding it. They offer limited lodging options, but **North Park** has copious restaurants, nightlife, and craft beer options and is a preferred hangout among local creative types. Sitting along the park's western border, the relatively quiet **Bankers Hill** is walking distance from the park's center, better suited to those avoiding the action.

· **...An Escape:** Though it technically sits at the northern tip of a very skinny peninsula, **Coronado** often calls itself Crown Island, and it can definitely feel removed from the real world in the way only a resort island can. It's a fine place to rent bikes and beach gear and organize occasional bouts of eating and activity around your busy relaxation schedule.

HOTELS
DOWNTOWN

lounges offer a nice respite from exploring the dozens of bars, clubs, and restaurants within a five-block radius.

Map 1: 521 Market St., Gaslamp, 619/525-1531, www.sandiegohostels.org

HOTEL INDIGO SAN DIEGO $$

Overlooking Petco Park, this pet-friendly, LEED-certified hotel isn't just an environmentally friendly place to bring your dog and catch a ballgame. It's also centrally located to explore downtown or just to relax on the rooftop lounge. Prices vary with a range of sleeping and view options, including rooms with a clear view of the Padres at work.

Map 1: 509 9th Ave., East Village, 619/727-4000, www.hotelinsd.com

HOTEL REPUBLIC $$

Refurbished in 2017, this clean, contemporary hotel property is ideally situated for travelers visiting San Diego without a car. It sits two short blocks from downtown's Santa Fe Depot train station and trolley stop, and it's a 10-minute walk from Little Italy, the Marina District, and the Gaslamp Quarter. The property features a casual on-site restaurant and roof-deck bar, and each of its elegantly simple rooms welcomes guests to the SoCal lifestyle by making yoga mats available.

Map 1: 421 W. B St., 619/398-3100, www.hotelrepublicsd.com

★ LA PENSIONE HOTEL ❸❸

A central Little Italy location gives this clean and simple hotel a leg up, whether or not you opt for a room with a harbor view. A trolley stop is a couple of blocks away, and a short walk gets you to the USS *Midway* Museum and Maritime Museum of San Diego, not to mention all the great restaurants in the neighborhood, starting with a pizza place and café in the shared courtyard. Biggest drawback? Limited daily parking on a first-come basis.

Map 1: 606 W. Date St., Little Italy, 619/236-8000, www.lapensionehotel.com

MANCHESTER GRAND HYATT ❸❸❸

Steps from the marina, Seaport Village, San Diego Convention Center, and USS *Midway* Museum, the dual high-rises of this bayfront hotel overlook downtown. The large rooftop pool and cabanas are a favorite of the celebrities working Comic Con each July, and the luster seems to hold most of the year. Other rooftops feature tennis, basketball, and volleyball courts, and a separate lap pool. The business-friendly place has an excellent hotel bar, the penthouse Top of the Hyatt, known for panoramic views and a mostly sophisticated clientele.

Map 1: 1 Market Pl., 619/232-1234, www.manchestergrand.hyatt.com

★ MUDVILLE FLATS ❸❸

Experience the quaint appeal of San Diego's gorgeous Craftsman homes by renting one of the fully furnished apartments of this 1905 boutique hotel. Rooms feature the built-in shelves and wood detailing that make Craftsmans so appealing, plus private kitchens and one amenity few of those cottages can claim: air-conditioning.

Map 1: 747 10th Ave., East Village, 619/232-4045, www.mudvilleflats.com

OMNI SAN DIEGO HOTEL ❸❸❸

Best known for having a sky bridge granting direct access to Petco Park, this luxury high-rise hotel has some rooms that actually overlook the field along the third-base line, so having a ticket to the game or concert may not even be necessary. A spacious rooftop terrace with pool offers views of the Coronado Bridge and the convention center across the street. The lively Gaslamp is out the front door, the edgier East Village is nearby, and a trolley stop is even closer than home plate.

Map 1: 675 L St., East Village, 619/231-6664, www.omnihotels.com

Top: two hundred year old buildings combine to form the Horton Grand. Bottom: the lavish lobby of the U.S. Grant Hotel.

PENDRY SAN DIEGO $$$

This ambitious boutique property in the center of the Gaslamp has a large urban hotel feel to it, courtesy of its many chic venues. It's equipped with both upscale and casual restaurants, a cocktail bar, an exclusive nightclub, and an expansive beer hall featuring plenty of local craft beverages—plus a spa and rooftop pool deck. Everything's dressed with incredible attention to style, so that each pristinely comfortable guest room seems a relaxing escape.

Map 1: 550 J St., Gaslamp, 619/738-7000, www.pendryhotels.com

PORTO VISTA HOTEL $$

This pet-friendly urban boutique hotel with a rooftop deck offers a variety of options at reasonable rates. The on-site restaurant has a nice view of the harbor, which some rooms also share. It's in a great neighborhood with quick trolley and freeway access.

Map 1: 1835 Columbia St., Little Italy, 619/544-0164, www.portovistasd.com

SOLAMAR HOTEL $$$

Situated just between the Gaslamp Quarter and the East Village, this stylish, modern hotel sits right in the middle of the action, whether you're going to a game at Petco Park, attending an event at the convention center, or hitting the local nightlife. The hotel has a comfortable and hip rooftop pool and lounge, along with an excellent restaurant, J Six. The hotel hosts a complimentary happy hour (daily 5pm-6pm), serving local wine and beer. Pet-friendly and allergy-free rooms are available.

Map 1: 435 6th Ave., Gaslamp, 619/819-9500, www.hotelsolamar.com

URBAN BOUTIQUE HOTEL $$

This independently owned boutique lodging, renovated in 2017, doesn't stand out or thrill, but neither does it disappoint. Affordability, location, and a dog-friendly first floor warrant consideration for those looking to stay within Little Italy and who don't mind parking in a nearby pay lot. It's a quick walk to a trolley stop, the Maritime Museum, and Waterfront Park, in a neighborhood with great, walkable streets, bars, and restaurants.

Map 1: 1654 Columbia St., Little Italy, 619/232-3400, www.urbanboutiquehotel.com

U. S. GRANT HOTEL $$

Built by the family of the 18th president and named in his honor, the U. S. Grant opened in 1910 with much pomp. This classic century-old hotel offers a grand entrance: An elegant lobby presents marble floors and silk carpets, with high ceilings furnished with crystal chandeliers. A 2006 restoration renewed glamour to the place, with 47 luxurious suites. Standard rooms go for reasonable rates, considering the style and location, though pricey parking ($40 per day) can eat into that.

Map 1: 326 Broadway, 619/232-3121, www.usgrant.com

THE WESTGATE HOTEL $$

Old European elegance is on display at this central Gaslamp hotel. The lobby features vintage furniture, a curved staircase, and a grand piano; on weekends a high tea comes complete with a harpist. A third-floor roof deck adds an outdoor lounge, a swimming pool, and even a small running track—all benefit from the views of downtown and the harbor. Good-sized comfortable rooms figure nicely into the continental motif, and many share a private foyer with the room next door, which is great for groups booking rooms together.

Map 1: 1055 2nd Ave., Gaslamp, 619/238-1818, www.westgatehotel.com

Balboa Park

Map 2

INN AT THE PARK $$

Across the street from Balboa Park and within walking distance of Hillcrest restaurants and nightlife, this all-suite historic 1926 hotel property in Bankers Hill offers 82 suites ranging from studios to two bedrooms. With high ceilings, Sealy Posturepedic mattresses, and fully stocked kitchens, the spacious, classically tasteful rooms feel like home, even while adhering to the vintage building's original apartment-building layout.

Map 2: 525 Spruce St., Bankers Hill, 619/291-0999, www.shellhospitality.com/Inn-at-the-Park

KEATING HOUSE $$

With only nine rooms within this 19th-century Victorian mansion, each has its own peculiar charm—and private bath. The romantic and affordable bed-and-breakfast stands a mere four blocks from the western edge of Balboa Park in a quiet part of Bankers Hill. Aside from a little gold-leafing, the home's colorfully painted exterior and interior adhere to its original 1888 palette. A full breakfast is made from scratch each morning, using mostly natural and organic ingredients. Room prices remain constant year-round.

Map 2: 2331 2nd Ave., Bankers Hill, 619/239-8585, www.keatinghouse.com

ITH ZOO HOSTEL SAN DIEGO $

A game lounge, library, and sheltered courtyard add to the community vibe of this hostel near Balboa Park, and it's bolstered by daily—and nightly—organized activities geared toward sharing a few of the fun outings available to young adults in San Diego. Dorm bed counts range 2-6 per room, including all-female options.

Map 3: 3751 6th Ave., Hillcrest, 619/955-7723, http://ithhostels.com/san-diego-zoo-hostel

★ LAFAYETTE HOTEL $$

North Park has emerged as one of San Diego's hippest neighborhoods, but the Lafayette was here long before it was cool. When it first opened in 1946, it was a popular destination for celebrities and jet-setters. Amid the recent resurgence, this historic hotel has been redesigned to bring its amenities up to par with its vintage charm. Contemporary decor and comfortable beds make all the bungalows and suites desirable—but especially those sitting poolside. Today, the Lafayette can be quite the scene, hosting pool parties in the summer, with occasional live music events during holiday weekends. Within a few blocks are North Park, Hillcrest, Normal Heights, and University Heights restaurants and bars.

Map 3: 2223 El Cajon Blvd., North Park, 619/296-2101, www.lafayettehotelsd.com

Old Town and Mission Hills Map 4

COSMOPOLITAN HOTEL $$

To get into the spirit of Old Town, reserve one of the 10 guest rooms in this 19th-century hotel located within the historical park. Rooms are outfitted with furnishings from the era, such as claw-foot tubs, with views of San Diego's original city center. Guests should pose for a photograph in the hotel's vintage saloon.

Map 4: 2660 Calhoun St., Old Town, 619/297-1874, www.oldtowncosmopolitan.com

WESTERN INN OLD TOWN $

Don't expect the moon at this budget-friendly hotel. Do expect clean, conscientious lodging within a couple blocks of historic Old Town. What it may lack in character it makes up for with accessibility—the hotel offers instant freeway access, and a 10-minute walk gets you to the **Old Town Transit Center** (4005 Taylor St.), where bus and trolley lines routinely depart for beach towns, downtown, and to the border of Mexico.

Map 4: 3889 Arista St., Old Town, 619/298-6888, www.westerninn.com

BAHIA RESORT HOTEL $$

Just a short distance from Belmont Park, the Bahia fronts Mission Bay, offering a laid-back bit of beachfront in contrast to the lively boardwalk and amusement park scene. Both the price point and the calm waters of the bay suit families with young children, and the resort offers some mellow activities, including a steamboat ride to the Catamaran, its sister resort across the bay.

Map 5: 998 W. Mission Bay Dr., Mission Bay, 858/488-0551, www.bahiahotel.com

BANANA BUNGALOW $

Located in the center of the action with a community patio overlooking the rowdy PB boardwalk, Banana Bungalow hostel offers coed dorms or private rooms, each with a bath, plus beach rentals and 24-hour access. Nobody ever recommends a youth hostel based on its rooms, but if you're going the low-budget backpacker route, you'll never get closer to the sand than this.

Map 5: 707 Reed Ave., Pacific Beach, 858/412-5878, www.bananabungalowsandiego. com

CATAMARAN RESORT HOTEL AND SPA $$$

Inspired by a trip to Hawaii, the Catamaran captures a tropical resort atmosphere with leafy plants, colorful birds, and twice-weekly luaus along its bayside beach. Water activities are available on the placid bay, and a short walk across Mission Boulevard takes you to the Pacific side of the peninsula.

Map 5: 3999 Mission Blvd., Pacific Beach, 858/488-1081, www.catamaranresort.com

CRYSTAL PIER HOTEL $$

How central to Pacific Beach do you want to be? Crystal Pier juts right out from the center of PB, and these historic, moderately appointed guest cottages sit right on top of the pier itself. Cottages feature kitchenettes and decks, with prime views of the surfers and beach life below.

Map 5: 4500 Ocean Blvd., Pacific Beach, 800/748-5894, www.crystalpier.com

PACIFIC TERRACE HOTEL $$$

The 73 rooms at this beachfront hotel aim for a "Tommy Bahama" vibe, which suits the vacation feel offered by playful surrounding Pacific Beach. The hotel lies on the northern, quieter end of the beach, and most of the rooms have at least a partial view of the water. A light breakfast is served around the small pool each morning. The many bars and restaurants within walking distance provide nourishment and entertainment.

Map 5: 610 Diamond St., Pacific Beach, 858/581-3500, www.pacificterrace.com

PARADISE POINT RESORT & SPA ⑤⑤⑤

Many of the comfortable rooms in this bayfront resort look right out at Mission Bay. Guests can rent equipment from the on-site water-sports company or take advantage of the miniature golf, basketball, tennis, croquet, bocce, and Ping-Pong on offer. The spacious property is peppered with myriad water features, including ponds, fountains, and swimming pools. Calm, shallow beaches surround most of the hotel, with bonfire pits for relaxing evenings.

Map 5: 1404 Vacation Rd., Mission Bay, 858/274-4630, www.paradisepoint.com

SURFER BEACH HOTEL ⑤⑤

It's tough to find fault with this moderately priced, pet-friendly boutique hotel right on the boardwalk at Pacific Beach. Standard rooms feature king or double beds, some with balconies. Amenities include on-site parking ($15) and a heated pool. Access to the surf is almost immediate, and the nightlife of PB is a just a few minutes' walk.

Map 5: 711 Pacific Beach Dr., Pacific Beach, 858/483-7070, www.surferbeachhotel.com

★ TOWER23 HOTEL ⑤⑤⑤

A Tempur-Pedic mattress in every room ensures this designer boutique hotel remains the most comfortable place to sleep in Pacific Beach. Its location fronting the boardwalk gives you plenty to do and see to earn that sleep. Guests may enjoy the view from their balconies or the shared rooftop deck, or step onto the beach from the hotel's well-appointed JRDN restaurant and bar. With surf lockers available and beach and bike rentals on-site, it's a chic home base for a beachy stay in this lively part of town.

Map 5: 723 Felspar St., Pacific Beach, 858/270-2323, www.t23hotel.com

Ocean Beach and Point Loma

Map 6

HUMPHREYS HALF MOON INN ⑤⑤⑤

This tropical, bayfront hotel offers a unique set of views. In the distance is the San Diego skyline; look a little closer to admire the San Diego Yacht Club boats moored just outside. But the real views are of the city's best summer concert venue. The intimate outdoor stage sits right on the water and attracts some of the world's most celebrated musicians and comedians. Room packages may be paired with front-and-center seating, and some suites open up to a balcony with the best view in the house. Regardless of whether there's a show scheduled, this is one of the most enjoyable hotels in the city.

Map 6: 2303 Shelter Island Dr., Shelter Island, 619/224-3411, www.halfmooninn.com

THE INN AT SUNSET CLIFFS $$$

If you like the idea of chillin' poolside on a cliff overlooking the Pacific, check out this cozy midcentury gem. It's almost impossible to sleep closer to the ocean than this, whether you opt for a simple individual room or a decked-out hot-tub suite. The soothing sound of breaking waves more than makes up for the hotel's only flaw—it's a good 10-minute drive from the nearest freeway, but it's an optimal choice if you plan to relax in the area.

Map 6: 1370 Sunset Cliffs Blvd., 619/222-7901, www.innatsunsetcliffs.com

OCEAN BEACH HOTEL $$

Mixed reviews about the condition of some of the rooms occasionally tarnish this hotel's reputation, but that kind of fits the OB zeitgeist—ask to inspect available rooms at check-in. Its location cannot be beat—smack on the corner of action-packed Newport Avenue, right where it hits the sand. Modest pet-friendly rooms, sweet ocean views, and proximity to the lively world of Ocean Beach will keep you living like a local: up late, rowdy, and never wanting to leave the neighborhood.

Map 6: 5080 Newport Ave., Ocean Beach, 619/223-7191, www.obhotel.com

USA HOSTELS OCEAN BEACH $

Backpackers and world travelers are just as woven into the fabric of OB as surfers and Volkswagen buses blasting "Hotel California" from their cassette players. This place is like a Hostel California, where a constant flow of curious young people gather, regardless of language, to sleep in bunk beds and embrace the countercultural SoCal beach lifestyle. Adventurers tend to find an engaging temporary home here.

Map 6: 4961 Newport Ave., Ocean Beach, 619/223-7873, www.usahostels.com

THE PEARL $$

Believe it or not, there's a hip place to stay in Point Loma that doesn't command a harbor view. The Pearl is central to Shelter Island but makes its mark through stylish decorating at modest rates and the sort of local-friendly hotel scene that makes dinner in the courtyard worth dressing for. In summer, the hotel hosts movie screenings, projecting cult and comedy classics on a blank wall over the swimming pool. It's a surprisingly fun way to watch a movie, and smiling crowds of savvy locals attending couldn't agree more.

Map 6: 1410 Rosecrans St., Point Loma, 619/226-6100, www.thepearlsd.com

Clockwise from top left: Tower23 Hotel; Cosmopolitan Hotel; Crystal Pier Hotel.

THE BED & BREAKFAST INN AT LA JOLLA $$

To feel at home in La Jolla, stay in one of the 13 distinctive rooms or two suites of this gourmet and wonderfully situated bed-and-breakfast. Amenities add a sense of warmth: Laptop desks and down pillows are available, and there's complimentary wine and cheese at sunset. The quiet location, just steps from the beach and village center, will seem ideal after a day in the middle of the action.

Map 7: 7753 Draper Ave., La Jolla Village, 858/456-2066, www.sandiegolajollabnb.com

HOTEL LA JOLLA $$

This high-rise hotel sits a 10-minute walk from the beach at La Jolla Shores and a short drive down the hill from La Jolla Village. While this doesn't make it incredibly convenient to either location, it does make it a much easier process for getting in and out of the La Jolla area and back to the freeway. You can sense the design in the comfortable, contemporary decor of the rooms and public areas of the hotel, including the great **Cusp Dining & Drinks** restaurant and bar, which, like many rooms on the upper floors, commands a terrific ocean view.

Map 7: 7955 La Jolla Shores Dr., La Jolla Shores, 858/551-3600, www.hotellajolla.com

LA JOLLA BEACH & TENNIS CLUB $$$

Instant beach access—along with tennis courts—makes this gated La Jolla Shores resort a pretty cushy vacation destination. It's the kind of place that comps beach chairs and umbrellas, lets you upgrade to a cabana, and even go so far as to outfit and cater a beach barbecue (for a fee). Plenty of kids' activities allow more time for Mom and Dad to play or relax or catch an elegant meal at one of the highly rated hotel restaurants, including the vaunted **Marine Room.** To make the most of the property's private beach, aim for a beachfront deluxe suite or cottage.

Map 7: 2000 Spindrift Dr., La Jolla Shores, 858/454-7126, www.ljbtc.com

LA JOLLA COVE SUITES $$

Specializing in oceanview suites, this resort hotel offers some reasonable rates considering the rooftop deck, heated swimming pool, and other amenities. Grab one of the few single rooms without a view for a really good deal, but you might be cranky when you realize what you're missing: a chance for balcony views of Scripps Park and the ocean off La Jolla Cove.

Map 7: 1155 Coast Blvd., La Jolla Village, 858/459-2621, www.lajollacove.com

LA JOLLA RIVIERA INN $$

A few blocks from the beach at La Jolla Shores, this small apartment building-turned-suite hotel offers a reasonable option for families looking

Top: The Lodge at Torrey Pines. Bottom: La Jolla Cove Suites.

to keep costs down. Homey dwellings include full kitchens, dining areas, and living rooms with foldout couches, plus access to a small heated pool.

Map 7: 2031 Paseo Dorado, La Jolla Shores, 858/224-7600, www.lajollarivierainn.com

LA JOLLA SHORES HOTEL $$

The best thing about this hotel is its location—right on La Jolla Shores, one of the best family beaches in San Diego. Guest rooms come with patios or balconies, and an on-site restaurant hosts a Sunday brunch buffet. With a pool, Ping-Pong tables, and plenty of beach activities on hand, there's little chance of getting bored. A courtesy shuttle can whisk you into downtown La Jolla when you're ready to shop or dine.

Map 7: 8110 Camino Del Oro, La Jolla Shores, 858/923-8058, www.ljshoreshotel.com

LA JOLLA VILLAGE LODGE $$

A lot changes if you move a few blocks east of La Jolla Cove—at least the hotel rates do. This pet-friendly spot won't win any design awards; it doesn't have a pool, and there are no luxury suites. However, complimentary parking and affordable rates make it feel like a steal this close to the action.

Map 7: 1141 Silverado St., La Jolla Village, 858/551-2001, http://lajollabythesea.com

LA VALENCIA HOTEL $$$

With a central location in downtown La Jolla, this high-end hotel overlooks the lovely Scripps seaside park on one side and the many shops, galleries, and restaurants of Prospect Street on the other. The Spanish Colonial beauty was built in 1926, but 2015 updates ensure its guests experience contemporary comforts, whether from an oceanview or garden-view room. A terraced layout keeps the entire property open to sunlight and ocean air, lending a Mediterranean feel that's tough to improve upon.

Map 7: 1132 Prospect St., La Jolla Village, 858/454-0771, www.lavalencia.com

★ THE LODGE AT TORREY PINES $$$

Sitting on the 18th hole of the famous Torrey Pines Golf Course atop cliffs overlooking the Pacific, this beautifully designed Arts and Crafts hotel offers a wealth of amenities, including spa services, access to hiking trails in Torrey Pines State Natural Reserve, and a shuttle to La Jolla's nearby village or idyllic shores. It also boasts one of the city's most highly regarded restaurants, **A.R. Valentien**, and a more casual restaurant, **The Grill**. It's rare to encapsulate so much of the San Diego experience in so luxurious a package, though none will appreciate it more than the golfers in your party. One of the hotel's greatest perks is its preferred tee times for guests at the always-booked-solid Torrey Pines Golf Course.

Map 7: 11480 N. Torrey Pines Rd., Torrey Pines, 858/453-4420, www.lodgetorreypines.com

PANTAI INN $$$

Combine the exoticism of Bali with the oceanfront appeal of La Jolla and you'll get this boutique hotel with a bevy of well-appointed oceanview rooms and suites. The Southeast Asian furnishings stand out among high-end properties in the area, and while the hotel may lack a pool or restaurant, the quality of the rooms speaks for itself. Suites feature sun porches and kitchens, and with a cozy little beach out front and all of La Jolla in back, you may decide you've found a second home.

Map 7: 1003 Coast Blvd., La Jolla Village, 858/224-7600, www.pantai.com

Coronado

Map 8

CHEROKEE LODGE $$

No two rooms are alike in this 1896 "bed and board" just a block off Orange Avenue and a short walk from Coronado Beach. The 12-bedroom property doesn't serve breakfast, instead sending guests a few doors down for a complimentary meal at Panera Bread. There's also no designated parking, though plenty of charm makes up for it—along with some of the more affordable rooms in the area.

Map 8: 964 D Ave., 619/437-1967, www.cherokeelodge.com

GLORIETTA BAY INN $$

The one-time mansion and residence of John Spreckels, one of the wealthiest and most influential men in San Diego history, the Glorietta Bay Inn may not seem so grandiose sitting in the shadow of the Hotel del Coronado across the street. However, opt for one of the 11 mansion rooms and you'll experience a taste of what life may have been like for the real-estate magnate. A spate of modern accommodations offers the same bayside location at more affordable rates, but all guests enjoy the splendor of the mansion's sitting room, where you can take your coffee with a little old-world opulence.

Map 8: 1630 Glorietta Blvd., 800/283-9383, www.gloriettabayinn.com

★ HOTEL DEL CORONADO $$$

Historically one of San Diego's finest resorts, the Hotel Del doesn't come cheap, but it delivers a great number of amenities and charm in addition to its incredible beachfront location. Accommodations fall into a few distinct categories. While most people may gravitate toward the rooms filling the 19th-century halls of the original all-wood Victorian structure, these may not be the best choice for everyone. Those traveling with families might prefer the poolside **California Cabanas,** which offer more space, easier access, and more modern comfort. The modern architecture of the **Ocean Towers** may seem less appealing, but with the best ocean views and an adults-only pool, couples may prefer this to the main building. The gated

Best Family Hotels

Traveling with children presents a different set of requirements for a good hotel. Most San Diego hotels accommodate children; however, some do so a bit better or more conveniently than others.

- **Bahia Resort Hotel** (998 W. Mission Bay Dr., Mission Bay, 858/488-0551, www.bahiahotel.com). From this hotel on the calm bay side of the Mission Beach peninsula, you can still walk over to the Pacific Ocean, which happens to sit next to the amusements of Belmont Park. The resort beach sees zero waves; a small strip of sand runs along the gentle waters, offering all the fun of sandcastle building without the fickle currents.

- **Catamaran Resort** (3999 Mission Blvd., 858/488-1081, www.catamaranresort.com). This might be a better option for older kids. The bayside hotel offers some water activities on its beach, and north Mission Beach can be reached by crossing Mission Boulevard.

- **La Jolla Shores Hotel** (8110 Camino Del Oro, La Jolla Shores, 858/923-8058, www.ljshoreshotel.com). Set right on top of La Jolla Shores, this hotel has easy access to the family-friendly beach, surf schools, kayaking and snorkeling rentals, and a pretty great playground.

- **Hotel del Coronado** (1500 Orange Ave., 619/435-6611, www.hoteldel.com). The beach resort caters to kids and families, with a nice pool, beach toys at the ready, and an ice cream shop on-site.

- **Handlery Hotel** (950 Hotel Circle N., Mission Valley, 619/298-0511, www.sd.handlery.com). Every family doesn't have to stay at the beach. The Handlery sits a short freeway hop inland and offers good budget accommodations with a bit of greenery and a generous pool.

**HOTELS
CORONADO**

Victorian Village is an exclusive little neighborhood of high-end villas featuring its own restaurant, parking lot, pools, and jetted tubs. Wherever you stay, you'll have access to the hotel's restaurants and shops, beach rentals, and spa services. The hotel is ideally situated to enjoy Coronado village and downtown San Diego just across the bay, but many visitors seem content to spend their entire trip within the memorable landscape of the Del's 28 acres, just as so many of Hollywood's elite have done during the resort's 125-year history.

Map 8: 1500 Orange Ave., 619/435-6611, www.hoteldel.com

1906 LODGE $$$

Named for the year it was built, this century-old lodge was actually refurbished in 2009, including additional suites and a basement garage. Designed by noted local architect Irving Gill, the Arts and Crafts beauty features abundant structural charm—be sure to note the unique leaded-glass window built into the middle of the chimney. Each distinctive room has been decorated with early-20th-century period furniture and vintage photographs pertaining to Coronado history. Orange Avenue is just a couple of blocks away, or make use of complimentary bikes and golf carts to get around.

Map 8: 1060 Adella Ave., 619/437-1900, www.1906lodge.com

VILLA CAPRI BY THE SEA $$

A small boutique motel with a big neon sign, the instantly recognizable Villa Capri boasts a luxury hotel location with budget accommodation prices and not too many frills. Given the area, the parking alone is practically worth the price of a standard room. Suites and weekly rates may make you consider longer stays at this well-maintained inn.

Map 8: 1417 Orange Ave., 619/435-4137, www.villacapribythesea.com

Greater San Diego
Map 9

HANDLERY HOTEL $$

One of San Diego's better budget options is this hotel tucked between I-8 and the Riverwalk Golf Course. With 217 rooms, a large pool, on-site dining, and occasional entertainment, it's a decent place to relax even if its greatest asset is easy access to other San Diego attractions with a quick hop on the freeway.

Map 9: 950 Hotel Circle N., Mission Valley, 619/298-0511, www.sd.handlery.com

Excursions

Look for ★ to find
recommended sights and activities

Highlights

★ **Best Place to Lose a Bet:** Horses running in circles shouldn't be this fun, but the ocean breeze and the thunderous hooves of the racetrack at the **Del Mar Fairgrounds** seem to pair well (page 244).

★ **Best Place for Kids: Legoland** turns brightly colored plastic blocks into an entire universe to explore (page 254).

★ **Best of the Missions: Mission San Luis Rey de Francia** is the king of the missions, and it shows (page 255).

★ **Best Place to Run Wild: San Diego Zoo Safari Park** gives animals what we all want for them—more room to run (page 261).

★ **Best Brew with a View:** Everybody comes to **Stone World Bistro & Gardens** for the same reason: They love to drink great beer—and talk about drinking great beer—surrounded by a beautiful park-like setting (page 261).

★ **Best Wine-Tasting in Southern California:** Only an hour from San Diego, **Temecula wine country** provides an elegant escape to the hills (page 265).

★ **Best International Adventure:** Right across the border, **Tijuana** hums with urban arts, nightlife, and tacos (page 276).

Legoland

S an Diego's a large city, but it only takes an hour or two on the road to find a drastic change of scenery.

A short drive in any direction reveals charming beach towns, wine country, gorgeous natural landscapes, or adventures south of the border.

Northwest along the coast, metropolitan sprawl gives way to a series of independent beach communities: Del Mar, Encinitas, Carlsbad, and Oceanside. These beautiful little towns, with breathtaking beaches interspersed among estuaries, lagoons, state parks, and campgrounds, make for desirable day trips, even among locals.

Heading due north takes you to inland valleys, where towns around Escondido and San Marcos nurture the craft beer scene, and Temecula boasts Southern California's premier wine country.

Nature lovers may want to look east, where San Diego County crosses chaparral-covered mesas, pine-strewn forests, and mountain ridges into arid desert landscapes. The faded gold rush town of Julian provides a charming base to explore the Laguna Mountains. Farther on, Borrego Springs basks under the clear skies of the Anza-Borrego Desert.

Of course, you'll need a passport to cross into Mexico, where Tijuana offers a glimpse of border town life and an entryway into the state of Baja California.

PLANNING YOUR TIME

North County beach towns appear one after another as you drive north on I-5. It's possible to make a full day of stopping at all the North County beaches (hop on US 101 at Via de la Valle and enjoy the coastal route), or drive straight to Oceanside in the morning and keep the Pacific on your right as you retrace your way south to Del Mar. But I recommend picking

Previous: tigers at the San Diego Zoo Safari Park; vineyards in Temecula.

Choosing Excursions

- **Del Mar:** Bet on your horse at this seaside track and feel the thrill as they come galloping down the stretch so hard you feel it in your chest. Stick around for a free concert after the last race, Friday afternoons at 5pm.

- **Encinitas:** The beautiful cliffside beaches of Encinitas represent the ideal backdrop for Southern California life. The city is within reach, but nobody can think of a reason to go there.

- **Carlsbad:** Cast your eyes on the gold coastline of Carlsbad, then look the other direction for the startlingly vivid Flower Fields, which bloom each summer.

- **Oceanside:** Mission San Luis Rey de Francia is a turn-of-the-19th-century California mission in whitewashed glory, a commingling of Spanish Colonial architectural styles, and an active friary.

- **Escondido:** The San Diego Zoo Safari Park is the zoo blown up to a grand scale, recreating global habitats where animals, including tigers, rhinos, and gorillas, can run and raise families.

- **Temecula:** Don't miss a trip to Southern California's preeminent wine country. The cute 19th-century Old Town is a fun bonus.

- **Julian:** Come for the cider, stay for the pie. This apple-growing small

one general area and soaking it in. None of these trips require an overnight stay, though it's certainly an option, and especially warranted if you plan to enjoy a couple of beach-filled days on the coast.

Del Mar appears first, just 30 minutes from downtown, with another beach town every 5-10 minutes farther north. There are enough beaches, restaurants, and shopping that Del Mar and **Solana Beach** can fill a day on their own, perhaps more if there's an event at the track or the fairgrounds.

Encinitas and **Cardiff** may possess the best stretch of coastline in the county, with clean beaches braced against sandstone cliffs. A lack of great hotels makes them better to do as day trips. Both communities are roughly 40 minutes by car from downtown San Diego.

Carlsbad and **Oceanside** offer beachside hotels, with state beaches in Carlsbad open to camping and RVs. Oceanside's main beach stretches over 1.5 miles south from its harbor, though there are few amenities other than around its central-to-downtown pier. Legoland and Mission San Luis Rey de Francia are the draws here. Carlsbad could make a nice two-night beach getaway if you pace yourself. Expect a 45-minute drive from downtown San Diego to either city.

San Onofre is for those seeking great surf; head straight for waves in the morning, and stop at one of the beach towns for lunch on the way back.

Anza-Borrego Desert State Park

town sprang up during a short-lived gold rush, and its old-timey downtown is filled with sweet thrills of the fruit and baked goods variety.

- **Anza-Borrego Desert State Park:** If you enjoy hiking, wildflower-viewing, funky sculptures, and stargazing, you'll enjoy the ethereal beauty of this desert park.

- **Tijuana:** San Diego's sister-city has come into its own in recent years. Cross the border into Mexico for delicious tacos, great beer, and fun shopping—for a fraction of Cali costs.

From downtown San Diego, count on at least 50 minutes to get here, or longer with traffic.

Visiting inland North County means driving either west via Highway 78 from Oceanside or north on I-15 from downtown. The best reason to visit **Escondido** is the San Diego Zoo Safari Park, followed by a visit to Stone Brewery, or a pint at The Lost Abbey in neighboring **San Marcos.** Plan on 35-45 minutes of driving, or more if you encounter rush-hour traffic.

About an hour's drive north of San Diego, **Temecula** sits just on the other side of the Riverside County line. While its 19th-century Old Town offers tourist-friendly shopping and dining, most visit the area for its forty-some wineries. Vineyards cluster a few minutes east of the highway, many offering fine dining and lodging.

Julian is a gold-mining town turned apple producer, offering a good reason to visit the mountains east of San Diego. While you'll encounter delicious apple pie and cider, a little on-foot exploration of the 19th-century town offers a glimpse into frontier life. From downtown San Diego, expect a little over an hour's drive in good conditions.

Northeast of Julian, the mountains drop into a desert valley, where the small town of **Borrego Springs** offers limited amenities for those visiting **Anza-Borrego Desert State Park.** A roughly two-hour drive from San

Diego, the area is best known for arid hiking and desert flower blooms that add color to the area each spring.

Every border town has its counterpart, and San Diego looks across the international line to **Tijuana.** Once a lowbrow drinking and clubbing destination, TJ has shifted its focus in recent years. While most parts remain economically depressed, new upscale dining and drinking establishments lure San Diegans into taking a 20-minute drive across the border for excellent low-cost meals and craft beer crawls.

North County Beaches

San Diegans consider anything north of La Jolla to be North County, home to a wide swath of vast, suburban communities. North County coastal towns and their pristine beaches make the region an enviable place to live. The Southern California lifestyle flourishes here, with stereotypical surfers and sunbathers scheduling their lives around water, sun, and sand. Spend a little time here living as the locals do and you'll find yourself caring less about the problems of the outside world too.

DEL MAR AND SOLANA BEACH

Del Mar is an upscale residential community nestled between the cliffs of Torrey Pines and the San Dieguito Lagoon. A Tudor-style village spreads out from the central beach, with a smattering of high-priced shops and restaurants. The town is best known for its namesake fairgrounds and racetrack.

Less than three miles north is Solana Beach, a small town independent of Del Mar though close enough to feel almost like a suburb. Solana Beach is best known for shopping in the Cedros Avenue Design District, which offers furniture, designer antiques, and various high-end stores for the home decorator. Solana Beach anchors the North County music scene at its Belly Up nightclub.

Sights
★ DEL MAR FAIRGROUNDS

The San Diego County Fair takes place each June at the **Del Mar Fairgrounds** (2260 Jimmy Durante Blvd., 858/755-1161, www. delmarfairgrounds.com), culminating in a big Fourth of July celebration. Along with the typical fair fare—attractions, rides, farm animals, and fried food—the fair hosts concurrent events such as the San Diego International Beer Festival as well as concerts headlined by internationally known artists. The annual KAABOO music festival is held here in mid-September. The fairgrounds share an address with the racetrack, often featuring horse shows and competitions.

North County

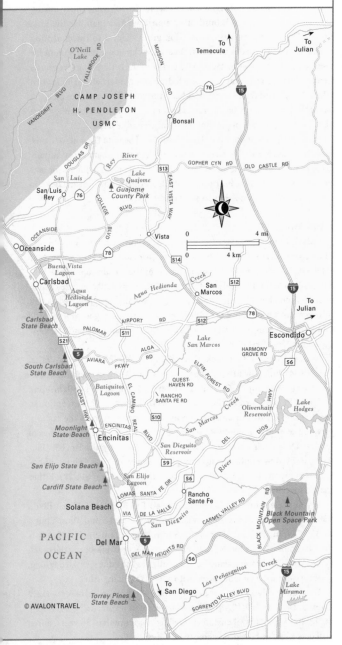

Sports and Activities

"Where the surf meets the turf," the **Del Mar Racetrack** (2260 Jimmy Durante Blvd., 858/755-1141, www.dmtc.com; $6-50) comes alive during the summer racing season (mid-July-Labor Day) and again for the Bing Crosby Season (Nov.). Basic admission grants access to the charming coastal facility. Upgrades allow entrance to the clubhouse, with options for reserved seating or dining tables with a view of the action. The track hosts free concerts after Friday races, including some internationally known talent. On Saturdays concerts and beer and food festivals take place. A day at the track can be rousing fun even for those who don't gamble, and it offers women the rare opportunity to wear elaborate hats.

For a closer look at the natural life within San Dieguito Lagoon wetlands, hike the **Coast to Crest Trail** (www.sdrp.org). Part of what may eventually become a 70-mile trail culminating in the mountain town of Julian, for now this section starts where Jimmy Durante Boulevard meets the San Dieguito River and extends east 2.5 miles to El Camino Real.

Restaurants

Del Mar's known to have a lot of upscale restaurants, but none do fine dining as well as the five-star, five-diamond **Addison** (5200 Grand Del Mar Way, 858/314-1900, www.addisondelmar.com; Tues.-Thurs. 6pm-9pm, Fri.-Sat. 5:30pm-9:30pm; $98-125). The refined tastes and disciplined kitchen of renowned chef William Bradley send seasonally designed dishes to a dining room sitting above the 18th green of the exclusive golf course of the Grand Del Mar resort, complete with a Mediterranean-style patio to enjoy the sommelier's best picks.

Not far from the racetrack, **Cucina Enoteca** (2730 Via De La Valle, 858/704-4500, www.urbankitchengroup.com; Mon. 5pm-9pm, Tues.-Thurs. 11:30am-10pm, Fri.-Sat. 11:30am-10:30pm, Sun. 11:30am-9pm; $15-36) offers its own brilliant wine selection, served with exceptional, creative Italian dishes at a more reasonable price. Across the lagoon, elevated pub fare and outdoor dining pair with craft beer and games of leisure at **Viewpoint Brewing Company** (2201 San Dieguito Dr., 858/356-9346, www.viewpointbrewing.com; Mon. 5pm-9pm, Tues.-Thurs. noon-9pm, Fri. noon-10pm, Sat. 11am-10pm, Sun. 11am-9pm; $14-27). Either makes a terrific post-race option.

If you prefer your meals coastal, **Jake's Del Mar** (1660 Coast Blvd., 858/755-2002, www.jakesdelmar.com; Mon. 4:30pm-9pm, Tues.-Thurs. 11:30am-9pm, Fri.-Sat. 11:30am-9:30pm, Sun. 10am-9pm; $20-36) is famous among locals for its Sunday brunch directly overlooking the beach at Del Mar's Powerhouse Park, but it actually has the same view all day long, serving California cuisine mixed with a few Hawaiian dishes.

For a quick, cheap bite, the beachy sandwich shop **Board & Brew** (1212 Camino Del Mar, 858/481-1021, www.boardandbrew.com; daily 10am-6pm; $5-10) has kept its loyal customers well fed for more than 35 years, and it still gets a line out the door come lunchtime.

Catching a movie in Del Mar may be worthwhile just to check out **Cinéopolis** (12905 El Camino Real, Ste. K1, 858/794-4045, www. cinepolisusa.com). The luxury cinema chain offers cushioned, reclining seats in small, uncrowded theaters, showing first-run films with table service, including cocktails if you attend a dedicated 21-and-over screening.

Nightlife

You'll find a little evening action on Cedros Avenue. One of the county's best rock venues, **Belly Up** (143 S. Cedros Ave., Solana Beach, 858/481-8140, www.bellyup.com) offers nightly shows ranging from tribute bands to indie rockers to music legends that fill the intimate venue with devoted fans.

Across the street from Belly Up, check out the urban winery **Carruth Cellars** (118 S. Cedros Ave., Ste. C, Solana Beach, 858/847-9463, www. carruthcellars.com; daily 11am-9pm), which brings grapes from up north to make wine right here amid the ocean-scented breeze.

Hotels

Those wishing to stay near the beach in Del Mar may opt for the **Hotel Indigo** (710 Camino Del Mar, 858/755-1501, www.hotelindigosddelmar. com; from $150), which offers ocean views, spa services, and comfortable accommodations from the cliffs on the south side of town. Closer to sea level is a highly rated luxury resort, **L'Auberge Del Mar** (1540 Camino Del Mar, 858/259-1515, www.laubergedelmar.com; from $250), nestled between the village and the beach.

For unmatched opulence, nothing compares to the **Grand Del Mar** (5300 Grand Del Mar Ct., 866/305-1528, www.thegranddelmar.com; from $400). The extravagantly built resort overlooks the 4,000-acre Peñasquitos Canyon Preserve, giving the whole place the feel of a country estate. Marble columns and parquet floors set off breathtaking rooms filled with beautiful yet comfortable furniture. It's the kind of place where the Presidential Suite has hosted actual presidents.

Practicalities

Del Mar lies about 20 miles north of downtown San Diego. The easiest way to get here is by car; take I-5 north for about 20 miles and exit at Villa de la Valle, about a 30-minute drive.

For public transit options, you can take the **Amtrak Pacific Surfliner** (www.amtrak.com) route from the downtown **Santa Fe Depot** (1050 Kettner Blvd.) or **Old Town Transit Center** (4005 Taylor St.) in Old Town. Much cheaper is the **Coaster** service (760/966-6500, www.gonctd.com/ coaster; $4-12) offered by the North County Transit District. The nearest Coaster stop is **Solana Beach Station** (105 N. Cedros Ave., Solana Beach). From there, buses travel regularly to the Del Mar Fairgrounds and Del Mar village. The Coaster generally takes 10-15 minutes longer than driving.

Top: Del Mar Racetrack. Bottom: Cardiff-by-the-Sea.

The idyllic coastal city of Encinitas sprawls between lagoons north of Solana Beach. One of these communities, Cardiff-by-the-Sea, features a beautiful state beach, a popular destination for campers that possesses an epic reef break favored by longboarders. Downtown Encinitas features artsy shops that run parallel to breathtaking cliffside beaches, including the area's top surf spot—Swami's. Spend a couple of hours anywhere along this stretch and you'll start plotting ways to uproot your life and move here.

Sights

SAN DIEGUITO HERITAGE MUSEUM

To learn more about the area, pick up some history at the **San Dieguito Heritage Museum** (450 Quail Gardens Dr., Encinitas, 760/632-9711, www.sdheritage.org; Thurs.-Sun. noon-4pm; free). Entertaining stories include how Moonlight Beach got its name during the Prohibition era.

SAN DIEGO BOTANIC GARDEN

Don't miss the chance to wander the unique and expansive **San Diego Botanic Garden** (230 Quail Gardens Dr., Encinitas, 760/436-3036, www.sdbgarden.org; daily 9am-5pm; $14 adults, $10 seniors, students, and military, $8 ages 3-12, $2 parking). A stroll through the gardens almost feels like a geography lesson. Plants and flowers range from desert cacti to tropical rainforest plants, plus the nation's largest collection of bamboo.

SELF-REALIZATION FELLOWSHIP RETREAT AND GARDENS

Tough to miss while driving along the Coast Highway is the **Self-Realization Fellowship** (939 2nd St., Encinitas, 760/436-7220, www.encinitastemple.org; Tues.-Sat. 9am-5pm, Sun. 11am-5pm; free). Its gold-pointed domes call attention to the spiritualist center, while just next door is the tranquil, manicured meditation garden (215 K St.). All of it sits high on a cliff overlooking the region's most beloved surf spot, consequently named **Swami's**.

Sports and Activities

Beautiful **Moonlight State Beach** (400 B St., Encinitas, 760/633-2740, www.parks.ca.gov; daily 5am-10pm) is a great place to see true California beach living at its finest. But one of the great features of Encinitas is the presence of other state beaches and campgrounds.

Longboarders love the famous reef break at **Cardiff State Beach** (2050 S. Coast Hwy. 101, Cardiff-by-the-Sea, 760/753-5091, www.parks.ca.gov; dawn-sunset). Adjoining **San Elijo State Beach** (2500 S. Coast Hwy. 101, 760/753-5091, www.parks.ca.gov) may not be as well known, but it offers its share of fun, uncrowded waves below its campground, and **Eli Howard Surf School** (760/809-3069, www.elihoward.com) offers lessons and overnight surf camps at this location.

Encinitas and Cardiff-by-the-Sea

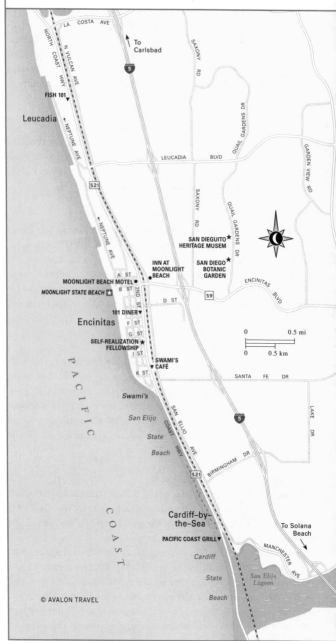

Between the campground and central Encinitas is Swami's (end of 2nd St., Encinitas), the sort of surf spot where you find local pros at play when it's really firing. Swami's is right below the Self-Realization Fellowship (which gives Swami's its name), and the cliffs above offer a terrific vantage point for spectators. On mediocre days the waves remain crowded with those looking to reach that top echelon someday. Due to its competitive nature, Swami's is not a place beginners want to try, but it can turn up some excellent days for visiting surfers with etiquette and skill who want a memorable San Diego surf experience.

For an overhead view of North County's beaches, book a hot air balloon tour with Compass Balloons (1969 Villa Cardiff Dr., 760/704-7407, www. compassballoons.com; 9am-7pm; $179 pp, $1,000 private ride for two). The sunset rides view the county from above, serving champagne and soft drinks as the sun dips below the ocean horizon.

Restaurants

Encinitas boasts a half dozen good coffee shops. For atmosphere, visit the old train station building housing San Diego's original coffee roaster, Pannikin Coffee (510 N. Coast Hwy. 101, 760/436-5824, www. pannikincoffeeandtea.com; Mon.-Fri. 6am-6pm, Sat.-Sun. 6:30am-6pm), which offers a lovely patio setting for coffee and tea. Down the road, Lofty Coffee Company (97 N. Coast Hwy. 101, 760/230-6747, www.loftycoffeeco. com; Mon.-Fri. 6am-6pm, Sat.-Sun. 7am-6pm) roasts organic specialty coffee at a beachy yet design-savvy café on a hillside, leaving its patio open to ocean breezes in the summer, when a Kyoto-drip cold-brew iced coffee proves ideal.

For breakfast with your coffee, try local favorite Swami's Café (1163 S. Coast Hwy. 101, Encinitas, 760/944-0612, www.swamiscafesd.com; daily 7am-4pm; $8-12), known for its unique varieties of eggs Benedict (I'm partial to the avocado and Mexican chorizo sausage combo). For old-school diner-style grub, stop in at 101 Diner (552 S. Coast Hwy. 101, Encinitas, 760/753-2123, www.101diner.com; Mon.-Fri. 6am-1:30pm, Sat.-Sun. 6am-2pm; $8-10) to enjoy traditional egg dishes along with apple-baked pancakes and stuffed waffles.

Funky little taco shop Haggo's Organic Taco (1302 N. Coast Hwy. 101, Ste. 101, Encinitas, 760/753-6000, www.haggosorganictaco.com; Tues.-Sun. 11am-3pm; $8-15) captures the laid-back spirit of the region while using organic ingredients.

To take advantage of this gorgeous coastline, reserve a patio table at Pacific Coast Grill (2526 S. Coast Hwy. 101, Cardiff-by-the-Sea, 760/479-0721, www.pacificcoastgrill.com; Sun.-Thurs. 11am-4pm and 4:30pm-9pm, Fri.-Sat. 11am-4pm and 4:30pm-10pm; $25-50). Set on top of gorgeous Cardiff State Beach, this surf-and-turf restaurant lets you dine about as close to the ocean as you can without getting sand in your lap. In addition to the spectacular view, the kitchen provides a worthy dining experience, with strips of ahi tuna and a fillet you sear yourself on a sizzling hot stone. Follow it up with a fish perfectly cooked sous vide while you enjoy the sunset.

Arts and Culture

Rumored to be the first rural theater to show "talkies," **La Paloma Theater** (471 S. Coast Hwy. 101, 760/436-5774, www.lapalomatheatre.com) still shows first-run movies. The best times to go are during premieres of new surfing films. Seeing great surfing and big waves on the large screen is a treat, and some of the pros featured in the flicks are likely to show up at the occasional premiere party.

Hotels

For a good spot to spend the night, look no farther than the **Inn at Moonlight Beach** (105 N. Vulcan Ave., Encinitas, 760/450-5028, www. innatmoonlightbeach.com; from $150). This lovely bed-and-breakfast puts you within walking distance of great beaches and restaurants. You can also find a good, clean stay at the charming and central **Moonlight Beach Motel** (233 2nd St., Encinitas, 800/753-0623, www.moonlightbeachmotel. com; from $160), which seems to complement the feeling of this laid-back beach town.

For roughing it next to the ocean, reserve a campsite at Cardiff's **San Elijo State Beach** (2500 S. Coast Hwy. 101, Cardiff-by-the-Sea, 760/753-5091, www.parks.ca.gov; $35-70). Car camping and RV spots line the cliffs overlooking the beach. Designated spaces are close together but fill up fast; reservations are available seven months in advance at the first of each month.

Practicalities

Cardiff-by-the-Sea is just five miles north of Del Mar via US-101 or I-5; Encinitas is just 1.5 miles farther north. From downtown San Diego, plan for the 25-mile drive to take about 35 minutes, without traffic. From I-5, take the Birmingham Drive exit for Cardiff-by-the-Sea or the Encinitas Boulevard exit for Encinitas.

The **Coaster** (North County Transit District, 760/966-6500, www. gonctd.com/coaster; $4-12) departs from the downtown **Santa Fe Depot** (1050 Kettner Blvd.) or **Old Town Transit Center** (4005 Taylor St.) and stops at the **Encinitas Coaster Station** (25 E. D St., Encinitas). Buses and taxis provide further options.

CARLSBAD AND OCEANSIDE

Carlsbad is a pretty huge place, large enough to have its own airport (though it offers flights only to LAX). Seaside Carlsbad Village serves as the city center, but the presence of Legoland in South Carlsbad has put the place on the map and lured a rising number of visitors to its plum seven miles of coastline.

Five miles north, Oceanside grew up next to the Marine Corps Base

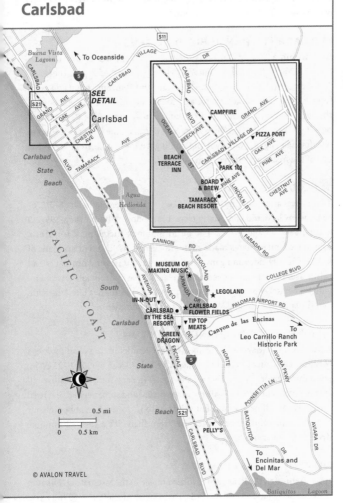

Camp Pendleton. Young marines and their families have lived here dating back to World War II, drawn to its many miles of residential beachfront and a downtown area close to a fishing harbor and pier.

Sights
THE FLOWER FIELDS

The Flower Fields (5704 Paseo Del Norte, 760/431-0352, www.theflowerfields.com; Mar. 1-May 10 daily 9am-6pm; $16 adults, $14 seniors, $8 ages 3-10) are endlessly beautiful during the spring bloom, with more than 50 acres devoted to the giant ranunculus. Just check the online calendar before visiting to make sure you don't miss the flowers in bloom; otherwise, you'll be left to stare at empty fields.

LEO CARRILLO RANCH HISTORIC PARK

Built within a 27-acre canyon is the historically preserved **Leo Carrillo Ranch** (6200 Flying LC Ln., 760/476-1042, www.carlsbadca.gov; Tues.-Sat. 9am-5pm, Sun. 11am-5pm; tours Sat. 11am and 1pm, Sun. noon and 2pm; free). Hollywood character actor and conservationist Leo Carrillo bought the 19th-century hacienda in 1937, consciously preserving its historical buildings. Part time capsule, part garden preserve, the lovely grounds are worth exploring on your own, but you'll get a lot more history by taking one of the free tours offered each weekend.

★ LEGOLAND

The biggest attraction in Carlsbad is **Legoland** (1 Legoland Dr., 877/376-5346, www.legoland.com; daily from 10am, closing hours vary, $95-119 adults, $89-113 ages 3-12). The building-block theme park features a miniature United States made of interlocking plastic and offers loads of kiddie-friendly rides and games incorporating pirates and dinosaurs and using laser blasters to recover stolen treasure. Base admission gets you in, with higher ticket prices adding park attractions like the Sea Life Aquarium and the splashy Legoland Water Park (spring-summer only).

MARINE CORPS MECHANIZED MUSEUM

Located on the Marine Corps Base Camp Pendleton, the **Marine Corps Mechanized Museum** (6212 Vandegrift Blvd., Oceanside, 760/725-5758, www.themech.org; Mon.-Thurs. 8am-4pm, Fri. 8am-1pm; free) features all manner of armored trucks, all-terrain vehicles, and some very large retired ordnance. You'll need to present valid photo ID for each member in your party to gain admittance to the base; from there, it's a 15- to 20-minute drive to the museum.

MUSEUM OF MAKING MUSIC

A stroll through the history of recorded music in the fascinating **Museum of Making Music** (5790 Armada Dr., Carlsbad, 760/438-5996, www.museumofmakingmusic.org; Tues.-Sun. 10am-5pm; $10 adults, $7 seniors, students, military, and ages 6-18) reveals hundreds of vintage instruments and even a few modern ones. Trace the advent of modern instruments and listen to snippets of popular recordings made at the time of their inception. Along the way, a few hands-on instruments allow you to make your own music (or noise), including my favorite corner of the museum: an exhibit devoted to the electric guitar.

OCEANSIDE MUSEUM OF ART

Stop in to enjoy the contemporary and conceptual art collection of the **Oceanside Museum of Art** (704 Pier View Way, Oceanside,

military and students, free 1st Sun. each month). A rotating calendar of
programs and events complements a series of modern and contemporary art exhibitions.

CALIFORNIA SURF MUSEUM

The small **California Surf Museum** (312 Pier View Way, Oceanside,
760/721-6876, www.surfmuseum.org; Fri.-Wed. 10am-4pm, Thurs. 10am-8pm; $5 adults, $3 seniors, military, and students, free under age 12) has
plenty to say about local surfing history. Exhibits depict the evolution of
the surfboard as well as well-known riders, including soul surfer Bethany
Hamilton.

★ MISSION SAN LUIS REY DE FRANCIA

Oceanside's top attraction is the **Mission San Luis Rey de Francia** (4050
Mission Ave., Oceanside, 760/757-3651, www.sanluisrey.org; Mon.-Thurs.
9:30am-5pm, Sat.-Sun. 10am-5pm; $5 adults, $4 seniors and ages 6-18, free
military), the 18th of California's 21 Franciscan missions. It was founded
in 1798 by French missionary Fermín Lasuén, successor to Junípero
Serra. Also known as the "King of Missions," it's the largest of the group.
Simply walk around and ogle the whitewashed walls and Spanish Colonial
architectural styles or take one of the tours to learn more about the history
of the National Historic Landmark.

Sports and Activities

Two state beaches bear similar names in Carlsbad. Found at the end of
Poinsettia Lane, **South Carlsbad State Beach** (7201 Carlsbad Blvd.,
760/438-3143, www.parks.ca.gov, dawn-sunset) is partly reserved for
coastal campsites, but a free day-use parking lot offers access to sandy
beachfront and spaced-out, intermediate surf breaks.

There's a free lot at **Tamarack Surf Beach** (101 Tamarack Ave.), as well as
fun beginner to intermediate surf most of the year, even on many summer
days when the rest of the county is flat. The family-friendly, sandy beach
slopes a bit, making surfers seem a lot closer than they actually are.

North of Oceanside, one of the top surf breaks in the county is at the
northern edge of Marine Corps Base Camp Pendleton, one of the largest
military bases in the world. Only military personnel have access to the 16
miles of coastline and other land around the freeway, but farther north,
just as you enter Orange County, is **San Onofre State Beach** (Old Hwy. 101
at Basilone Rd., 949/492-4872, www.parks.ca.gov/sanonofre; Apr. 15-Sept.
daily 6am-10pm, Oct.-Apr. 14 6am-8pm; $15), home to Trestles.

Named for a trestle bridge that surfers used to cross underneath to reach
the world-class breaks, **Trestles** is most easily accessed by entering the
San Onofre State Beach Campground (www.reservecalifornia.com). A
1.5-mile nature trail connects the campground to Trestle Beach. While

camping has its own merits, people come here to seek the surf, which remains crowded despite the complicated access.

While beaches get a fair amount of use, many visitors come to bike the **Coast Highway** (US 101), which picks up just south of Marine Corps Base Camp Pendleton and rides with the ocean on your right 20 miles down to San Dieguito Lagoon near Del Mar. Great scenery and cool ocean breezes make this one of the county's most popular cycling routes; it's particularly well-trafficked on weekends.

Hikers may spot large water birds and other tidal wetland inhabitants along **Batiquitos Lagoon Trail** (7489 Gabbiano Ln.), an easy 3.3-mile trail winding through 610 acres of trees and marshes in the Batiquitos Lagoon reserve.

Golfers will appreciate the challenging 18-hole, par-72 **Aviara Golf Club** (7447 Batiquitos Dr., Carlsbad, 760/603-6900, www.golfaviara.com; daily 7am-5pm; $120-240 Mon.-Thurs., $140-260 Fri.-Sun.), with 7,000 gorgeously maintained yards of fairway. Its rolling green hills seem so far removed from the rest of the area that you might forget where you are.

Restaurants

Close to Legoland and the Flower Fields, European restaurant and imported foods grocer **Tip Top Meats** (6118 Paseo Del Norte, 760/438-2620, www.tiptopmeats.com; daily 6am-8pm; $6-15) serves mostly German meals in a traditional setting, including an all-you-can-eat sausage breakfast and a host of value-priced regional specialties throughout the day. Inside a stately, colonial brick building nearby, **Green Dragon Tavern & Museum** (6115 Paseo Del Norte, 760/918-2421, www.greendragontavernca.com; Mon.-Sat. 11am-9pm, Sun. 10am-8pm; $11-27) adopts the wooded style of American Revolution-era taverns, right down to its traditional English pub menu. You may take your drinks to peruse the corresponding history museum next door.

This area also offers a good opportunity to grab an **In-N-Out Burger** (5950 Avenida Encinas, Carlsbad, 800/786-1000, www.in-n-out.com; Sun.-Thurs. 10:30am-1am, Fri.-Sat. 10:30am-1:30am; $5-10). The classic California drive-through burger chain makes an honest-to-goodness fast-food burger with a well-known "secret menu" of upgrades. Go "Animal Style" for a saucy burger with grilled onions, pickles, and everything else.

The best restaurant in Carlsbad Village is **Campfire** (2725 State St., Carlsbad, 760/637-5121, www.thisiscampfire.com; Mon. 5pm-11pm, Tues.-Thurs. 11:30am-11pm, Fri. 11:30am-1am, Sat. 10am-1am, Sun. 10am-11pm; $14-36). Its wood-fired kitchen creates savory dishes for a woodsy, semi-outdoor space, bolstered by delicious cocktails. Closer to the beach, **Park 101** (3040 Carlsbad Blvd., 760/434-2217, www.park101carlsbad.com; Mon. 4pm-close, Tues.-Fri. 11am-close, Sat.-Sun. 9am-close, deli hours Sun.-Thurs. 7am-3pm, Fri.-Sat. 7am-6pm; $10-20) offers casual outdoor dining to go with several service counters featuring barbecue, drinks, or sandwiches to go. Also offering casual bites, **Board & Brew** (201 Oak Ave.,

Clockwise from top left: a cyclist on the Pacific Coast Highway in North County; the California Surf Museum; Mission San Luis Rey de Francia.

Hops Highway

Collectively, the cities of North County are home to more than 50 craft breweries. Most of them sit on or near Highway 78, which is why it's better known around these parts as the Hops Highway. The best way to experience them is to stay nearby and visit several at a time with the help of a brewery tour, ride share, or designated driver.

Many of the smaller breweries have plenty to offer, but these are a few not to miss. In San Marcos, **The Lost Abbey** (155 Mata Way, Ste. 104, San Marcos, 800/918-6816, www.lostabbey.com; Mon. 1pm-6pm, Tues.-Wed. 1pm-7pm, Thurs. 1pm-8pm, Fri. 1pm-9pm, Sat. 11:30am-8pm, Sun. noon-6pm) has a huge reputation for producing some of the best Belgian-style beers this side of the Atlantic, in addition to regional favorite IPAs. Nearby, newcomer **Wild Barrel Brewing** (692 Rancheros Dr., San Marcos, 760/593-4785, www.wildbarrelbrewing.com; Sun.-Wed. 11am-9pm, Thurs. 11am-10pm, Fri.-Sat. 11am-11pm) is quickly catching up.

While in San Marcos, plan to spend time at **URGE Gastropub and Common House** (255 Redel Rd., San Marcos, 760/798-8822, sm.urgegastropub.com; Sun.-Wed. 11:30am-9pm, Thurs. 11:30am-10pm, Fri.-Sat. 11:30am-11:00pm), which brews beer by the name Mason Ale Works and fills out its huge one-acre facility with a massive restaurant, beer garden, and boutique bowling alley decorated after the film The Big Lebowski. A little to the west, **Rip Current Brewing** (1325 Grand Ave. #100, San Marcos, 760/481-3141, www.ripcurrentbrewing.com; Mon.-Thurs. 3pm-8pm, Fri. 3pm-9pm, Sat. noon-9pm, Sun. noon-7pm) is much smaller, one of the reasons it won a best very small brewery championship (terrific hoppy and German-style beers are the other reasons).

In Vista, you'll spot Native American-owned **Indian Joe Brewing** (2123 Industrial Ct., 760/295-3945, www.indianjoebrewing.com; Wed. 4pm-9pm, Thurs.-Fri. 3pm-10pm, Sat. 1pm-10pm, Sun. 1pm-6pm) from the highway; it serves beers of every style. A few blocks south of there, about a dozen small

Carlsbad, 760/434-4466, www.boardandbrew.com; daily 10am-8pm; $5-10) is a local sandwich favorite.

Elsewhere in the village, beer drinkers have had plenty of award-winning beers to celebrate over doughy pizza at the shared tables of **Pizza Port** (571 Carlsbad Village Dr., 760/720-7007, www.pizzaport.com; Mon.-Thurs. 11am-10pm, Fri.-Sat. 11am-midnight, Sun. 11am-11pm; $10-25).

It's well worth veering into south Oceanside for dinner to sit at the "unorthodox sushi" counter of **Wrench and Rodent Seabasstropub** (1815 S. Coast Hwy., Oceanside, 760/271-0531, www.seabasstropub.com; Mon. 4pm-9pm, Tues.-Sun. 4pm-10pm; $10-95). Don't be deterred by the name: Innovative chef Davin Waite assembles sushi unlike anyone else, sourcing sustainable seafood and locally sourced—or foraged—produce. Creative dishes abound, including house-made ramen noodles.

In downtown Oceanside, your best bet for beer and pub fare is **Bagby Beer Company** (601 S. Coast Hwy., Oceanside, 760/512-3372, www.bagby-beer.com; Mon.-Thurs. 11am-10pm, Fri.-Sat. 11am-11pm, Sun. 10am-10pm; $10-16), where truly exceptional house beers go with burgers, tacos, and

The Lost Abbey brings Belgian style beers to the Hops Highway.

breweries cluster around a large complex of industrial parks in south Vista. You can dive in and find a fun tasting experience at any of them.

Another option is to head into Vista Village, where a couple of them have opened tasting rooms amid the restaurants and shops of Vista's quaint city center. Mother Earth Brew Co. may be Vista's best known brewery, and its **Mother Earth Tap Room** (206 Main St., Vista, 760/726-2273, www.motherearthbrewco.com; Mon. noon-9pm, Tues.-Thurs. noon-10pm, Fri. noon-11pm, Sat. 11am-11pm, Sun. 11am-9pm) comes alive nights and weekends. Belching Beaver Brewery isn't far behind, and its village brewpub, **Belching Beaver Tavern and Grill** (302 E. Broadway, Vista, 760/295-8599; Mon.-Wed. 3pm-9pm, Thurs. noon-10pm, Fri.-Sat. noon-11pm, Sun. noon-8pm) offers meals to wash down the San Diego-style beer.

Belgian fries. Fans of chain **Ruby's Diner** (1 Oceanside Pier, Oceanside, 760/433-7829, www.rubys.com; Sun.-Thurs. 7am-9pm, Fri.-Sat. 7am-10pm; $10-15) will find a particularly fun outpost at the end of the 1,954-foot Oceanside Pier.

Hotels

Oceanside hotel options are limited, but a reasonable oceanfront stay may be found at the **Southern California Beach Club** (121 S. Pacific St., 760/722-6666, www.southerncalifbeachclub.com; from $150), which offers clean studios and condos that include full kitchens and views, plus direct access to the beach.

Stay on the beach in Carlsbad at the **Tamarack Beach Resort** (3200 Carlsbad Blvd., Carlsbad, 800/334-2199, www.tamarackresort.com; from $200), or treat yourself to the **Beach Terrace Inn** (2775 Ocean St., Carlsbad, 760/729-5951, www.beachterraceinn.com; from $250). Each offers direct beach access and locations within easy walking distance of village shops and restaurants.

For a more affordable stay, try the **Carlsbad by the Sea Hotel** (850 Palomar Airport Rd., Carlsbad, 760/438-7880, www.carlsbadhotelbythe-sea.com; from $100), which puts you within reach of Legoland and the beach. It's a short walk from the Flower Fields.

For top-tier hospitality, no one tops **La Costa Resort & Spa** (2100 Costa Del Mar Rd., Carlsbad, 760/438-9111, www.omnihotels.com; from $250). Located slightly inland, the terra-cotta luxury resort, spa, and gold-medal golf course is a vacation unto itself. Expect exquisite comfort and service, as well as swimming pools, tennis courts, fitness classes, and activities for kids and teens.

Beach campsites may be reserved in advance at the **South Carlsbad State Beach Campground** (7201 Carlsbad Blvd., 760/438-3143, www.reservecalifornia.com; $35-50). Hundreds of cliffside spaces are set up for car camping or for RVs and trailers, with stairs leading down to a long, beautiful, undeveloped beach with plenty of swimming and surfing options.

Practicalities

Carlsbad and Oceanside are best accessed by car. Carlsbad is 35 miles north of downtown San Diego via I-5, about a 40-minute drive. Carlsbad Village lies at the north end of town and is best accessed by exiting at Carlsbad Village Drive. Oceanside is 40 miles (45 minutes) north of downtown via I-5. San Onofre is even farther north, close to 60 miles from downtown San Diego and at least a 50-minute drive.

The **Coaster** (North County Transit District, 760/966-6500, www.gonctd.com/coaster, $4-12) accesses the region from downtown's **Santa Fe Depot** (1050 Kettner Blvd.) or **Old Town Transit Center** (4005 Taylor St.). Carlsbad has two stops: the **Poinsettia Station** (6511 Avenida Encinas, morning and afternoons only) in South Carlsbad or in **Carlsbad Village** (2775 State St.). At the end of the line is **Oceanside Transit Station** (195 S. Tremont St.), which deposits you within walking distance of the pier and beach.

Escondido and Vicinity

Said to mean "hidden water," Escondido has become the place of not-so-hidden beer. While there's plenty to see and do in Escondido, the presence of Stone Brewing probably inspires more 40-minute drives from San Diego than any other local feature. Once a rural outpost, the town has grown rapidly; its quaint downtown district now sits within suburban sprawl. An old section of Grand Avenue (between Centre City Parkway and Ivy Street) features shops and restaurants old and new to provide a couple hours' worth of exploration.

However, the nearby community of Rancho Bernardo offers better food

options, and watching wild animals roam the hillsides is still the best overall reason to visit the area.

Sights

★ SAN DIEGO ZOO SAFARI PARK

San Diego Zoo Safari Park (15500 San Pasqual Valley Rd., 760/747-8702, www.sdzsafaripark.org; daily 9am-7pm, hours vary seasonally, $54 ages 12 and up, $44 ages 3-11, safari tour tickets $54-125 additional) might be related to the zoo at Balboa Park, but it does things differently. Here the animals have a lot more space to roam, with the landscape made to more closely resemble the natural habitats of a number of African species, including lions and elephants. Options to see these creatures include riding around in a jeep and getting a close-up look at some pretty majestic animals.

★ STONE WORLD BISTRO & GARDENS

Stone World Bistro & Gardens (1999 Citracado Pkwy., 760/294-7899, www.stonebrewing.com; Sun.-Thurs. 11am-10pm, Fri.-Sat. 11am-11pm) serves as a monument to craft beer, presented Southern California style, with a large desert garden rolling off its generous outdoor patio and bar. You may opt for a brewery tour (to see how these guys do what they do), stay for dinner, or fill some growlers. Mainly, you'll want to check out the huge tap list and drink world-class beers.

CALIFORNIA CENTER FOR THE ARTS

Set on a large property next to Escondido City Hall is the multi-faceted **California Center for the Arts** (340 N. Escondido Blvd., 760/839-4138, www.artcenter.org; Tues.-Sat. noon-6pm, Sun. noon-5pm; ticket prices vary). The voter-created cultural center stages musical and theatrical performances, hosts seasonal museum exhibitions, and offers performing arts classes for adults and children. The vast complex boasts three galleries and a sculpture court; a 1,500-seat concert venue; a 400-seat theater; plus art and dance studios. Check online for a calendar of events covering a wide variety of artistic mediums and genres.

BERNARDO WINERY

"Southern California's oldest operating winery," **Bernardo Winery** (13330 Paseo Del Verano Norte, Rancho Bernardo, 858/487-1866, www.bernardowinery.com; Sun.-Thurs. 10am-6pm, Fri. 10am-9pm) features a cluster of wine and gift shops, a tasting room, and a small vineyard. The old-timey "village" delivers on charm and can make a relaxing and fun stopover on the way back from the Safari Park.

Restaurants

Dining at **Stone World Bistro & Gardens** (1999 Citracado Pkwy., 760/294-7899, www.stonebrewing.com; Sun.-Thurs. 11am-10pm, Fri.-Sat.

11am-11pm; $15-30) is a given. But if you make it into downtown Escondido, Parisian-style bakery **Delight of France** (126 W. Grand Ave., 760/746-2644, www.adelightoffrance.com; daily 8am-2pm; $8-15) serves up great croissants and baguettes, plus sandwiches, quiches, and pastries the locals love. For caffeinated sips, check out **Kettle Coffee and Tea** (119 E. Grand Ave., 760/738-8662, www.kettlecoffeeandtea.com; Mon.-Wed. and Fri. 6:30am-6:30pm, Thurs. 6:30am-8:30pm, Sat. 7:30am-5pm).

One of Escondido's oldest restaurants is charming **La Tapatia** (340 W. Grand Ave., 760/747-8282, www.latapatia.net; daily 11am-9pm; $10-15), a Mexican family restaurant dating back to 1932. Take it up a notch at **Bellamy's Restaurant** (417 W. Grand Ave., Escondido, 760/747-5000, www.bellamysdining.com; Tues.-Thurs. 11:30am-9pm, Fri. 11:30am-10pm, Sat. 4pm-10pm; $22-36), which imbues California cuisine with French influence.

A little south, in Rancho Bernardo, **The Cork and Craft** (16990 Via Tazon, Rancho Bernardo, 858/618-2463, www.thecorkandcraft.com; Tues.-Thurs. 11am-9pm, Fri. 11am-10pm, Sat. 3pm-10pm, Sun. 10am-9pm; $21-36) combines creative, upscale dining with both wine and beer made in-house. A couple exits away, the more casual **Brothers Provisions** (16451 Bernardo Center Dr., 855/850-2767, www.brosprovisions.com; Mon.-Wed. 11am-9pm, Thurs.-Sat. 11am-10pm, Sun. 11am-8pm; $8-20) offers counter service including hot and cold sandwiches, coffee, flatbreads, and cheese boards.

Hotels

Accommodations within Escondido are not always the most welcoming, but you can hit pay dirt close by in Rancho Bernardo at the **Rancho Bernardo Inn** (17550 Bernardo Oaks Dr., Rancho Bernardo, 855/574-5356, www.ranchobernardoinn.com; from $200). The upscale resort offers golf and spa services amid a beautiful, tranquil setting. Otherwise, there are a few chain motels, and an under-construction Stone Hotel is being built near the brewery, due to open in 2018 or 2019.

Practicalities

Escondido is in North County. From San Diego, take I-15 north for about 35 miles; Rancho Bernardo is reachable in about 25 miles. This is a heavily traveled commuter highway, so avoid rush hour and expect the trip to take an hour or longer. The North County Transit District offers the **Sprinter** (www.gonctd.com/sprinter) commuter train from Oceanside through San Marcos to the **Escondido Transit Center** (796 W. Valley Pkwy.).

Top: giraffes at San Diego Zoo Safari Park. Bottom: Old Town Temecula.

Temecula

Just north of San Diego County, the Temecula Valley has established itself as Southern California's preeminent wine country. Only a couple hours removed from Los Angeles, and about an hour from San Diego, the region's 40-plus wineries have become a major weekend attraction, attracting an estimated three million visitors each year.

The name Temecula comes from the Luiseño Native American term for "sunshine through the mist," and the valley's idyllic weather lives up to the assessment. The valley is surrounded by a ring of mountains that block out any coastal fog that creeps into the town's neighbors to the west—as may be seen during the valley's popular early morning hot air balloon tours. The Pechanga band of Luiseño still reside in the area, and its casino south of town is the largest in California.

Sights

OLD TOWN TEMECULA

Dating back to 1859, **Old Town Temecula** (Old Town Front St. between 1st St. and Morena Rd., www.visittemeculavalley.com) encompasses 12 tourist-friendly blocks of antiques shops, restaurants, and gift boutiques, such as **Temecula Olive Oil Company** (28653 Old Town Front St.) and **Temecula Lavender Co.** (28561 Old Town Front St.). Lined by sidewalks made from wooden railroad ties, Old Town's redwood water towers and storefronts evoke frontier times, when Temecula grew from a railroad stop between San Diego and Riverside into a ranching town, nearly 100 years before its grape-growing reputation took off. Today, the cars of weekend visitors line up outside the welcome gates on either side of town to spend a few hours exploring.

TEMECULA VALLEY MUSEUM

Delve into the history of the area in the **Temecula Valley Museum** (28314 Mercedes St., 951/694-6450, www.temeculavalleymuseum.org; Tues.-Sat. 10am-4pm, Sun. 1pm-4pm; $5 suggested donation), which features cultural artifacts and photographs from Temecula's early days, along with histories of its native inhabitants.

TEMECULA CHILDREN'S MUSEUM

Also known as Pennypickle's Workshop, the kooky **Temecula Children's Museum** (42081 Main St., 951/308-6376, www.pennypickles.org; two-hour sessions Tues.-Sat. 10am, 12:30pm, and 3pm, Fri. 5:30pm, Sun. 12:30pm and 3pm; $5 pp) comprises 7,500 square feet of interactive science exhibits. Visits are split into two-hour sessions throughout the day to keep crowds down.

PECHANGA RESORT AND CASINO

With a casino floor measuring 188,000 square feet, the **Pechanga Resort and Casino** (45000 Pechanga Pkwy., 951/693-1819, www.pechanga.com)

stakes a claim as California's largest casino, with more than 4,000 slot machines, 150 table games, and a bingo parlor big enough to fit 700. The recently expanded resort hosts live music, theater, and comedy and offers a pool complex and spa services to visitors staying in its more than 1,000 guest rooms.

★ Wineries

More than 40 wineries currently populate the Temecula Valley, ranging from rustic boutique wineries to elegant vintner estates. The first grape seeds were planted back in 1968, when the hills east of Old Town were known as the Valle de los Caballos, but now dozens of varietals are prevalent, though the local climate tends to favor temperate fruit originating from Spain, Italy, and the Rhone Valley of southern France. Winery tasting rooms tend to close by 6pm, so the best way to enjoy wine country is to stay at one of the wineries and use it as a launching point to visit multiple vineyards between lunch and dinner, via shuttle or with a designated driver.

Visiting multiple wineries is easy, as all of them reside within only a few square miles; two of the oldest are found only a mile apart. Each dating to 1969, **Mount Palomar Winery** (33820 Rancho California Rd., 951/676-5047, www.mountpalomar.com; Mon.-Thurs. 11am-5pm, Fri.-Sat. 11am-7pm) is known for smooth and complex wines like the Italian red sangiovese, French white, and viognier; while **Callaway Vineyard and Winery** (32720 Rancho California Rd., 951/676-4001, www.callawaywinery.com; daily 10:30am-6pm) makes balanced, fruit-forward wines with more than a dozen varietals, including popular reds like cabernet and zinfandel, and whites such as chardonnay and sauvignon blanc. Each offers a restaurant on-site, and as at many wineries in the area, their beautiful grounds make desirable wedding destinations.

The best known in Temecula is **South Coast Winery** (34843 Rancho California Rd., 877/743-8303, www.southcoastwinery.com; daily 10am-6pm), the only winery in California to win the California State Golden Bear Winery of the Year Award four times. Its resort, spa, and restaurant host many visitors, with good reason. Its expertly produced vintages include cabernets, syrahs, and merlots. Across the street, its sister winery **Carter Estate Winery** (34450 Rancho California Rd., 844/851-2138, www.carterestatewinery.com; daily 11am-6pm) is one of two local producers to make sparkling wines practicing Méthode Champenoise—the traditional method used in champagne. The other, **Thornton Winery** (32575 Rancho California Rd., 951/699-0099, www.thorntonwine.com; daily 10am-8pm), hosts live music on summer weekends on its Mediterranean-inspired terrace.

For a less Mediterranean, more California feel, try **Ponte Winery** (35053 Rancho California Rd., 951/694-8855, www.pontewinery.com; daily 10am-5pm). To experience a more intimate, small-scale winemaker, visit **Hart Winery** (41300 Avenida Biona, 951/676-6300, www.hartfamilywinery.com;

daily 9am-5pm), where the focus is on enjoying several styles of wine and enjoying the scenery from a terrace overlooking the valley.

You can put together winery tours—including transportation—with **Grapeline Wine Tours** (951/693-5755, http://gogrape.com/temecula; $119-149 pp); you may also take tours by jeep with **Sunrider Wine & Beer Jeep Tour** (951/551-1516, www.sunriderjeeptours.com; $125 pp) or by limo with **Temecula Limo Wine Tasting** (951/402-3595, www.temeculalimowinetasting.com; $220 for group of 4).

There are a great many experiences to choose from, so it can be fun merely to explore the area. Consult the **Temecula Valley Winegrowers** website (www.temeculawines.org) for detailed information about all the Temecula wineries.

Sports and Activities

The Temecula wine country used to be called Valle de los Caballos, and it's still horse country. The two countries come together with **Wine Country Trails by Horseback** (34225 Rancho California, 951/506-8706, www.winecountrytrailsbyhorseback.com; Wed.-Sun. by reservation), which offers guided horseback rides along trails between vineyards. If you'd rather not sit atop a horse, you may sit behind one. **Temecula Carriage Company** (40001 Berenda Rd., 858/205-9161, www.temeculacarriageco.com; Fri.-Sun. 10am-2pm; $39 pp) offers wine tours by carriage ride.

Or you could simply watch the horses at the racetrack, **Galway Downs** (38801 Los Corralitos Rd., 951/303-0405, www.galwaydowns.com), which features racing and dressage events throughout the year, as well as concerts.

Perhaps the most exciting way to tour Temecula is by hot air balloon. **California Dreamin' Balloon Adventures** (33133 Vista Del Monte Rd., 951/699-0601, www.californiadreamin.com; $148 pp and up) meets at Vindemia Winery in the predawn hours, then trucks to a suitable launch site to rise above the entire valley, viewing vineyards, the surrounding mountains, and beyond.

Restaurants

Dining options in Temecula range from full-service winery restaurants to fast food. In between there are a few spots in Old Town worth checking out. For breakfast and lunch, check out the red vinyl booth Americana at **Swing Inn Café** (28676 Old Town Front St., 951/676-2321, www.swinginncafe.com; daily 5am-9pm; $9-15); it's mostly customary diner food, but the cinnamon rolls are massive. To deviate a bit, try **Havana Kitchen** (41955 5th St. #101, 951/699-7300, www.havanakitchen.com; Mon. 8am-6pm, Tues.-Thurs. 8am-8pm, Fri.-Sat. 8am-11pm, Sun. 9am-7pm; $6-16), a Cuban coffee shop that serves breakfast, pastries, and traditional stewed meat dishes like *ropa vieja*.

The Gambling Cowboy Chophouse (42072 5th St., 951/699-2895, www.ilovethecowboy.com; Tues.-Thurs. 11am-9pm, Fri. 11am-10:30pm,

Sat. 9am-10:30pm, Sun. 9am-9pm; $31-60) captures the local flavor in steak house form, serving surf and turf in a Western-style dining room. For something rustic yet modern, hit the patio of **1909 Temecula** (28656 Old Town Front St., 951/619-1909, www.1909temecula.com; Mon.-Thurs. 11am-10pm, Fri. 11am-2am, Sat. 9am-2am, Sun. 9am-11pm; $11-30) for gourmet burgers, chops, charcuterie, or vegetarian dishes. For crusty artisanal pizza made from scratch, drop in on **The Goat & Vine** (41911 5th St., Ste. 100, 951/695-5600, www.thegoatandvine.com; Sun.-Thurs. 11am-9pm, Fri.-Sat. 11am-10pm; $11-30).

Your finest dining will be found at the wineries. The lunchtime views are phenomenal from the **Falkner Winery** hilltop restaurant **The Pinnacle** (40620 Calle Contento, 951/676-8231, www.falknerwinery.com/restaurant; daily 11:30am-3pm; $16-28). The restaurant at **Leoness Cellars** (38311 De Portola Rd., 951/302-7601, www.leonesscellars.com; Sun.-Thurs. 11:30am-5pm, Fri.-Sat. 11am-8pm, Sun. 11:30am-6pm; $20-40) pairs a gorgeous vineyard setting with adventurous contemporary cuisine and decor.

Hotels

The usual chain hotels and motels crop up along the freeway outside of Old Town, and most make an affordable home base for winetasting adventures. For a more interesting stay that's inside Old Town, hunker down in the Old-West-style rooms of **The Hotel Temecula** (42100 Main St., 951/972-8500, www.thehoteltemecula.com; from $275). Built in 1891, it probably doesn't look much different these days, though it's a lot more comfortable.

South of town, there's never a shortage of options at the **Pechanga Resort and Casino** (45000 Pechanga Pkwy., 951/693-1819, www.pechanga.com; from $199), which comes with swimming pools, spa services, and many kinds of entertainment. At nearby **Temecula Creek Inn** (44501 Rainbow Canyon Rd., 844/791-6073, www.temeculacreekinn.com; from $120), stylish amenities include a fitness center and golf course.

The best choice for a wine tasting excursion is to stay where the wine is. **South Coast Winery Resort & Spa** (34843 Rancho California Rd., 877/743-8303, www.southcoastwinery.com; from $199) offers rooms and villas with porches backed up against the vineyards, which get quite peaceful at night. The next property over, **Ponte Vineyard Inn** (35001 Rancho California Rd., 951/587-6688, www.pontevineyardinn.com; from $260) offers sustainability, spa services, a fitness room, and a duck pond.

Practicalities

The best way to get to Temecula from San Diego is by car—it's a pretty straight shot 60 miles up I-15 and takes about an hour in light traffic. It's also accessible by bus via **Greyhound Bus Lines** (28464 Old Town Front St., Ste. B, 951/676-2059, www.greyhound.com; $20-25 one-way from San Diego).

From Gold to Golden Delicious

While herding cattle back in 1869, Santa Ysabel rancher A. E. Frederick Coleman stopped to water his horse and recognized a glint of gold in the creek bed. Formerly enslaved in Kentucky, Coleman had joined the Northern California gold rush before settling in the rural outskirts of San Diego, where the majority of the county's black population lived at the time. The agricultural potential of the area held greater opportunity than the minority population found in central San Diego, which was just starting to move out of Old Town.

Coleman's discovery brought a new kind of opportunity to the African Americans in the community: business ownership in a new town. He immediately formed a mining company; when word got out, the boom was on, attracting prospectors and opportunists from around the country. Coleman City sprang up around his claim but dissipated once the source of the gold was discovered farther east. Ironically, it was a pair of former Confederate soldiers who lent their name to Julian. The Julian brothers came west from Georgia to follow the expansion of the railroad to San Diego. Beating the track builders to California, their party came across the **gold rush** and began mining. Within a few years, the population grew from nearly nonexistent to more than 600 people, with hotels, restaurants, stores, liveries, and saloons opening around a newly formed Main Street. The Hotel Robinson, opened in 1887 by another formerly enslaved person, Albert Robinson, and his wife, Margaret, remains open today as the **Julian Gold Rush Hotel,** the oldest continuously operating hotel in Southern California, older than Hotel del Coronado by about a year.

Like Coleman City, most gold towns turned to ghost towns once the gold ran out. However, Julian endured for a couple of reasons: the sense of community that arose during the 20-30 years of the gold boom and the tightly knit bunch of men and women who'd met, married, and begun raising families. Even without the gold, they wanted to stay.

Fortunately, the favorable agricultural conditions that first brought people like Coleman to Julian were also ideal for growing apples. East Coast native James Madison planted some apple trees in the early 1870s, and by the early 20th century, large and firm Julian apples were winning blue ribbons at world's fairs around the country. Today, Julian apple pies and ciders are standout regional treats, and apple picking is a popular late-summer activity. The **Julian Apple Days Festival** (www.julianmerchants.org; early Oct.) celebrates the annual harvest that has kept Julian a happy little mountain town for nearly 150 years.

Julian

An adventurous day trip takes you to this little mountain town that sprang up after Fred Coleman discovered gold in a creek running through nearby Santa Ysabel. The ensuing gold rush didn't last long, but by the time it faded, Julian was established and the apple trees planted then literally bore fruit. While a little strip of Main Street still has the facade of a mining town, today's gold is made from apples. Julian apple pie is coveted countywide as a true regional delicacy. You can get it at lower altitudes, but it's less fresh and fun.

California Wolf Center

With a mission to preserve the presence of wolves in California, the **California Wolf Center** (K Q Ranch Rd., 760/765-0030, www. californiawolfcenter.org; tours summer Mon. 10am, Fri. 3pm, Sat. 2pm and 4:30pm, Sun. 10am; winter Mon. 10am, Fri. 2pm, Sat.-Sun. 10am and 2pm; $15-20) provides a home to several packs of gray wolves, including animals from Alaska and Mexico. Regularly scheduled tours include educational presentations and guided observations of two wolf packs. Reservations are required.

Eagle Mining Company

Offering a glimpse into Julian's gold rush past, the **Eagle Mining Company** (2320 C St., 760/440-6352, www.theeaglemining.com; Mon.-Fri. 10am-4pm, Sat.-Sun. 10am-5pm; $10 adults, $5 ages 5-13, $1 under age 5) offers tours 1,000 feet into the mile-deep mine, as well as gold-panning activities and insights into milling operations. Located close to the center of town, it provides a fun and educational couple of hours' worth of activities.

Julian Mining Company

Another place offering gold-panning activities is **Julian Mining Company** (4444 CA-78, 951/313-0166, www.julianminingcompany.com; Sat. 10am-5pm, Sun. noon-5pm; $9 adults, $7 under 12), a short way down the road from downtown Julian in the community of Wynola.

Julian Pioneer Cemetery

Dating to the 1870s and still in use, the **Julian Pioneer Cemetery** (Farmer Rd. at A St., 760/765-0436, www.juliancemetery.org) holds the final resting places of multiple generations of Julian natives. Perched on a hill at the north end of Main Street, the cemetery provides a beautiful if solemn vantage point to look out over Julian and the surrounding area.

Julian Pioneer Museum

The history of Julian is on display at the **Julian Pioneer Museum** (2811 Washington St., 760/765-0227, www.julianpioneermuseum.org; Thurs.-Sun. 10am-4pm; $3 adults, free under age 7), mostly in the form of 19th-century clothes, furniture, and mining equipment. You'll also find early photos of the people and town, as well as a horse buggy and information about the original Native American inhabitants of the area.

Santa Ysabel Mission

Technically an *asistencia*, this sub-mission was built in 1818 to serve those who could not regularly make it to the Mission Basilica San Diego de Alcalá. About eight miles northwest of Julian, **Santa Ysabel Mission** (23013 Hwy. 79, Santa Ysabel, 760/765-0810, www.missiontour.org) actually had a greater conversion rate among the Diegueño and Luiseño people. The original mission structure is long gone, with a more modern white-brick chapel built on the site in 1924 and a small museum revealing insights into the *asistencia*'s long history.

SPORTS AND ACTIVITIES

Apple and pear picking late summer-early fall can be a fun way to occupy your trip to Julian. There are more than 100 years of history behind **Peacefield Boutique Orchard** (3803 Wynola Rd., 855/936-2775; Sat.-Sun. 10:30am-3:30pm). Pears have made a strong showing in recent years, and they can be picked at **O'Dell's Pear Orchard** (1095 Julian Orchard Dr., 760/765-1174; Sat.-Sun. 11am-4pm). If you prefer organic produce, pick the apples and pears at **Apple Starr Orchards** (1020 Julian Orchard Dr., 760-305-2169, www.apple-starr.com; Sat.-Sun. 10am-5pm). Seasonal harvests vary annually but typically begin in late August. Picking opportunities tend to be on weekends only, though orchards may accept weekday appointments on a case-by-case basis.

RESTAURANTS

The **Julian Café & Bakery** (2112 Main St., 760/765-2712, www.juliancafe.com; Mon.-Thurs. 8am-7:30pm, Fri. 8am-8:30pm, Sat. 7am-9pm, Sun. 7am-8:30pm; $10-15) was built in 1882 but burned down in 1957. Nevertheless, this rebuilt structure from 1978 tries to capture that old-time spirit, complete with an extensive breakfast menu and apple pies. Just up the street, the **Miner's Diner** (2134 Main St., 760/765-3753, www.minersdinerjulian.com; Tues.-Thurs., 10am-5pm, Fri.-Sat. 8am-6pm, Sun.-Mon. 8am-5pm; $8-15) has more of a 1950s look and feel, with burgers and malts, good coffee, and, of course, apple pies.

For a slice of famous Julian pie, try selections from the **Julian Pie Company** (2225 Main St., 760/765-2449, www.julianpie.com; daily 9am-5pm; $8-12) or **Mom's Pies** (2119 Main St., 760/765-2472, www.momspiesjulian.com; Mon.-Thurs. 7am-5pm, Fri.-Sun. 7am-5:30pm; $17 for whole pie). Both offer traditional apple pies plus variations featuring local berries, including strawberry and boysenberry. If you're struggling to decide, get a slice from Mom's and a whole pie to go from Julian Pie Company.

Further satisfy your sweet tooth with a visit to the **Julian Cider Mill** (2103 Main St., 760/765-1430, www.juliancidermillinc.com; Mon.-Thurs. 9:30am-5pm, Fri.-Sun. 9:30am-5:30pm). The shop serves delicious cider as well as preserves and candy. It's pretty much a sweet tooth's idea of heaven.

Beer fans should head to **Nickel Beer Co.** (1485 Hollow Glen Rd., 760/765-2337, www.nickelbeerco.com; Mon.-Thurs. 2pm-7:30pm, Fri. 11:30am-8:30pm, Sat. 11am-8:30pm, Sun. 11am-7:30pm), where Tom Nickel, one of the original brewers who put San Diego on the craft beer map, makes beer in a small house with a big patio loaded with fresh air.

If your drinking interests skew more toward wine, visit the local station of urban winemaker **Blue Door Winery** (2608 B St., 760/765-0361, www. thebluedoorwinery.com; Thurs.-Mon. noon-5pm), or sample locally produced wine at the **Orfila Tasting Room** (2000 Main St., 760/765-0102, www.orfila.com; Thurs.-Mon. 11am-5:30pm).

Down the road a few miles in Wynola, several businesses operate tasting rooms at **Julian Station** (4470 Julian Rd., 760/885-8364, www.julianstation.com; Sun.-Wed. 11am-7pm, Thurs.-Sat. 11am-8pm), including hard cider, wine, chocolate, and mead businesses. It also operates a bar and hosts live music.

HOTELS

An overnight stay in Julian doesn't get more central than the **Julian Gold Rush Hotel** (2032 Main St., 760/765-0201, www.julianhotel.com; from $95). The "oldest continuously operated hotel in Southern California" appears in the National Register of Historic Places, though it has been upgraded since 1897 to include amenities like air-conditioning and Wi-Fi. Only slightly less central is the more modern and dog-friendly **Julian Lodge** (2720 C St., 760/765-1420, www.julianlodge.com; from $100), just a block off Main Street.

The highest-rated stay in Julian can be found at **Orchard Hill Country Inn** (2502 Washington St., 760/765-1700, www.orchardhill.com; from $250). Located just uphill from the center of town, the lodge rooms and cottages of this Four Diamond property are country hospitable, right down to the patchwork quilts.

A few miles outside of town in a quiet, natural setting, the **Observer's Inn** (3535 Hwy. 79, 760/765-0088, www.observersinn.com; from $150) boasts a comfortable stay with a bonus: astronomy. The B&B offers "Sky Tours," setting up telescopes for guests to stargaze at the dark night sky. **Wikiup Bed & Breakfast** (1645 Whispering Pines Dr., 800/694-5487, www. wikiupbnb.com; from $150) doesn't show you the stars, but if you prefer a hot tub, massage, and carriage rides, this comfortable woodsy lodge might be for you.

PRACTICALITIES

You will need a car for the day trip to Julian, which is 60 miles northeast of San Diego and about a 1.5-hour drive. From San Diego, take I-8 east for about 25 miles (about 40 minutes), then head north on Highway 79 for 25 miles (another 30 minutes) to Julian. The mountain town is also doable as a side trip from Escondido; Highway 78 leads west to Julian in about 40 miles (one hour).

Top: buildings in Julian. Bottom: sculptures by Ricardo Breceda in Galleta Meadows.

Borrego Springs

Past Julian, on the other side of the Laguna mountain range, the tiny town of Borrego Springs isn't much of a destination on its own. However, because it provides access to the ethereal beauty of Anza-Borrego Desert State Park, it receives a fair amount of nature-loving visitors from San Diego each year. It's a great overnight trip for those seeking unlit skies to enjoy meteor showers and other astronomical events. But its biggest draw is the desert flower bloom each spring.

As in any arid landscape, you'll find a couple of golf courses, but the most intriguing discoveries around Borrego Springs are life-sized metal animal sculptures spread out across the desert plain. Bear in mind—this is a desert, and temperatures may reach and exceed 100°F. Merely standing outside in the extreme dry heat can dehydrate a person in minutes. Bring plenty of water and sun protection.

SIGHTS
Anza-Borrego Desert State Park
The annual spring bloom adds color to the desert floor of the 640,000 acres of **Anza-Borrego Desert State Park** (300 Palm Canyon Dr., 760/767-4205, http://www.parks.ca.gov). The timing, length, and size of the bloom depends on how much or little rain the area receives in the winter—you can find updates on the park's website or that of the **Anza-Borrego Foundation** (http://theabf.org). Plan your visit around the **Anza-Borrego Desert State Park Visitors Center** (300 Palm Canyon Dr.), which offers parking and more detailed information about hiking, safety, and the red, purple, yellow, orange, white, and pink flowers around the park. Visit early during bloom season—not only do visitors fill up the park after 10am, but lower morning temperatures make for floral activity.

Galleta Meadows
Artist Ricardo Breceda made a *Tyrannosaurus rex* for his dinosaur-fan daughter in 2001, and in the time since he's been commissioned to add more than 100 life-sized metal sculptures of animals, many of them scattered across the Borrego desert. Wandering **Galleta Meadows** (the fields surrounding Borrego Springs Rd. and Big Horn Rd., www.abdnha.org) turns up mythical beasts—including a mesmerizing sea dragon—horses, elephants, and animals native to the region. He's made this desert one of the world's best sculpture gardens.

Borrego Art Institute
A gallery at the **Borrego Art Institute** (665 Palm Canyon Dr., 760/767-5152, www.borregoartinstitute.org; Tues.-Sun. 10am-5pm) brings rotating shows, mostly of desert artists, featuring anything from pottery to paintings and photography.

SPORTS AND ACTIVITIES

Desert hiking proves the top activity around Borrego Springs, with a mix of easy valley and canyon hikes, plus others that climb higher into high desert. For an easy taste of Borrego hiking, start at the **Anza-Borrego Desert State Park Visitors Center** (300 Palm Canyon Dr.) for its all-access trails. A paved path heads north 0.7 mile to the Palm Canyon Campground, with signs highlighting local flora and fauna as you go. To the right of the visitors center, a 0.3-mile loop on compacted dirt offers an opportunity to see a rare desert fish, the pupfish, which can survive in extreme temperatures and high salinity.

Start at the west end of the Borrego Palm Canyon Campground for the three-mile, two-hour **Borrego Palm Canyon** hike (200 Palm Canyon Dr.), the park's most popular. The canyon follows a stream 600 feet up to a desert oasis, and you may spot *borregos*—a.k.a. bighorn sheep—along the way. Rather than turn back at the 1.5-mile mark, there's an option to climb another couple thousand feet in altitude to the top of Indian Head, passing a waterfall and capturing an expansive view of the desert valley. Expect 6-8 hours round-trip for this rigorous hike.

A family-friendly 1.2-mile loop delivers a valley view from the **Kenyon Overlook** (1.9 miles north of CA-78 on Yaqui Pass Road, 60 yards from mile marker 2) and takes about an hour. For something more involved, plan on four hours to complete the six-mile, out-and-back hike to **Hellhole Canyon and Maidenhair Falls** (0.8 mile south of Palm Canyon Dr. on Montezuma Borrego Hwy.). The scary-sounding canyon is truly misnamed; it's a relatively pleasant 1,000-foot climb to the 18-foot cascade of Maidenhair Falls.

RESTAURANTS

There aren't very many dining options in Borrego Springs. The local favorite is **Red Ocotillo** (721 Avenida Sureste, 760/767-7400; daily 7am-8:30pm; $10-16), a breezy casual restaurant offering burgers, sandwiches, salads, and pasta. Located at the Borrego Art Institute, **Kesling's Kitchen** (665 Palm Canyon Dr., 760/767-7600; daily 11am-9pm; $10-15) offers from-scratch Mediterranean food but is best known for its wood-fired pizzas.

For Old West saloon style, opt for **Big Horn Bar & Grill** (221 Palm Canyon Dr., 676/767-5341, www.palmcanyonrvresort.com; Oct.-Jun. Sun. and Thurs.-Fri. 11:30am-8pm, Fri.-Sat. 11:30am-9pm; $8-22). The Palm Canyon Hotel serves a small menu mostly of hot sandwiches, and its country-style dining patio offers gorgeous views of the surrounding landscape. One caveat: It's closed during the hot summer months. For a divey, biker bar atmosphere, check out the from-scratch burgers, grinders, steaks, and salads at **Carlee's Place** (660 Palm Canyon Dr., 760/767-3262, www.carleesplace.com; Sun.-Thurs. 11am-10pm, Fri.-Sat. 11am-midnight, $9-16).

HOTELS

Lovingly restored midcentury architecture awaits you at **The Palms at Indian Head** (2220 Hoberg Rd., 760/767-7788, www.thepalmsatindianhead. com; from $139), which claims Marilyn Monroe, Bing Crosby, and Cary Grant as guests during its original heyday. Today the visually sumptuous lobby and pool area continue to enjoy enviable proximity to the desert park, though rooms are in short supply, so plan ahead. Midcentury meets the Wild West at charming **Palm Canyon Hotel & RV Resort** (221 Palm Canyon Dr., 760/767-5341, www.palmcanyonrvresort.com; Mon., from $80), where you can rent a Southwestern-style room or a vintage Airstream trailer.

Stylish and comfortable rooms aren't the only draw to **La Casa Del Zorro** (3845 Yaqui Pass Rd., 760/767-0100, www.lacasadelzorro.com; from $109); the resort offers large pools, tennis courts, a fitness center, yoga studio, and spa services. A PGA-sanctioned 18-hole golf course is the chief draw to **Borrego Springs Resort** (1112 Tilting T Dr., 760/767-5700, www.borregospringsresort.com; from $116), which also offers poolside cabanas, bicycles, free shuttles, tennis, and spa services.

A true desert resort, the adobe **Borrego Valley Inn** (405 Palm Canyon Dr., 760/767-0311, www.highwaywestvacations.com; from $235) offers perks such as in-room fireplaces or Jacuzzis on a property that perfectly matches the lure of the desert park.

For those looking to rough it in the desert, the **Borrego Palm Canyon Campground** (200 Palm Canyon Dr., 760/767-4238, www.reservecalifornia.com; Oct.-Apr.; $20-25 campsites, $35 RVs) is near the entrance of the desert park and offers more than 100 sites. Reservations are recommended during the spring bloom.

PRACTICALITIES

It takes about two hours by car to make the 80-plus mile drive to Borrego Springs from San Diego. From San Diego, take I-8 east for about 25 miles (about 40 minutes), then head north on Highway 79 for 25 miles (another 30 minutes) to Julian, then CA-78 east for 31 miles (45 minutes).

While bus service is offered on lines 891 and 892 from the **El Cajon Transit Center** (352 S. Marshall Ave., 619/233-3004, www.sdcommute. com), eastbound routes of each line are limited to Thursday and Friday at 2:30pm, departing Borrego Springs at 7:45am, also Thursday and Friday. Each trip takes about three hours.

October-April is the best time to visit Borrego Springs, particularly during the spring bloom. The rest of the year, the Anza-Borrego Desert gets extremely hot, with temperatures often exceeding 100°F, so it's important to carry lots of water and stay hydrated. Surprisingly, summer monsoons also make the desert prone to flash floods during that time. It's a potentially dangerous time to explore, even before you consider this is a native habitat for rattlesnakes.

Borrego Springs itself sits at about 600 feet above sea level, while mountain portions of Anza-Borrego Desert State Park reach an elevation of 4,000 feet. You may experience climate shifts with elevation, and the temperatures fluctuate greatly from daytime to nighttime. Plan accordingly.

Tijuana, Mexico

One of San Diego's greatest cultural assets is its proximity to Mexico; the multi-faceted border-town wouldn't be the same without its sister-city to the south, Tijuana (or, as we like to call it, TJ). Tijuana is the second largest city in the state of Baja California, Mexico, with a population of 1.8 million. Twenty miles south of downtown San Diego, the sprawling TJ hugs the entire length of the U.S. border, from beach to mountains, and offers a tantalizing glimpse of the sights, sounds, and flavors of Mexico. Millions of tourists visit annually to revel in the city's colorful souvenirs, folk music, spicy food, cheap beers, and extreme bargain shopping.

While Tijuana got its start in the late 19th century, it didn't really boom until the U.S. made alcohol illegal in the 1920s, which drove Americans across the border in search of booze and good times, which often included gambling, prostitution, and narcotics. Tijuana learned to profit off lurid appetites, and sadly, many Americans still visit with the same intentions, particularly teenagers taking advantage of the lower legal drinking age.

In recent years, however, Tijuana has emerged as one of the region's most talked-about destinations for dining, performance, and visual arts. Its emerging, progressive cultural identity has proven a refreshing change from its years of being known as a corrupt party town.

Present-day Tijuana exists within this strange duality: On the one hand, it's a culturally rich city of nearly two million people, home to emerging artists, creative entrepreneurs, and celebrity chefs. On the other, it's a seedy adult resort, serving cheap beer and street tacos (the best in the West) late into the night. Whichever Tijuana you prefer to visit, you can expect to have a blast.

Due to a relatively depressed economy, the costs of doing anything in TJ are considerably less than in the U.S. Most visitors stick to the urban center, Zona Centro, adjacent business hub Zona Rio, or venture west to uncrowded beaches, Playas de Tijuana.

SIGHTS
Avenida Revolución
It's only a couple thousand feet from U.S. soil, but **Avenida Revolución** is the living center of Tijuana, as far as tourists are concerned. Referred to in loving shorthand as La Revu, it's a wide avenue of shops, bars, clubs, tobacconists, and casinos. Historically, the active street has catered to often unsavory American appetites, but in recent years, the locals have started

catering to themselves instead. A creative entrepreneurial culture has consequently emerged in the form of street art, music, breweries, and a new generation of businesses emanating gritty cosmopolitan charm. However, the signature cheap souvenirs of La Revu are still hawked here, as are cheap beers and photo-ops with the street's famous "zonkeys" (donkeys painted with stripes to resemble zebras).

Tijuana Arch & Plaza Santa Cecilia

The most immediately visible sites as you enter Tijuana are an enormous Mexican flag flying over the border and El Arco del Milenio, better known as the **Tijuana Arch** (Av. Revolución at Calle Primera). Erected in 2000 and loosely inspired by the St. Louis Arch, the Arch stands as an ornamental entryway to La Revu. More recently, it's been wired up with a large video screen. Just below the arch is the colorful **Plaza Santa Cecilia,** the original city center. The plaza is now a tourist-friendly market square punctuated on busy days by *papel picado* décor, live mariachi music, and folk dance performances.

Centro Cultural Tijuana

Referred to locally as CECUT (pronounced like say-coot), the **Centro Cultural Tijuana** (9350 Paseo de los Héroes, Zona Rio, 52-664/687-9600, www.cecut.gob.mx; daily 9am-9pm; adults US$2.75/MX$48, children US$1.50/MX$27, students and teachers US$1.60/MX$29), this government sponsored cultural center serves as Tijuana's top museum. It shows permanent and rotating art exhibitions, focused on Baja works as well as International touring shows. It occasionally stages musical, dance, and theater performances; and has an IMAX theater in the massive dome out front.

Guided Tours

Guided tours of Tijuana will provide updated local insights to a city that's humming with new street art, hip bars, star chefs, and hip drinking spots in addition to transportation and border-crossing assistance. Contact ¡**Let's Go Clandestino!** (letsgoclandestino.net; from US$125/MX$2300) to arrange a curated private trip around Tijuana and even down to Baja wine country if a greater excursion is desired. It also offers occasional larger, public outings, often revolving around food and drink festivals.

SPORTS AND ACTIVITIES

Perhaps the most unique spectacle sport in all of Mexico is Luche Libre, or masked wrestling. The 150-year-old form of entertainment involves colorfully masked luchadores, beloved characters who create dramatic storylines ahead of high-flying wrestling bouts. Friday night matches take place in the southeast section of town at **Auditorio Municipal Fausto Gutierrez Moreno** (Blvd. Gustavo Díaz Ordaz at Blvd. do las Americas, 52/664/250-9015). Tickets and schedules may sometimes be found at ticketing website

Ticket Móvil (www.ticketmovil.com.mx), but it's easy to buy cheap tickets at the door ahead of shows starting at 8:30pm.

The matadors (almost) always win the bullfights at the Bullring by the Sea, officially known as **Monumental Plaza de Toros** (Av. Del Pacífico 4, Playas de Tijuana, 52/656613-1182, www.monumentalmexico.com), right beside the U.S. border in Playas de Tijuana. However, the state of Baja California, Mexico came close to banning bullfights in 2016, and no fights were scheduled here in 2017. They are rumored to return in 2018, with fighting season stretching sporadically from March to August.

Even U.S. soccer fans follow Club Tijuana in the Liga MX México Primera División. The pro team is more commonly known as the Xolos (pronounced cholos), as their mascot is the famous Mexican hairless dog breed, Xoloitzcuintle. The team plays home games August-April south of Zona Rio at **Estadio Caliente** (12027 Blvd. Agua Caliente, Hipodromo Agua Caliente).

Another Tijuana pro sports team, the Toros, play minor Mexican league baseball April-August in the southeast portion of the city at **Estadio Gasmart** (Mision de Santo Tomas at Rio Eufrates, 52/664/635-5600, www.torosdetijuana.com).

Gambling is legal in Tijuana for those 18 and older, and all of the casinos are owned by the family of **Caliente Casinos** (www.calientecasino.com.mx). They're easy to find on La Revu, particularly **Casino Jai Alai** (1100 Av. Revolución, Zona Centro, 52/664/638-4308; daily 24 hours), built within the city's historic Jai Alai Palace, easily recognized for its Moroccan inspired architecture and the giant red "Jai Alai" sign. Close to the border crossing, the snazziest new casino venue is **Hotel Pueblo Amigo** (9211 Vía Rapida Oriente, Zona Río, 52/664/624-2700, www.hotelpuebloamigo.com; daily 24 hours).

Both the Monumental Plaza de Toro and the Jai Alai Palace double as concert venues.

★ RESTAURANTS

Tijuana's rich array of dining options ranges from unforgettable Mexican street food to fine dining for a fraction of the price of equivalent meals in San Diego. The city's greatest culinary claim to fame is **Caesar's** (1059 Av. Revolución, Zona Centro, 52-664/685-1927, www.caesarstijuana.com; Mon.-Tues. 11:30am-10pm, Wed. 11:30am-11pm, Thurs.-Sat. 11:30am-midnight, Sun. 11:30am-9pm; US$15-25/MX$280-470), the historic birthplace of the Caesar salad. This classic, American-style steak house on La Revu is trimmed in dark wood and hosts jazz performances on weekends. Highlights of the deep menu include the beef wellington, a terrific bone marrow *sope,* and the signature salad, which is made tableside.

A block away, Zona Centro's best contemporary restaurant is the overachieving gastropub **La Justina** (1232 Av. Revolución, Zona Centro, 52-664/638-4936, www.facebook.com/lajustinatj; Tue.-Thurs. 2pm-1am, Fri.-Sat. 2pm-2am, US$12-20/MX$220-370), which handles burgers and craft beer with the same deftness as it does craft cocktails and addictive *tiraditos*—Latin America's answer to sushi.

For the best fine dining, look to Zona Rio, and particularly to **Mision 19** (10643 Misión de San Javier, Zona Río, 52/664/634-2493, www.mision19. com; Sun.-Thurs. 11am-10pm, Fri.-Sat. 11am-midnight; US$9-16/MX$165-300). Chef Javier Plascencia, face of the Baja-Mediterranean movement, puts out dishes adeptly blending simplicity and great ingredients *a la* the Mediterranean with rustic Mexican culinary traditions, resulting in dishes like dry-aged ribeye steaks, Baja farmed oysters, and grilled octopus. Between the fine wines, attentive table service, and elegant décor, Mision's dining rooms feel a world removed from Tijuana's urban street life.

If you only eat one thing in Tijuana, it should be tacos—lots of them. Make a pilgrimage to Taco Alley, a.k.a. **Las Ahumaderas** (9770 Guilermo Prieto), a cluster of taco shops that have attained local cult status over the past half century. The latest obsession is the busy Zona Rio taco counter at **Tacos El Franc** (9013 Blvd. Sánchez Taboada, Zona Rio, 52/667/142-2955, www.tacoselfranc.com; Mon.-Thurs. 4pm-1am, Fri.-Sat. 3pm-3am, US$3-6/MX$55-110). The street tacos sell for less than a buck-fifty apiece, and the sloppy *al pastor* rotisserie pork might be the tastiest thing in the city. Save some room for a stop across the street at TJ mainstay **Tacos El Gordo** (9210 Blvd. General Rodolfo Sánchez Taboada, Zona Rio, www.tacoselgordobc. com; Sun.-Thurs. 8am-2am, Fri.-Sat. 8am-4am, US$3-8/MX$55-150); it serves a long list of regional favorites as well as *antojitos.*

For a classic Tijuana seafood experience near La Revu, head to **La Corriente Cevicheria Nais** (803 Flores Magón, Zona Centro, 52/664/685-0555, www.palmcanyonrvresort.com; July-Sept. Mon.-Wed. 11:30am-10pm, Thurs. 11:30am-11pm, Fri.-Sat. 11:30am-midnight, Sun. 11:30am-9:30pm, Oct.-Jun. Thurs.-Fri. 11am-9pm, Sat.-Sun. 8am-9pm; US$4-10/MX$75-185), a beachy, thatched-roof restaurant that has served over 200,000 red snapper ceviche tostadas. Definitely try one of those, along with other ceviches and *aguachiles,* shrimp and other seafood cocktails, fish and shrimp tacos, and anything octopus. Find similar offerings on the border of Zona Rio at the food truck **Mariscos Ruben** (Calle 8va Miguel Hidalgo and Av. Andrés Quintana Roo, Zona Rio; daily 10am-6pm, US$4-8/MX$75-150), which has earned so much cachet over decades at this spot that it's the first seafood stop for every famous chef visiting Tijuana.

The Baja culinary community tends to lift each other up, and nowhere is that better displayed than the rise in cooperative food courts, where up-and-coming chefs serve from individual food counters around a shared dining space. On La Revu, step into an alley leading into **Colectivo 9** (1265 Av. Revolución, Zona Centro, 760/767-5341, www.colectivo9.com; Tues.-Thurs. 1pm-8pm, Fri.-Sat. 1pm-midnight, Sun. 1pm-8pm; US$4-8/MX$75-150), where you'll find food counters serving hamburgers, pasta, sushi, coffee, beer, and wine. At the Plaza Rio mall, skip the food court in favor of the **Foodgarden** (11821 Av. Vía Rápida Poniente, Zona Rio., 52/664/634-1087, www.foodgarden.mx; Sun.-Thur. 10am-10pm, Fri.-Sat. 10am-11pm;

Clockwise from top left: Plaza Santa Cecilia; Mexican candies at Mercado Hidalgo; businesses along La Revu.

US$4-12/MX$75-220), offering Mediterranean, Italian, ramen, and rotis-serie chicken. The best of the bunch is the food truck and beer garden col-lectively known as **Telefonica** (8924 Blvd. Aguacaliente, 52/664/684-8782, www.carleesplace.com; Mon.-Wed. 8am-10pm, Thurs. 8am-11pm, Fri.-Sat. 8am-11:30pm, Sun. 8am-9pm; US$4-10/MX$75-185). A craft beer taplist pairs with your choice of street foods, including vegan tacos, gourmet sau-sages, *tortas,* seafood, and *barbacoa.*

★ NIGHTLIFE

Tijuana's famously raucous nightlife centers around the collective city blocks known as **La Sexta** (Calle 6ta Flores Magón at Av. Revolución, Zona Centro)—so called because it's on *Calle Sexta,* or "Sixth Street." Step east of La Revu onto La Sexta and you'll find a dozen bars and clubs compet-ing for your attention with music and drink specials. The one must-visit destination is **Dandy del Sur Cantina** (8274 Flores Magón, Zona Centro, 52/664/688-0052; daily 9am-3am), the heart and soul of La Sexta. It's an intimate dive of dark polished wood, known for its jukebox, stiff cocktails, and inimitable ambiance.

Across the street, **La Mezcaleria** (8267 Calle Sexta Flores Magón, 52/664/688-0384, www.palmcanyonrvresort.com; Tue.-Thurs. 6pm-2am, Fri.-Sun. 6pm-3am) is a relative hole in the wall, and has become a favorite stop of Tijuana and San Diego urbanites, thanks to its cheap-shots tour of up to 17 mezcal varieties, including *mezcal de pechuga,* which draws distinctive flavor during a distillation process featuring raw chicken. For more mezcal in cozier surroundings, look behind **La Corriente Cevicheria Nais** for its sister bar **El Tinieblo Mezcal Room** (221 Calle Sexta Flores Magón, Zona Centro, 52/664/685-0555; Thurs. 7pm-2am, Fri.-Sat. 5pm-3am), where DJs provide a smoother soundtrack.

To seek out TJ's larger dance club environments, go back on La Revu, just south of La Sexta; most weekends will be lively at **Las Pulgas** (1127 Av. Revolución, Zona Centro, 52/664/685-9594, www.laspulgas.mx; daily noon-6am). When Zona Centro really gets going, however, it's worth the experience to explore its "mega nightclub," **Coko Bongo** (1656 Av. Revolución, Zona Centro, 52/664/638-7353, www.cokobongo.com; daily 8pm-5am), offering multiple dancefloors so you can find the vibe you like. Ladies are strongly encouraged to use the buddy system visiting these spots.

To see where Tijuana's creative crowd drinks, head to the rooftop of **Cine Tonalá** (1317 Av. Revolución, Zona Centro, 52/664/688-0118, www. cinetonala.com; Tue.-Sun. 1pm-2am), which offers live music and DJ's, cocktails, and reasonably upscale dining in a classy open-air environment. Meanwhile, the cinema downstairs plays documentaries and art films and hosts live speakers.

To enjoy a beer while exploring La Revu, check out the **Mamut Brewing Co.** tasting room at **Pasaje Rodriguez** (906 Av. Revolución, Zona Centro) or head upstairs through **Foreign Club Parking Structure** (Calle Salvador Díaz Mirón 4ta, a half block west of Av. Revolución) to drink beers with a fifth story view of the city at **Norte Brewery** (52/664/638-4891, www. nortebrewing.com; Mon.-Thur. 2pm-10pm, Thurs.-Sat. 2pm-midnight). But the best place to experience Tijuana's craft beer scene is **Plaza Fiesta** (9440 Erasmo Castellanos Q., Zona Rio, 52/664/202-7267, www.thepalm-satindianhead.com; plaza open daily 24 hours, most businesses noon-2am), a cooperative of bars and brewery tasting rooms unlike anything you'll find in the U.S. The favorite local beermakers to check out here include **Insurge Cervecería Insurgente, Border Psycho Brewery**, and **Madueño Brewing Co.**

★ SHOPPING

Tijuana never runs out of souvenirs; you'll find them at every turn, particularly along La Revu and Plaza Santa Cecilia. But the best place to find them is **Mercado de Artesanías** (621 Av. Melchor Ocampo, Zona Centro; daily 6am-6pm), a loose collection of shops with low prices on Mexican crafts, including clothes, leather products, talavera tiles, pottery, housewares, and textiles. To get a taste of local tastes, visit the sprawling **Mercado Hidalgo** (2 Guadalupe Victoria, Zona Rio, 52/664/684-0485; Mon.-Sat. 6am-6pm, Sun. 6am-4:30pm), loaded with stalls selling local fruits and vegetables, Mexican sweets, spiced nuts, dried chilis, cooking oils, dairy products, meats, and sausages.

A new generation of artists and entrepreneurs have sprung up around La Revu in recent years, resulting in a cluster of small, independent shops off the main street. The murals and galleries alone are worth a visit to **Pasaje Rodriguez** (906 Av. Revolución, Zona Centro; Mon.-Sat. 9am-10pm, Sun. 9am-8pm), but it's also got a craft brewery, a used bookstore, a record store, a bike shop, and some terrific spots to drink coffee.

Zona Rio's resident shopping mall, **Plaza Rio** (96-98 Paseo de los Héroes, Zona Rio, 52/800704-5900, www.palmcanyonrvresort.com; daily 10am-10pm) is modeled after the suburban American shopping mall, complete with food courts and movie theaters. **Outlets at the Border** (4463 Camino De La Plaza, San Ysidro, 619/651-8018, www.outletsattheborder.com; Mon.-Sat. 10am-9pm, Sun. 10am-7pm) actually sits on the American side of the border wall, but the populations on both sides are drawn to the collection of popular brand outlets.

HOTELS

To stay right on Avenida Revolución, try the boutique lodging at **One Bunk** (920 Av. Revolución, Zona Centro, www.onebunk.com; from US$32/ MX$600); it's stylish but stays cheap thanks to the unstoppable street noise of La Revu. A few blocks up, **Hotel Ticuan** (3845 Yaqui Pass Rd., 760/767-0100, www.lacasadelzorro.com; from US$74/MX$1400) is larger and provides a quieter stay, offering the equivalent of an American three-star hotel experience.

For a central stay that's also close to the border, the bare-boned but clean **B My Hotel** (221 Palm Canyon Dr., 760/767-5341, www.

palmcanyonrvresort.com; from US$40/MX$750) offers quick highway access in any direction and sits within walking distance of both Zona Centro and Zona Rio. Casino-goers may benefit from a stay at **Hotel Pueblo Amigo** (9211 Vía Rapida Oriente, Zona Río, 52/664/624-2700, www.hotelpuebloamigo.com; from US$68/MX$1300), part of a multi-million dollar Caliente Casino property.

Zona Rio proves the place to go for more executive-friendly lodgings, led by a familiar brand at **Hyatt Place Tijuana** (10488 Blvd. Agua Caliente, Zona Rio, 52/664/900-1234, tijuana.place.hyatt.com; from US$115/MX$2200), with well-appointed rooms and free parking. The **Hotel Lucerna Tijuana** (10902 Paseo de los Héroes, Zona Rio, 52/664/633-3900, www.hoteleslucerna.com; from US$115/MX$2200) sits on a large and picturesque property, offering a great bang for your buck. Its adjacent sister hotel, **K Tower** (10902 Paseo de los Héroes, Zona Rio, 52/664/633-7500, www.ktowerhotel.com; from US$200/MX$3750), costs a bit more, but is still a tremendous bargain; it delivers luxurious furnishings, a sushi restaurant, and a rooftop pool deck with a panoramic view.

Those looking for a cheap stay by the beach or for a quieter experience can find hostel-style accommodations at **LifeStyle Hostel** (820 Av. Del Pacifico, Playas de Tijuana, 52/664/976-8244; from US$17/MX$310 dorm, US$40/MX$740 private). It's a long cab ride from Zona Centro, but both the transportation and hostel fares are far cheaper than those in American beach communities.

PRACTICALITIES
Language
Spanish is spoken by nearly the entire local population of Tijuana; many locals, especially those working in the city's frequently-touristed areas, speak some amount of English, but the majority do not. It will be helpful to know a few basic Spanish phrases before visiting.

Money
The official currency of Mexico is the peso, though most businesses gladly accept the U.S. dollar as currency for a favorable approximation of the current exchange rate (usually 14-20 pesos/1 dollar). Those approaching the border crossing on foot will find it surrounded by money exchanges and ATMs issuing pesos in paper currency in denominations of 20, 50, 100, 200, and 500. Coins are issued in 20-and-smaller denominations.

Poverty rates in Baja California exceed 40%, and many of its residents come to Tijuana seeking income. Tipping is a vital practice towards supporting Tijuana's service industry, usually 10-20% at restaurants, 10-15 pesos per drink at bars, and 25-50 pesos each morning for hotel housekeeping. Taxi drivers do not expect tips.

Haggling for consumer goods is alive and well in Tijuana; within many shops and markets, prices may be negotiable.

Drinking

The drinking age in Mexico is 18; beer, wine, and cider may be served to those 16 years and older. Speaking of drinking: the tap water in Tijuana is not entirely safe for outsiders to drink and can cause digestive distress. As a precaution, drink only bottled water and other packaged beverages and only from glasses with no ice.

Safety

Crime has historically been a concern in Tijuana, ranging from petty crimes to serious incidents. On the petty side, pickpockets and purse-snatchers prey on crowds, and street hustlers are very much a part of daily life around La Revu. The aggressive requests for tourist attention are usually harmless attempts to attract business, but some may be more persistent and nefarious. Take care not to wander farther north than Calle Primera, or you'll find yourself in Zona Norte, Tijuana's red light district, where the aggressive offers turn to prostitution and drugs.

The city's more serious issues include high rates of sexual assault and kidnapping. The city also received a lot of attention in 2017 when its murder rate nearly doubled. By far the majority of these killings involved members of local gangs and drug cartels and took place well outside the tourists zones referenced within this guide. However, entering Tijuana does carry the assumption of more personal risk when compared to San Diego.

To avoid potential trouble, follow these four rules: don't wander alone, don't flaunt any valuables, stick to well-lit public spaces in tourist-friendly areas, and take a taxi or car-sharing service at night.

Finally, a history of corruption within the Tijuana police force has resulted in stories from tourists being forced to bribe both real and fraudulent uniformed officers with cash and possessions to avoid arrest. While the city has made strides in mitigating this practice, it is recommended not to behave in a way that may attract negative attention from local police.

To contact police and emergency services while in Tijuana, dial the number 066.

Getting There

Tijuana sits about 20 miles south of San Diego on the other side of the U.S. border with Mexico. You may enter Mexico by land or air, but either way, it requires a passport and baggage inspection. It does not, however, require a visa for citizens of the United States, Canada, and many other places. For detailed visa information visit https://consulmex.sre.gob.mx/sanfrancisco/index.php.

Crossing back from Tijuana into the United States often requires a more rigorous inspection and longer waits. It always requires a passport and any necessary visas for non-U.S. citizens.

The major crossing point for both cars and pedestrians is the **San Ysidro Port of Entry** (720 E San Ysidro Blvd., 619/690-8900, www.cbp.gov; daily

24 hours), located at the southern terminus of both the Interstate 5 and Interstate 805 freeways. It's the busiest border crossing in the western hemisphere, and most of that is traffic entering the U.S.: 25,000 pedestrians and 50,000 vehicles cross northbound each day—more than 2,000 per hour.

A less busy, alternate crossing point may be found 5.5 miles to the east, at the **Otay Mesa Port of Entry** (9777 Via De La Amistad, 619/690-7696, www.cbp.gov; daily 24 hours), where CA-905 and CA-125 meet.

Individuals in possession of a valid **SENTRI Pass** (Secure Electronic Network for Travelers Rapid Inspection) may enter through special lanes that cross into the U.S. at a much faster rate. Several SENTRI compatible Trusted Traveler programs are administered by **U.S. Customs and Border Protection** (ttp.cbp.dhs.gov), cost US$100-$200 in fees, require an in-person interview, and take several weeks to obtain. All passengers in a car attempting to cross through a designated SENTRI lane must possess a SENTRI pass in order for the car to pass into the U.S. Pedestrians with SENTRI access may enter through designated Ready Lanes at on-foot crossing points.

CAR

Due to the long wait times, the legal requirements of driving in Mexico, and the confusing nature of Tijuana roads, it is not recommended to drive into Tijuana unless you plan to continue south into the state of Baja. It's much cheaper and easier to get around in a taxi or car share.

That said, passing into Mexico by car takes only a few minutes most times of day at **San Ysidro Port of Entry**—the major exceptions being afternoon rush hours (particularly on Friday) and weekend mornings, when waits can be up to an hour. However, passing back into the U.S. by car can take up to a two and a half hours, with the worst times being mornings, evenings, and some weekend nights. The shortest wait times, often under 20 minutes, occur very late at night. A $740 million Port of Entry expansion pledges to significantly reduce wait times upon completion in 2019 or 2020, but early results indicate long lines may continue due to increased demand.

While somewhat shorter vehicle wait times are standard in both directions at the less busy **Otay Mesa Port of Entry,** the drive from central Tijuana typically adds twenty minutes or more.

Current estimated wait times at both locations may be checked via phone line or web site set up by **US Customs and Border Protection** (619/690-8999, bwt.cbp.gov).

Every car entering Mexico is required to carry Mexico-specific car insurance, typically at a rate of US$25-30 per day, with lower rates for weekly or monthly premiums. Kiosks selling insurance may be found by following signs to take the last freeway exit before the international border: **Camino de la Plaza** at San Ysidro, **Siempre Viva Road** at Otay Mesa. Car insurance may also be purchased in advance through websites such as **Baja Bound** (619/702-4292, www.bajabound.com). Some U.S. rental car agencies allow cars to be driven into Mexico with additional insurance policies.

Drivers with a valid U.S. driver's license may drive in Mexico, in addition to anyone with an International Driving Permit, which may be acquired in the United States through the **American Automobile Association** (877/735-1714, www.aaa.com).

The Tijuana River sits between the border crossing of Tijuana's downtown areas of Zona Centro and Zona Rio, and it wreaks havoc on the poorly planned city by weaving a maze of traffic circles, one way streets that double back on themselves, and four lane highways that abruptly fork in four different exit lanes. Consequently, at any moment, a car or pedestrian may suddenly veer into your lane, or violate your right of way, and a wrong turn can get you lost in an instant.

Street parking may be available, but it's quite affordable and advisable to park in secured, paid lots. When visiting Avenida Revolución, you may find reliable paid lots on Zona Centro's 4th street at the **Foreign Club Parking Structure** (Calle Salvador Díaz Mirón 4ta, half block west of Av. Revolución) and 8th street at the **Hotel Ticuán** (Calle Miguel Hidalgo 8va, half block west of Av. Revolución).

ON FOOT

To enter Tijuana on foot, visitors have the option to drive to the border and park or take public transportation.

When driving to the border to cross on foot, it's imperative to follow the freeway signs to take the "Last U.S. Exit"—**Camino de la Plaza** at San Ysidro, **Siempre Viva Road** at Otay Mesa. Paid parking is available at several private lots surrounding each border crossing point, charging a flat rate of US$6-10 for 24 hours on weekdays and US$20-25 on Fridays and weekends.

The Blue Line of the **San Diego Trolley** (619/557-4555, www.sdmts.com; US$2.50 one way) terminates with a station closer to the San Ysidro border crossing than any parking lot. The Blue Line departs from downtown every 15-30 minutes daily, from just after 4am until midnight. The trolley regularly departs San Ysidro from 5am daily, with the last train of the night leaving at 12:58am.

Crossing the border into Tijuana on foot requires a fair amount of walking—expect 10 minutes to walk a little less than a half-mile, not counting time at customs. Wheelchairs may be provided for those requiring accessibility assistance.

The San Ysidro Port of Entry now features two pedestrian crossing points. To the east of the freeway is the original pedestrian crossing point at **San Ysidro** (720 East San Ysidro Blvd.; daily 24 hours), which exits on the Tijuana side in front of **Plaza Viva Tijuana** (Avenida de la Amistad and Frontera). Pedestrians can access the path to the U.S. from the same location.

The newer crossing at **Pedwest** (499 Virginia Ave., San Ysidro; daily 6am-10pm) sits west of the freeway, beside the Outlets at the Border mall.

It exits to a pick up and drop off location called **Garita El Chaparral** (471 José María Larroque). Pedestrians can access the path to the U.S. from the same location.

AIR

Tijuana International Airport (Carretera Aeropuerto, 52/664/607-8200, www.tijuana-airport.com) primarily offers flights to and from other destinations in Mexico and Central/South America. It's an easy taxi ride into downtown Tijuana, though the airport sits right on the US border and recently opened Cross Border Xpress (www.crossborderxpress.com), a border crossing into the United States only available to those flying in or out of the airport.

Getting Around

Most sights in Zona Centro are a 15-30 minute walk from the U.S. border, accessed via a pedestrian bridge over the Tijuana River and through **Plaza Viva Tijuana** (Avenida de la Amistad and Frontera). But first-time visitors may feel more comfortable hiring a car. Public transportation within Tijuana revolves around taxis and car shares. A taxi stand outside each border crossing serves as an active pick-up and drop-off point.

The easiest car-sharing app to use here is **Uber** (www.uber.com), which offers precise and affordable transportation with short trips within the city center typically costing US$1.75/ MX$28. The Uber English option ensures your driver speaks English, but it may take longer to get a car. Consult your mobile carrier for cellular and data roaming packages within Mexico.

A more flexible cash option will be several types of taxi. The best bet is a taxi marked as **Taxi Libre,** driven by independent contractors. Negotiate a price up front to get to your destination, or request the driver use a meter. Either way, expect to pay US$3/ MX$54 or less to reach destinations within the city center from the border. As a rule of thumb, don't expect taxi drivers to offer exact change. Tipping is rare, but up to you.

Another option will be **yellow taxis,** though these drivers often charge twice a Taxi Libre, and likewise receive commissions if they can steer you towards specific businesses that may not be on your agenda. If you must take a yellow (or off color) taxi, definitely agree to a firm price for an explicit destination before you get in the car.

A third taxi option, **route taxis,** or *taxis de ruta* are vans that navigate the suburban lengths of the sprawling city on specific routes, much like buses, except you flag them down like taxis rather than wait at established stops. These can be useful to get you long distances—from city center to Playas de Tijuana, for example—likely for less than US$1/ MX$18. However, it can be confusing to understand the routes if you're not a local. This site offers the closest to a published map: http://contactoruta664.wixsite.com/ruta664/mapa.

Background

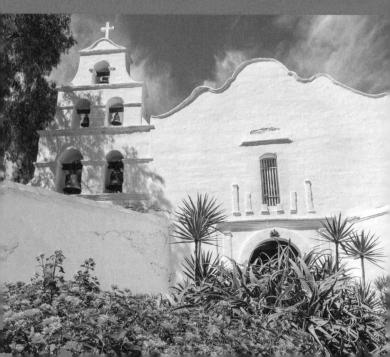

The Landscape

GEOGRAPHY

San Diego may be famous for its gorgeous Pacific coastline, but east of the city are the Laguna, Palomar, and Cuyamaca **mountain ranges,** responsible for keeping those beaches sunny and welcoming almost year-round. Part of the Peninsular Ranges, which extend from central California south into Mexico, these mountains act as a buffer against the clouds, maintaining San Diego's almost constant sunshine.

Santa Ana Winds

In fall and winter, high air pressure funnels through the mountain passes with such force that it dries out and warms up, forming what are known as Santa Ana winds. The **Santa Anas** account for some of the scorching-hot days San Diego sometimes experiences in the fall and even the winter. When the Santa Anas are blowing, the coast may actually be warmer than inland areas. The resulting offshore winds can carve some nice waves for surfers, but they also bring a lot of dry heat to an environment considered at high risk for **wildfires.**

Plants

The San Diego area is classified as semiarid. Aside from the mountain ranges, the landscape is dominated by **chaparral,** a drought-resistant and low-lying shrubland. Plants characteristic of chaparral tend to have evergreen leaves with oily skins that help retain moisture. Unfortunately, they are also highly flammable, making them fast fuel for wildfires.

Low-lying **coastal sage scrub** dominates close to the beach in environs typified by nature reserves such as the San Elijo and Batiquitos Lagoons, Peñasquitos Canyon, and Torrey Pines. The five-needle **Torrey pine** is one of the rarest pines in the United States. This endangered species grows only in the Torrey Pines State Natural Reserve, north of La Jolla, and on one of the Channel Islands, a loose archipelago off the California coast.

Much more common are **eucalyptus** trees, an invasive species that thrives in drought conditions and salty soil. The Australian native arrived in California with the gold rush, in an attempt to plant fast-growing hardwood for rail ties. Unfortunately, the soft wood was unusable, and instead proved to edge out native species. The heavily aromatic leaves and peeling gray bark are common indicators of their presence near canyons and parks.

Bays and Waterways

The original shifting course of the **San Diego River** proved too unreliable

Previous: sea lions at La Jolla Cove; Mission Basilica San Diego de Alcalá.

a water source for the growing city, A dam went up in the 1870s to form the El Capitan Reservoir (about 30 miles east of Mission Bay), and a fixed river channel was made for the runoff. The San Diego River flows out to the Pacific Ocean between Ocean Beach and Mission Beach, though it doesn't always look like much, particularly in the summer when dry conditions lower water levels to near wetland status.

Mission Bay used to be a vast system of wetlands known as False Bay; then 25 million cubic yards of sand and silt were dredged from the marshy area in the 1950s. There are still plenty of tidal marshes, estuaries, and lagoons along San Diego's North County coastline; these low-lying bodies of saltwater are not deep enough to be bays or inlets, yet not quite solid enough to form firm ground.

San Diego Bay is the city's most indelible asset. Large and outwardly protected by the partially overlapping Coronado and Point Loma peninsulas, this naturally protected harbor is what ultimately molded San Diego into the city it is today.

CLIMATE

San Diego enjoys 150 sunny days a year, with approximately 130 "partly cloudy" days (more like partly sunny) and 10 inches of annual rainfall. Summers are warm with cool nights, while winters are warm or cloudy during the day with colder nights.

In late May and June, a marine layer often rolls in over the city—a blanket of clouds held low in the sky by the pressure of an inversion layer. Locals call this phenomenon May Gray and June Gloom. During cool nights in fall and winter, fog creeps in over the ocean and covers the city in a gauzy overcast that lasts most of the day. East of I-5, this layer may dissipate into cloudless sunshine—a perfect example of San Diego's regional microclimates. Temperatures may rise 15 degrees just a few miles from the ocean. On average, inland San Diego and North County will be 10 degrees warmer on most days.

ENVIRONMENTAL ISSUES

California suffered a severe drought for several years, which eased thanks to historic rainfall in the winter of 2016. While statewide drought restrictions on water use subsequently have eased, the semiarid climate of San Diego continues, so it's considered practical to keep water waste to a minimum. For visitors, this means that hotels will launder towels and linens only by request; water is not served at restaurants unless specifically requested.

When it does rain, water runoff can pollute the beaches in and around the Pacific Ocean, making contact unsafe for up to 72 hours. Entering the water at this time puts you at risk of ear and throat infections and, the nastiest of all, staph infections. Anyone with an open wound or a weakened immune system is particularly at risk, especially children and the elderly. To confirm water safety, consult the county of San Diego's **Beach Water**

Clockwise from top left: a cactus in Balboa Park; the unique needles of the Torrey Pine tree; a sea cave at La Jolla Cove.

San Diego at a Glance

- **Average Annual Rainfall:** 9.9 inches (25 centimeters)

- **Average Daily Temperatures (High/Low):** 70/57°F (21/14°C)

- **City Land Area:** 325 square miles (842 square kilometers)

- **City Population:** 1.41 million

- **Coolest Months:** January-February at 65/48°F (18/9°C)

- **County Land Area:** 4,207 square miles (10,900 square kilometers)

- **County Population:** 3.3 million

- **Hotel Tax:** 10.5 percent

- **Hottest Month:** August at 76/66°F (24/19°C)

- **Incorporated:** 1850

- **Median Age:** 34.9 years

- **Median Household Income:** $63,400

- **Population Density:** 4,325 per square mile (1,670 per square kilometer)

- **Sales Tax:** 7.75 percent

- **Time Zone:** Pacific time

- **Wettest Months:** January-February, with 2 inches (5.1 centimeters)

Quality Hotline (619/338-2073, www.sdbeachinfo.com) to find out which beaches may be affected.

History

THE MISSION PERIOD

When Spanish conquistador Juan Rodríguez Cabrillo led the first Spanish ship into San Diego Bay in 1542, he encountered the region's original Native American inhabitants, the Kumeyaay people. The Kumeyaay wore clothing made from animal skins, reeds, or woven bark, and they lived in small thatched huts. At that time, the Kumeyaay were spread out among 30 clans connected by trade; some lived near the coast and would canoe miles offshore to fish. They would then trade with inland clans, who built dams and used fire to clear land for agriculture. A particularly large and central clan grew as a trade center along the San Diego River where the more robust waterway of the time drained into Mission Bay. In 1769, the landing party of Franciscan friar Junípero Serra chose this spot to establish California's first mission; the location gave him the chance to convert the greatest number of Kumeyaay people to Roman Catholicism.

The Mission Basilica San Diego de Alcalá was the first permanent European settlement in the expansive area that would become Alta California, claiming the region for Spain and opening the door to the establishment of 20 more missions throughout the state. Along with Serra came a garrison of Spanish troops who established a presidio (fort) along with the mission. Within five years, the mission moved several miles inland, but the presidio stayed where it was. As the Spanish presence grew, some retiring soldiers began building homes at the base of Presidio Hill. In 1821, after Alta California became part of Mexico following an 11-year war for independence from Spain, this cluster of adobe structures became the small village of San Diego. Its small population of ethnically mixed Californios developed the Mexican pueblo we know today as Old Town.

While Old Town survived for decades, it didn't exactly thrive. During the 1830s, the population fluctuated and the presidio fell into abandoned disrepair due to complications of transporting supplies from the nearest boat landing at Point Loma.

STATEHOOD

The Mexican-American War began in 1846 over border disputes in Texas and quickly encroached on California, which the United States coveted for coastal trade. The victory at the Battle of San Pasqual, in what is now north San Diego County, cemented the U.S. annexation of the territory. In 1848, Alta California was ceded to the United States, and in 1850, California became the 31st state. At the time, San Diego's population was around 650, which qualified it to become a county seat.

BOOM AND BUST

In the early 1860s, San Diego suffered floods, drought, a massive earthquake, and a smallpox epidemic. However, the city's natural harbor gave it great potential as a port of call for ships making the long journey around South America. In 1867, used-furniture dealer Alonzo Horton arrived in San Diego from San Francisco and bought 800 acres next to San Diego Bay for $265. He would go on to spend $45,000 to build a wharf that finally established a permanent shipping port. He sold 500-square-foot lots in what was then New Town San Diego, and by 1870, the population had grown to 2,300 people.

During a time of incredible growth, the new city boomed in size to nearly 40,000 people. With a promised connection to the transcontinental railroad, speculators were eager to invest, and public works projects saw the installation of electric streetlights, streetcars, and a flume that transported

Famous San Diegans

Many folks have contributed to the convoluted history of San Diego, but these names tend to show up around town on buildings, parks, and museums.

- **Juan Rodríguez Cabrillo:** During the 16th century, Cabrillo fought his way through Mexico and Guatemala with the Spanish conquistador Hernán Cortés. Following many years living and working in Guatemala, he led an exhibition to explore the coast of California. His was the first ship to enter San Diego Bay, which he apparently preferred to call San Miguel. Though he died before completing his expedition, Cabrillo Point in Point Loma marks the location where he may have first laid eyes on California.

- **William Heath Davis:** Davis is credited with having the idea to move San Diego from Old Town to a "New Town" beside the harbor. In 1850, he gathered investors to buy 160 acres and build a wharf in what is now downtown. However, a depression that hit in 1851 is blamed for dashing his plans. Aside from the house he built for himself (and never lived in), most of the buildings Davis and his investors built were torn down for scrap.

- **Irving J. Gill:** San Diego's most prominent turn-of-the-20th-century architect, Gill moved to San Diego in 1893 and enjoyed great esteem and a lengthy career that saw him design homes for statured residents like George Marston and Ellen Browning Scripps, as well as small economical cottages for working-class people. He's seen as a pioneer of the Arts and Crafts movement, and the effects of his influence may be seen in Craftsman homes throughout the city.

- **Alonzo E. Horton:** Horton managed to fulfill the "New Town" dream of William Heath Davis. In 1867, Horton took a steamboat from San Francisco to San Diego and wound up purchasing 800 acres at auction. He returned to San Francisco and diligently sold lots, sight unseen, to people inspired by the idea of the "American Riviera." He built a wharf and several buildings to cement his property next to the harbor as the new and permanent center of San Diego.

water from the Cuyamaca Mountains 35 miles away. However, this massive boom was followed by a colossal bust. As the railroad passage was rerouted, San Diego's spot on the map was relegated to a coastal spur line from Los Angeles. By the late 1880s, the population had dropped to 16,000 as the overzealous speculation failed to pay off.

THE 20TH CENTURY

Over the next 20 years the population would steadily creep back up. Local entrepreneurs and philanthropists spearheaded a movement to host an exposition commemorating the opening of the Panama Canal, which would make San Diego a much busier shipping destination. The Panama-California Exposition opened in 1914 at the newly developed Balboa Park,

- **George W. Marston:** Marston moved from Wisconsin to San Diego in 1870 at the age of 20. He dusted the coats of guests at the Horton House Hotel, then worked as a bookkeeper for a general store. Within 10 years, he owned the city's only department store. He was instrumental in developing Balboa Park, and he bought Presidio Hill in order to preserve the site of the city's original settlement.

- **Ellen Browning Scripps:** Scripps was a great philanthropist, and San Diego was her chief beneficiary. When the British-born newspaper publisher retired to La Jolla in 1896 at the age of 60, she had a mind to spread her wealth to the region. She lived in La Jolla for 35 years and spent millions on schools, hospitals, and gardens; established the Scripps Institute of Oceanography; and created the Natural History Museum at Balboa Park, among many other endeavors.

- **Junípero Serra:** Serra was a Franciscan friar who founded nine of the 21 California missions, starting with the Mission Basilica San Diego de Alcalá in 1769. He's credited with creating the first permanent European settlement in California.

- **Kate Sessions:** Known as the "Mother of Balboa Park," Sessions came to San Diego as a schoolteacher in 1884. In 1892, she leased land in Balboa Park to start a nursery, on the condition that she would plant 100 trees per year within the park and 300 more around the city. She is credited with introducing cypresses, oaks, pepper trees, and jacarandas to a city that had previously lacked them.

- **John D. Spreckels:** Spreckels had a massive impact on San Diego. After visiting San Diego in 1887, he built a wharf at the end of Broadway. Over the decades, he would become the richest man in San Diego, owning the ferry, streetcar, and local rail systems, both San Diego newspapers, Belmont Park, and most of Coronado, including the Hotel del Coronado. He built office buildings, theaters, and dams and contributed to the establishment of Balboa Park.

effectively announcing San Diego's return to prominence. The city had impressed at least one exposition visitor: Assistant Secretary of the Navy Franklin Delano Roosevelt.

In 1919, the Marine Corps Recruit Depot was built to be the marines' West Coast training depot, and after the 1941 bombing of Pearl Harbor, the headquarters of the Pacific Fleet was moved to San Diego. During this period, Camp Pendleton further established military presence in north San Diego County, where it remains the Marines' largest training base. During and after the war, great numbers of servicemen came through San Diego, and the defense industry followed, creating an anchor industry for the San Diego economy.

In the 1950s and 60s, the establishment of biological research institutes such as the Salk Institute, Scripps, and the San Diego branch of the University of California created a talent pool that attracted the burgeoning biotech industry, which also flourishes to this day.

San Diego's population has continued to grow ever since, becoming home to defense contractors, technology companies, and sun-worshippers alike.

Local Culture

It's tempting to peg San Diego as a surf spot, military base, or bilingual border town. But a city doesn't become the nation's eighth largest by attracting any type of person; San Diego lures a variety of people from other parts of the United States and abroad. Some come for opportunities, some for the lifestyle, and some because their orders tell them to.

NATIVE AMERICANS

The Native American population in San Diego is estimated to be a little more than 1 percent of the total, or about 20,000 people; the number is roughly the same as when Spanish ships first sailed into San Diego Bay. Along with the city's original inhabitants—the Kumeyaay people—other nations include the Luiseño, Cupeño, and Cahuilla. During the late 19th century, a government executive order forced these nations to move to reservations on the outer boundaries of San Diego County, including Lakeside, Campo, Pala, and Valley Center. San Diego County has more reservations than anywhere else in the country (a dubious distinction), though only a small percentage of self-identifying Native Americans currently live on reservation land.

LATINOS

San Diego is home to a huge Latino population that makes up more than 25% of the population. Spanish is the city's unofficial second language, and in many pocket neighborhoods, it's the first. Most of the Latino community in San Diego runs several generations deep; some can trace their ancestry back to the original Californio settlers of Mexican Old Town. While some communities may not be fully or equitably integrated, the sound of Mexican folk songs and the flavors of Mexican cuisine remind all San Diegans of home.

IMMIGRATION

While significant numbers of foreign refugees have moved to San Diego to escape political, ethnic, or religious persecutions in their native lands—including many Eritreans, Somalis, Sudanese, Vietnamese, Laotians, Burmese, and Chaldean Iraqis—other ethnic populations date back to the city's origins. Chinese immigrants arrived in the late 19th century to work construction and lay track for local railroad lines. Though the Chinatown

Clockwise from top left: Surfing is one of San Diego's biggest attractions; Pelicans regularly pop up in San Diego Bay; Old Town preserves the artifacts of San Diego's early days.

that originally formed near the harbor was dismantled a century ago, ethnic Chinese people remain a part of the city's cultural makeup. Asian populations account for approximately 16 percent of the city's population.

Many people of African heritage came to San Diego along with the Spanish colonials as the original settlement developed. When California became a U.S. state in 1850, slavery was outlawed, and in the years leading up to and during the Civil War, the city became a destination for many freed men and women. During World War II, many African American servicemen and -women stationed in the city also chose to stay. Today, San Diego's African American population hovers around 6 to 7 percent.

Portuguese and Italian fisherfolk arrived in San Diego in the late 19th and early 20th centuries and established communities in Point Loma and Little Italy, respectively. Little Italy retains its *tricolore* heritage, with many influences commemorating its history and culture. In recent years, a growing Brazilian and Portuguese population has mingled around Point Loma and Ocean Beach, though businesses in these neighborhoods do not represent this influence.

SUBCULTURES
Surfers

San Diego is home to hundreds of thousands of surfers—it can get pretty crowded out in the water sometimes. The classic image of a lean, bronzed, sun-bleached blond carving up the waves does exist, and you'll see it often, but surfers come from all ethnicities and walks of life. While the majority may be born-and-bred locals, many picked up the sport upon arriving in San Diego from elsewhere and became instant devotees. The lone unifying factor is the stoke they feel any day that a great swell hits.

Military

Up to 150,000 people move to San Diego each year from other parts of the country, and many are with the U.S. Navy and Marine Corps. Most are under age 30 and represent the diversity found in the military. Many are stationed at a huge North County base, Marine Corps Base Camp Pendleton, or, for a short time, at the Marine Corps Recruit Depot. Naval bases are also located in Coronado, Point Loma, Miramar, and National City.

Homelessness

By some counts, San Diego has the fourth-largest homeless population among U.S. cities. The vast majority of the city's estimated 9,000 homeless are found downtown, particularly in the East Village, with a second sizable population around Point Loma and Ocean Beach. Ongoing programs sponsored by the city aim to provide shelter and treatment for those in need, but progress is slow. Homeless help and services are available through **San Diego County** (1200 3rd Ave., 619/236-5990, www.sandiego.gov) and by calling the city's info line (619/230-0997 or 211).

Spring

EARTH FAIR

One of the world's largest Earth Day celebrations, the Earth Fair (Balboa Park, 858/272-7370, www.earthdayweb.org, Apr.) is presented by San Diego EarthWorks and attracts ecologically minded individuals. Booths highlight products and technological innovations in the world of conservation and sustainability that are both educational and inspirational.

ETHNIC FOOD FAIR

The House of Pacific Relations in Balboa Park features 21 cottages representing 34 foreign nations. In May, they host the Ethnic Food Fair (HPR Cottages, Balboa Park, www.sdhpr.org, May), offering traditional food from each host country in an afternoon sure to delight the taste buds and push the limits of your stomach.

FIESTA OLD TOWN CINCO DE MAYO

Cinco de Mayo is celebrated in Mexico as a day of national pride, and the three-day Fiesta Old Town Cinco de Mayo (Old Town, www.oldtownsandiegoguide.com, May) is the "largest of its kind." You'll find food, music, traditional attire, costumes, shopping, lowriders, and, if you look hard enough, some tequila.

ROCK 'N' ROLL MARATHON

It's easy to think that the Rock 'n' Roll Marathon (6th St. and Quince St., Balboa Park, www.runrocknroll.com, May, $90-130) isn't serious, what with all the bands, costumes, and drinking. While it may be a good time for onlookers, the participants are running a 26-mile marathon, a 13-mile half marathon, and a two-person relay (6 and 7 miles).

CHICANO PARK DAY

Commemorating the 1970 community stand that preserved a slice of green space for what is predominantly a Latino community, Chicano Park Day (1949 Logan Ave., Barrio Logan, www.chicano-park.com, Apr., free) features live music and dance performances, a lowrider car show, kids' crafts, and curated food and drink.

Summer

LA JOLLA FESTIVAL OF THE ARTS

Amid all the food, beer, wine, jazz, and folk music, one might easily forget that the annual La Jolla Festival of the Arts (UCSD, 3453 Voigt Dr., La Jolla, 619/744-0534, www.lajollaartfestival.org, June) is about the artists and their work. Providing an elegant atmosphere for hands-on appreciation, it gives art lovers a chance to mingle with artists and enjoy a La Jolla summer day.

OB STREET FAIR

Up to 70,000 people gather in Ocean Beach for the kooky, boozy **OB Street Fair** (locations vary, Ocean Beach, www.oceanbeachsandiego.com, June, free). Live music, a chili cook-off, an art walk, and carnival rides and attractions are hallmarks of the occasion, while a beer garden keeps it lively. Each year, kids and amateur artists paint one square of a community mural, which usually results in a patchwork-quilt seascape. Murals from previous years dot the neighborhood.

SAN DIEGO COUNTY FAIR

From the second week of June through July 4 the **San Diego County Fair** (2260 Jimmy Durante Blvd., Del Mar, 858/755-1161, www.sdfair.com, June) offers food, music, rides, animals, car shows, and one or two beer festivals. And if that isn't enough, it's held right beside the racetrack in Del Mar.

SAN DIEGO INTERNATIONAL BEER FESTIVAL

The West Coast's largest beer festival offers more than "400 beers" and "one glass." The **San Diego International Beer Festival** (Del Mar Fairgrounds, Del Mar, www.sandiegobeerfestival.com, June, free with fair admission) brings together more than 200 breweries—local and international—to give more than 10,000 craft beer lovers a place to immerse themselves in fermented hops, yeast, barley, and wheat. Five separate sessions keep it from getting too crowded, but some people attend them all and still can't get to all the beers.

SHAKESPEARE FESTIVAL

Reason enough for theater fans to visit San Diego, the **Shakespeare Festival** (Balboa Park, 619/234-5623, www.theoldglobe.org, June-Sept.) usually offers two or three productions, primarily the celebrated work of the Bard and occasionally a well-known modern play that lives up to the legacy of the English language's prolific genius. Hosted in the outdoor venue of The Old Globe theater complex, it's a special way to enjoy the evening air while nourishing your need for culture.

COMIC CON

Year after year, **Comic Con** (111 W. Harbor Dr., www.comic-con.org, July) is the biggest event at the downtown San Diego Convention Center. What began as a modest celebration of comic books has exploded into an entertainment juggernaut, drawing all manner of sci-fi fans, cosplayers, video-game buffs, and celebrities. More than 125,000 people descend on San Diego to attend 600 staged events and 1,500 exhibitor booths. Take note when Comic Con takes place; it sells out far in advance, as do most of the hotels anywhere near downtown and at triple their normal rates.

Possibly the most organized annual drinking game, the **Over the Line Tournament** (Fiesta Island Rd., Mission Bay, www.ombac.org, July, free) has been at it for more than 60 years. Teams of three gather at Fiesta Island in Mission Bay to compete (and drink) in this goofy miniature version of softball, while their friends watch and also drink. Of the 1,200 teams that compete each year, most have raunchy or suggestive names—all in the spirit of BYOB fun.

SAN DIEGO LGBT PRIDE

San Diego's lesbian, gay, bisexual, and transgender community congregates around Hillcrest, its de facto hub, to stage the **San Diego LGBT Pride** parade (University Ave., from Normal St. to Upas St., 619/297-7683, www.sdpride.org, July, free) to Balboa Park and back. Weekend festivities include live music, rallies, and a massive block party that attracts thousands of people from all orientations to join in the joy, hope, and pride of a civil rights movement that has made incredible strides.

SUMMERFEST

Chamber music receives special attention when the La Jolla Music Society presents **SummerFest** (locations vary, La Jolla, 858/459-3724, http://ljms.org, July-Aug.), a number of special engagements in area venues, including a free "Under the Stars" performance held beside La Jolla Cove. Most shows charge admission to see some of the world's top talents perform some of classical music's most heralded pieces.

BIKE THE BAY

One Sunday in mid- to late August, half of the Coronado Bridge closes to cars for **Bike the Bay** (619/269-6873, www.bikethebay.net, Aug., $45-55), a community bike ride over the iconic arched bridge. The ride continues around the mostly flat Bayshore Bikeway and offers a great way for cyclists to see a bit of the town (and the view from the bridge).

STONE ANNIVERSARY CELEBRATION

San Diego's beloved Stone Brewing throws the **Stone Anniversary Celebration and International Beer Festival** (333 S. Twin Oaks Valley Rd., Escondido, www.stonebrewing.com, Aug., $45-85), a massive weekend-long birthday bash. Stone invites 60 or so of its favorite craft-brewing friends from around the country to participate. More than 100 beers are on hand; guests can opt to taste special releases from some of their favorite brewers or discover something new.

Fall
FESTIVAL OF SAIL

Labor Day weekend, San Diego Bay brings another era back to life with the **Festival of Sail** (1492 N. Harbor Dr., www.sdmaritime.org, Sept.). Beautiful vintage tall ships parade across the bay, firing cannon salutes and coming to dock. A lot of food, beer, and nautical-themed attractions keep the event family friendly and engaging for everyone who likes boats.

SAN DIEGO MUSIC THING

Similar to Austin's South by Southwest festival, **Music Thing** (locations vary, 619/381-8789, www.sandiegomusicthing.com, Sept.) takes over live music clubs all over town, setting feature lineups of local up-and-comers as well as a few better-known headliners. Music industry workshops and networking take place during the day, providing a chance for creative folk to mingle and music lovers to learn about show business.

SAN DIEGO RESTAURANT WEEK

Twice a year during **San Diego Restaurant Week** (locations vary, www.sandiegorestaurantweek.com, Sept. and Jan.), restaurants all over town offer special pricing on selected menus, giving a chance for foodies on a budget to check out new restaurants they might otherwise miss. Prices and availability vary; check online to secure a spot at the city's best eateries in advance.

HALLOWEEN FAMILY DAY

Each Saturday before Halloween, selected Balboa Park museums open their doors for **Halloween Family Day** (Balboa Park, 619/239-0512, www.balboapark.org, Oct.). From 11am to 3pm, children ages 12 and under can explore spooky hands-on displays that complement the usual educational and cultural fare. Parents don't get in for free, but reduced rates typically are available.

LA JOLLA ART & WINE FESTIVAL

The **La Jolla Art & Wine Festival** (Girard Ave., La Jolla Village, www.ljawf.com, Oct., free) shuts down a portion of Girard Avenue for two days to exhibit local artwork, gourmet fare, and excellent wine, as well as local beer. Proceeds support arts programs at area schools.

SAN DIEGO FILM FESTIVAL

Over 100 films screen at theaters around the city during the annual **San Diego Film Festival** (www.sdfilmfest.com, Oct.), including early screenings of wide-release films and occasional world premieres. The four-day festival includes parties and awards shows honoring actors, filmmakers, and other celebrities.

MCAS MIRAMAR AIR SHOW

Federal funds permitting, aviators put on a dazzling show during the **MCAS Miramar Air Show** (Marine Corps Air Station Miramar, Miramar Way, http://miramarairshow.com, Oct., free). The event is held over the airfield at the Marine Corps Air Station Miramar and attracts an estimated 700,000 each year. There are Harrier and Osprey demonstrations, vintage plane shows, parachute teams, and, of course, the headliners, the Blue Angels.

DÍA DE LOS MUERTOS
Día de los Muertos (Old Town San Diego State Historic Park, 619/297-9327, http://sddayofthedead.org, Nov. 1-2, free) isn't a street-fair kind of festival but rather a celebration of the traditional Mexican holiday that honors the dead. Old Town becomes the site of 50 altars as well as enlightening booths dedicated to face painting and *papel picado* (a Mexican folk art), offering an opportunity to engage in other traditional practices before a candlelit procession to El Campo Santo Cemetery.

SAN DIEGO BAY WINE & FOOD FESTIVAL
The **San Diego Bay Wine & Food Festival** (Embarcadero Marina Park North, www.sandiegowineclassic.com, Nov.) is a gourmand celebration of the city's local culinary scene, with a little beer thrown in for good measure. Special tasting events, celebrity chef panels, and cooking classes are some of the many events staged during the weeklong fest.

SAN DIEGO BEER WEEK
The second week of November is a great time to drink beer—at least that's what we tell ourselves when **San Diego Beer Week** (locations vary, www.sdbw.org, Nov.) kicks up. Events are tailored around seasonal and special-release beers that could be the best new ale or stout in town. It's a great time for beer tourists to sample some of the best local brewing.

Winter
BALBOA PARK DECEMBER NIGHTS
Billing itself as the "largest free community festival in San Diego," the annual **Balboa Park December Nights** event (Balboa Park, www.balboapark.org, Dec.) draws hundreds of thousands of people to Balboa Park. Holiday lights and decor provide the main attraction, though special performances, food, and free museum entry (5pm-9pm) help make this an every-year tradition for many locals. The event is usually the first Friday and Saturday evenings of December.

HOLIDAY BOWL PARADE
The Rose Parade in Pasadena may be the best-known event associated with college football, but 100,000 people line up to see San Diego's **Holiday Bowl Parade** (locations vary, http://sandiegobowlgames.com, Dec.), kickoff to the Holiday Bowl. "America's largest balloon parade" runs along Harbor Drive and features hundreds of floats and, yes, balloons. You haven't lived till you've seen a pneumatic Cookie Monster float past the tall clipper ships of the Maritime Museum.

Even the La Jolla Village loves a parade. In December, it stages the **La Jolla Christmas Parade & Holiday Festival** (Girard Ave., La Jolla, 858/922-4046, www.ljparade.com, Dec.), complete with floats, equestrians, vintage cars, beauty queens, and marching bands. The parade route moves down Girard Avenue before turning south on Prospect Street, where a decorated Christmas tree marks the spot of the festival, along with food, games, and entertainment.

OCEAN BEACH HOLIDAY PARADE

OB has a unique character, so it's little surprise that it has a unique holiday parade. The **Ocean Beach Holiday Parade** (Newport Ave., Ocean Beach, https://oceanbeachsandiego.com, Dec.) features floats and marching bands with the occasional countercultural twist, whether it's a team of Roller Derby women or the parade of surf-car classics known as woodies.

SAN DIEGO BAY PARADE OF LIGHTS

Some neighborhoods are popular every year for their Christmas lights. San Diego Bay is one of these; however, instead of houses and lawns, it's the festively decorated boats of the **San Diego Bay Parade of Lights** (locations vary, 619/224-2240, www.sdparadeoflights.org, Dec.). The two Sunday evenings before Christmas, dozens of boats parade through the bay—from Shelter Island to Harbor Island, the Embarcadero, and all the way around to the Coronado Ferry Landing. Pick your spot on the bay, and let the lights come to you.

Essentials

Transportation

GETTING THERE
Air
Also known as Lindbergh Field, **San Diego International Airport** (SAN, 619/400-2404, www.san.org) is a centrally located urban airport a mere three miles from the city center. While the location makes it a little noisy for those living in neighborhoods under the flight path, it makes getting to and from the airport a quick trip from most parts of the city. The airport is split into two major terminals plus a small commuter terminal, hosting 20 airlines and subsidiaries.

The opening of a pedestrian bridge border crossing makes **Tijuana International Airport** (TIJ, +52 664/607-8200, www.tijuana-airport.com) a convenient option for travelers visiting San Diego from cities without direct flights to San Diego, or those wishing to fly on more affordable airlines, including **Aeroméxico** (800/237-6639, www.aeromexico.com), **Interjet** (866/285-8307, www.interjet.com), **VivaAerobus** (888/935-9848, www.vivaaerobus.com), and **Volaris** (855/865-2747, www.volaris.com). Passports are required to cross the border.

Bus
Greyhound Bus Lines (800/752-4841, www.greyhound.com) has its terminal (1313 National Ave., 619/515-1100) in downtown San Diego's East Village, with the option to stop in **Oceanside** (205 S. Tremont St., 760/722-1587) or **Escondido** (700 W. Valley Pkwy., 800/231-2222).

Train
Amtrak (800/872-7245, www.amtrak.com) offers daily service to and from San Diego on its **Pacific Surfliner** route, which extends up the coast connecting to Los Angeles, Santa Barbara, and San Luis Obispo. Trains depart from the downtown **Santa Fe Depot** (1050 Kettner Blvd.), with stops in **Solana Beach** (105 N. Cedros Ave.) and **Oceanside** (235 S. Tremont St.).

Some Surfliner trains also make stops at the **Old Town Transit Center** (4005 Taylor St.), **Sorrento Valley** (11170 Sorrento Valley Rd.), and at two stations in **Carlsbad** (6511 Avenida Encinas; 2775 State St.). Consult schedules online for these additional stops.

Car
San Diego is bisected by **I-5**, which provides access to the North County coast and downtown San Diego and continues south to Tijuana in Mexico. From Los Angeles, I-5 is a direct shot 120 miles south to downtown San

Previous: the Old Town Trolley Tours bus in the Gaslamp Quarter; the San Diego Central Library.

San Diego by Air

The following airlines provide service to and from San Diego:

- **Air Canada** (888/247-2262, www.aircanada.com, Terminal 2)

- **Alaska Airlines** (800/252-7522, www.alaskaair.com, Terminal 1)

- **Allegiant Air** (702/505-8888, www.allegiantair.com, Terminal 2)

- **American Airlines** (800/433-7300, www.aa.com, Terminal 2)

- **British Airways** (800/247-9297, www.britishairways.com, Terminal 2)

- **Condor** (866/960-7915, www.condor.com, Terminal 2)

- **Delta Airlines** (800/221-1212, www.delta.com, Terminal 2)

- **Edelweiss Air** (877/359-7947, www.flyedelweiss.com, Terminal 2)

- **Frontier Airlines** (800/432-1359, www.flyfrontier.com, Terminal 1)

- **Hawaiian Airlines** (800/367-5320, www.hawaiianairlines.com, Terminal 2)

- **Japan Airlines** (800/525-3663, www.ar.jal.com, Terminal 2)

- **JetBlue Airways** (800/538-2583, www.jetblue.com, Terminal 2)

- **Lufthansa** (800/645-3880, www.lufthansa.com, Terminal 1)

- **Southwest Airlines** (800/435-9792, www.southwest.com, Terminal 1)

- **Spirit Airlines** (801/401-2222, www.spirit.com, Terminal 2)

- **Sun Country Airlines** (800/359-6786, www.suncountry.com, Terminal 2)

- **United Airlines** (800/864-8331, www.united.com, Terminal 2)

- **Virgin America** (877/359-8474, www.virginamerica.com, Terminal 2)

- **WestJet** (888/937-8538, www.westjet.com, Terminal 2)

Diego. The drive can take 2-3 hours in light traffic but up to five hours in rush hour or otherwise congested traffic.

I-15 provides access to San Diego from the northeast and runs to Escondido, Riverside County, and eventually into Nevada and Las Vegas. This freeway is the most direct route to inland North County; in light traffic, it can take 30 minutes to an hour to drive the 30 miles north from downtown to Escondido. However, I-15 suffers from impacted rush-hour traffic as commuters return home to Miramar, Mira Mesa, Poway, and Rancho Bernardo.

I-8 connects east to El Centro before crossing to Yuma, Arizona, in about 175 miles. In Arizona, I-8 connects to I-10 south of Phoenix.

CAR RENTALS

Most car rental agencies operate near the San Diego International Airport. The closest are **Hertz** (3355 Admiral Boland Way, 619/767-5700, www. hertz.com), **National** (3355 Admiral Boland Way, 888/445-5664, www.nationalcar.com), and **Avis** (3355 Admiral Boland Way, 619/688-5000, www. avis.com). All are a short shuttle ride away, so Thrifty and even farther-away Enterprise are accessible enough. From the train station, **Avis** (1670 Kettner Blvd. Ste. 1, 619/231-7137, www.avis.com) is within short walking distance.

GETTING AROUND
Public Transportation

San Diego's public transportation is operated by the **Metropolitan Transit System** (MTS, 619/557-4555, www.sdmts.com), which includes buses and a trolley system. The **trolley** ($2.50 one-way, $5 day pass) operates daily, offering three color-coded routes that make a good option for visiting downtown (all lines), Old Town and Mission Valley (Green Line), or Tijuana (Blue Line). While the bus system ($2.25 one-way) is extensive and runs countywide, it can be complicated and slow; the uninitiated should plan the trip in advance online.

The **North County Transit District** (NCTD, 760/966-6500, www.gonctd.com) operates the **Coaster** (operating hours and schedules vary, $4-5.50 one-way), a commuter rail line that extends from downtown San Diego to Oceanside; it's a great way to visit Solana Beach, Encinitas, or Carlsbad. NCTD also runs the **Sprinter** (Mon.-Fri. 4am-9pm, Sat.-Sun. 10am-6pm, $2 one-way), a rail line from Oceanside to Escondido; a bus system ($1.75 one-way) serving mostly suburban areas; and a reservation-based shuttle, **Flex** (855/844-1454, call 30 minutes in advance, $5), which may be a handy option for those looking to get around between Encinitas and Solana Beach.

A regional **route-planning website** (www.sdcommute.com) encompassing both MTS and NCTD can help you plan your trip.

Car
DRIVING

San Diego is a freeway town, but getting around will be a lot less frustrating—and safer—if you know where you're going and how to get there before you hop on the road. GPS navigation services help, but the city is constantly bisected by canyons and waterways; the quickest way to get somewhere is often not a straight line.

San Diego Trolley Map

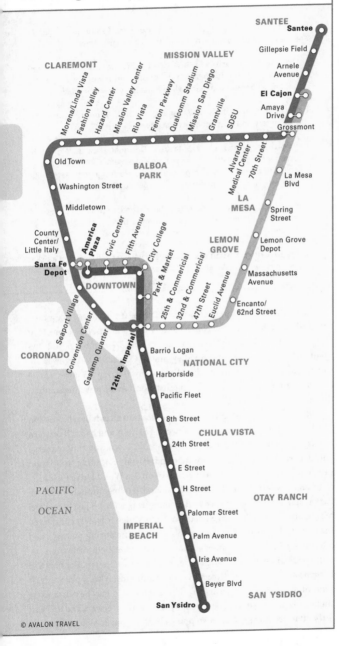

SANTEE

Santee

Gillepsie Field

Arnele Avenue

El Cajon

Amaya Drive

Grossmont

MISSION VALLEY

CLAREMONT

Morena/Linda Vista

Fashion Valley

Hazard Center

Mission Valley Center

Rio Vista

Fenton Parkway

Qualcomm Stadium

Mission San Diego

Grantville

SDSU

Old Town

BALBOA PARK

Alvarado Medical Center

70th Street

La Mesa Blvd

Washington Street

Middletown

LA MESA

Spring Street

County Center/ Little Italy

America Plaza

Civic Center

Fifth Avenue

City College

LEMON GROVE

Lemon Grove Depot

Santa Fe Depot

DOWNTOWN

Park & Market

25th & Commercial

32nd & Commercial

47th Street

Euclid Avenue

Massachusetts Avenue

Encanto/ 62nd Street

Seaport Village

Convention Center

Gaslamp Quarter

12th & Imperial

Barrio Logan

NATIONAL CITY

Harborside

Pacific Fleet

8th Street

CHULA VISTA

24th Street

E Street

H Street

OTAY RANCH

Palomar Street

CORONADO

PACIFIC OCEAN

IMPERIAL BEACH

Palm Avenue

Iris Avenue

Beyer Blvd

San Ysidro

SAN YSIDRO

© AVALON TRAVEL

California Traffic Laws

In addition to typical traffic laws seen elsewhere, California stringently enforces a few less common rules with tickets and steep fines.

- **Do not phone or text while driving.** You may use a sanctioned hands-free device to speak on the phone, but if you are in any way holding a phone in your hand while you drive, you will be cited.

- **Wear a seatbelt.** This law applies to both front- and back-seat passengers, and it's mandated for safety.

- **Avoid carpool lane violations.** Designated carpool or high-occupancy vehicle (HOV) lanes require a minimum of 2-3 passengers to access (the exact number is posted). These are designed to ease traffic congestion and are especially enforced during rush hours.

- **Check car seat requirements.** Children under age 8 must be secured in a car seat in the back seat of a car unless they are taller than 4 feet, 9 inches.

- **No littering.** Tossing any trash out of your car will earn you a ticket worth at least several hundred dollars.

I-5 stretches through downtown San Diego, from the Mexican border north to La Jolla and the North County beach towns. I-5 connects to Highway 163 north through Balboa Park to both I-8 and I-805, to I-805 again farther north in Sorrento Valley, and in Oceanside to Highway 78, which leads east to San Marcos and Escondido. Driving I-5 north of Del Mar can be a traffic nightmare during rush hour. Avoid traveling south in the morning or north in the afternoon.

Within San Diego, **I-8** offers east-west access to Ocean Beach, Mission Beach, and Mission Valley before connecting to I-805 and I-15 at its eastern points. Note that while I-5 crosses I-8 near Old Town, you cannot merge onto I-8 westbound from I-5 southbound; if you're heading to Mission Beach or Ocean Beach from the north, exit on Sea World Drive instead.

I-805 runs parallel to I-5 a few miles inland, passing through the North Park neighborhood in Uptown and reconnecting with I-5 just before Del Mar at Sorrento Valley. Take heed: Sorrento Valley is widely considered the city's tech hub and has the region's worst traffic during morning and afternoon rush hours (Mon.-Fri. 7am-9:30am and 3:30pm-6:30pm).

If you're unfortunate enough to see rain, drive cautiously. For one, San Diegans are not the best drivers in rainy conditions. Also, since we don't get a lot of rain, for a time after the first rain the road may be a little extra slippery. Dense coastal fog occasionally reaches the freeways and makes it difficult to see cars slowing or stopping ahead of you; drive with caution.

Navigating Surface Streets

San Diego has its fair share of dead-end streets, which can make getting from point A to point B a challenge. Following are some major thoroughfares to help you avoid them, and a few alphabetical schemes to keep track of which direction you're going.

Numbered avenues run north-south and increase sequentially from west to east.

Alphabetical streets run east-west and start downtown at A Street, going in order to L Street as you head south. Broadway replaces D Street and Market Street replaces H Street.

Alphabetized groupings reflect streets named after trees (downtown, Balboa Park), birds (Mission Hills), and gemstones (Pacific Beach). Downtown, this grouping begins with Ash Street, which runs parallel with, and one block north of, A Street.

The San Diego airport is located on **Harbor Drive,** which runs south through downtown and along the bay all the way to the Coronado Bridge. The road connects with a few key parts of town—Harbor Island, downtown, the Embarcadero—without too much cross traffic.

Broadway is the major west-east thoroughfare through downtown. There are a lot of buses and stoplights, and you may never be allowed to turn left, but chances are you'll need to drive it. Harbor Drive crosses Broadway at its western terminus.

A one-way street, **6th Avenue,** runs along the western edge of Balboa Park and is the most reliable passage through Bankers Hill into Hillcrest, where it meets University Avenue.

The wide, heavily used **University Avenue** runs east-west the length of the Hillcrest and North Park neighborhoods, with popular restaurants and bars scattered along the way. As University Avenue runs east, it crosses Park Avenue shortly east of the Highway 163 overpass.

The intersection of University and Park Avenues is the geographic center of Uptown. **Park Avenue** runs north through University Heights and south through Balboa Park to the East Village downtown, the only direct route to do so.

University Avenue crosses **30th Street** in North Park; this intersection is sometimes referred to as Restaurant Row. As 30th Street continues north, it crosses El Cajon Boulevard and Adams Avenue, streets with increasing notoriety for shopping among younger generations.

ON-DEMAND CAR RENTALS

An alternative to traditional car rentals, **Zipcar** (619/546-9654, www.zipcar. com) plants a small number of multiple-passenger cars in key locations around the city for on-demand use as hourly rentals. Users must return the car to one of the company's designated spaces, though not necessarily to its original location. This can be a viable option when you need a car to visit multiple places within a single day.

HIRED CARS AND TAXIS

While numerous taxis may still be spotted in populous areas, car-for-hire services operated by smartphone apps tend to be quicker, and often cheaper, alternatives. Two services, **Uber** (www.uber.com) and **Lyft** (www.lyft.com), operate the same way: Drivers are recruited from the public and cruise the streets shuttling people around at the touch of a button. Simply pinpoint your location on a smartphone app to request a ride; the savvy GPS system will determine the nearest available car and send it your way. Rides tend to be clean and the drivers pleasant. Charges are processed to the user's credit card through the app, which means no money changes hands (no cash tips).

For those wishing to stick with traditional taxis, try **San Diego Cab** (619/226-8294) or **Yellow Cab** (619/239-8061). For traditional limos and hired cars, contact **Flex Transportation** (619/796-3539, www.flextranspo.com) or **City Captain** (619/800-3515, www.citycaptain.com).

Pedicabs for hire shuttle visitors around the Gaslamp Quarter, Marina District, and East Village; they offer convenient transport between different parts of downtown, but only when flagged down like a taxi.

Ferries

San Diego has two major ferry routes; both run to and from Coronado. **Flagship Cruises** (619/234-4111, www.flagshipsd.com, $4.75 each way) operates the Coronado Ferry from two locations: the Broadway pier (between the USS *Midway* Museum and the Maritime Museum of San Diego) and the 5th Avenue pier (south of the San Diego Convention Center). The 15-minute trip runs daily approximately 9am-9pm, arriving at the Coronado Ferry Landing. The ferry ride can be a scenic activity in its own right, especially if you bring a bicycle to explore the opposite shore.

Travel Tips

WHAT TO PACK

The first thing you should pack is a swimsuit. Fancy attire isn't a priority unless you plan to attend a theater production, business event, or upscale restaurant. Most locals remain comfortable with warm-weather clothing, and you can do the same. Long shorts, short to mid-length skirts and dresses, short sleeves, and tank tops are common. For fall, winter, or nighttime, when temperatures cool, pack jeans, casual pants, and a long-sleeved shirt or light sweater to add layers.

Bring comfortable shoes for walking around and some sandals or flip-flops for the beach. Sunglasses are a must, preferably those with UV protection. Either pack or purchase sunscreen, especially if you're fair-skinned and haven't seen a lot of sun in a while.

Bring a valid ID for going out to breweries, bars, and clubs; local law enforcement cracks down on underage drinking, and businesses will card even those in their forties to avoid steep fines. If you're planning to hop across the border to Mexico, you'll need a valid passport to return.

Top: San Diego trolleys. Bottom: Santa Fe Depot train station.

VISITOR INFORMATION

For in-person conversations and all the pamphlets you could ask for, stop by one of San Diego's many regional tourism offices: the **San Diego International Visitor Information Center** (996 N. Harbor Dr., 619/236-1242, daily 9am-4pm), downtown at the Embarcadero; **Coronado Visitor Center** (1100 Orange Ave., 619/437-8788; Mon.-Fri. 9am-5pm, Sat.-Sun. 10am-5pm); or the **California Welcome Center** (928 North Coast Hwy., Oceanside, 760/721-1101; daily 9am-5pm). Information is also available online at www.sandiego.org.

FOREIGN TRAVELERS

Foreign travelers entering the United States must have a valid passport, and most must have a visa issued by a U.S. Consular Official. Citizens of certain countries may be eligible to visit for 90 days without a visa pending the Electronic System for Travel Authorization (ESTA). To find out if you are eligible, consult the updated U.S. Customs and Border Patrol website (www.cbp.gov/travel/international-visitors).

The currency used in San Diego and the rest of California is the U.S. dollar ($), issued in paper bills with denominations of $1, $5, $10, $20, $50, and $100.

Tipping is a common and expected practice in the United States, particularly for waiters, waitresses, and others in the service industry. Standard tips range 15-20 percent for table service, $1-2 for bar or counter service, 15 percent for taxis, $1-2 to carry luggage, and $1-2 per day for housekeeping services in hotels or vacation rentals.

Standards of measurement differ from most countries, as the United States is not on the metric system. Distance is measured in inches (1 inch is 25.4 millimeters), feet (1 foot is 30.48 centimeters), yards (1 yard is 0.91 meter), and miles (1 mile is 1.6 kilometers). Weight is measured in ounces (1 ounce is 28.35 grams) and pounds (1 pound is 0.45 kilogram). Volume is measured in fluid ounces (1 ounce is 29.57 milliliters), pints (1 U.S. pint is 0.47 liter), and gallons (1 U.S. gallon is 3.79 liters).

Electrical outlets in San Diego operate at 120 volts, 60 hertz, using a plug with two parallel flat prongs and often a third, round prong that functions as a safety ground.

English is the language spoken in San Diego, although a large number of locals are fluent or proficient in Spanish.

ACCESS FOR TRAVELERS WITH DISABILITIES

Travelers with special needs may require extra planning and may have to skip a few of the city's harder-to-reach attractions; however, there's more than enough to reward your efforts. A growing number of attractions have become compliant with the Americans with Disabilities Act (ADA), and the city itself is currently in the process of making sweeping upgrades to make it more accessible. For a comprehensive list of accessible sights and assistive services, consult **San Diego Tourism Authority** (800/350-6205, www.sandiego.org).

A few different transportation options may be available to those in wheelchairs or requiring assistance. Local transportation agencies offer ADA-compliant programs in San Diego, such as **MTS Access** (www.sdmts.com) and North County's **Lift** (www.gonctd.com/lift). Each may require prior registration with **ADA Ride** (www.adaride.com). For private rides, contact **Super Shuttle** (800/258-3826, www.supershuttle.com), which operates daily 24 hours. Specially equipped van rentals are available from **Wheelchair Getaways** (800/642-2042, www.wheelchairgetaways.com) and **Better Life Mobility Center** (888/540-8267, www.betterlifemobility.com).

The **San Diego Central Library** (330 Park Blvd., 619/236-5800, www.sandiego.gov; Mon.-Thurs. 9:30am-7pm, Fri.-Sat. 9:30am-6pm, Sun. noon-6pm) includes the Oliver McMillan Center, which offers a wide range of assistive devices to help connect special needs individuals with computers and other technology.

Beachgoers may want to take advantage of **free beach wheelchairs,** available by calling ahead for a reservation at any of the following beaches: Coronado Beach (619/522-7346), La Jolla Shores (619/221-8899), Mission Beach (619/980-1876), Ocean Beach (619/221-8899), and Silver Strand State Beach (619/435-0126).

Mission Bay Aquatic Center (1001 Santa Clara Pl., 858/488-1000, www.mbaquaticcenter.com; daily 8am-6pm) operates an Accessible Watersports program that offers sailing, kayaking, and waterskiing lessons to people with disabilities. Activities usually involve adaptive devices or adjustments to accommodate different needs. Call ahead to reserve individual lessons (available year-round) or to find out about group events scheduled throughout the summer.

TRAVELING WITH CHILDREN

Many hotels and attractions in San Diego cater to children and families, often with reduced admission costs or kid-friendly programs. Several surf schools and water-sports rental agencies offer child-specific classes or even day camps that will keep kids active. In addition, these top playgrounds in the city should help:

- **Waterfront Park** (1600 Pacific Hwy., downtown; daily 6am-10pm) lies between Little Italy and the harbor, with a playground, cooling water-jet fountains, and a pleasant view of the boats at the Maritime Museum.

- **Pepper Grove Park** (Park Blvd. at Space Theater Way, Balboa Park; daily 6am-10pm) is a scenic little park with a large playground split into areas for older and younger children.

- **Trolley Barn Park** (Adams Ave. at Florida St., Uptown; daily 24 hours) is a small grassy park with a large playground in the pleasant walking neighborhood of University Heights.

- **Kellogg Park** (6200 Camino del Oro, La Jolla; daily 4am-10pm) playground sits on a grassy park right behind the sand at La Jolla Shores beach.

- **Spreckels Park** (Orange Ave. at 7th St., Coronado; daily 24 hours) offers plenty of green grass, shady trees, a gazebo, and a playground for children.

SENIOR TRAVELERS

Travelers over age 65 (in some cases over age 60) may enjoy discounts and other benefits to attractions all over San Diego. In addition to discounted admission, hotel rooms, and public transportation fares, seniors may find dedicated spaces such as the **Senior Lounge** (Casa del Prado, Ste. 105, Balboa Park). Transportation assistance may be available by consulting the organization **FACT** (888/924-3228, www.factsd.org).

TRAVELING WITH PETS

San Diego loves dogs, and the city furnishes a number of off-leash parks, including several beaches. There are plenty of dog-friendly patios and even hotels that allow dogs, with some restrictions.

OB Dog Beach (W. Point Loma Blvd. at Voltaire St.) is the best stretch of sand in town, or try **Fiesta Island** (1590 E. Mission Bay Dr.) in Mission Bay if your dog is less into playing with others and more about running around. If your socially fit pup would rather run on grass, head over to **Nate's Point Dog Park** (2500 Balboa Dr., Bankers Hill), **Morley Field Dog Park** (2225 Morley Field Dr., North Park), or **Grape Street Dog Park** (1998 28th St., South Park).

Pet-friendly accommodations include Hotel Indigo and the U. S. Grant Hotel downtown; Porto Vista Hotel in Little Italy; the Ocean Beach Hotel in OB; Surfer Beach Hotel in Pacific Beach; La Jolla Village Lodge in La Jolla; the Hotel del Coronado (within walking distance of the Coronado dog beach); and the Grand Del Mar resort in Del Mar.

For an extensive directory of pet-friendly restaurants, hotels, and events—including a Surf Dog competition (Aug. or Sept.)—visit **San Diego Happy Dogs** (www.sandiegohappydogs.com).

URGENT-CARE CLINICS

U.S. health care runs primarily on private insurance, meaning there are general-practice physicians and specialists all over town, but they are expensive without insurance coverage, and they are usually booked up weeks and months in advance. If you're traveling and in need of medical attention for minor illness or injury (sports injury, illness, digestive or skin problems), the best way to see a doctor is to visit one of these urgent-care clinics. Waits tend to be shorter than at an emergency room, and you may receive the treatment you need to keep your vacation going.

- **Sharp Rees-Stealy Downtown** (300 Fir St., 858/499-2600, www.sharp.com; daily 8am-8pm)
- **Rady Children's Urgent Care** (4305 University Ave. Ste. 150, Uptown, 619/280-2905, www.rchsd.org; Mon.-Fri. 4pm-10pm, Sat.-Sun. 1pm-10pm)
- **Anderson Medical Center** (1945 Garnet Ave., Pacific Beach, 858/224-7977, www.andersonmedicalcenter.com; Mon.-Fri. 8am-8pm, Sat.-Sun. 8am-4pm, call for holiday hours)
- **Scripps Clinic Torrey Pines** (10666 N. Torrey Pines Rd., La Jolla, 858/554-9100, www.scripps.org; Mon.-Thurs. 7am-7pm, Fri. 7am-5pm, Sat.-Sun. 8am-noon)
- **Carlsbad Urgent Care** (295 S. Rancho Santa Fe Rd., San Marcos, 760/720-2804, https://carlsbadurgentcare.com; Mon.-Fri. 9am-9pm, Sat.-Sun. 9am-5pm)

EMERGENCY SERVICES

If an immediately life-threatening situation occurs, call **911** on any phone for emergency help, and an ambulance will respond quickly. If the ill or injured person is mobile enough to travel, you may also drive to the nearest of these emergency rooms:

- **UCSD Medical Center** (200 W. Arbor Dr., Hillcrest, 619/543-6222, http://health.ucsd.edu)
- **Scripps Memorial Hospital La Jolla** (9888 Genesee Ave., La Jolla, 858/626-4123, www.scripps.org)
- **Sharp Coronado Hospital** (250 Prospect Pl., Coronado, 619/522-3600, www.sharp.com/coronado)
- **Scripps Memorial Hospital Encinitas** (354 Santa Fe Dr., Encinitas, 760/633-6501, www.scripps.org)

Clockwise from top left: OB Dog Beach; public bikes for rent; a lifeguard tower.

Swimming

Most, though not all, San Diego beaches post **lifeguards** during daylight hours; however, there may be some gaps in coverage around sunrise and sunset. When in the water, watch for **strong waves.** Even small waves can get the better of inexperienced swimmers, and it only takes six inches of rushing water to bring you down. **Rip currents** are a little tougher to spot. You might see a little ripple on the ocean surface or spot a section on the edge of the waves where nothing is breaking. These may be indications a strong rush—or rip—is forming to suck water from the beach back into the ocean. If you find yourself caught in a rip current, don't try to swim against it; a deep enough rip could carry away a small elephant. Instead, try to escape the rip by swimming across it, perpendicular to whichever direction it tries to carry you. And try to signal a lifeguard.

Sharks may be the most feared creatures in the sea, but shark attacks in San Diego are very uncommon and usually take place in deeper water. More common dangers come from **jellyfish** and stingrays. The jellies are tough to see and may surround you before you realize it. Jellyfish stings hurt, but lifeguards know how to treat them. Further treatment should only be necessary in the event of an allergic reaction.

Stingrays hurt quite a bit more. Stingrays tend to shuffle along the sand in shallow waters. La Jolla Shores, for example, is a stingray habitat. When you step on one, the stingray responds by whipping you with a venomous stinger on its tail, almost like a giant bee sting. To avoid being stung, kick up the sand as you walk along the ocean floor; the stingray will feel you coming and get out of your way. If stung, seek medical treatment right away to prevent serious infection.

Sun Protection

The beaches get really crowded in the summer, but you can always spot those who forgot to wear sunscreen by their bright-pink faces and reddish-purple backs. Here's a tip: Use **waterproof sunscreen** on any exposed surface, SPF 30 or higher, and reapply it every two hours. Failing that, you may go from tanning to burning in 30 minutes; by the end of your beach day, you'll need to bathe in an aloe-based ointment, the only treatment for sunburn. It's only mildly effective.

Wildlife

There are a few natural predators in San Diego, but most aren't a danger to humans. **Hawks** occasionally swoop down to carry off small pets, and **coyotes** may group together to attempt the same. If you spot a hawk, pick up any dog less than 7 or 8 pounds. If you spot a coyote, corral your pets; there may be more coyotes lurking nearby. Coyotes can tease dogs into traps by appearing to be hurt or vulnerable. Coyotes fear humans, though, so make a loud or aggressive noise and they'll settle for watching you from a safe distance.

Rattlesnakes are a more formidable threat. Though snakes tend to hibernate in winter, in summer they may be found in any natural area and even residential ones. A heavy tread while hiking will help you avoid surprising a dozing rattlesnake; if it senses you coming, it'll usually slither out of your path. If someone in your party receives a rattlesnake bite, seek medical attention immediately. Bites can be lethal within 30 minutes.

Black widow spider bites can be quite dangerous. The shiny black spider with a bright-red hourglass on its abdomen lives all over San Diego, but the nocturnal creatures will do their best to stay out of the way and out of sight. If one is encountered (a rare occurrence), keep away from the spider and it will do the same. If someone is bitten, seek urgent care; if a child, an elderly person, or a pregnant woman is bitten, go to the emergency room.

CRIME

San Diego is one of the safest large cities in the country, but it's still a large city, and unsavory people may try to prey on out-of-town guests. Use common sense: Avoid handling large amounts of cash in public and keep purses and wallets zipped or latched and close at hand. When driving, keep car doors locked; in hotels, keep valuables in a hotel safe. Do not bring hard-to-replace items to the beach—credit cards, electronic devices, jewelry, passports, or other valuables—it's impossible to keep an eye on your things while you play in the waves. If you do encounter violent individuals or theft, call the police by dialing 911.

Resources

Suggested Reading

Amero, Richard W., and Mike Kelly. *Balboa Park and the 1915 Exposition.* Charleston, SC: The History Press, 2013. Delve deeper into the coordinated efforts of local civic leaders and philanthropists to produce the Panama-California Exposition, which effectively created Balboa Park and arguably put San Diego on the world map.

Carrico, Richard. *Strangers in a Stolen Land: Indians of San Diego County from Prehistory to the New Deal.* San Diego: Sunbelt Publications, 2008. The history of San Diego's indigenous Kumeyaay, Luiseño, Cupeño, and Cahuilla peoples, beginning long before the Spanish ever set foot in California, through the U.S. government's sometimes forced removal to outer-county reservations.

Davis, Mike, Kelly Mayhew, and Jim Miller. *Under the Perfect Sun: The San Diego Tourists Never See.* New York: New Press, 2003. A glimpse into behind-the-scenes political machinations of San Diego, where life ain't always sunshine, water sports, and beachwear.

Elwell, John C., and Jane Schmauss. *Surfing in San Diego.* Mt. Pleasant, SC: Arcadia Publishing, 2007. A thorough and visually rich telling of local surfing history, dating back to the days of George Freeth, by longtime surf historian Elwell in collaboration with Schmauss, a founder of the California Surf Museum in Oceanside.

Engstrand, Iris Wilson. *San Diego: California's Cornerstone.* 2nd edition. El Cajon, CA: Sunbelt Publications, 2016. A comprehensive history of San Diego written by a historian at UC San Diego, ranging from the earliest known human presence to the 21st century.

Griswold del Castillo, Richard. *Chicano San Diego: Cultural Space and the Struggle for Justice.* Tucson: University of Arizona Press, 2008. A recounting of San Diego's omnipresent Chicano culture and the ways it has manifested in the city throughout, and in some ways before, its civic history, including a detailed telling of the events establishing Chicano Park.

Hendrickson, Nancy. *San Diego Then and Now.* London: Pavilion, 2016. Primarily a photographic history of the city, juxtaposing vintage and current-day photographs of buildings and neighborhoods to highlight the changes over time.

Innis, Jack Scheffler. *San Diego Legends: Events, People, and Places That Made History.* 2nd edition. San Diego: Sunbelt Publications, 2014. Engaging survey of the parade of politicians, religious cults, and larger-than-life characters that contributed to San Diego's development as a left-coast city.

Lee, Murray K. *In Search of Gold Mountain: A History of the Chinese in San Diego.* Virginia Beach, VA: Donning Co., 2010. Lee, curator of the Chinese American History Museum, reveals the fascinating history of San Diego's Chinese and (once naturalization was finally allowed in 1943) Chinese American population, including a detailed account of the decline of Chinatown.

Lindsay, Diana, Paula Knoll, and Terri Varnell. *Coast to Cactus: The Canyoneer Trail Guide to San Diego Outdoors.* San Diego: Sunbelt Publications, 2016. Affiliated with the San Diego Museum of Natural History, the Canyoneers organization routinely leads hikers on trails throughout the county. Their discoveries are documented here, with everything you could want to know about a hike's location, distance, difficulty, and accessibility, plus detailed lists of any flora and fauna you might encounter.

MacPhail, Elizabeth C. *Kate Sessions: Pioneer Horticulturist.* San Diego: San Diego Historical Society, 1976. Biography of local figure Sessions, the "Mother of Balboa Park," responsible for introducing a startling number of trees and plants to the once barren region.

McGaugh, Scott. *The Military in San Diego.* Mt. Pleasant, SC: Arcadia Publishing, 2014. A photo-rich survey of San Diego's long-standing symbiotic relationship with the U.S. military, written by a local military historian and curator.

McLaughlin, David J. *Soldiers, Scoundrels, Poets & Priests: Stories of the Men and Women Behind the Missions of California.* Scottsdale, AZ: Pentacle Press, 2006. Compiled histories of the 21 California missions established by Spain in the 18th and 19th centuries, with the first three chapters devoted to Juan Rodríguez Cabrillo, Gaspar de Portolà, and Junípero Serra, three men who cemented Spain's temporary conquest of San Diego.

Smythe, William Ellsworth. *History of San Diego, 1542-1908.* Altenmünster, Germany: Jazzybee Verlag, 2017. A comprehensive history of the

Internet Resources

Balboa Park

www.balboapark.org

Check out this Balboa Park site to keep up with museum special exhibits, find park day passes, and discover special events that happen in the park periodically throughout the year.

Bands in Town

www.bandsintown.com

Find updated concert listings and local music recommendations with the handy app from this company, which happens to keep an office in Little Italy.

City of San Diego

www.sandiego.gov

Providing information and access to all city departments, this city site is especially useful for researching the Parks and Recreation department, including specific rules, regulations, and amenities for all city beaches, including lifeguard information.

Lyft

www.lyft.com

Similar to Uber, Lyft drivers pick up riders in most of the city within five minutes, for personal or shared rides.

San Diego City Beat

www.sdcitybeat.com

One of the city's free alt-weekly publications, keeping up with relevant cultural happenings, including music and politics.

San Diego Eater

www.sandiego.eater.com

A local food and dining blog, this site keeps up with new restaurant openings and foodie special events. It also offers features relating to some top local chefs.

San Diego Golf

www.sandiegogolf.com

A useful place to look into all San Diego golfing opportunities, including help reserving tee times at in-demand courses around town.

San Diego History Center
www.sandiegohistory.org

A terrific resource for anyone interested in San Diego history. Besides the San Diego History Center in Balboa Park, it represents the Junípero Serra Museum on Presidio Hill in Old Town.

San Diego Reader
www.sdreader.com

One of San Diego's free alt-weekly papers, with updated music, news, and theater information, plus recent food reviews, beer news, and coffee features written by yours truly.

San Diego Tourism Authority
www.sandiego.org

Primarily a visitor information website, this group highlights goings-on at attractions all over town, including detailed explanations of cultural events and nice ideas for family activities.

San Diego Union-Tribune
www.signonsandiego.com

San Diego's long-established newspaper of note, the *Union-Tribune* offers comprehensive news coverage of the region, as well as international stories contributed by the paper's news partners. The website is designed as a portal to local information and resources.

Taphunter
www.taphunter.com

Beer hunters will love this app, which keeps track of which terrific craft beers are currently on tap at nearby and popular restaurants and bars. Search by location or specific beer.

Thrillist
www.thrillist.com/san-diego

Probably the best way to keep up with the ever-changing trend of San Diego's nightlife, the San Diego branch of this global website covers food, music, cool happenings, and sights, written in Internet parlance by young people.

Uber
www.uber.com

Getting an inexpensive ride somewhere can happen in minutes with Uber's app. An Uber driver will locate you and get you to where you're going. It's especially handy for beer tourists—think of it as a designated driver on demand.

Index

Restaurants Index

Nightlife Index

Shops Index

Hotels Index

Photo Credits

PORTLAND

SEATTLE

TUCSON

VANCOUVER

Explore the city, escape into nature,

75 GREAT HIKES SEATTLE

101 GREAT HIKES SAN FRANCISCO BAY AREA

CALIFORNIA CAMPING

COLORADO CAMPING

OREGON CAMPING

PACIFIC NORTHWEST CAMPING

WASHINGTON CAMPING

WEST COAST RV CAMPING

or go where the road takes you....

CALIFORNIA Road Trip

PACIFIC COAST HIGHWAY

PACIFIC NORTHWEST Road Trip

SOUTHWEST Road Trip

SEVEN GREAT CITIES ONE STEP AT A TIME

MOON

AMSTERDAM WALKS
SEE THE CITY LIKE A LOCAL

MOON

BARCELONA WALKS
SEE THE CITY LIKE A LOCAL

MOON

BERLIN WALKS
SEE THE CITY LIKE A LOCAL

MOON

LONDON WALKS
SEE THE CITY LIKE A LOCAL

MOON

NEW YORK WALKS
SEE THE CITY LIKE A LOCAL

MOON

PARIS WALKS
SEE THE CITY LIKE A LOCAL

MOON

ROME WALKS
SEE THE CITY LIKE A LOCAL

MOON
CITY WALKS

Visit moon.com for travel inspiration and guidance.